The
Complete Herbalist

The Complete Herbalist

Volume Two

Prof. O. Phelps Brown

LOGOS PRESS
New Delhi-110 002

ISBN-13: 978-81-7268-190-6 (Set)
ISBN-10: 81-7268-190-9 (Set)

ISBN-13: 978-81-7268-191-3 (Vol. I)
ISBN-13: 978-81-7268-192-0 (Vol. II)
ISBN-10: 81-7268-191-7 (Vol. I)
ISBN-10: 81-7268-192-5 (Vol. II)

2009

Printed and Published by

LOGOS PRESS

Building No. 4788-90, Street No. 23, Ansari Road,
Darya Ganj, **New Delhi**-110 002 (India)

Phone : 23272187

Email : mail@logospressindia.com
Website : www.logospressindia.com

CONTENTS

Volume One

PART–I

Herbal Materia Medica

Plants

Essays on Hygiene, etc.

How to Assist the Doctor

Volume Two

PART–II

TREATMENT OF CHRONIC DISEASES

The Author's Speciality

PART–III

RECIPES

NATURE'S HERBAL REMEDIES

Volume Two

PART II.

DISEASES.

THE great difficulty of treating disease, by those who are not physicians, is the liability to mistake the character of the affection, being unable through obscurity of the symptoms to ascertain the organ or tissue affected. Without entering minutely into diagnosis, the author will endeavor to simplify the study of morbid conditions of the human body, so that the unscientific may more readily ascertain the disease and apply the appropriate remedy or treatment.

1. General condition pertaining to:
   a. Temperature and dryness of skin.
   b. Condition of pulse—full and quick, or slow and weak.
   c. Appearance of tongue.
   d. State of bowels and kidneys.
   e. Desire for food and drink.
2. The general appearance of the patient.
   a. Size—emaciation or increase, general or local.
   b. Aspect of face or expression.
   c. Changes of color of skin.
3. The position or posture.
   a. In bed—the manner of lying, on the back or either side, quiet, restless, etc.
   b. Out of bed—posture, gait, stiffness, loss of power of limbs, etc.
4. The sensations of the patient.

Whenever any of these conditions are at variance with the normal state, the presumption, or rather certainty, is that some organ or tissue is assailed by disease. Some of the general indications of the patient in many cases often make known the character of the affection, when not suggested by other symptoms. For instance, the skin is remarkably moist and soft in delirium tremens; the perspiration profuse and sour in acute rheumatism; exhausting sweats in the latter stages of consumption or profuse suppuration; the crackling feeling of emphysema, and the pitting under pressure in dropsy.

The pulse is hard and wiry in abdominal inflammations; in acute hydrocephalus its frequency is very great, slow and labored in brain diseases, irregular in disease of the heart, almost imperceptible in cholera or in the latter stages of the low fevers.

The tongue covered with a thin white layer is indicative of disorder of the stomach; when patchy, the stomach is considerably irritated; when yellow, the patient is bilious; when shining, glazed, and chapped, it indicates long-continued inflammation or ulceration of the bowels; aphthous patches indicate imperfect nutrition, etc.

In cholera the stools resemble rice-water; when clay-colored, it denotes a deficiency of bile; when yeast-like, fermentation takes place instead of digestion.

The urine is dark-colored in fevers, very limpid and abundant in hysteria, scanty in dropsies, acid in rheumatism.

The *aspect* is often very significant. In scrofula the corners of the nose and lips are swollen, in chlorosis a waxy pallor is observed, in malignant diseases a sallow hue, in heart-diseases a blue color of the lips, in pneumonia a dusky flush, in phthisis a hectic flush. When the expression is anxious, it indicates disease of the heart and dyspnœa; when pinched and contracted, there is much suffering, as in the low forms of fever; the skin is white in anæmia, yellow in jaundice and malignant cases; it has a muddy hue in splenic diseases, blue in cholera, and livid in commencing mortification.

If the patient's head is elevated by choice in bed, it denotes heart-disease; when he is very feeble he lies on his back; in peritonitis the knees are drawn up; in cramps or pain of the abdomen, he lies on his side.

In order that the reader may not have a confused idea of what is meant by inflammation, I will describe it insomuch as to give its phenomena. These are *redness*, *heat*, *swelling*, and *pain*. When all these are present it constitutes *inflammation*. When a fever or disease partakes of this character, it is inflammatory. Chronic inflammation is characterized by all the essential conditions of the acute form, differing, however, in this, by being preceded through all its changes with symptoms so mild that it is only after a certain time that the patient is much inconvenienced constitutionally. Inflammation always denotes increase of activity of the vascular system. When of a localized character, the increase is noticed in the capillary circulation; when general, as in fevers, or of some important organ, the whole circulatory apparatus is abnormally active.

MIASMATIC FEVERS.

These, as signified by name, owe their origin to, or are caused by, a peculiar principle to which the name of *malaria* or *miasm* has been given. Of the chemical nature of miasm we literally know nothing; but we have abundant evidence that it is a specific cause of disease. There are practically, two kinds of malaria: First, *koino-miasmata*, the product of vegetable decomposition, or terrestrial emanations; second, *Idio-miasmata*, the deleterous effluvia originating from the decomposition of matter derived from the human body. Both of these are prolific causes of disease, yet the profession, owing to the subtile nature of the miasms, are in a great degree ignorant as to the manner of operation. These two causes may act separately, and produce their different symptoms, or they may operate together, causing a confusion of morbid phenomena.

"Marsh gas," or the product of vegetable decomposition, owing to its diversification, is of course the greater cause of disease. Two requisites, heat and moisture, are necessary for its production; and hence, where these abound in any quantity, so proportionably is the miasm evolved. For this reason, low, marshy lands are at certain seasons very unhealthy, while those regions at a greater elevation are peculiarly healthy in this respect. Wherever vegetation is profuse, and to which abundant heat and moisture are contributed, there we may reasonably expect a plentiful product of miasm and consequent disease. Experiments have proved that in decomposition of vegetable matter, animal matter—infusoria—is produced in very rapid succession, having an exceedingly short-lived existence. These infusoria are inhaled at every breath, as the air contains swarms of them, but which are imperceptible to any of the senses. It is reasonable to suppose that they, in a great measure, contribute largely to periodic fevers. The diseases generally classed as Malarial are Intermittent, Remittent, Yellow, and Typhus Fevers.

INTERMITTENT FEVER.

This is commonly called *Fever and Ague*, or *Chills and Fever*. As the name implies, the fever is not constant, as in the continual fevers, but *intermits*, so that in its career there are well-marked periods of absence of febrile symptoms. It is a fever characterized by a succession of attacks, with equal *intervals* and *intermissions*, that are complete, but irregular, owing to the paroxysms being of uncertain duration. By *interval* is meant the time from the beginning of one paroxysm to the beginning of the next, and by *intermission* the period of time between the close of one paroxysm to the beginning of the next. The length of the interval determines the variety of ague. When the interval is twenty-four hours, it is called *quotidian*; thirty-six hours, *tertian*; and when seventy-two hours, it is called *quartan*. These varieties duplicate, and are then called double quotidian, etc.

The disease is announced by a paroxysm which has three stages, the cold, the hot, and the sweating. The cold stage is well marked; the patient yawns, has a feeling of weakness, stretches, no appetite, and no inclination to move. Paleness is observed in the face and extremities; the patient shakes, the teeth chatter, and the skin shrinks causing *horripilation* or "goose-flesh."

When this stage declines, the hot stage comes on, which is characterized by a high fever. This is followed by the sweating stage, which increases from a mere moisture at first to a profuse perspiration. After this the body returns to its natural temperature, and apparent health returns.

During the cold stage the circulation is thrown upon the internal organs, the spleen becomes congested, which organ is enlarged, causing what is known as the *ague cake.*

A quotidian begins generally in the morning, a tertian at noon, and a quartan in the afternoon. The cold stage is shortest in the quotidian, and longest in the quartan. Intermittent fever is more common in the spring and autumn than at other seasons of the year, and in fall more severe and dangerous.

TREATMENT.—Commence treatment with a cathartic, as senna or the Renovating Pill. In the cold stage give hot drinks, and even stimulants may be of service. Induce warmth and comfort by extra covering, foot-baths, bottles filled with hot water applied to the surface, etc. In the hot stage, cooling drinks and anything that mollifies febrile action.

When an intermission ensues, administer Peruvian bark, or, preferably, one of its active principles, quinine. This can be given in a large dose, or smaller doses repeated. Fifteen grains may be given at once or in successive doses. It may be taken in pills or in solution with elixir of vitriol. Quinine is a specific in this disease, and it rarely ever fails in curing every case, if the patient be placed under its influence. Peculiar head symptoms and buzzing in the ears denote the influence of this admirable remedy. My experience has not taught me that there is much danger in an overdose, and I consider it more or less harmless; yet, like every other remedy, it must be judiciously and intelligently administered. The web of the black spider rolled up in five-grain pills, and taken, one pill at a time every two hours, is a valuable domestic remedy. Decoctions of dogwood bark are successful in many cases; so also of the bark of the tulip tree.

REMITTENT FEVER.

This is commonly called *Bilious* Fever. It is a disease whose attack is generally sudden and well marked, without prominent premonitory symptoms, if any, at all times. There is sense of languor and debility for a few days previous to the onset; slight headache, lack of appetite, furred tongue, bitter taste in the mouth in the morning, pain in the joints, and a feeling of uneasiness.

The first onset is announced by a rigor or chill, distinct in character, though generally brief and sometimes slight, but at times severe and prolonged. Sometimes the chill is first felt in the feet; at other times commences at the shoulder-blades, or in the back, running from thence through the whole body. Usually there is but one well-marked chill; the paroxysms of fever returning subsequently, and seldom preceded by a cold stage.

The symptoms of this disease intensify at certain periods of the day; preceded occasionally, but not generally, by a chill. Between this period of severity in the febrile symptoms and a similar period following there is generally a decrease in the violence of the symptoms, during which the fever moderates, but does not, as in intermittent fever, totally disappear. It remits in severity, and hence the name. The pulse in the hot stage ranges from one hundred to one hundred and thirty. The pains in the head, back, and limbs are almost insufferable. The covering of the tongue is yellowish or dirty white, and in severe cases, in the advanced stage, the tongue is parched, brown or nearly black in the centre, and red at the edges. Food is distasteful, and nausea and vomiting ensue, with frequently pain, upon pressure, in the epigastrium. The bowels are at first costive, but become loose, and the fæces are dark and offensive.

TREATMENT.—Give an emetic or cathartic in the formative stage. When the disease is fully developed, sponge the body all over several times a day with cold or tepid water, whichever is most grateful to the patient, and give cooling drinks, as the effervescing draught. When the fever is high, moderate it with tincture or fluid extract of green hellebore, in doses of from three to ten drops. Dover's powder should be given as a diaphoretic. Ice-water can be drunk at pleasure. A mustard poultice should be placed over the pit of the stomach whenever tenderness exists.

Quinine is the great remedy in this disease also, and should be administered in the same manner as advised in fever and ague. It is to be given in a remission. Whenever the fever has been subdued by large doses of quinine, its administration should not be abruptly ceased, but be continued in smaller or tonic doses for several weeks afterward.

There is a form of fever called *Congestive*. It is also called *pernicious fever*. It is not essentially remittent, but may also be intermittent in character. The congestion may only operate upon one of the internal organs, or upon all of them. Congestion may ensue in the earlier or later stage of the disease. There is usually congestion of the brain, and profound stupor follows. It assumes all types of periodic fevers, but is more frequently quotidian or tertian. The first attack generally simulates a simple attack of intermittent, and excites but little attention. The second attack is severe, producing great coldness, and the patient has a deathlike hue of face and extremities. As the disease advances, the heat of the skin becomes pungent. The skin also becomes dry, husky, and parched, followed, after a time, by a cold, clammy sensation. The eyes are dull and watery, and at times glassy;

the countenance dull, sleepy, and distressed; the tongue trembles upon protrusion, indicating weakness, and is at first covered with whitish fur, which changes to either brown or black; the breathing is difficult, and inspirations often thirty to the minute. Pressure over the liver, stomach, or bowels occasions pain; and the mind is often disturbed, and falls into lethargy and stupor, or is delirious.

The treatment is the same as in remittent fever. Quinine and the other remedies are of the some signal service. In stupor friction is to be made along the course of the spine with spirits of turpentine or ammonia.

In convalescence the diet must be light and nutritious, and as strength returns may be increased. Exercise out of doors should be encouraged. If recovery be slow, it should be hastened by wine, ale, or brandy, and the usual vegetable tonics.

Any person who is suffering from almost a continuity of the disease, or the so-called chronic form of malarial fever, desirous of corresponding with me on the subject, I should be most happy to reply to, for in the vast and beneficent domain of Herbalism there are many remedies that can be advised as curative, to mention which would occupy too much space in a volume of this size. We can be eclectic in Nature's laboratory.

YELLOW-FEVER.

The first symptoms of this fever seem identical with remittent, often well marked by periodicity, but finally reaction occurs, and it assumes a typhoid character. The disease is ushered in generally with a chill, severe at times, though usually moderate, of short duration, and rarely repeated. The chill is followed by slight fever, with increased heat of surface; but this rarely rises to any considerable height, and continues only for two or three days, when, in cases likely to prove fatal, it is succeeded by coldness of surface, etc. Sweating exists in many cases. The pulse is singular in character, but rarely rises above a hundred, the tongue is moist and white for the first few days, but as the disease advances it becomes red, smooth, shining, and dry, having a black streak in the middle. The most prominent symptoms are nausea and vomiting. In fatal cases the vomiting is persistent, and towards the termination the green biliary matter thrown up changes to a thin black fluid, having a sediment like the grounds of coffee. This is the terrible *black vomit* (vomita-nigra) of yellow-fever. The bowels are generally costive, and the abdomen tender upon pressure. Severe headache generally exists, and the countenance bears a singular expression, in which a smile seems to play upon the lips, but the rest of the face bears a wild or sad look. Restlessness is common to this disease night and day. Blood often escapes from the nose, gums, ears, stomach, bowels, and urinary passages. The skin bears a tinged color similar to that in jaundice. The disease appears both endemically and epidemically. At first the disease is hard to recognize, presenting but the usual symptoms of fevers in their incipient stage, with no symptoms to distinguish the disease, or, if any, very obscure; but when the severe pain in the back and loins exists, the conjunctiva injected, and a red flush of the face and forehead is present, the identity of the disease is no longer in doubt, especially when extraneous circumstances, calculated to suggest the probability of an attack of yellow-fever, are also present.

TREATMENT.—In the early stage of the attack it should be treated, as regards medicines, the same as a case of malarial fever. If any derangement of the stomach exists, a gentle emetic is proper; this rouses the nervous system from its lethargy, promotes the action of the liver, and, by determining the blood to the surface, restores the capillary circulation. The best emetic for this purpose is lobelia combined with boneset. The febrile stage requires a thorough bath with tepid water and whiskey over the entire surface, with friction by rubbing with a towel or the hand. Large mustard-poultices should be placed over the spine and abdomen. Immediately upon the decline of fever, if the symptoms denote urgency, administer the antiperiodic remedies advised in intermittent and remittent fever. The sulphate of quinia may be combined with tannin, because the astringent properties of the tannin have a beneficial effect in subduing inflammatory action of the mucous membranes. This remedy should not be delayed a moment if the patient is in a period of prostration, and its retention by the stomach should be favored by anodynes, carminatives, or stimulants, as the case may require. Oil of turpentine and Cayenne pepper can also be combined with advantage in this disease. The strength of the patient must be supported by every means that can be employed—gruel and weak animal broths, bread-water, my nutritive fluids, milk and water, etc , are important means for this object. The revulsive influence of a blister over the stomach is of great service in this stage. If reaction is induced and convalescence established, the remaining strength of the patient must be carefully husbanded by proper tonics and wholesome and digestible diet, increasing the quantity as the patient gains strength.

All exposed to yellow-fever should avoid the night-air and sudden changes of temperature; they should sleep in the highest part of the house; be moderate in taking exercise; they should take nutritious but not stimulating food, and never expose themselves to infected air with empty stomachs or when fatigue.

TYPHUS FEVER.

This is also called *Hospital*, *Jail*, *Camp*, *Putrid*, and *Ship* Fever. It is usually preceded by lassitude, debility, and loss of appetite, and ushered in by rigors and chills, and characterized by frequent exacerbations and declines during its progress. It generally presents itself as an epidemic, and runs a uniform course. From the third to the seventh day of the fever the peculiar *petechial* eruption occurs. It is of a florid, reddish, or reddish-pink color, disappearing on pressure, which distinguishes it from the petechiæ of typhoid. The breathing is hurried, the skin dry and hot, the tongue thickly coated, and the thirst urgent. There is great distress about the head, which often results in delirium. This stage of excitement continues generally, with little increase or abatement in the symptoms, for some time. The fever is greatest towards evening, least in the morning. The bowels are generally costive, and if it continues for some time, all the secretions become vitiated, the body exhaling a nauseous odor, and the tongue, gums, and teeth become coated with a dark-brown slime. Collapse generally follows, voluntary powers depressed, surface relaxed, and diminished in temperature, often covered with a clammy sweat; pulse small and tremulous. The tongue becomes black and dry, voice faint, breathing short, feeble, and very anxious. The mental functions become greatly disordered, the patient is restless and fearful, his delirium is low-muttering, and he lies in a state of stupor from which he can be scarcely aroused. Often an irritating cough is present, coming on as if in convulsive paroxysms. In this stage of collapse the patient is disposed to lie on his back, with his feet drawn up, and there is a great tendency in his body to slide towards the foot of the bed. As the disease progresses, all the symptoms of prostration increase. A convulsive motion of the tendons, as as in typhoid, is observed; his stupor becomes fixed; hiccough, involuntary discharges from the bowels, a cadaverous smell of the body, generally occur towards the close of the disease. Death, in violent cases, is generally preceded by extreme prostration, cold, clammy sweats, involuntary fecal discharges, and a discharge of grumous blood from the mouth, nose, and anus; or by convulsions.

This is a contagious disease, and emphatically one of poverty and low life.

TREATMENT.—Place the patient in a well-ventilated apartment, wash the body with soap and water, and give an emetic and cathartic, if the patient's condition requires it. Then give quinine in two or three grain doses every two or three hours, until its effects are observable. Control the fever with veratrum, as advised in typhoid cases. If great prostration is present, add capsicum or prickly-ash to the quinine, which should be continued in regular doses throughout the greater part of the course of the disease. A decoction of ladies'-slipper, or, preferably, cypripedin, in two or three grain doses every two hours, should be given in delirium or tendinous convulsions. Support the strength with iced-milk, chicken-broth, beef-tea, milk-punch, etc. The bladder should receive attention, and, if distended, should be evacuated by the influence of a sitz-bath, or by a catheter. In cases of cerebro-spinal congestions, make counter-irritations along the course of the spine, apply cold water to the head, and bottles of hot water to the feet. Convalescence is to be aided by the proper tonics, as golden-seal, columbo, etc., and complete repose should be allowed to the convalescent.

ERUPTIVE OR EXANTHEMATOUS FEVERS.

These are all characterized by fever and the usual constitutional disturbances, together with an eruption or exanthem distinguishing each variety. They owe their origin to animal or vegetable malaria, or both combined, and the peculiarities of this class are, that they, when once affecting the system, render the patient comparatively exempt from any future attack of the disease.

Typhoid Fever.

This is a very insidious disease, its commencement being scarcely perceptible. The patient has a sense of indisposition, but is unable to describe his condition. He feels slight debility, a dull and heavy feeling in the head, which increases and terminates in violent frontal headache. At full development of the disease, the limbs are weak, accompanied by lameness, and sometimes rheumatic pain. The bowels may at first be constipated, but in a few days the tendency is to diarrhœa. The pulse is quickened, a creeping, chilly sensation is felt, and the skin is dry and warm. The tongue is but slightly coated, and the appetite often remains until the disease is fully developed. After the full development, a number of small vesicles, called *sudaminæ*, may be observed on the abdomen. They are small, and may escape notice unless carefully observed. On the fifth day after the occurrenee of these, another eruption occurs, which consists of small red or purple spots, resembling flea-bites. These spots are called *petechiæ*. If these are observed, the disease is unmistakably typhoid fever. When the abdomen is percussed, it yields a drum-like resonance, and a gurgling may be heard on the right side, a little below the navel. Nervous symptoms arise, frequently delirium, great pain in different parts of the body, stupor, and a buzzing noise in the head are often complained of. The tongue becomes red, and is protruded with much difficulty, pulse increases, eyes have a watery appearance, and remain partly open when asleep. The breathing becomes difficult, mouth half open, and a black substance (*sordes*) collects on the teeth. The urine becomes nearly suppressed, and has a dark-red appearance. The bowels bloat, and evacuations of frothy and watery excrement are frequent. If the disease is about to terminate unfavorably, the patient becomes stupid, with low, muttering delirium, his muscles jerk, hiccoughs, picks at bed-clothes, and labors under profound coma. The anatomical character of this disease is ulceration of certain glands, called *Peyerian*, of the intestines, which are sometimes perforated by the process, when, of course, death inevitably follows. The course of the disease is from 11 to 21 days.

TREATMENT.—If the disease is suspected, the patient should be placed in bed, and his bowels evacuated by warm-water injections, if costive. If indigestible food is contained in his stomach, an emetic of lobelia should be administered. Rice-gruel should then be given. The tincture of American Hellebore should, on the approach of the febrile paroxysm, be given until the pulse becomes less frequent, and perspiration ensues. Lye and slippery-elm poultices should be applied to the abdomen as long as bowel symptoms prove troublesome. Quinine and Hydrastin should be exhibited, with a view to overcome the periodicity of the fever. At the same time a cold infusion of marsh mallow, acacia, and flax-seed, should be taken. Apply cold water to the head, and keep the feet warm. Control the fever throughout its whole course with the veratrum or aconite. If the patient is restless and unable to sleep, give a little morphine in a decoction of Ladies'-slipper. If the diarrhœa is persistent, let the patient take a decoction of rhus and cranes-bill. When the red tongue is noticed, administer the spirits of turpentine, in from six to ten drop doses, three or four times a day. Beef-tea, brandy, etc., should be given to support the strength through the course of the disease. During convalescence care should be taken that the patient does not eat hearty food. Convalescence should be assisted by golden-seal and other tonics. The danger in the treatment of this disease is over-medication, and hence only such agents as are chemically called for should be given, and the patient's strength well supported throughout the course of the fever.

DIPHTHERIA.

Diphtheria is scarcely more than a modification of scarlet fever. The patient first complains of lassitude, headache, loss of appetite, has rigors and chills, active and quick pulse, a light furred tongue, redness of the back of mouth, enlargement of the glands about the neck, a hot, dry, and pungent skin, and in most cases an exudation upon the mucous surfaces of the upper air-passages. This soon becomes organized into a tough, white membrane, covering the soft palate and tonsils. These sometimes degenerate into ulcers. The breathing in consequence of this membrane becomes hurried and difficult, pulse quick, and frequently the asphyxia ensuing ends in death; it generally reigns as an epidemic and is regarded as contagious.

TREATMENT.—The first step in the treatment should be a thorough emetic and an active cathartic; free perspiration should be produced by aconite or veratrum, and the kidneys should be kept in vigorous operation. Flannel cloths, wet with the compound tincture of capsicum, myrrh, and lobelia, should be applied to the neck, changed every half hour, and applied as hot as the patient can bear it. Jugs of hot water should be applied to the feet. The inflammation of the throat should be subdued by a gargle of a hot decoction of golden-seal. If the disease assumes an unfavorable aspect, give a powder containing one grain of quinine, one-half grain of capsicum, and one grain of hydrastin every two hours. If the patches ulcerate, use a gargle of sumach and wild indigo. For the difficulty of breathing give sanguinaria and lobelia in emetic doses for the purpose of dislodging the membrane. The secretions should be increased even to ptyalism by irisin, the effect of which will be to overcome the adhesiveness of the membrane. The "Herbal Ointment" used for this purpose, and also to subdue the local inflammation, acts specifically and should be used in all cases.

During convalescence the diet should be nutritious, and baths, fresh air, and a liberal amount of fresh fruits ordered.

SMALL-POX (*Variola*).

The symptoms are divided into four periods. The period of invasion occupies about three days, and is marked by languor, lassitude, restlessness, stretching, gaping, petulance, sullen mood; these are followed by chills and rigors. Towards evening the skin becomes hot and dry, pain attacks the head, loss of appetite, nausea, and frequently lumbago. On the third day, heat, fever, flushed face, headache, and in children sometimes convulsions. The period of eruption commences on the fourth day (often on the third), with the appearance of a series of small red circular points (papulæ). They do not rise above the surface then, but can be seen in it, and felt by the finger. They are situated in the substance of the skin, and roll about under the finger, the size that of a small pin's head. These gradually enlarge, the patient in the mean time suffering severely, until the period of suppuration arrives. The fever is now great, the hands, feet, and face swell, and salivation is profuse and constant. There is hoarseness and pain, and the saliva emits a most disagreeable odor. Then comes the period of recovery. The pustules scab, the fever and other unpleasant symptoms gradually disappear, and, if all goes right, the danger is over from the twelfth to the fifteenth day after the eruption.

What is known as *confluent* small-pox is when the pustulus are very numerous and running together; and when all the symptoms are very severe, the disease is known as *malignant*. Variola patients emit a peculiar fetid odor, which is characteristic, and distinguishes it from Varioloid.

TREATMENT.—An active purge should be given at the outset. For this purpose a combination like the "Renovating Pills" should be selected. as the catharsis produced is thorough and unattended with subsequent debility or costiveness. Diaphoretics should be given to promote early appearance of the eruption. The patient should be placed in a cool and well-ventilated room, and frequently sponged with tepid water. Not much treatment of a medicinal character is required. The fever should be controlled by aconite or veratrum, as in all active fevers. If complicated with pneumonia, pleurisy, etc., the treatment necessary is such as is advised in those diseases. Pitting to a great extent may be avoided by sweet-oil applied to hands and face.

Varioloid is but modified small-pox. It has all the essential characteristics of the disease except its virulence. The treatment is the same as advised for small pox.

The utility of vaccination is a mooted question. It has unquestionably done great harm, as in many cases scrofulous and syphilitic taints have been implanted. Aside from this, however, it has been the means of almost banishing the dreadful plague from existence, and its practice should be encouraged. Great care, however, should be exercised in the selection of the vaccine virus, so that its purity is unquestionably established before being used as an agent of prevention.

Chicken Pox (*Varicella*).

This is a very mild eruptive disease, characterized by a slight fever of short duration, aud followed by vesicles which desquamate about the fifth or sixth day. The fever is sometimes ushered in by slight rigors, though there is seldom any chill. There is often headache, and vomiting occasionally. The eruption appears in one or two days after the inauguration of the fever. It consists of red spots at first, which quickly become vesicular, and are frequently attended with itching.

Treatment.—Very little treatment is required, except in cases of feeble vitality, when the disease often assumes a severe character. In such cases the stomach and bowels should be well cleansed, the surface sponged with hot water, and the fever controlled with arterial sedatives Tonics should be given if the patient is enfeebled. The diet should be nutritious, but composed of easily digested articles.

Measles (*Rubeola*).

This is an acute inflammation of the entire skin, of an infectious and contagious nature. It is ushered in with chills, followed by heat, drowsiness, pain in head, back, and limbs, sore throat, dry cough, and other symptoms common to febrile action, growing in violence until the fourth day. Then the eruption appears, producing heat and itching. The breaking out appears in patches of half-moon shape, which distinguishes this disease from the other eruptive diseases. They reach their height at the fifth day on the face and neck. and on the legs about the seventh day. Their decline is in the same order as appearance, disappearing about the tenth day, when the scarfskin peals off in the shape of scurf.

TREATMENT.—If the attack be a mild one, all the treatment necessary consists in light diet, acid and demulcent drinks, as flaxseed-tea decoction of slippery-elm, etc. Sponging with tepid water is very grateful to the sufferer in all cases. If during the first stage the eruption should be tardy in its coming, it should be hastened by a warm bath, and sweating drinks made from saffron, mullein, pennyroyal, summer savory, etc. If tardy on account of excessive fever, give tincture of green hellebore, ipecac, lobelia, snake-root, etc. In enfeebled constitutions stimulants are necessary.

SCARLET FEVER (*Scarlatina*).

Also a contagious disease. The eruption is in the shape of pimples of a scarlet hue, displayed in patches over the whole surface. The fever is usually more intense than in measles, and accompanied by sore throat, swollen face, and coated tongue. The greatest degree of redness is attained at the third or fourth day. The decline is the same as in measles. Scarlet fever is distinguished from other diseases by the swollen condition of the flesh, which spreads out the fingers peculiarly The throat becomes ulcerated, and swallowing is attended with pain and difficulty. There is no cough, which also distinguishes it from measles.

The following will show the difference between scarlet fever and measles :—

In Scarlet Fever.	*In Measles.*
The eruption is bright scarlet.	The eruption is dark-red color.
It appears on the second day.	Does not appear till the fourth day.
Is quite smooth to the touch.	Is raised.
Is in small round spots.	Is larger and crescent-shaped.
Disappears on pressure.	Does not disappear.
The face is quite dry.	Face swelled ; running from the eyes and nose.

TREATMENT.—This should be cooling in its nature, cooling drinks, sponging with cold water, etc. In ordinary cases little more is required, excepting a few drops of tincture of belladonna may be given several times per day. When high fever exists, give the remedies advised in measles. Hot foot-baths are advisable. As this is a prostrative disease, beef-tea and the ordinary stimulants should be given from the first. What is called malignant scarlet fever is only a severer form than the above. Gargles of sage and Cayenne pepper are used to allay the throat affections. The abscesses in the region of the ear, and consequent deafness, can be obviated by subduing the inflammation of that part by the usual methods.

Nettle Rash.

This commences with fever, lasting two or three days; then itching pimples, diversified in shape, appear, which go off during the day and come again at night. Teething causes it sometimes, while at other times it is due to improper diet.

Treatment.—This is indicated by the cause. If due to indigestible food, the stomach must be unloaded by an emetic of blood-root or ipecacuanha. A lotion of vinegar and water is of service. Tonics and simple diet will complete the cure.

Erysipelas.

This disease commences with languor, aching or soreness of the limbs, chilliness, alternating with flushes of heat. The pulse is quick, skin hot, tongue foul, appetite gone, thirst, nausea sometimes; vomiting, headache, restlessness, sore throat, swelling and tenderness of the glands of the neck, arm-pits, or groin, according to the seat of the cutaneous inflammation. The eruption usually makes its appearance, about the third day of the fever, in the form of a small reddish spot, somewhat elevated, painful or tender to the touch. This occurs most frequently upon the face, especially on the side of the nose, cheek, or rim of the ear. In some instances the inflammation advances slowly, in others it spreads quickly over large portions of the body, accompanied by tumefaction, and a burning and stinging pain in all cases. About the third day of the inflammation small blisters, filled with yellow serum, appear, which break about three days afterward. On the fifth or sixth day they begin to dry, and on the seventh or eighth form crusts or scabs, which desquamate, and a new skin forms. In phlegmonous erysipelas the inflammation involves not only the skin, but the subcutaneous tissues also, and the symptoms are all severer. It often assumes a very malignant type, and is then a disease of a most fatal character. It is liable to attack wounds; and those who are nursing patients suffering with erysipelas should never wait upon a woman who has been but recently confined, as she will be very liable to contract puerperal peritonitis, a very fatal disease.

Treatment.—Give a lobelia emetic, a mild purge, and a hot bath at the commencement. In the mild form cover the inflamed patch with collodion, and renew every two or three hours. The emetic and purge should be followed with quinine in two or three grain doses every three hours. The inflamed surface should also be washed with a decoction of the bark, or a solution of quinine. Bruised cranberries are a good application. Cloths wrung out of a hot decoction of white-oak bark and golden-seal should be applied to the inflamed part to prevent spreading. In wounds apply lint saturated with compound tincture of myrrh and capsicum. If the fever is violent, treat it as in all other febrile cases. A nutritive diet should follow medical treatment as soon as the disease has passed its active career.

ROSE RASH (*Roseola*).

This is an eruptive disease of little importance. The febrile symptoms are slight, more or less attended with gastric derangement, which continues two or three days before the rash appears and subsides with it. The eruption generally commences upon the face, is of uniform redness, and causes itching or tingling. The rash continues from one to five days, and is followed by a slight scaling off of the skin. It is often the accompaniment of dentition and is not contagious.

TREATMENT.—Little more is necessary than a warm bath and a few drops of veratrum. If the eruption is troublesome, two or three drops of tincture of Belladonna should be added to a tumbler of water, and a teaspoonful given occasionally.

ERYTHEMA.

The eruption of this disease is of superficial redness, generally in irregular patches, slightly elevated, and attended with heat, tingling, and sometimes slight pain. It may be local or owing to constitutional disturbance. It may be caused by friction of contiguous surfaces, as in the groin and arm-pits, in fat infants, particularly when not frequently washed. When owing to constitutional causes, it usually appears on the face, breast or limbs. It lasts from a few days to a week or longer.

TREATMENT.—If the cause can be ascertained, it should be removed by the proper remedies. Anoint the affected part with a little lime-water and sweet-oil, or bathe with a strong decoction of golden-seal. Glycerine may also be applied, but if you can procure the "Herbal Ointment" (see page 472) I advise its application, as it is a specific for this and kindred affections.

GLANDERS.

This may be contracted from the horse, and is a very malignant disease. It is characterized by a purulent and sometimes bloody discharge from the nose, a peculiar pustular eruption, and by tumors in different parts of the body. Its initial stage is the same as in all eruptive fevers, attended with neuralgic pains in the limbs. In the course of four or five days the eruption makes its appearance in different parts of the body, usually most abundant upon the face and limbs. The discharge from the nose ensues in the course of a week or ten days, being at first yellowish, afterwards bloody, and very offensive. The body finally exhales a fetid odor, the mind wanders, delirium and coma follow, and by the end of the second week, or during the third, it generally proves fatal, if not arrested sooner in its course. It is fortunately very rare;

and attendants upon a horse affected with glanders should be very careful that they do not come in contact with the virus. The affected horse should be shot, as the disease is very seldom cured.

TREATMENT.—Support the strength of the patient, and stimulate the emunctories. This can be best achieved by a thorough alcoholic vapor bath, followed by an active lobelia emetic and a brisk cathartic. After this give quinine, three grains, and baptisin, two grains, every two or three hours, for a day or two. The nostrils should be syringed with warm water, to which a few drops of creosote has been added, three or four times a day. The throat may be gargled with the same preparation. Support the strength with chicken-broth, rice-gruel, cream, punch, porter, ale, etc. If this course is not effectual, repeat every three or four days.

DANDY FEVER (*Dengue*).

This disease occasionally prevails as an epidemic in the southern seacoast towns. There is pain, stiffness of the neck, back, and loins, and swelling of the muscles of the limbs and joints. Intolerance of light, restlessness, chilliness, fever, headache, a full and quick pulse, red eyes, a hot and dry skin, and an intense thirst prevail. The fever usually lasts from one to two days, when a gradual remission occurs, and the patient feels quite comfortable. After an interval of two or three days the fever returns, the pains are increased, the tongue is thickly coated, the stomach irritable, and the patient becomes dejected and fretful. Nausea is a prominent symptom, but seldom any vomiting occurs. About the sixth or seventh day an eruption, resembling scarlatina, appears, and gives relief to the distressing symptoms. It disappears after two or three days, the color of the skin gradually fading, with slight desquamation. The duration of the disease is about eight days. The causes are evidently miasmatic poison, in concert with epidemic influence.

TREATMENT.—Essentially the same as in scarlatina, accompanied with such remedies as advised in rheumatism. Quinine, in antiperiodic doses, should also be administered, and the anodynes should be given if the pains are severe. Tonics may be required in some cases; and in convalescence, frequent baths, a generous diet, and out-door exercises should be prescribed.

PURPURA.

This affection is characterized by a greater or lesser number of livid spots on the skin, from extravasated blood. In simple cases the effusion is confined to the skin and cellular tissues, mostly occurring on the arms, legs, and breasts. The spots at first are small, and resemble flea-bites. The countenance is pale, and the patient complains of debility, loss of appetite, irregularity of the bowels, and periodic fever. If allowed to progress, it will assume a form known as *purpura hemorrhagica*, in which the spots are longer, and resemble whip-marks or violent bruises. They are bright red at first, but become purple or livid. A great variety of symptoms are presented by each case, and the disease is a very singular one.

TREATMENT.—In the simple form a very liberal diet of fresh vegetables, out-door exercise, and some simple tonic, are all that is necessary. In the hemorrhagic character, quinine, in one or two grain doses, should be given every three hours. Diet should consist of green vegetables, salt meats, eggs, and the free use of lemonade. A liniment of camphor, whiskey, and turpentine should be externally applied. If internal hemorrhage occurs, give oil of erigeron, in five-drop doses, every half hour; or matico, in from five to ten grain doses, may be administered every twenty minutes until it ceases.

ANATOMY OF THE ORGANS OF DIGESTION.

Mouth.—The mouth is separated from the nose by the hard and soft palate, and communicates. It is bounded in front by the lips, and its sides by the cheeks. The space between the lips and teeth is called the vestibule. The mouth is lined by a mucous membrane, which is covered by numerous glands, some being mucous and some salivary. The mouth contains a double row of teeth, thirty-two in the aggregate, performing the first process in digestion, the *mastication* of food.

Tongue.—The tongue is an oblong, flattened, muscular body, which varies in size and shape; it is the organ of taste, and also of importance in speech and mastication. Its posterior extremity or root is attached to a bone, called the *hyoid*, by yellow fibrous tissue. Its anterior extremity is called the *tip;* its intervening portion its *body*. The mucous covering of the tongue is very thick upon its upper surface, and very thin upon its under surface. Upon its upper surface are a number of projections, of various sizes and shapes, called *papillæ*. The largest are eight or nine in number, called *papillæ maximæ*, and are situated at the posterior portion of the tongue, in two convergent lines. The smallest papillæ are fine and pointed, and are found near the middle of the tongue, and are termed *filiform*. The intermediate papillæ are most abundant, some of which are *conical*, others *fungiform*. The tongue assists in the process of deglutition.

Palate.—The palate separates the back portion of the nose from the mouth, and is divided into two parts. The *hard palate*, of a bony base, covered by mucous membrane, which is continuous with that of the mouth; the soft palate is the membranous separation between the back portion of the mouth and nose. From the middle the *uvula* projects, about three-quarters of an inch in length; from each side of the uvula there are two divergent crescentic folds of mucous membrane, which are called *lateral half-arches;* the space between which constitutes the *fauces.*

Between the anterior and posterior arches of each side is the *tonsil gland.* The tonsils are about the size of an almond, and consist of a collection of large mucous follicles.

Salivary Glands.—The salivary glands are of light pink color, and their secretion is of great service in mastication and digestion. These are three in number — the parotid, submaxillary, and sublingual. The *parotid* is the largest; it lies on the side of the face in front of the ear, and beneath the skin. The submaxillary lies in a depression on the internal face of the lower jaw-bone. The *sublingual* is the smallest of the three; it is situated under the tongue.

Pharynx.—The pharynx is a muscular and membranous sac, communicating with the mouth, nose, œsophagus, larynx, and the tube (Eustachian) leading to the ear. Its length is about five inches, although this varies by extension and contraction. Its uses are for deglutition, respiration, and modulation of the voice.

Œsophagus.—This is the canal that conveys the food from the pharynx to the stomach. Its length is about nine or ten inches, and its diameter is not uniform, gradually increasing (as it descends). Its upper portion is the narrowest part of the alimentary canal; and hence foreign bodies which are too large to pass through the alimentary canal are generally arrested in the neck. It never contains air. Deglutition is performed by the contraction of the longitudinal fibres of the œsophagus, which shorten the passage, and by contraction of its circular fibres successively from above downward.

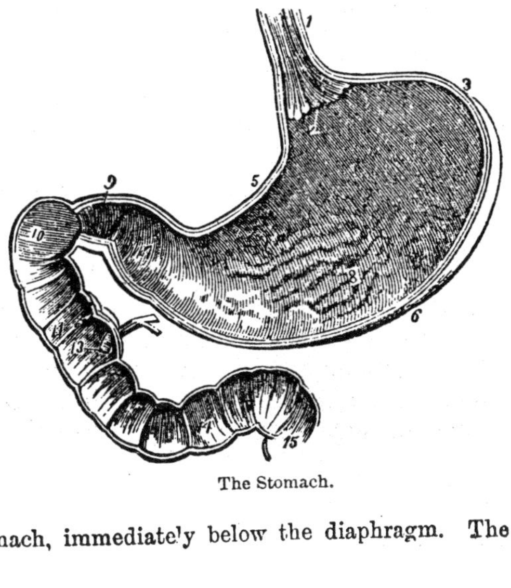

The Stomach.

Stomach.—The stomach is a conoidal sac, somewhat bent or curved, and situated below the breast-bone or in the epigastric region. The left[1] extremity is much the larger, and terminates in a rounded sac; at the upper portions of this extremity is the *cardiac* orifice[2] where the œsophagus is continued into the stomach, immediately below the diaphragm. The right extremity is continuous with the intestines, and its orifice is called the *pyloric*. The structure of the pylorus is much thicker than that of any other portion. The stomach is held in its position by the œsophagus[1] and the duodenum,[10] as well as by reflexions of the peritoneum. The upper and lower curvatures of the stomach are called the greater and lesser cuvatures.[5 6] Near the pyloric extremity of the stomach is a small dilatation[7] called the *antrum pylori*. The dimensions of the stomach are variable, depending upon the mode of life. It has four coats; the peritoneal, muscular, cellular and mucous.

In the stomach the food receives the admixture of the gastric juice, which is the solvent agent of digestion. The fluids taken into the stomach are for the most part absorbed from it; the solids, with the exception of the insoluble parts, are by the action of the gastric juice reduced to a substance called *chyme*, which in general is grayish, semi-fluid, homogeneous, with a slightly acid taste and smell. The chyme is then poured into the duodenum through the pyloric orifice for the subsequent action of the intestines.

Intestines.— The intestinal canal is from thirty to thirty-five feet in length, and is divided into *large* and *small* intestines. The small intestine is four-fifths of the length of the whole canal, reaching from the pylorus to the large intestine; it is cylindrical, and about one inch in diameter; there is a gradual diminution in calibre as it descends. Its coats are the same as those of the stomach. The mucous coat is very vascular, and its absorbents are very numerous. The glands are the crypts or follicles of Lieberkühn, the glands of Peyer, the solitary glands, and Brunner's glands.

The small intestine is divided into duodenum, jejunum, and ileum.

The *Duodenum* commences at the pylorus, and is about twelve inches long. The common duct formed by the junction of the bile and gall ducts opens into it about four or five inches from the pylorus. The *Jejunum* (from jejunus, *empty*) constitutes the upper two-fifths of the small intestine, and the *ileum* the remaining three-fifths.

The large intestine reaches from the ileum to the anus, and is one-fifth in length of the whole canal; it differs much from the small intestine, and has a sacculated appearance. It likewise has four coats. It is divided into cæcum, colon, and rectum

The *Cæcum* is a cul-de-sac or blind sac, and the commencement of the large intestine, and hence often called the *caput coli*. At the inferior portion is a worm-like process called *the appendix vermiformis*. On the side of the cæcum is the *ileo-cæcal* valve, an elliptical opening whereby the small intestine empties into the large.

The *Colon* is the largest portion of the large intestine; gradually diminishes in diameter until it terminates in the sigmoid or S-like flexure on the left side. It ascends on the right side, and forming an arch transversely, descends upon the left side. The *Rectum* is the terminating portion of the large intestine, and reaches from the sigmoid flexure to the *anus*. It is somewhat barrel-shaped, being larger in the middle than at either end.

DISEASES OF THE DIGESTIVE ORGANS.

STOMATITIS.

This is characterized by inflammation of the mouth. It may involve the whole membrane, or be confined to isolated portions. The first prominent symptom is a loss of taste, and a sensation similar to that produced by scalding liquids. The surface is red, very tender, and painful. The inflammation may extend to the fauces, nasal passages, and Eustachian tube. The stomach often becomes irritable, bowels loose, and the patient debilitated and emaciated. When caused by vitiated secretions, produced by the disturbed condition of the lymphatics while suckling, it is known as "*nursing sore-mouth*," or technically, *follicular stomatitis*. It may then extend to the stomach and bowels, causing ulceration, diarrhœa, dyspepsia, dysentery, and great prostration of the nervous system; and if not arrested, the mucous membranes of the air passages are involved, producing cough, expectoration, tuberculous degeneration and death. The teeth may fall out, and the gums be absorbed.

Aphthæ or Thrush is another form of stomatitis. It is generally characterized by small ulcers scattered over the surface, or in patches of white exudation, which may become thick and absorbed, and leave a raw-looking surface, or a foul spot. Children are very liable to it, and it is generally caused by acidity of the stomach, or general derangement of that organ by improper diet or unhealthy milk.

TREATMENT.—This depends upon the cause, which, if ascertained, should be removed. If due to carious teeth, they should be removed, and if owing to dyspepsia, the proper remedies should be given. The mouth should be frequently washed with a warm decoction of golden seal. The system should be supported with tonics, a generous diet, and a liberal use of fresh succulent vegetables, as grapes, etc., should be prescribed. Sage-tea gargles are very useful. The mother should also pay attention to her diet, so as not to supply the babe with improper milk. If due to acidity of the stomach, the necessary absorbents should be administered.

GLOSSITIS.

This is inflammation of the substance of the tongue, involving its muscular structure. It usually commences with a throbbing pain in the tongue, followed soon after with redness and swelling. In the course of a few hours the tongue enlarges so much as to fill the whole mouth, forces open the jaws, and protrudes from the mouth. Some fever usually accompanies it. Swallowing is usually almost impossible, speech gone, abscesses may form, and the tongue may even become mortified.

TREATMENT.—If due to a disordered state of the stomach, an active lobelia emetic should be given, and followed with an anti-bilious purge, like the Renovating Pill. If due to scalds or burns, the mouth should be washed with mucilage of flaxseed and slippery elm. If due to mercury, vapor baths should be taken, a free use of the syrup of stillingia resorted to, and equal parts of charcoal and yeast used as a gargle.

QUINSY (*Tonsillitis*).

This consists of inflammation of the tonsils, which may in many cases extend to the adjacent tissues. It usually commences with a slight chill, followed by much febrile excitement, uneasy feeling in the throat, and difficulty of swallowing, which increases in severity very rapidly, until at last deglutition becomes almost impossible. There is a constant disposition to swallow, in order to free the fauces from a tenacious, colorless mucus which adheres to that part. The respiration is not much affected unless in bad cases. From the commencement there is fever, severe headache, and a rapid pulse. The termination is usually an abscess, which at length opens, and a discharge of very fetid pus ensues, which affords relief. The duration of the disease is usually about a week, and is scarcely ever fatal.

TREATMENT.—Administer a free lobelia emetic, and anoint the throat thoroughly with the Herbal Ointment. In ordinary forms this will be sufficient. If an abscess, however, forms, it should be evacuated by an incision. In malarial districts, quinine in anti-periodic doses may be necessary, and if the fever is severe, veratrum should be given. The throat should be gargled with a decoction of golden seal, and to prevent termination into induration and permanent enlargement, alteratives should be given, especially in strumous habits.

PHARYNGITIS.

This is characterized either by acute, sub-acute, or chronic inflammation of the pharynx. There is slight pain upon pressure, or in the act of swallowing. It is seldom attended with fever, but in severe cases abscesses may form, causing great difficulty in swallowing and breathing. In the acute form the inflammation is usually limited to the mucous membrane, and simply constitutes an erythematic affection. The chronic form is known as "*clergyman's sore throat*," and is attended with a dry, hacking cough, hoarseness, and a sense of fatigue of the vocal organs after a slight exercise.

TREATMENT.—The treatment of simple pharyngitis is but little more than merely to regulate the stomach and bowels, the external application of cold packs, and a few days' rest. In the chronic form an invigorating and tonic course of treatment should be pursued, in connection with rest, baths, and pure air. To relieve the local difficulty, one grain of stillingia may be mixed with a drachm of sugar, divided into ten powders, of which one should be taken every two hours. The inhalation of hot vapor from bitter herbs is to be recommended. Blood-root in connection with constitutional treatment is highly beneficial. Patients will find that my "Acacian Balsam" in the chronic form is a virtual specific; the Herbal Ointment should also be outwardly applied. If owing to a complicated constitutional disorder, or if it exists in association with catarrh, it constitutes an affection requiring the most skilful treatment, and those who may wish my advice in such cases may refer to page 390 for general directions for consultation.

PAROTITIS (*Mumps*).

Mumps is an inflammatory affection of the salivary glands, especially the parotids. It generally commences with slight fever, stiffness of the jaws, and a slight pain or swelling in one or both parotid glands. The parts are hot, painful, and very tender upon pressure. Mastication and swallowing become painful, which causes considerable nervous irritability. Metastasis to the breasts of the female and to testicles of the male is liable to occur, especially if the patient is subjected to undue exposure. Inflammation of the brain may occur in some cases. It reaches its height in about four days, disappearing entirely about the seventh.

TREATMENT.—Keep the patient quiet, and give a mild purge. For external application a liniment of goose-fat and camphor is very beneficial. If there be much fever, resort to the usual anti-febrile treatment. If inflammation of the brain should ensue, resort to active cathartics, and give small doses of macrotin and quinine. The "Herbal Ointment" will be found a superior remedy, see page 472.

ŒSOPHAGITIS.

This is an inflammation of the œsophagus, or that portion of the alimentary canal which conveys the food from the pharynx to the stomach. Heat and pain, increased by swallowing, at some point along the tube, are the earliest symptoms. Occasionally there is pain between the shoulders, and, perhaps, tenderness on pressure, with more or less difficulty in swallowing. Hiccough, an eructation of glairy mucus, and vomiting, are sometimes present. There is also more or less constitutional disturbance. Ulcers and abscesses may form. It may become chronic, and stricture of the canal at any part of its passage may result, which may so effectually prevent deglutition as to cause death by starvation.

TREATMENT.—In the acute form, the stomach should be cleansed by a lobelia emetic, and the bowels opened by a purge. The surface should be sponged with hot water, and sufficient tincture of veratrum given to maintain a gentle diaphoresis. In the chronic form the alteratives are to be administered, and the bowels occasionally purged. The patient should be confined mostly to a vegetable diet of fluid character. Frequent sips from a decoction of golden seal and slippery elm should be taken. Stricture of the œsophagus should only be treated by a competent physician, as the means employed for its cure might do more harm in improper hands than any possible good.

INFLAMMATION OF THE STOMACH (*Gastritis*).

This usually commences in the acute form with violent vomiting and a burning pain in the region of the stomach. Swallowing becomes difficult, thirst is intense, tongue is dry and smooth, headache often violent, delirium and prostration are present. If the stomach only is inflamed, there is constipation; but if the bowels also are affected, there is diarrhœa. The attendant fever is as common, and the disease may assume such a gravity that death inevitably ensues, especially in perforation of the stomach. Chronic gastritis is a common disorder. It is generally of a mild character, unless of long continuance, when it may occasion considerable organic disorder. Its approach is gradual, presenting a variety of symptoms, but may be known from dyspepsia in there being more pain at some particular point, and more frequent vomiting after taking food.

TREATMENT.—Give an emetic, and cleanse the stomach by means of large draughts of warm water. Counter-irritation should be resorted to over the stomach. The vomiting may be checked by opium, and the tincture of crawley may be given to control the fever. If produced by a corrosive poison, the necessary antidotes will, of course, be required. All solid foods should be withheld, and the drinks should be mucilaginous, as marshmallow, slippery elm, gum-water, etc.

The treatment of chronic gastritis is not so easily stated. It depends greatly upon associated conditions and complications. Diet is an important element in the treatment. My "Restorative Assimilant" internally, and "Herbal Ointment" externally, generally cure each case; but some cases are of such a serious character that a cure can only be effected by special symptomatic treatment. Those desiring to consult me are referred to questions, page 390.

CANCER OF THE STOMACH.

The early symptoms of cancer of the stomach are usually similar to chronic gastritis. The appetite is impaired, and frequent nausea and vomiting supervene. The pain in the stomach is of a lancinating character. The gastric functions are impaired, and the mucous discharges become sour and purulent, finally bloody, and if subjected to microscopical examination, cancer cells are found. The complexion has a yellowish-white, waxen appearance, which distinguishes cancer from other diseases of the stomach.

TREATMENT.—The treatment consists chiefly in combating the symptoms as they occur. Cundurango should be given a fair trial in all cases. If the disease has reached a certain stage, no remedy will produce a radical impression; but I have the assurance that I have cured many cases of well-defined cancer of the stomach, in more or less advanced stages of the disease, by the employment of consistent and energetic chemical treatment.

HEART-BURN (*Gastralgia*).

Two forms of heart-burn are commonly observed: one, attended by acid eructations, causing irritation of the throat and fauces; and in the other, the ejections from the stomach are rancid and alkaline. and connected with a gnawing pain and distention of the stomach. It principally occurs during digestion, and may be of every grade of severity. It is caused by excess of acid, or an accumulation of gas, in the stomach.

TREATMENT.—This depends upon the cause. If acid, administer pulverized charcoal, with a little magnesia, or, what is just as good, compound spirits of lavender. If alkaline, give lemon-juice as often as required.

GASTRALGIA, OR GASTRODYNIA.

This is a neuralgic affection of the stomach, and is often a symptom of dyspepsia. The appetite is generally impaired, though sometimes remains good. There is a gnawing pain in the stomach, and a strong disposition to vomit. The tongue is usually foul, the skin cool, and pulse quite disturbed.

TREATMENT.—If owing to long-continued use of indigestible or improper food, abandon it, and change to other articles. Take quinine. and a little cherry laurel water, to subdue the neuralgic affection, and tonics to restore the tonicity of the stomach.

SPASM OF THE STOMACH.

This consists of a sense of pain, stricture, or contraction, occurring in paroxysms. The stomach feels as if rolled into a ball, or drawn towards the back. It assumes different degrees of violence, being often exceedingly painful.

TREATMENT.—It is instantly relieved by a dose of some preparation of wild gum, in combination with a fourth of a grain of gelsemin. External application of the "Herbal Ointment" acts equally as specifically.

WATER-BRASH (*Pyrosis*).

This also occurs generally in paroxysms. The pain is intense, and of a burning character. An eructation of a thin, insipid, watery liquid occurs, and, when discharged, affords momentary relief.

TREATMENT.—Quinine and the general tonics will remove this difficulty. Certain habits, as inebriety, anxiety of mind, etc., are to be overcome, and a generous diet indulged in.

DYSPEPSIA, OR INDIGESTION.

This is one of the most common affections in the whole catalogue of diseases. Scarcely a human being lives that has not or will not be a victim to this harassing disease. In simple indigestion, the symptoms vary much in nature and severity. One may suffer severely, while another has merely slight depression of spirits. Loss of appetite, nausea, vomiting, constipation alternating with diarrhœa, furred tongue, foulness of breath, palpitation of the heart, pains in various parts, dull headache, hypochondriasis, etc., are present in all cases. The patient's appetite may at one time be wholly lost; at other times it is morbid and ravenous, which, if indulged in, will only add to his misery. There is seldom any healthy feeling of hunger, but, in place of this, the patient has a most miserable sensation of hollowness or sinking at the region of the stomach. Nausea and vomiting are the most distressing symptoms of dyspepsia; the former may occur soon after the food is swallowed, or it may be deferred for an hour or two. The matter ejected is most frequently sour, and mixed with bile, often having the flavor of rotten eggs, which is due to a gas known as sulphuretted hydrogen. This gas, in ascending, often brings the solid food into the throat and mouth, making the patient almost a ruminant animal. Suffering is experienced when the stomach is full or empty, though it differs in various cases. Sometimes not much uneasiness is felt until several hours after eating, when all its attendant horrors are manifested. This is due to fermentation of the food. Water-brash, gastralgia, spasm of the stomach, etc., are constant companions of the dyspeptic, and his days are most miserably spent, while his nights are not much better, because his sleep is not refreshing; the body is not reposed, and he is the frequent victim of horrible nightmares. A dyspeptic patient suffers from every variety of indisposition, and it is easy to learn from his dejected countenance and woe-begone look that he yearns for that comfortable human existence that only a healthy digestive apparatus affords to man. He is fretful and peevish, dissatisfied with others and with himself; has individually no comfort, and allows but little to those around him; everything that was formerly bright and cheerful now bears a gloomy aspect; his smiles are derisive, his opinions cynical; and everything that is bright, cheerful, and lovable has gone with the enjoyment of good health. The disease is in fact a malady that embraces in its symptoms and consequences nearly every physical and mental torture known to mankind.

TREATMENT.—When it arises from inertia of the stomach, it may be removed by stomachics. If produced by bad habits, it can only be corrected by strict adherence to the physiological laws controlling the digestive functions. When it occurs from softening of the mucous membranes and a deficiency of the gastric secretion, alnuin is a good remedy; and chelonin acts well in chronic inflammation of the organ. When dependent upon nervous debility, herbal phosphorus and cypripedin act well. Constipation should be relieved by leptandrin and similar cathartics. Diet and hygiene form a very important part in the treatment, and these should receive very careful attention. Fresh air, baths, friction, out-door exercise, careful avoidance of overloading the stomach, are indispensable adjuncts to all treatment. It is but just to myself, and eminently due to my readers, to acquaint them with my mode of treating dyspepsia, and which, I confidently assert, is attended with as specific results as can be expected from any medicinal agents. It is my sincere belief that failure is impossible if the remedies are taken faithfully, for a reasonable length of time. I advise in all cases and in all forms of the disease, my "Restorative Assimilant," "Renovating Pills," and "Herbal Ointment." The Assimilant is taken internally, in prescribed doses, three times a day; the pills are taken as occasion requires, to keep bowels regular, and the Herbal Ointment is rubbed externally, once or twice a day, over the region of the stomach and bowels. The philosophy of this treatment is obvious; the Assimilant restores the tonicity of the digestive organs, increases secretion of gastric juice, promotes chymification, stimulates the accessory organs of digestion, and, by its assimilative properties, increases the functional action of the absorbents, and restores the chemical process of digestion to its healthy state. The pills increase the peristaltic motion of the bowels, augment biliary discharges, stimulate the mesenteric glands, while, at the same time, they give tonic power to the whole alimentary canal. The ointment, by its discutient properties, removes all inflammation, localizes healthy blood to the organs and tissues, and prevents centralization of morbific agents.

These remedies at once assert their value, and gain complete mastery over the disease in a short time; and should any of my dyspeptic readers, though faithless in medicinal relief from repeated failures, be pleased to give them a trial, the author is confident that the medicines will cure them and restore them to vigorous health, so that they may once more enjoy the boon of healthy digestive organs. (See page 469.)

ANATOMY OF THE LIVER.

The liver is the largest glandular organ in the body; its office is to secrete bile. It is oblong and oval in shape, and occupies the position on the right side, under the lower ribs. It weighs from four to five pounds; it measures from ten to twelve inches transversely, and from six to seven antero-posteriorly; its greatest thickness is from four to five inches. On the upper surface it is convex, and on the lower concave. Its *color* is of a reddish-brown, with occasional spots of black.

The under surface of the liver presents a deep fissure, called umbilical or longitudinal, reaching from the anterior[16] to the posterior[17] notch, containing the remains of the umbilical vein of fœtal life. Sometimes this fissure is converted into a foramen,[7] or opening, the right and left lobes being connected. At right angles to this fissure is another, called the *transverse*[11] fissure, containing the portal vein, hepatic artery, and hepatic duct, bound together by the *capsule of Glisson*, a membrane of cellular tissue. The *gall-bladder*[10] lies in a deep depression upon the under surface of the right lobe of the liver. The *lobulus quadratus*[3] is that portion of the liver included between the depression occupied by the gall-bladder and the longitudinal and transverse fissures. At the posterior and inferior portion of the liver is a triangular lobe called the *lobulus Spigelii.*[4] The elongated ridge running from the lobulus Spigelii outwardly is the *lobulus caudatus.*[5] These lobules are, however, all contained in the two lobes of the liver. The *right lobe*[1] is the largest and thickest, and the *left*[2] terminates in a thin cutting edge. The *structure* of the liver may be seen by tearing the liver of any animal. This will show a granulated arrangement, and each of these granules is usually called an *acinus*. These acini consist of a terminal branch of the portal vein and hepatic artery, together with the incipient radicles of the hepatic duct and hepatic vein, and in the capillary network thus constituted are numerous cells, which secrete the bile.

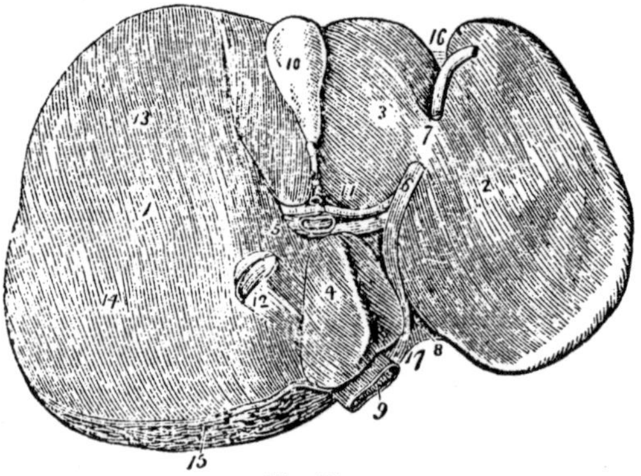

The Liver.

The liver is liable to a variety of disorders, and, when affected, exerts a marked influence on the organs and tissues of the body. The functions of the organ are so important that impairment arising from any organic cause quickly disturbs the harmony and health of the whole economy. Its office is to eliminate the superfluous carbon from the blood. This carbon enters into chemical combination with other substances, forming the compound known as bile, and which is poured into the duodenum, or upper bowel, where it assists greatly in the process of digestion.

DISEASES OF THE LIVER.

HEPATITIS.

Inflammation may be confined to its outside covering, or involve the entire substance of the liver. It usually makes its appearance with sympathetic fever, pain, a sense of tension on the right side, inability to lie on the left side, difficulty of breathing, a dry cough, vomiting, and a troublesome cough. As the morbid action increases, high fever, with hot skin, thirst, and scanty urine is observed. The pain is acute and lancinating, and is apt to run up to the right collar-bone, and to the top of the shoulder. The pain is increased by coughing, breathing, and lying on the left side. A soreness is felt by pressing over the liver, and usually, when enlarged, is readily recognized by the touch. The pulse is full and hard, bowels costive, stools clay-colored, and the tongue is covered with a dark-brown, or even black coat, and there is a bitter taste in the mouth.

TREATMENT.—Evacuate the stomach and bowels, and apply hot packs, rubefacients, or even vesicants in some cases, to the region of the liver. The purges should be such that will thoroughly evacuate the bowels with watery discharges, as jalap, elaterium, etc. Promote perspiration by a spirit vapor bath, or by American hellebore, or other diaphoretics. When the urine is red and scanty, an infusion of marsh-mallow, pumpkin-seeds, or trailing arbutus should be given. Quinine, gelsemin, and irisin may be necessary in some cases.

CHRONIC HEPATITIS.

Chronic inflammation of the liver usually involves the entire organ, and may be the result of the acute form, although it exists independently of it. It is a disease very common in the South and West, and is evidently owing to malarial poison, in connection with heat and atmospheric vicissitudes. It is a very insidious disease, and the whole organ may assume a pathological condition before attracting any special attention. The most common symptoms are a disordered stomach, occasional vomiting, a sense of fulness and weight in the right side, irregular bowels, pains in one or both shoulders, unhealthy stools, yellowness of skin, eyes, and urine, a short dry cough, disturbed appetite, febrile exacerbations towards night, and general emaciation. The patient is generally despondent, his temper is irritable and peevish, and he is frequently the prey to the dread of some impending evil. The exercise of his mental faculties is often impossible in a literary or argumentative direction, and the loss of the cherished attribute of manhood is most frequently added to his misery. If the patient be a female, sexual congress becomes to her a revolting union, and her husband's approaches create in her only a feeling of disgust and scorn.

TREATMENT.—The diet should be regulated, outdoor exercise should be taken, baths liberally used, and chafing liniments applied over the liver; keep the bowels open with leptandrin, or decoction of the plant, and give one-tenth of a grain of gelsemin with two grains of quinine, every three or four hours, until about twenty doses have been taken. This may be followed by dandelion and blackroot in small doses four or five times a day. An alterative like irisin may also be given. I also most strongly advise my "Restorative Assimilant," "Herbal Ointment," and "Renovating Pills;" to be used about the same as ordered in dyspepsia. The pills, especially, exercise specific control over morbid conditions of the liver, and frequently cure the disease, unaided by other remedies.

It is frequently the case that chronic inflammation of the liver is so complicated that it will not respond to any ordinary treatment. In such cases a careful analysis of the symptoms and general condition of the patient must be made, and the treatment so modified and varied as to suit all the conditions of the case. In these cases it is difficult to designate the required treatment, as each individual case is characterized by its own pathological phenomena, and requires essentially particular treatment. My success in the treatment of these stubborn cases has exceeded even my own anticipations in many instances, and I now like to combat the "bilious" foe with my herbal weapons — and the laurels generally rest on my brow. Those who wish to cousult me are referred to page 390.

CIRRHOSIS.

The result of chronic inflammation of the areolar tissue of the entire organ is often induration or cirrhosis of the liver. The tissues become so firm, and ultimately so constricted, as to diminish the caliber of the portal vein, hepatic artery, and duct, resulting in the wasting away or atrophy of the lobular structure, and the hepatic cells become studded with fat. This condition sadly interferes with the circulation of the blood through the portal vein, producing inflammation of gastric and intestinal linings. It is the *hob-nailed* liver of some writers. The usual symptoms are constipation, a dry skin, high-colored urine, fickle appetite, and derangement of the nervous system. The spleen often becomes enlarged, while the liver diminishes in size, the pain becomes more intense, and frequently the kidneys are also involved. Digestion is feeble, chills, hectic fever, and night-sweats are often present, and frequently a dropsical condition of the lower limbs and abdomen is observed.

TREATMENT.—All alcoholic stimulants should be avoided, and the action of the liver aroused by prickly ash, leptandrin, dandelion, emetics, etc. The tonics should be given, and Indian hemp should be administered in sufficient quantities to maintain a gentle influence upon the bowels and kidneys The alteratives, if indicated, should be exhibited, and continued as long as required.

This disease is certainly an unfavorable one for treatment in its advanced stages, but my treatment in well-defined cases has been attended with the most favorable results, and I hope ere long that the result of my investigations into the morbid character of the disease in all its phases, that I have made for many years, will enable me to still more rob the disease of its formidable nature.

GALL-STONES.

These concretions are generally oval or pear-shaped, and formed in the gall-bladder or hepatic ducts. They vary in size, from that of a small pea to a fowl's egg, and in chemical composition present cholesterine, coloring matter, and the salts of lime, magnesia, etc. They occur oftener in females than in males, from the fact that their inactive life is more conducive to their formation. They give rise to a dull, heavy pain in the region of the liver, and more or less febrile excitement. In their passage through the duct they cause the most excruciating pain, which is accordingly intensified in proportion to the size of the stone. Impaction of the cystic duct, with complete obstruction and inflammation, ulceration, and perforation of the duct and bladder may occur, giving rise to great difficulties.

TREATMENT.—To reduce the spasm, Dover's powder, or other anodynes, should be given, and hot packs or fomentations should be applied externally. A vapor bath and lobelia emetic often afford great relief. Belladonna plasters should be applied over the region of the liver, as they dilate the cystic duct, and alleviate the pains. Thoroughwort is a good remedy, and should be freely taken. If the stones can be found in the alvine discharges, their chemical character should be definitely ascertained, and the proper chemical treatment resorted to in order to prevent their re-formation. Those who may desire my services in this respect can forward to me the stones, and on receipt I will carefully analyze them, and suggest the proper treatment.

JAUNDICE (*Icterus*).

The most prominent symptoms are yellowness of the skin, eyes, and urine, owing to the deposit of the coloring matter of the bile in the blood. The appetite is impaired, the food is loathed, an uncomfortable feeling of a load at the pit of the stomach is felt. The stomach is sour, sometimes there is sickness and vomiting, a bitter taste in the mouth, a dull pain at the right side, sleepiness, and an uncomfortable feeling of lassitude at all times distresses the patient. The urine is heavily tinged with bile, and the stools clay colored. It is usually idiopathic, but may be a concomitant of other diseases. Torpidity of the liver is the chief cause, yet any functional disorder of the organs may cause it.

TREATMENT.—If caused by inactivity of the liver, the organ should be aroused by a lobelia emetic and active antibilious purges. I can certainly advise no better cathartic for this purpose than my Renovating Pill. The liver should be further stimulated to action by the application of an irritating plaster over the region of the liver. Tonics, like quinine, poplar, and liriodendron, may be necessary in some cases. The diet should consist of fresh vegetables, and as much out-door exercise should be taken as the patient can bear.

The liver is the seat of many other diseases, but as they are more or less rare, of difficult detection, and treatment difficult, I deemed it prudent not to enter upon any consideration of them. The organ may hypertrophy or atrophy, its blood-vessels may become diseased, it may be affected by syphilitic taint, it may become fatty, it may degenerate into a waxy or albuminous mass; disease may change it into a pigment or nutmeg liver; it may be the seat of hydatids or parasites, tumors or cancer may assail it, and finally it may be the seat of tuberculous matter of a miliary character. The symptoms produced by these morbid conditions are so obscure, and many of them the common property of all, that none but a skilful physician is capable of recognizing the identity of the affection; and I advise all patients who are suffering from any liver disease that presents phenomena not recognizable in the simpler affections of the organ, to intrust his case to a competent physician.

I have devoted nearly a lifetime to the study of liver diseases, and I am ready to maintain that my success in their treatment is greater than by any other system of medication. I am daily consulted with reference to some chronic disease of the liver, both in person or by letter, and patients under treatment are scattered in all sections of the country. Constant communication by correspondence enables me to treat such cases as satisfactorily as by personal interview, as is attested by the gratifying success achieved in all cases. (See page 390.)

ANATOMY OF THE SPLEEN.

The organ [2 1 3], occupying the right of the following cut, is the spleen. It is a soft vascular organ, of a purplish color. It is not a true gland, as it has no duct.

The shape of the spleen is irregular and variable, but it is generally the section of an ovoid, with a convex surface resting against the dia-

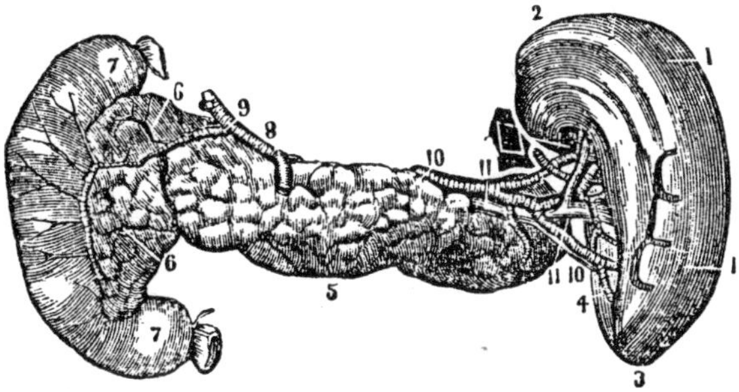

Spleen and Pancreas.

phragm, opposite the ninth, tenth, and eleventh ribs, and a convex surface directed towards the stomach.

It varies in size more than any other organ in the body. It is generally five inches long and three wide, and weighs from five to seven ounces. The proper substance of the spleen is a soft, pulpy mass, of a reddish-brown color, resembling grumous blood. Its office in the economy is not well understood, but is evidently concerned in the blood-depurating process. It is numerously supplied with lymphatics. The long and flat gland lying between the spleen and duodenum, in the left of the cut, is the *Pancreas*, or *sweet-bread.* It is of a light-pink color, and is about seven inches long. Its right extremity [6], or *head* is much the thickest part, and is often called the *lesser pancreas.* Its left extremity gradually diminishes in breadth until it touches the spleen [8 9 10]. The superior edge has a groove for the passage of the splenic artery. Its structure is conglomerate. Its excretory duct is called the *duct of Wirsungius.*

Its secretion is somewhat similar to saliva, hence it is often called the *abdominal* salivary gland. Its secretion contains a larger amount of solid matter than the saliva, and assists in the process of digestion.

SPLENITIS.

The functions of the spleen have formerly been the cause of much controversy, nor are they better understood at the present day; but the organ is evidently concerned somewhat in the blood-making process;

but that it performs a very important part is doubtful, as the whole organ has been removed without affecting the health in the least. In some countries, the practice of removing the spleen in pigs, for the purpose of facilitating the fattening practice, has been resorted to, which fact has suggested to some over-confident analogists the propriety of removing the spleen in the human subject as a remedy for debility.

Splenitis prevails most in malarious districts, and is a frequent result of chills and fever. A feeling of weight, tightness, sometimes pain in the left side, which is increased by pressure, or an attempt to lie on the left side, are the earliest symptoms. The organ enlarges—sometimes so much that it can readily be felt by the hand. It is known by the name of "ague-cake," and causes numbness and weakness of the legs, difficulty of breathing, palpitation of the heart, obstinate constipation, vomiting of food, piles, dry skin, and occasionally dropsical affections.

TREATMENT.—This does not differ much with the treatment advised for acute and chronic inflammation of the liver. Quinine, in combination with leptandrin and irisin, is indicated in all cases. Counter-irritation should also be made over the splenic region, and, when complicated with dropsy, the required directions should be administered. My "Restorative Assimilant," "Herbal Ointment," and "Renovating Pills" cure every case, if taken for a reasonable length of time.

The spleen may also be affected with dropsy, or become studded with tuberculous matter. In such events the treatment is the same as for dropsy and tubercular depositions of any other internal organ.

DISEASES OF THE PANCREAS.

The pancreas is rarely the seat of disease. The symptoms of its morbid conditions are usually obscure. It may be affected by inflammation, passive or acute. In typhoid, typhus, and puerperal fevers, it occasionally becomes involved in inflammation. The symptoms of disease of this gland are usually pain in the epigastrium, enlargement and tenderness, a sensation of heat and constriction, salivation, nausea and vomiting, diarrhœa, loss of appetite, despondency, chills, alternated with flushes of heat, and debility, with great emaciation. The vomiting in some instances is very obstinate; the matters ejected are thin, ropy and of a sour or saltish taste. Jaundice is often observed.

TREATMENT.—Control the disease by equalizing the circulation with hot packs, veratrum, aconite, mild purges, etc. In the chronic form, administer mandrake, blue flag, and poke-root, as these remedies are known to increase the functions of this gland. Lobelia and capsicum, in some cases of chronic congestion and inflammation, act with decided benefit. In all diseases of this gland it would be well, however, to intrust the treatment to a competent herbal physician.

DISEASES OF THE BOWELS.

The intestinal tube is very seldom affected throughout its whole extent but inflammation may involve any portion of it at one time. If the duodenum is affected it is called *Duodenitis*, if the cæcum or blind gut is inflamed, it receives the name of *Typhilitis*, if it involves the small intestine, it is called *Enteritis*. These diseases are very rare, however, and their consideration as separate affections is of not much importance, except to the nosologist. The treatment is upon general principles and corresponds withthat given in all inflammatory affections of the intestinal mucous membrane. Dysentery is a typical case of enteric inflammation, hence we will commence with the consideration of it.

DYSENTERY (*Colitis*).

This is also known as bloody flux, and consists of an inflammation of the membrane of the colon and rectum, and characterized by small mucous or bloody evacuations, griping, and straining. The disease comes on with loss of appetite, costiveness, lassitude, shivering, heat of skin and quick pulse. These are followed by griping pain in the bowels and a constant desire to go to stool. The passages are mostly small in quantity, and composed of mucus mixed with blood. These passages are attended with severe griping and straining, technically known as *tormina* and *tenesmus*. Nausea and vomiting sometimes attend the early stages. When the natural fæces pass off, they are usually formed in round compact balls, called *scybala*. Fever is commonly present, with a feeble, almost thread-like pulse. The discharges have but little odor at first, but become exceedingly offensive as the disease advances. The chronic form is characterized by frequent small evacuations, consisting mostly of mucus, but sometimes mixed with pus, bile, fæces and blood. The symptoms are the same, but less intense than in the acute form Emaciation, debility, dropsy, and consumption result, if not arrested. When the liver and stomach become disordered at the commencement, it is called *bilious* dysentery. Various forms of the disease are known as adynamic, intermittent and remittent, typhous, rheumatic and epidemic dysentery; but it is not necessary to classify the disease under these heads.

TREATMENT.—A free lobelia emetic may be given at the outset, and the bowels evacuated by a purge; castor-oil with laudanum is the best for this purpose. After the purge, take twenty grains of quinine and one drachm of leptandrin, divide into six powders and take one every hour until all are taken. The tenesmus should be relieved by injecting into the rectum five or six ounces of starch water, containing about twenty drops of laudanum, as often as is necessary. Ipecacuanha is a superior remedy. Gelsemin may be given afterwards, and if required the fever should be controlled by veratrum. The patient should lie quietly in bed, and his diet should consist of grapes, baked apples, flour porridge, bread, rice, coffee, beef-tea and ripe fruit. The astringents are of course necessary, and for this purpose tannic and gallic acids, kino, rhatany, opium, capsicum, cranesbill, etc., can be given. Tonics should be combined when the patient is weak, and if the debility is very great the alcoholic stimulants should be administered. I can with safety recommend my "Restorative Assimilant" as a sure cure for both acute and chronic dysentery, as well as for all bowel complaints. The Herbal Ointment should be rubbed externally on the whole abdomen to relieve the inflammation. In the chronic form, the astringents, with such other remedies as may be indicated by the symptoms, are all that is necessary.

Diarrhœa.

This common disorder is characterized by frequent and urgent demands to evacuate the bowels. It is usually preceded by a sense of indigestion, fulness of stomach, flatulency, and more or less colic pains. The pain generally subsides after an evacuation, and returns as an indication of another discharge. The discharges may be thick, consisting of ingesta, or they may be serous, or of a rice-water appearance. Sometimes they consist of disintegrated mucous membranes, blood, and bile. There is usually a disagreeable sinking sensation in the abdomen along with the discharge, with exhaustion, a cool skin, and a feeble irregular pulse. It may be attended with fever, indicating extensive irritation of the mucous coat. The urine is usually scanty. When the discharges are composed of serum, and highly colored with either yellow or green bile, it is called *bilious* diarrhœa; when composed principally of mucus, it is known as *mucous* diarrhœa, and when of a thin, watery character, the name of *serous* diarrhœa is given to it. The disease may become chronic.

Treatment.—If it occurs in children, a little paregoric, or essence of peppermint or spearmint, usually cures in a short time. Opium in combination with ipecac, as in the Dover's powder, is an excellent remedy. The astringents are all indicated. Starch injections, as advised in dysentery, should also be resorted to, and counter-irritation of the abdomen is also serviceable. In the chronic form the tonics should be combined with the astringents. I cannot recommend my "Restorative Assimilant" (see page 469.) too strongly. It is certainly an admirable remedy for this complaint, relieving it most instantly.

Chronic diarrhœa may often be so dependent upon a vitiated condition of the system that it becomes quite difficult to cure. In such cases the most careful treatment is necessary to overcome the disease. During the war, and also afterwards, the author was consulted for this affection by those who contracted it in the army in thousands of cases; but under proper treatment all recovered.

CONSTIPATION.

By this is understood a collection of excrementitious matters in some part of the intestinal tube. It is marked by unfrequency of stool, and by the recurrence of fulness and tension in parts of the abdomen. It occurs in patients of a lax and weak habit of body, or it may arise from rigidity of the muscles. It may also be due to imperfect functional action of the stomach, liver, pancreas, etc., in which case the intellectual faculties are dull, the complexion is sallow, the skin dry, urine scanty, acidity of the stomach, and headache. Sometimes the accumulation of fæcal matter is so great that the masses can be felt through the abdominal walls. It is frequently caused by an atonic condition of the muscular structure of the intestines, and in very many cases it results from neglect to attend to the calls of nature. These calls should be imperative, and whenever the desire arises they should not be disregarded, but obeyed as quickly as opportunity allows. I once knew a sea-captain who only evacuated his bowels when in port, and who remarked to me that when he "battened down the hatches of his vessel, he also battened down the hatches of his body, and no matter how long the voyages, no stools are made." The consequences were, that whenever he came to port he had a hard time to be relieved of his fæcal accumulations. In many other cases no movement of the bowels was observed for ten or twelve weeks. Constipation is attended with various sympathetic affections, and finally deranges the blood, impairs the health, tone, and vigor of the whole system. It is frequently the cause of piles, strangury, dysmenorrhœa, amenorrhœa, leucorrhœa, apoplexy, epilepsy, dyspepsia, insanity, etc.

TREATMENT.—The cause of the difficulty should be carefully studied, and the proper treatment resorted to. The diet should be composed of laxative articles of food, as fresh fruits, unbolted-flour bread, etc. If dependent upon a lax state of the muscular fibres, golden seal, in combination with mandrake and blackroot are the proper remedies, and when due to vitiated secretions of the stomach, liver, etc., the American Columbo should be given. In atony of the bowels, nux vomica should be carefully administered with the cathartics. Cathartics and enemas are of course indicated for present relief in all cases, and those should be selected which operate sufficiently, without causing irritation of the mucous membranes. Kneading the bowels often overcomes habitual constipation. There exists no better remedy than my "Renovating Pills," they cure every case of habitual constipation. The bowels may become obstructed from other causes, *Intussusception*, or invagination of the bowels, or when one part of the bowel is drawn into another portion, produces complete closure of the canal. The bowels also become twisted. These conditions may be known by the vomiting of stercoraceous or fæcal matter, and when this is observed, instant medical aid should be called for, as the condition is one of great danger, and requires intelligent treatment.

INTESTINAL WORMS.

Every animal seems to be a nest for other animals, and man is no exception to the rule. There are five varieties of intestinal worms, all more or less familiar to every one of my readers.

1. *Ascaris lumbricoides.*– This worm resembles the common earthworm, and is supposed to belong to the same species. It varies in size from four to eighteen inches in length; it also varies in color, having in some instances a whitish pink hue, and in others a dull, dirty-yellow color. It feeds on the chyme found in the intestines, upon absorption from which the growth of the human system depends. They are generally found in the smaller intestines.

2. *Ascaris vermicularis.*—This worm is sometimes improperly called the thread-worm, for there is another variety more like a thread than this. It is commonly called the maw-worm, and is the smallest known. The male is exceedingly small, but the female is about half an inch long. It is very slender, and about the size of small sewing-thread. From the fact that it inhabits the rectum chiefly, it is often called the *seat-worm*. This is the animal so troublesome and annoying to children, but is occasionally also found in adults. The child infested with them runs about during the day apparently well, but when night comes it complains of itching in the rectum, which is sometimes excessively annoying.

3. *Tricocephalus dispar.*—This is the long thread-worm, from one to two inches in length, but sometimes reaches a length of four inches. It is like a small thread, except at the posterior extremity, where it is enlarged. It is not so often found as the others. It is of light color. The male is smaller than the female, and differs little in shape. It is common to all parts of the intestinal canal.

4. *Tœnia solium* or *vulgaris.*—This is the common tape-worm. Of this family there is but one variety in the United States, though there is another peculiar to other parts of the world. It varies greatly in length and size. The ordinary length is from seven to fifteen feet, but it sometimes arrives at the enormous length of one hundred feet. It is of a flat, ribbon-like shape, about one-quarter of an inch in breadth in the largest places, and tapers to almost a mere thread at the caudal extremity. Its color is whitish or yellowish; and it is made up of numerous segments or joints, which are most distinct and perfect at a distance from the head. These segments resemble a gourd-seed, and are four-sided. The head is smaller than most of the body, with a small point in the centre with openings. It is supposed that this animal can exist or reproduce itself if but a single joint exists, but this is doubtful

unless the head exists. When the head is evacuated the remainder will decay and be also expelled. This animal is hermaphrodite, and impregnates itself. It inhabits the small intestines. Persons affected with this worm frequently pass joints, but it often remains in the body for a long time without its presence being thus revealed.

5. *Tænia lata*, or *bothriocephalus latus*.—This is the broad tape-worm, and does not exist in this country unless imported. It is found in Central and Western Europe. It is much broader, and the joints are shorter than in the common long tape-worm. The joints are more per-

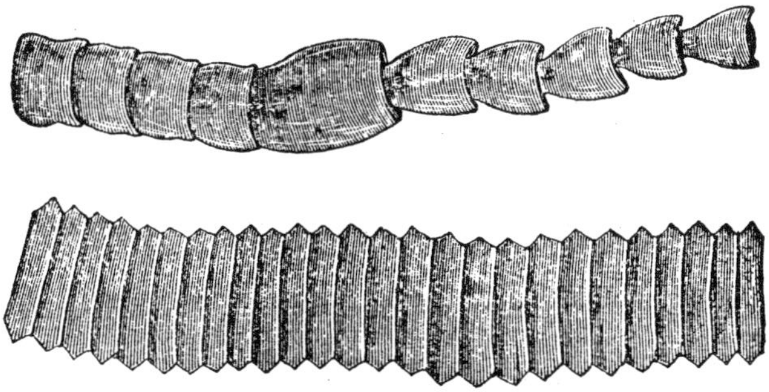

Sections of the Tape Worm.

fect, well developed, and thrown off in connected rows, and by a cavity in the centre, and not in the border of the joint. It varies in length from one to twenty feet.

Almost every variety of symptoms is found to result from the irritation that worms produce in the human system. The symptoms, however, occur mostly in children, and are generally produced by the long, round, or common worms. The abdomen is prominent, full or bloated; the appetite variable and capricious; sometimes deficient and sometimes voracious. The breath is usually offensive, the tongue has a white-coated appearance, and often the upper lip will be much swollen. The eyelids also swell often, sometimes so much that the child can barely see; and occasionally swollen patches will present themselves in other parts of the body. Children troubled with worms are apt to pass restless nights, and frequently start in their sleep. Paleness around the mouth, extending up the sides of the nose, is another common symptom. Itching of the anus is the most common and only particular effect produced by the small worms. St. Vitus' dance and epilepsy often result from verminous irritation, but the latter is usually harmless when properly treated. A dry, choking cough is a symptom peculiar of worms. Itching of the nose is a common symptom, and the child is almost incessantly rubbing that member.

The symptoms of tape-worm are somewhat peculiar, and deserve a brief notice. Persons of all ages are subject to them, but they are most common to middle age. The disturbance they occasion is that of great uneasiness and distress, which often, sooner or later, destroys the general health. Uneasiness in the head, sometimes pain, slight giddiness and ringing in the ears, are the symptoms most complained of. The countenance changes frequently from a flushed to a pale condition; twitching of the muscles, especially those at the mouth, and a pinched, contracted appearance of the nostrils, accompanied with itching, are peculiar symptoms of tape-worm. The appetite is variable, the eyelids swollen, the breath offensive, etc., and other symptoms common to other worms are present also in tape-worm. Nausea occurs at times, with ejections of frothy mucus. The patient grits his teeth in sleep; and the abdomen seems full, with contraction of the navel. After a night's sleep there is a sensation of an animal moving about in the bowels, accompanied by darting pains, which subside after eating. The patient becomes weak and nervous, and finally, worn out with excitement, gets hypochondriacal and even deranged. Of course, the most unequivocal symptom is a discharge of joints of the worm.

TREATMENT.—This varies with the symptoms of each case. If convulsions exist, the first step should be to subdue these by brisk friction and warm applications along the spine and abdomen. Anti-spasmodics in these cases should be given; also sweating drinks. If these symptoms are relieved, the compound powder of senna and jalap may be given with pink and wormwood in sufficient doses to produce free evacuations of the bowels. This is to be repeated for two or three days, and is usually successful. It is equally reliable in the treatment of the long thread-worm. The powder is composed of three drachms each of the above herbs decocted in a pint of water; dose, a tablespoonful. It produces sometimes alarming symptoms, but these, however, are harmless and of short duration. Pinkroot and wormwood are good remedies, however, given in any form. The melia azedarach, or the Pride of China, given in decoction, is a favorite remedy; so also is the burr of the red cedar, the efficacy depending upon the turpentine it contains. Santonine in doses of three or five grains is efficacious, and very serviceable because it is tasteless, and therefore readily administered. Blue vervain is a good remedy, and for this reason my "Restorative Assimilant" is so efficient for the expulsion of worms. Seat, or maw-worms, are best expelled by injections of moderately strong salt and water, or soap-suds. Turpentine in emulsion also makes an efficient injection.

For tape-worm various remedies are used. Kousso, pumpkin-seeds, and turpentine have each a good reputation. Male Fern, however, is the most specific remedy that can be used. It is certain to dislodge the distressing enemy.

My "Male Fern Vermifuge" is without doubt the best vermifuge ever compounded and offered to the public. It instantly expels the minor worms, and the tape-worm is quickly dislodged by it. It is composed of such articles as make it applicable to every variety of worms, and it is veritably infallible in its effect. (See page 471.)

I admonish all persons to avoid eating pork that is not well cooked, for it is an established and indisputable fact that tape-worm is caused by eating raw pork, provided that it is not in a healthy condition. That which is commonly known as "measly pork" contains the germs of tape-worm, and should not be eaten unless thoroughly cooked. Tape-worm is most prevalent among the peasants of Central Europe, as they subsist largely on raw pork.

PERITONITIS.

This is an inflammation of the serous membrane lining the abdominal cavity, and investing the viscera, and may be either acute or chronic. During the early stages of the disease there is a feeling of lassitude, pain in the back and limbs, chills alternating with flushes of heat, headache and a feeling of uneasiness about the abdomen. As soon as the febrile action is established, the pain becomes sharp and severe. The abdomen is very tender, the slightest pressure by the hand causing most intense pain. The patient lies on his back, with his knees drawn up and shoulders elevated, finding that this relaxes the abdominal muscles, and prevents pressure by the bedclothes. Nausea, vomiting, thirst, constipation and suppression of urine, are frequent symptoms. The face is pale and contracted, respiration is oppressed, each inspiration aggravates the pain; pulse is frequent and small, tongue moist, and the patient is generally wakeful. The abdomen becomes tympanitic, and when a fatal termination is approached it becomes very much distended. The pulse also becomes feeble and quick, and the countenance assumes a ghastly appearance. It is very rapid in its course, death sometimes occurring within twenty-four hours. Puerperal peritonitis is only another variety of this disease, and attacks women in child-bed. It may arise idiopathically, or it may be caused by wounds, blows, falls, etc.

TREATMENT.—The stomach and bowels should be evacuated by an emetic and purge. If associated with malarial influence quinine should be given. The fever should be controlled by veratrum. A large mustard plaster or turpentine stupe should be applied to the abdomen. Large doses of opium to allay the pain are also indicated. The patient should drink freely of marsh-mallow or flaxseed tea, and be supported by tonics, beef-tea, etc.

SUMMER COMPLAINT (*Cholera Infantum*).

This is a complaint which usually attacks children between the ages of two months and three years; it occurs in the warm season, and is chiefly confined to cities. It is very fatal. It commences with a profuse diarrhœa, stools thin and variously colored. The stomach becomes irritable, and rejects everything. Loss of flesh, languor, and prostration follow, and stools become colorless and odorless, skin is dry and harsh, head and belly hot, thirst is great, and fever at night-fall. Delirium is present in many cases, indicated by violent tossing of the head, etc.

TREATMENT.—The child should be removed to a vicinity abounding in pure air, if possible; otherwise, in a large and airy room, and may even be taken into the open air occasionally. Its food should consist of the farinaceous articles of diet, if weaned; otherwise, of its mother's milk; mucilaginous drinks can also be given. If the vomiting be obstinate, give camphor, or a little opium, or combined, as in paregoric. The astringents, as turmeric and cranesbill, must be given to check the diarrhœa. Rhubarb is a good remedy, also leptandrin, prepared chalk, etc. Lime-water is grateful, and should be given. Charcoal is the proper remedy when the stools are very offensive.

CHOLERA MORBUS.

This is characterized by violent purging and vomiting of bilious matter, attended with griping, sickness and a constant desire to go to stool. The attack is usually abrupt, but it is sometimes preceded by loss of appetite, nausea, headache, chilliness, colicky pains, etc. It occurs generally at night, and the vomiting and purging occur in quick succession. The evacuations are usually copious, consisting of the ingesta first, but afterwards of a sour, acrid, serous liquid, causing a scalding sensation in the throat; there is slight tenderness over the abdomen, hiccough, anxiety, restlessness and exhaustion. The pulse is quick, small and feeble, the skin cool and moist, or bathed in clammy perspiration. It is quite a serious disease and runs a rapid course—death often occurring within twenty-four hours.

TREATMENT.—If the stomach is overloaded with indigestible food a lobelia emetic should be given in connection with warm ginger tea. Hot packs or mustard plasters should be placed on the abdomen, and bottles of hot water to the feet. Lumps of ice should be placed in the mouth to allay the patient's thirst. Opium is a very good remedy, and may be given by mouth or by injection. A tea made of chamomile flowers or columbo often succeeds well. Where great exhaustion is felt, a brandy toddy should be given.

ASIATIC CHOLERA.

This is an endemic disease of India, and visits other lands by travelling in what is called the cholera cycle. The Hindoos call it *purrhee morlii* (rapid death); the Mahometans, *eunerum vaudi* (diarrhœa and vomiting); and the Arabs, *el houwah* (hurricane). It is evidently caused by a noxious malaria arising from human or animal decomposi tion. It is characterized by three stages. The first is marked by derangement of the digestive organs, rumbling in the bowels, pain in the loins or knees, twitching of the calves of the legs, impaired appetite, thirst, and especially a slight diarrhœa. These symptoms continue from a few hours to several days. The pulse is frequently very slow, the tongue is furred, and a sense of great debility is present in all cases. In the second stage vomiting occurs, and the characteristic rice-water stools make their appearance. These stools are thin and watery, and have a peculiar spermatic odor. The cramps become excessively severe, drawing the muscles into knots. The tongue is pale and moist, pulse feeble, the breathing hurried, with distress about the heart, great thirst, and the secretion of urine nearly stopped. The thin, colorless fluid discharged by vomiting and purging is the watery portion of the blood, and when so much has been discharged that the blood cannot circulate freely, the patient sinks into the third, or stage of *collapse*. This is characterized by great prostration, the pulse being hardly perceptible, skin cold and clammy, face blue or purple, eyes much sunken, hands dark-colored, looking like a washerwoman's, breathing short and laborious, a sense of great heat in the stomach, intense thirst, inanition, and death. Recoveries from the third stage seldom occur.

TREATMENT.—In the first place the diarrhœa should receive prompt attention. The patient should lie in bed, and from five to ten drops of laudanum every two or three hours should be given. The astringents should also be administered. Morphine can also be given. The diet should be carefully regulated, and every symptom promptly met with an appropriate remedy. In the second stage the treatment should be energetic, quinine should be given, and the sinking powers sustained with tonics, beef-tea, etc. A pill containing opium, camphor, and cayenne pepper should also be administered. Brandy may also be given freely. I also advise my "Restorative Assimilant" as a good remedy; it should be taken in full doses. Its success has been very gratifying wherever it has been used.

In the third stage the above remedies are to be pursued with increased energy, especially the stimulants, and every effort should be made to promote the warmth of the body.

PROLAPSUS OF THE RECTUM.

This is more common to children than to adults, and is frequently a sequel to protracted diarrhœa, the falling caused by the debility occasioned thereby. It is also associated with disease of the digestive organs, and is peculiar to persons of feeble habit, or of a scrofulous or tuberculous diathesis. It causes pain in the lumbar region, constipation, sometimes diarrhœa, cardiac irritation, and general prostration.

TREATMENT.—The bowels should be replaced as soon as possible to prevent inflammation, that would naturally follow. The bowel can be replaced with the finger, well greased with sweet oil, gently pressing the tumor within the fundament. Cold water should be applied to the parts, and a decoction of white oak bark should be injected. A T-bandage should be applied to restrain the bowel from protrusion.

ANAL FISTULA.

This consists of an abscess occurring in some portion of the cellular tissue around the anus. As suppuration occurs the pus can be detected by the touch, and which sooner or later makes its way to the surface, and is discharged. While the abscess is forming the patient is considerably feverish, and feels a tenderness about the anal region. At first the discharge is a bloody pus, which in time becomes watery and acrid, or sanious. The channel through which it passes is called the fistula. If it communicates with the rectum, the fistula is said to be *complete;* but if it does not perforate the mucous membrane, it is said to be *incomplete* or *blind.* Fistula is more liable to occur in scrofulous and consumptive persons than in others, though it may be caused by piles, habitual constipation, or the presence of foreign bodies in the rectum.

TREATMENT.—During the active inflammatory state the bowels should be evacuated by a mild purge, and if the pain is severe, an opiate may be given. Flaxseed poultices, or hot fomentations, should be applied, and as soon as fluctuation is quite evident, an incision should be made, and the pus evacuated. A weak decoction of white oak bark may then be injected, and the parts drawn together by adhesive straps. The poultices should be continued as long as there is any hope to prevent a fistulous opening. If the fistula does occur, it gives great annoyance, and is quite difficult to cure. The surgical treatment consists in introducing a ligature through the fistulous opening into the bowels and out the anus, securing it to a small piece of cork, and twisting it once or twice a day until it cuts through, or by dividing the septum by a knife, and healing it from the bottom. Others cauterize the fistula, and attempt to stimulate adhesive granulations in that way. I grant that success attends all these surgical operations, but I do not see the propriety of subjecting the patient to all the attendant pain and confinement to bed when a cure can be as radically effected in as short a space of time by purely medicinal treatment. I have cured very many cases, and in no instance have resorted to cauterization or the knife. Consultation, either in person or by letter, is free with reference to such cases. (See page 390).

PILES (*Hemorrhoids*).

By these are understood the existence of small excrescences within the rectum and around the anus, which are characterized by a varicose condition of the hemorrhoidal veins. They may be situated either internally or externally, and when blood is discharged they are called *bleeding* piles, if not, *blind* piles. The tumors vary in size from a pea to a hen's egg. They are more common in women than men, owing to the sedentary habits of the former. They are caused by obstruction of the portal circulation, drastic purgatives, habitual constipation, pregnancy, uterine misplacement, etc.

TREATMENT.—If costiveness exists, give some mild purgative, as senna and leptandrin, or the "Renovating Pill," and keep bowels gently open, so as to secure one passage a day. Thoroughwort, in decoction, is also very useful. A compound decoction, or an ointment made of witch-hazel, white oak bark, and sweet-apple tree, applied to the tumors, very often cures them. In congestion of the liver, or derangement of the portal circulation, resort to the treatment advised in chronic hepatitis. If there is much inflammation, apply a slippery elm, stramonium, or poke-leaf poultice. Daily injections of cold water are also very useful. The diet should be regulated, and fatigue should be avoided. As a remedy for either internal or external piles, I can recommend nothing better than my "Herbal Ointment." If thoroughly applied to the tumors about twice a day, it gives instant relief, and cures them in a short time.

DISEASES OF THE ABSORBENT SYSTEM.

These are diseases affecting the lymphatic glands. The lymphatic system is that particular system of organs inservient to the formation and circulation of lymph, and consists of glands and vessels. When any of these glands become inflamed, the affection is *lymphangeitis*, *angeioleucitis*, or *lymphadenitis*.

SCROFULA.

This is commonly known as "King's Evil," and derives its name from the Latin *scrofa*, a sow, because it was supposed that it also affects swine. It is most apt to occur in persons of sanguine temperament, with thick upper lip. When fully developed, it gives rise to a deposit of tuberculous matter. It is characterized by a morbid state of the system, manifested by glandular swellings, chiefly in the neck, suppurating slowly, and healing with difficulty. At first there appear small, hard, movable kernels about the neck, just under the skin. These are the affected lymphatic glands. No redness or soreness is perceptible at first, but when in course of time they reach the size from a filbert to a hen's egg, or even larger, they come to a head and break, discharging a watery fluid, or a mixture like whey and curd. No great pain is seldom if ever felt. When the ulcers heal, they are apt to leave a puckered condition of the skin, and ugly scars. There is scarcely any tissue or organ in the body that scrofula does not assail, and it forms the basis, in many cases of disease, of all their virulence and stubbornness. Strumous habits are very common, being mostly hereditary; but they may also be contracted by bad habits, or be the sequel to low vitality or prostrating diseases. The taint is apt to become universal if in marriage the health of either party is not considered of equal importance with affection, etc., etc. It impairs the functions of all the organs; it renders the mental faculties more or less imbecile; it gives to the patient a heavy, sullen, and forbidding appearance, and is destructive of all beauty of form or sprightliness of character. It is so serious a disease that no one affected with the taint, however slight it may be, should defer such rational treatment as will cure him of one of the greatest enemies of mankind.

TREATMENT.—How lamentable it is that we have no Kings now a days, whose "sacred touch" will cure the prevalent scrofula. In olden times persons believed that if the scrofulous patient could get into the presence of the King, and be touched by his royal hand, his disease would vanish in nothingness. Hence the name of "King's Evil." This folly reached its height in the reign of Charles II. and after the Restoration; the number who flocked to the royal palaces to receive the "touch" is said to have been immense—no less than *ninety-two thousand* in twelve years. If Kings are no longer divine, and whose sacred touch no longer cures, we are not left hopeless, for the products made by a divine hand as manifested in the herbal world afford us abundant agents of cure, if we but have the wisdom not to ignore them, and the intelligence to use them properly.

Rational treatment should be preventive and curative. The preventive treatment consists in regulating the diet and to supply all the chemical material lacking in the histogenic character of the tissues. The habits should be conformed to well-established hygienic laws, and the digestive and assimilative organs should especially be elevated in tonicity and healthfulness. Exercise and bathing are very important, and must not be neglected. When it manifests itself by its characteristic features, tumors, ulcers, etc., the herbal alteratives alone will effect the cure. The best of these are rock-rose, stillingia, corydalis formosa, yellow-dock, fig-wort, sarsaparilla, etc. If the system is debilitated the tonics should also be given to give tone to the various organs of the body. The ulcers should be treated as all chronic indolent ulcers—the best application to them being my "Herbal Ointment." My "Blood Purifier" (see page 471) is composed of the choicest alteratives known, and acts specifically in the cure of this disease, and ever since it has been given to the public, its success was asserted in every case in which it received a competent trial.

Certain cases of scrofula, in which nearly all the tissues and organs are involved, and where the vitality of the system is at a low point, energetic special treatment is necessary. In such cases the author can be consulted, according to directions given on page 390.

TABES MESENTERICA.

This consists of an engorgement and tubercular degeneration of the mesenteric glands, followed by emaciation and general disorder of the nutritive functions. It occurs particularly in children of a scrofulous diathesis, and in those who are weaned too soon, or fed on indigestible substances. The disease is often owing to irritation in inflammation of the lining membrane of the intestines, giving occasion to enlarg ment of the glands of the mesentery, or duplicature of the peritoneum. Diarrhœa, emaciation, loss of appetite, or sometimes immoderate appetite, hardness and swelling of the abdomen, and toward the end hectic fever, are the chief symptoms of this disease. Recovery is seldom from this disease, if it has attained such a stage in which the glands have become extensively disorganized.

TREATMENT.—Digestible food, fresh air, etc. must be provided for the patient, and the bowels should be kept soluble. The treatment advised in scrofula should be resorted to in this disease. The patient's strength is especially to be well supported by good food, tonics and stimulants. This disease is commonly known as "*opneme*" in certain localities, which literally means *taking of* or wasting away, and persons can yet be found who ascribe the miserable condition of the child to the power of witchcraft, and the celebrated "witch doctors" do yet find employment and supply their amulets or engage in heathenish incantations. I advise every mother when the first symptoms of this disease are recognized to at once engage skilful medical aid, and her child may oftentimes be saved.

ANATOMY OF THE RESPIRATORY ORGANS.

LARYNX.

The *larynx* is a canal formed of cartilages, whose various movements regulate the voice. It is situated in the median line in the upper and anterior part of the neck. It can readily be felt from the exterior, and is commonly called "Adam's Apple." It forms the commencement of the wind-pipe, and in shape is cylindrical below and prismatic above. It is larger in males than in females, which accounts in a measure for the different quality of the voice between the sexes.

It is composed of five cartilages; viz., thyroid, cricoid, two arytenoid, and epiglottis. The *thyroid* is the largest; it occupies the upper anterior portion of the larynx. The *cricoid* is next in size, and situated at the base of the larynx. Its form is that of a laterally-compressed thick ring. The *arytenoid cartilages* are two in number, pyramidal in shape, and situated at the upper and back portion of the larynx. The *epiglottis* is a thin, oval, cartilaginous plate, behind the root of the tongue, and attached to the angle of the larynx; it resembles a leaf in shape, and is perforated with numerous foramina or holes. During deglutition it is pressed over the *rima glottidis*, thus preventing either solids or liquids from entering the respiratory tract.

Within the larynx are two ligaments on either side. The *inferior* ligaments are usually called the *vocal chords*, though they are more properly ligaments. The space between them is called the *rima glottidis*, and the space between the *superior* ligaments is the *glottis*. The larynx is lined with mucous membrane, inflammation of which constitutes laryngitis.

TRACHEA.

The *trachea* [7] (see figure) is a cylindrical tube, four or five inches long, reaching from the larynx to the point of division into the bronchial tubes. It is formed of from sixteen to twenty cartilaginous rings, united by elastic ligamentous tissue. It is lined with mucous membrane continuous with that of the larynx, which is extremely vascular, and covered with numerous follicles.

The *bronchi* [8 9] or bronchial tubes are essentially of the same structure and arrangement as the trachea; the right bronchus is shorter and of larger diameter than the left. The bronchial tubes ramify into numerous sub-divisions, which finally terminate in the lobules of the lungs.

In front of the first two rings of the trachea and upon the sides of the larynx is the *thyroid gland*. It is sometimes much enlarged, constituting *goitre*.

THE LUNGS.

The lungs are the organs of respiration properly; they are two in number, and situated in the chest, placed side by side, being separated from the abdomen by the diaphragm.

The size varies with the capacity and condition of the chest, age, inspiration, expiration, and disease. They are conical in shape, are longer posteriorly than anteriorly, and have concave bases. The color of the lungs is of a pinkish gray, mottled with black; these black spots are more numerous in adult life than in infancy. The right lung is shorter but larger than the left, whose transverse diameter is somewhat diminished by the position of the heart. It has three lobes, the left having but two.

The structure of the lungs is spongy, and its compression between the fingers produces a crackling sound called *crepitation*. It consists of air-vesicles [20], held together by cellular tissue, called *parenchyma*, through which blood-vessels and air-vessels are ramified. A certain number of air-cells communicate with each other, and with a single branch of the bronchial tube ; these are separated from neighboring cells by partitions of parenchyma, and thus are formed the *lobules* in which the aëration of the blood is performed.

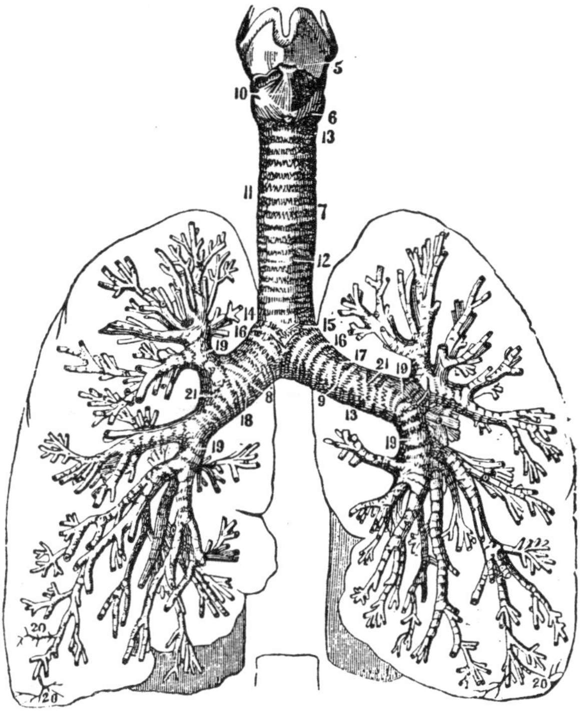

The Lungs.

PLEURÆ.

The pleura is a serous membrane investing each lung, and then reflected upon the walls of the chest. That portion in contact with the chest is called the *pleura costalis ;* that covering the lungs, the *pleura pulmonalis.*

DISEASES OF THE RESPIRATORY AND CIRCULATORY SYSTEMS.

CORYZA.

This is the "running at the nose" or "cold in the head," so frequently contracted. It consists of acute inflammation of the Schneiderian or mucous membrane of the nose, and the sinuses connecting with it. It causes considerable annoyance, and often creates some constitutional dis turbance. It is caused by the partial application of cold, as to the back of the head or neck, to the feet, etc., and the effect is especially apt to be produced after perspiration from heat or exertion. When it reigns epidemically it is called *influenza*.

TREATMENT.—It will usually subside without any treatment, but the subsidence can be greatly hastened by hot baths, a draught of ginger tea upon retiring, and the inhalation of some hot aromatic vapors, such as of balm, water-pepper, etc.

OZŒNA.

This consists of chronic inflammation of the nostrils, with an uneasy feeling, heat, and stiffness of the nose, swelling of the mucous membrane, and an offensive discharge. The nostrils are sometimes closed, owing to the thickness of the membrane. The discharge is often quite purulent, of a yellowish or greenish color, or sanious, and tinged with blood. It is very frequently associated with ulceration, and caries or necrosis of the bone. The breath is usually extremely offensive, and the sense of smell is occasionally lost. It is frequently the result of scrofulous, scorbutic, or syphilitic taint, and is a serious and disgusting disease.

TREATMENT.—The constitutional symptoms should receive special attention, and if owing to or connected with scrofulous or syphilitic taint the general treatment for those diseases should be given. The stomach and bowels should receive careful attention, the digestion being invigorated by alnuin, viburnin, etc. A salt water bath should be taken every morning to stimulate the emunctories. The vapors of tar, naphtha, astringent and narcotic herbs are very beneficial; an inhaling of mecca oil through an atomizer is successful and necessary in obstinate cases. Tonics, as quinine, etc., are necessary in some cases. Those persons who may wish the treatment to be directed by a competent physician, and who desire prompt relief and cure, may consult me, as I have given special attention to this disease, and have cured the most obstinate cases.

CATARRH.

We now come to a disease that is a bane to the existence of many a person. The catarrhal patient is never happy, for he knows that he is inseparably connected with a disease that is excessively annoying to himself and no less disagreeable to those with whom he comes in contact. It consists of inflammation of the mucous membrane lining the nose and sinuses or cavities connecting with it. It is a very common affection, arising from repeated colds, damp apartments, wet feet, insufficient clothing, hot rooms, a sudden check of perspiration, and a rheumatic or scrofulous disposition predisposes to an attack. The symptoms are weariness, pains in the back and limbs, frontal headache increased discharge from the nose, hoarseness, sore throat, impaired vision, fever, constant hawking, cough, and, if the disease continues, partial or complete deafness. By the constant dropping of the secretions into the throat, the catarrhal inflammation is made to extend to the mucous membrane of the throat and larynx, causing gastritis, tonsillitis, laryngitis, pharyngitis, and bronchitis. Consumption is not an unfrequent sequel to catarrh, and it may so undermine the vitality of the system that the most energetic and rational treatment will only reestablish it. A case that illustrates the ravages of catarrh in its ordinary severe forms is given in the following letter:—

MANCHESTER, April 3, 1871.

Prof. O. PHELPS BROWN.

RESPECTED SIR:—My catarrh, which had almost destroyed my power of speech, had nearly lost me the senses of smell and taste, and was rapidly extending to the lungs, by dropping down, has disappeared. I owe this great blessing to your course of treatment. I applied to you by advice of acquaintances, with many doubts; but a "drowning man catches at a straw," and I wrote you a full description of my sufferings. I cannot be too grateful to Providence for having directed me to do this. Use my name in any way you please for the benefit of others afflicted as I was, etc.

S. BROWN MILLS.

This patient describes the effect of nasal catarrh, as developed in himself, but partially. He has omitted to say that his breath was so offensive that people could not sit in the room with him; that the matter was discharged so copiously that it descended into the stomach, causing vomiting, reducing him in strength and flesh to a comparative skeleton; that he had inflammation and elongation of the soft palate (uvula); had lost his appetite, and was troubled with hectic fever.

He was subject to the usual despondency and hopelessness of patients suffering from long-standing catarrh, and it required every effort to arouse his drooping spirits to anything like natural vivacity. In fact, the symptomatic hopelessness and great depression of the spirits in catarrhal patients is often a greater barrier to speedy cure than the pathological condition of the disease itself.

TREATMENT.—In simple acute catarrh, a hot bath and a large draught of ginger tea will usually cure. The inhalation of the vapor of hops, water-pepper, etc., is also serviceable. The febrile excitement should be controlled by veratrum, the bowels evacuated by a mild purge. It is only in the chronic form that catarrh presents difficulties that require the most patient and skilful treatment to remove. Its condition should be thoroughly understood before treatment is attempted. It is not merely a local disease, but dependent upon a vitiated condition of the blood, hence merely local treatment will prove ineffectual. A combination of remedies are required: a remedy to cleanse the blood; a remedy for local application; a remedy to circulate the blood, thus arousing the system to action; and a medicine to stimulate the liver, to aid the system in throwing off the disease. The following treatment meets all these requirements and has proved effectual in curing many thousands of individuals—many of whom represented cases of long standing in the most advanced stages of this really dangerous complaint:

Accident first brought to my notice Dr. Lane's Catarrh Cure, and I tested it with perfect success in many instances, in conjunction with my Blood Purifier, Herbal Ointment, and Renovating Pills.

The following treatment is what I advise in cases of Catarrh: A course of the Blood Purifier, consisting of one large bottle taken internally to cleanse the blood. The Herbal Ointment well rubbed in at least once a day across the small of the back, sparingly over the stomach and bowels, and about the forehead and between the eyes to arouse action, assist digestion, soothe the nervous system, and remove irritation. The Renovating Pills taken only often enough to keep the bowels soluble and regulated to one passage per day. They arouse the liver to action, and thus aid in throwing off disease; and for local application three bottles of Dr. Lane's Catarrh Cure.

Having used this remedy for the past few years in my special practice, with universal success, I have no hesitancy in recommending it to the public as being the *only reliable* and effective preparation that I know of, for the immediate relief and *radical cure* of this most dangerous disease. One bottle of this medicine, "which lasts four weeks with ordinary use," will in many cases effect a cure, and will be sufficient to convince anyone of its rare merits. The use of two to four bottles has accomplished a permanent cure in the great majority of cases that I have met with in my practice. Inhaled through the nostrils it relieves headaches at once; used as a gargle it effects a speedy cure of ulcerated sore throat.

If Catarrh is neglected, the constant discharge of this purulent matter into the throat causes ulceration, the whole length of the nasal passage, and even hangs in festoons from the posterior nares, and ulcers or scabs form in the nostrils. Let me here add, that when the throat is affected as above described, *Dr. Lane's Catarrh Cure* should be thoroughly *used as a gargle* in addition to snuffing it up the nostrils twice a day. In many instances the ulcers penetrate the soft bones of the nose, when a thin straw-coloured fetid discharge ensues, and the sense of smell is impaired or entirely destroyed. In aggravated cases of *Chronic Catarrh* the discharge is attended with such an intolerable fetor or stench that a large room will become tainted in a very short time.

***Dr. Lane's Catarrh Cure* is the only known remedy that will certainly and effectually cure this troublesome and dangerous disease, instantly relieving headache and purifying the breath.**

Catarrh can be mastered by the above treatment, and I know of no other that will thoroughly eradicate it, as it will stimulate the Schneiderian membrane to healthy functional action.

Full and explicit directions accompany each bottle. The price of Dr. Lane's Catarrh Cure is 4*s.* 6*d.* *per bottle; three bottles* 11*s.* The catarrh cure may be snuffed up from the palm of the hand, or a small syringe may be used, as previously stated. By this local treatment and the purification of the blood and secretions with my Blood Purifier and Renovating Pills, the disease can always be cured, no matter how virulent its character.

In my professional career thousands of cases have come under my observation and treatment. It does certainly present insurmountable obstacles to the treatment of those whose opportunity of investigating and treating the disease has not been as extensive as mine, and hence you will find that the common practitioner generally pronounces it incurable, simply because *he* is unable to cure it. If rational treatment such as I advise and employ is engaged, and continued according to the requirements of each case, the disease is no more formidable than other chronic diseases, but is radically cured in a short time. Those desiring to consult me are referred to page 390.

LARYNGITIS.

This consists of an inflammation of the parts composing the larynx, especially the mucous membranes, and may be either acute or chronic. When it is known that in the larynx are situated the vocal organs, and that the aperture for the air to reach the lungs is situated at the apex, it can readily be conceived why inflammation impairs the voice or impedes the respiration. In the acute form there is hoarseness, a pain about the larynx or "Adam's apple," cough, and difficulty of swallowing. If the inflammation is violent the patient's life is in imminent danger from strangulation, caused by closure of the *rima glottidis.* The voice is often completely lost. In bad cases the patient starts up suddenly in bed begging for air; his lips assume a livid or purplish color, the surface becomes cold, the pulse frequent and feeble, the countenance ghastly, perspiration clammy, and finally death occurs from insufficient aëration of the blood. The chronic form is more common than the acute, and is generally associated with induration or ulceration of the mucous membrane. It causes great debility, emaciation, night-sweats, loss of appetite, vomiting and diarrhœa, and the patient often dies in a state of hectic exhaustion.

TREATMENT.—Control the circulation with veratrum, administer an emetic and purge, and apply hot packs to the throat Hot water should be used frequently as a gargle. The inhalation of hot vapors, as that of belladonna, lobelia, stramonium, mullein, sweet fern, etc.

gives great relief. Some practitioners use ice-bags in place of hot packs to the throat. They seem to answer the same purpose. In case of impending strangulation, no objection should be made to laryngotomy if in the opinion of the physician or surgeon it is deemed necessary. In the chronic form the disease demands the same treatment, though modified to suit the conditions of the case. A gargle of golden seal, and a syrup of Ceanothus Americanus, or frost-wort, taken internally, are very beneficial. Mecca oil is also used with great advantage. Tonics and stimulants become necessary if the strength is failing. I can offer to the patient an almost sure cure in my "Acacian Balsam," which is to be taken internally, and my "Herbal Ointment," applied externally.

If complicated, or owing to syphilitic contamination, special treatment (see page 390) is advised.

Bronchitis.

Inflammation of the bronchial mucous membrane is of common occurrence. Its severity is proportionate to the size of the tube involved. The disease may exist independently, but is often associated with lung diseases. It may exist either in the acute or chronic form. In the former variety, affecting the large and middle-sized tubes, coryza, sore throat, hoarseness, and slight chills are the first symptoms; lassitude and pain in the limbs are also present, and as the disease progresses there is a sensation of heat, soreness, and rawness of the bronchial surface, oppressed breathing, and a spasmodic cough and pain. The cough in the early stage is followed by a clear, frothy expectoration, with a saline taste, which changes to yellowish or greenish sputa, or it may be streaked with blood. If the small tubes are involved, the pulse is extremely frequent, great difficulty of breathing, blue appearance of the countenance, coldness of surface, and a tendency to asphyxia is noted. As soon as the disease becomes chronic the febrile symptoms disappear, but the pulse remains frequent, and the cough and dyspnœa are persistent, though to some extent relieved by free expectoration. The sleep is irregular, and night-sweats frequent, occasioning great debility. The cough becomes croupy, and diarrhœa often attests approaching dissolution.

Treatment.—A hot bath, hot packs, and veratrum will often terminate the career of the acute form at the outset. In the more severe forms an emetic should be given, and the hot packs or chafing liniments to the chest and throat frequently renewed. Blood-root and other expectorants should be given, and quinine should be administered if the disease is associated with malarial influence. The tonics may become necessary to sustain the strength. The vapors of mecca oil, goose-grease, and bitter herbs are beneficial. In the chronic form the treatment varies with the cause. If owing to syphilitic taint the treatment for that disease should be given, and if rheumatic in origin, colchicum, in connection with tonics, is the treatment indicated. The inhalation of the various vapors before alluded to should also be instituted, and the strength of the patient carefully husbanded by tonics, beef-tea, wine whey, etc. A remedy that combines both tonic and expectorant qualities is found in my "Acacian Balsam," which generally cures the worst cases very quickly. The "Herbal Ointment" should at the same time be thoroughly rubbed upon the chest, throat, and back. Consultations, either in person or by letter, will receive careful and prompt attention.

Croup.

Croup is an inflammation of the mucous membrane of the larynx and trachea, or windpipe. It is one of the scourges of childhood. False membranous croup is owing to an oozing of a peculiar fluid, which thickens into apparent membranes, and adheres to the surface of the windpipe. In membranous croup, there is much greater danger than in the simpler form.

The symptoms are, difficult breathing, hoarseness, loud and shrill cough, with fever. When the symptoms are violent at first, the disease will be in all probability not fatal, as the membranous croup comes on insidiously, and is scarcely ever ushered in by high inflammation.

Treatment.—An early and effective emetic is indicated in all cases. Some mechanical emetic, as ipecacuanha, alum, etc., should be preferred. Flaxseed poultices, my "Herbal Ointment," and irritating liniments should be applied to the neck. The Dover's powder should be given to promote perspiration and rest. Inhalation of vapor from hot water and mullein leaves is of great service. The bowels should be kept regular. In membranous croup, if the membrane cannot be dislodged by emetics, and suffocation is imminent, tracheotomy becomes necessary. Croup may often be prevented by tying a bag containing powdered rosin, which is electro-negative, around the throat at night.

Pneumonia.

This is commonly called *lung fever*. It is characterized by inflammation of the parenchyma or texture of the lungs. The patient is generally found lying on his back, complains of pain in his side, has more or less difficulty of breathing, a cough at first dry, but soon accompanied by bloody phlegm. As the disease becomes severe, the phlegm becomes very tenacious, so that it will adhere to the spit-cup if turned upside down. Three characteristic stages are observed in this disease, viz., *congestion*, *hepatization*, and *softening*. In the first stage the lungs become engorged with blood or congested, and if the lungs are percussed a dull sound is elicited, and if the ears are applied to the chest a minute crackling sound is heard, similar to that produced by rubbing fine hair between the fingers and thumb. It is only heard during inspiration, and is caused by the air breaking up the mucous adhesions. The urine is scanty and high colored. In the second stage the lungs become solid, or hepatized, resembling the liver. Some writers call it *red softening.* The dulness becomes more distinct upon percussion, and a whistling sound is heard if the ear is placed to the chest. The cough is more or less dry, but the fever is aggravated. There is great prostration, restlessness, complete loss of appetite, constipation, a loaded brown tongue, and the respiration is hurried and imperfect. In the third stage the lung softens and becomes filled with matter, and portions of the lung are apt to give way. The cavities may be detected by increased resonance at some parts by percussion, and the cavernous breathing by auscultation. There is also a metallic tinkling heard, and the sputum becomes more liquid, looking like prune-juice, and the general condition of the patient worse in every respect. If the disease advances into this stage, recovery is not very probable.

Pneumonia may be double or single; the right lung suffers, however, more frequently than the left. If pleurisy is associated with it, it is called *pleuro-pneumonia.* When characterized by great debility and prostration, and is of a low type, it is called *typhoid pneumonia.* The pneumonia of children is called *lobular*, as it is generally confined to one or two lobes of the lung.

TREATMENT.—Bleeding formerly was done in each case, and is again receiving attention by some physicians, but I deem it injudicious, as a general thing, though it may be of benefit in some plethoric cases. The treatment should be commenced with a mild cathartic, and the fever should be controlled with veratrum. The expectorants should be administered, and in cases of great prostration, beef-tea and alcoholic stimulants must be given. The chest should be blistered, and a cloth smeared with lard should be placed on the raw surface. Sleep should be promoted by lupulin or the opiates, and if great difficulty of breathing exists, turpentine should be poured on hot water, and the patient allowed to breathe the vapor. Fresh air, quietude, and rest, with frequent sponging of the body with tepid water, should not be neglected.

ASTHMA.

This is characterized by difficult breathing, occurring in paroxysms, accompanied by a wheezing sound, a great desire for fresh air, and unattended by fever or organic disease of the lungs or heart. It is evidently caused by an irritable condition of the cerebro-spinal system or medulla-oblongata, which deranges the nervous influence through the cervical and pneumogastric nerves. It is also called *Phthisic.* The attack generally comes on suddenly, but in some cases for a few days before the onset there is loss of appetite, flatulence, belching of wind, languor, chilliness, and drowsiness. The attack generally occurs at night, when the nervous system is at its lowest ebb. At first a sense of tightness, with a feeling of constriction about the chest, is felt, which intensifies into a fearful struggle for breath. The patient assumes various postures to facilitate in emptying and filling the lungs, and the feeling that he must have fresh air, induces him to rush to the window and put his head far out to catch the stirring breeze. The hands and feet are cold, the expression haggard and anxious, the body wet with perspiration, and the pulse irregular. The paroxysms usually last for some hours, when breathing becomes more easy. If the symptoms subside without expectoration it is called *dry asthma*, but when any phlegm is raised it is known as *humoral asthma*. The paroxysms may recur every night, remitting gradually in severity, before a final subsidence takes place. The very troublesome complaint, which seems to combine the peculiarities of asthma and coryza, occurring in some persons during hay-making, or even later, is called *hay asthma*. This complaint is often a distressing one.

TREATMENT.—During the paroxysm the inhalation of vapor of hot water, or that arising from a decoction of anti-spasmodic herbs, such as conium, belladonna, etc., lessens the severity of the spasm. The following preparation is a very good remedy: Ethereal Tincture of Lobelia ℥ ij; Tincture of assafœtida, ℥ i; laudanum, ℥ ss; fluid extract of stillingia, ℥ ij; simple syrup, ℥ iv; mix, and take a tablespoonful every two hours. Electro-magnetism, smoking stramonium leaves, inhaling the smoke from burning paper, dipped in a solution of saltpetre, are all beneficial. The anti-spasmodics, especially cherry-laurel water, should be taken to prevent the occurrence of frequent attacks. In hay asthma, changes of locality will often save the patient from an attack. The tincture of lobelia is a very good remedy. Quinine and nux vomica carefully administered are good remedies. Chloride of lime placed in a saucer in the sleeping-room often gives relief. My "Acacian Balsam" internally, and the "Herbal Ointment" rubbed externally on the chest, and up and down the spine, have cured many cases. Many interesting cases have come under my notice and treatment, but space forbids any allusion to them. By special treatment I think every case can be cured.

PLEURISY.

This is characterized by inflammation of the pleura or serous membrane enclosing the lungs. The disease usually commences with a chill, which is succeeded by a sharp, lancinating pain in the side; cough, short and quick breathing, and fever. The pain is usually called a ***stitch*** in the side, and is felt somewhere in the mammary region. It is increased by inspiration, cough, and motion, lying on the affected side, or by pressure. As the pain subsides, the effusion of a serous liquid occurs into the pleural cavity. The cough is usually short and dry, though a little frothy mucus may be expectorated. Severe pain often attends, and the patient tries to suppress the cough as much as possible. The breathing is more or less difficult in most cases, and the patient is said to have a catch in his breath. When the effusion is both sudden and copious, the function of one lung may be more or less suspended. The fever is usually considerable, and presents the usual phenomena of febrile affections. At some stages the patient's voice is said to be *ægophonous*, or similar to a goat's.

TREATMENT.—Commence with a mild cathartic, and though opposed to bleeding, yet if there is a human ailment requiring bleeding it is pleurisy, as it often gives prompt relief from pain. Sweating should be encouraged at the outset, and for this purpose the tincture of Virginia snake-root, in teaspoonful doses, every half-hour, is the best. It may be given in an infusion of catnip, balm, or pleurisy root. The affected side may be fomented with hops, tansy, wormwood, etc., applied very hot, or it may be blistered. The fever is to be controlled and the perspiration kept up with full doses of veratrum. Dover's powder may be given to procure sleep. The diet should be of the very lightest kind. The alteratives may be given if the effusion is not absorbed, and should these fail, the surgeon may perform *paracentesis*, or tapping of the side.

APNŒA, OR ASPHYXIA.

Literally the word asphyxia means pulseless, and was for a long time only used in that sense, but is now applied generally to all cases of *suspended animation*. It is produced by the non-conversion of venous or blue blood of the lungs into arterial, or red blood. Death is caused in all cases from want of oxygenized blood, and the stagnation that results in the pulmonary capillaries. There are several varieties of asphyxia; and as life can in many cases be revived, I shall state the procedure of resuscitation in each case.

ASPHYXIA BY EXTREME COLD.

When a person is subjected to extreme cold, the first symptoms are painful feelings, followed by sensations similar to those produced by inhalation of carbonic acid gas. He becomes benumbed, indifferent to the danger of his situation; the muscular system becomes enervated, step grows tottering, speech imperfect; and as these influences increase, the breathing becomes irregular and slow, the muscular powers fail, and he sinks into a state of insensibility and death.

TREATMENT.—Rub the person with snow if practicable, or the whole body may be submerged in cold water for a short time. These applications should be gradually increased in temperature until the surface approaches a natural state, or the muscles and joints are sufficiently relaxed to admit of free motion. Then resort to artificial respiration as in drowning.

Asphyxia by Inhalation of Gases.

Some gases cause death by spasmodic closure of the glottis, others by want of oxygen. Carbonic acid gas is the most common noxious gas.

Treatment.—Place the patient in a region where pure air abounds, and then practise artificial respiration.

Asphyxia by Submersion, Drowning.

Death in this case is not caused by the stomach and air passages being filled with water, but ensues in consequence of the person being plunged in a medium unfit for respiration. In no case where the body is recovered immediately after drowning, should the means of resuscitation be left unemployed. Life has been revived even in cases that were submerged half an hour.

Treatment.—1st. Treat the patient *instantly*, *on the spot*, in the open air, freely exposing the face, neck, and chest to the breeze, except in severe weather.

2d. Send for the nearest medical aid, and for clothing, blankets, etc.

3d. Place the patient gently on the face, the forehead resting on his wrist. This empties the mouth of fluids, and allows the tongue to fall forward, which leaves the entrance to the pipe free.

4th. Turn the patient slightly on his side, and apply ammonia, snuff, or other irritating substances, to the nostrils; then dash cold water on the face, previously rubbed briskly until it is warm. If there be no success, instantly—

5th. Replace the patient on his face, and turn the body gently, but completely, *on the side and a little beyond*, and then on the face, alternately; repeating these measures with deliberation, efficiency, and perseverance, fifteen times to the minute. When the patient reposes on the chest, this cavity is compressed and expiration takes place; the pressure is removed when turned on the side, and inspiration occurs.

6th. When in the *prone* position, make equable but efficient *pressure along* the spine, augment expiration, and remove it before rotation on the side, to facilitate inspiration.

7th. Induce circulation and warmth, while continuing these measures, by rubbing the limbs *upward* with *firm pressure* and with *energy*, using handkerchiefs, etc.

8th. Replace the patient's wet clothing by such other covering as can be instantly procured, each bystander furnishing a coat or waistcoat. Meantime, and from time to time, let the surface of the body be *slapped* freely with the hand, or let cold water be *dashed briskly* over the surface, previously rubbed dry and warm.

Let the patient often inhale diluted pure hartshorn, as this stimulates the respiratory organs.

CONSUMPTION (PHTHISIS).

This is a constitutional affection manifesting itself in most essential changes in the tissue of the lungs. It may be acute or chronic. The acute form, or *galloping consumption*, commences with chills, fever, rapid pulse, cough, pain and difficulty of breathing, which are soon followed by night-sweats, hectic fever, great emaciation, exhaustion, and if its course is not arrested, death. The chronic variety is, however, that which we usually meet with.

For the sake of convenience, I will class the symptoms of consumption into four general stages, viz., *the Incipient stage; the Solidification stage; the Maturation or Softening stage; and the Ulceration and Suppuration stage.*

The first stage of Tubercular Phthisis is generally stated to be that to which the *physical* signs indicate a *deposit* in the lungs. Evidently, however, there is, and must be, an antecedent state of disordered health before the most skilful observer can detect the *sound* which indicates the least shade or degree of solidification of the lungs, whether by means of the stethoscope, or other methods usually resorted to by the profession for such purpose. When the physical signs are observed, the use of the stethoscope, etc., may be regarded as little more than professional display, without a particle of advantage, except as developing in some degree the actual amount of lesion or injury then sustained by the tissues of the lungs. There must be a causative agent that originates the predisposition or tendency to the deposit of tubercles in the tissues, or which elaborates or prepares the material in the system, from which only tubercle is formed. *But we should not wait to see the physical signs developed if we would expect uniform and hopeful treatment of tubercular consumption.*

From my own long experience in the *specialty* of thoracic diseases, I do not hesitate to say that the *actual first set of symptoms* of consumption consists simply in the *wasting of flesh*, particularly if this is attended with, or by, a low scale of health and strength. Such loss of muscle, plumpness, as well as juices and fat, is first noticed in three principal places. The first region of flesh-consuming is usually the face; the second, the hands; the third, over the sacral or hip bones. The sacral region, where it first gives out, is lame and sore. The hands look poor and "scrawny;" the muscles of the arms and legs are soft and flabby.

If the face shows it first, the eyes stare; the brow, temples, and scalp look lean; the muscular tissues of all the limbs soon waste, and the pectoral muscles, as also all the chest muscles, waste away, and then the breathing is already become imperfect and weak.

The diminished respiration is soon attended with cough; then pains are felt through the breast or thorax.

The patient next is sensible of something wrong, and is conscious of a sense of general debility. The fact is, nutrition is lost. The vital powers are flagging, for the *wasting of the body*, in *spite of eating*, is *more rapid than the repair*.

Then comes a state of *spirit* depression—not the *cause* of consumption, but caused by the already deficient vitality, and all the more helping on the grand catastrophe; for it is a law of our being, that where *nerve* structure is not itself nourished, it, too, will fail in its work, just as surely as muscle fibre fails of power from the same cause. To recapitulate:—

1.—*Incipient stage.* This may present itself at a very early age, or may appear in middle age, and the first indications are, generally, a subdued and saddened feeling, the former buoyancy of spirits subsides, and the person becomes languid. The face begins to assume a sickly hue, and, to a practised eye, tells a sad tale. The skin becomes whiter, and a nervousness and sometimes irritable disposition of mind appears; and if any hint be given about consumption threatening, the person rebels against it, and will not tolerate such an idea. The appetite and digestion frequently become impaired, and may manifest itself in capricious fancies for certain sorts of food. A slight cold or any excitement will bring on diarrhœa. The breath is short, and the breathing hurried; running or walking up an incline, or ascending a flight of stairs, is unpleasant, and attended by a fluttering and palpitation of the heart. The strength and weight of the body diminish, but this varies. The sleep is disturbed, the skin becomes hot, there are burnings of the palms of the hands, and cold feet; a short, dry, teasing cough, or tickling, or hawking up of mucus from the throat appears. There is also a feeling of *feverishness* and uneasiness after meals, which are unfavorable symptoms, indicating the first *mal*-assimilation of the food, which, if not rectified, will inevitably deposit the germ of tubercles, and hence no time should now be lost in opposing the disease, before it lays siege to the citadel of the body.

2.—*Solidification.* The cough, which at first appeared very trifling, now begins to assume an anxious aspect, and becomes troublesome. It may not as yet be attended with expectoration, and if it be, the matter expectorated is of a ropy and viscid nature. The breathing becomes more impeded; hectic fever sets in, with chills and heats, while the weakness of both body and mind increases, although the intellect is sometimes extremely bright or sound to the very last. Pains, like those of *pleurisy*, are felt about the chest, and are indications of those *inflammatory* effusions and adhesions which attest the *progress* of the disease, and the infraction of the lung structure, and the impeding of the access of air to the cells of the lungs. The blocking up of the air-cells constitutes the stage of *Solidification*, and thus interferes with the due motives or functions of the chest, and, if not arrested, creates an afflux of fluid to the parts, thus promoting congestion and fresh deposits in the lungs.

3.—*Maturation and Softening.* In this stage, all the former symptoms are aggravated, and consumption is now confirmed. Fresh deposits in the lungs occur, and hasten the maturation and softening. These *local* lesions in their turn re-act on the system at large, aggravating the general infection and depressing the vital powers. Hence the advancing inertia of all the *vital* powers—the universal languor, loss of flesh, and strength, and weight. The cheeks and lips become blanched —painfully contrasting with the circumscribed *hectic* patch of the former. The expectoration is changed, and becomes more copious, opaque, and viscid, more massive, and frequently streaked with blood, or mixed with flocculent, wool-like, or curdy particles. It is most troublesome in the mornings, and when going to bed. The feverishness and general exhaustion increase; restless nights, with perspirations, hurried breathing, change in voice, and emaciation also increases. The appetite fails —either constipation or diarrhœa, more frequently the latter, comes on, with great increase of cough and vomiting after meals. If the disease advance to this stage, it will require much vigilance and judgment to arrest its progress, as the mischief in the lungs is now very great, and *ulcers*, rapidly forming, constitute what is called tubercles.

4.—*Ulceration and Suppuration.* The disease now assumes a totally different aspect, and becomes exceeding formidable in its nature and results. The cough becomes more severe, and the expectoration greenish, yellow, or even sometimes like tufts of wood chewed, appearing, when viewed in water, like jagged round balls. Hemorrhage, or bleeding from the lungs, is likely to come on, and the difficulty of breathing is very great. The patient can scarcely lie down; many times he must be kept with his head bolstered up in a chair, or in his bed, when sleep is desired. Sometimes the voice is reduced to a mere whisper, while in others it remains quite strong to the last. The perspiration, or night-sweats, are very copious, and very exhaustive of the vitality of the organism. The *ulcers* or tubercles in the lungs increase, causing large excavations, from which issue copious expectorations, sapping and undermining the foundation of the entire system.

The most unpractised eye can now at once detect the ravages of this disease in the altered appearance of the whole frame; the body is reduced to a mere skeleton; the eyes are sunken; cheek bones prominent, with sunken cheeks; the head bends forward; the chest is wasted, and the breathing becomes distressingly painful. The mental faculties generally become impaired; yet a gracious God, amid all this suffering, frequently permits the faculties to remain intact until the last ember burns out.

TREATMENT.—This resolves itself into such a management of the case as will tend to prevent the development of the disease, or its removal when it exists. It will be seen that consumption has its origin in a vitiated and defective condition of the general organism. This may occur as the result of hereditary predisposition, or from defective nutrition, or from imperfect development of either a part or the whole of the organic structure, and general disobedience to the physiological law of the general organism. Whenever this predisposition exists, the defective organization, as far as practicable, should be remedied by a faithful adherence to the laws of physiology and dietetics. Children possessing this organization should not be confined too closely in schools or to study, but should be reared in the country, and be exposed to fresh air and out-door exercise. Both boys and girls should be allowed to ramble through the fields, and indulge in those gymnastic exercises which tend to give strength and vigor to the system generally, such as jumping the rope, rolling the hoop, flying the kite, hoeing, wheeling, riding on horseback, etc., and not be studiously confined in-doors, because it is a "delicate child." Tidy mothers should not be horrified if they find their child of frail organization making mud-pies, or that he has torn his frock in climbing an apple-tree. Their diet should be plain and nutritious, consisting of bread and milk, oatmeal porridge, baked apples and milk, vegetables, and a liberal amount of meat once or twice a day. Their sleeping apartments should be well ventilated, and they should be warmly clad in all seasons. Misses, upon the approach of the catamenial flow, should be well instructed that the feet should be kept warm and dry, that washing and bathing in cold water should be avoided, and all exposure to cold and moisture is hurtful.

The medicinal treatment of consumption has been extensive, and to enumerate all that has been tried and recommended would fill a volume. Some recommend inhalations; these answer their purpose well for temporary relief. The disease must be treated upon general principles. The cough should be allayed by appropriate remedies, the occasional diarrhœa checked by the astringents, the debility removed by tonics, and vitality stimulated by alcoholic liquors. It is beyond question, that spirit-drinking has been beneficial in a number of cases, if taken regularly and moderately. Phosphorus is a good remedy, especially if given in a form as it exists in *erythroxylon coca*. External irritants, as Croton oil to the chest, answer very well. The blood of the consumptive contains too much oxygen, and too little carbon; hence to supply this deficiency cod-liver oil, which is a highly carbonaceous food, is excellent. It gives warmth to the body, and supplies the disease with material for destruction, without expense to the body. The chalybeates may also be given to give strength and enrich the blood in its red particles. Change of climate is rarely beneficial. The diet must be highly nutritious; fresh air, occasional baths, and plenty of friction, should not be neglected. While investigating the best means of treating this disease, I deemed that if a combination could be made that would prove remedial to all the morbid characters of consumption, that would antagonize each pathological condition as they arose, thus holding the disease in abeyance, and allow the forces of reparation and recuperation to mend the ravages of the disease, that such a combination would most surely cure the disease. After various experiments, I, finally, by intimate knowledge of the chemical elements of plants and the pathology of the disease, was led to compound the "Acacian Balsam," which has stood the test for years, and the thousands of testimonials of the permanent cure of many bad cases of consumption attest its virtues.

It is a superior exhilarant. It purifies all the fluids and secretions in the shortest reasonable period. It nourishes the patient who is too much reduced to partake of ordinary food. It will supply the place of food for a month at a time. It strengthens, braces, and vitalizes the brain. It heals all internal sores, tubercles, ulcers, and inflammations. It stimulates, but is not followed by reaction. It at once obviates emaciation, building up wasted flesh and muscle, as the rain vivifies and enhances the growth of the grass. It is without a rival as a tonic, and it immediately supplies electricity or magnetic force (as if it were a battery) to every part of the enfeebled and prostrate body. In conjunction with the balsam, I also advise external application of the "Herbal Ointment" (which answers all the purposes of counter-irritants) to the chest, throat and back, and the bowels regulated with the "Renovating Pill" (see page 469).

ANATOMY OF THE HEART.

The heart is a hollow muscular organ, surrounded by a membranous sac called the pericardium. It lies between the two pleuræ of the lungs, and rests upon the cord-like tendon of the midriff, in the cavity of the chest.

Its *shape* is conoidal, though it is somewhat flattened upon that side that rests upon the tendon of the diaphragm. Its apex inclines to the left side, touching the walls of the thorax between the fifth and sixth ribs. It *measures* about five inches and a half from its apex to its base, three and a half inches in the diameter of its base, and *weighs* about six or eight ounces. It contains *four cavities*, which perform two functions:

that of receiving the blood and emptying the blood into the lungs, and that of receiving it again after it has been oxygenated, and distributing it throughout the vascular system. The receptacles are *auricles*, and the *ventricles* propel the blood to the lungs and through the body.

The auricle and ventricle of the *right side* receive and propel the venous blood into the lungs. The auricle and ventricle of the *left side* receive and propel the arterial blood throughout the system.

The blood *circulates* as follows: The ascending and descending vena cavæ empty the blood (venous) into the right auricle; from here it passes to the right ventricle, through an opening protected by a valve, downwards; from the right ventricle it is propelled through the pulmonary artery, which divides into two branches, to the lungs; in the lungs it is oxygenated by the inspired air; it is then brought from the lungs, by four pulmonary veins, into the left auricle. The left auricle has an opening communicating with the left ventricle, protected by a valve opening downwards, and from the left ventricle it passes into the aorta, thence to be distributed throughout the body.

The *right auricle* is a cavity of irregular shape, somewhat oblong, and like a cube; anteriorly it has a convexity which is called its *sinus*; superiorly there is an elongated process resembling the ear of an animal, whence the term auricle. Its walls are thin, and composed of muscular fibres, which are called *musculi pectinati*, on account of their parallel arrangement, resembling the teeth of a comb. The superior [5], and inferior vena cavæ enter the auricle from behind. The elevation between the orifices is called the *tuberculum Loweri*. The *coronary* veins open into this cavity, and their orifices are protected by the *valves of Thebesius*. The opening to the ventricle is circular, and surrounded by a dense white line.

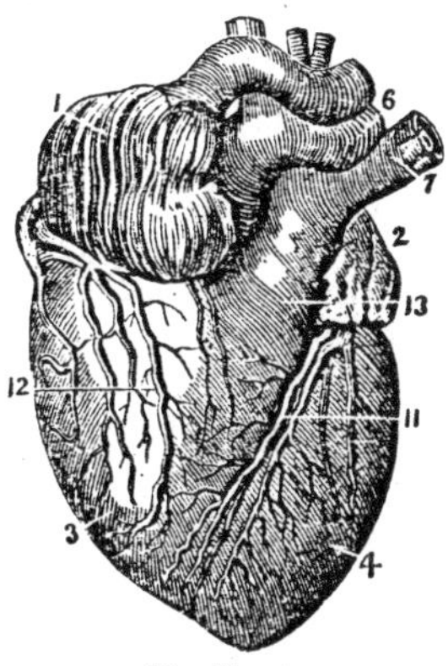

The Heart.

The *right ventricle* [3], is a triangular cavity, with thick walls, and of greater capacity than any other cavity of the heart. Its muscular structure is in the form of large fleshy bundles, called *columnæ carneæ*, from which proceed thin, white cords, called *chordæ tendineæ*, which are attached to the edge of the *tricuspid valve*. This valve is circular, having at its lower edge three spear-pointed processes, whence its name. It closes downwards, and prevents the blood from returning into the auricle, and, therefore, it passes out by the *pulmonary artery* [7]. The valves protecting the orifice of the pulmonary artery open outwards, and are called the *semi-lunar valves*. They are formed by three half-moon-shaped folds of the lining membranes, and their use is to prevent the blood returning from the artery to the ventricle, when it dilates. Behind each valve is a pouch or dilatation, called the *Sinus of Valsalva*, into which the blood flows by its reflux tendency upon the dilatation of the ventricle, and thus these valves are closed. The pulmonary artery is of the same diameter as the aorta, but its walls are thinner. After its origin it curves upwards and backwards, and divides into two branches. the right of which is larger than the left [7], and passes under the arch of the aorta.

The *left auricle* [2], is more concealed from its natural position than the right. The four pulmonary veins enter into it, which give it a quadrangular shape. Its walls are muscular and somewhat thicker than those of the right auricle. The partition between the auricles is not always perfect even in adult life.

The *left ventricle* [4], forms by its cavity the apex of the heart; it is like a cone in shape. Its walls are thick, and its *columnæ carneæ* numerous, strong and projecting; the *chordæ tendinea* are well developed, and attached to the *bicuspid* or *mitral valve.* This valve consists of two leaflets, one of which is much larger than the other. The contraction of the ventricle closes the valve, and the blood passes out by the aorta [6]. The heart is supplied with blood by the right and left *coronary* arteries [11 12]; the veins which accompany them empty by a common trunk into the right auricle.

It will thus be seen what a complex piece of machinery the human heart is, and how vital the organ must be. It will be apparent to every reader that the least interruption or derangement of its functional action is sure to be manifested upon the integrity of the general system. Any valvular derangement or breaking down of the septum between the auricles and ventricles will allow the commingling of arterial with venous blood, threatening death with asphyxia. Atrophy and hypertrophy interfere with the muscular action of the walls of the heart, and, in fact, it will be obvious from the complex character of the structural anatomy and the importance of the functional actions of the heart, that any disease assailing the organ is attended with danger.

In circulation the contraction of all the cavities is followed by their dilatation. The contraction is called the *systole;* the dilatation, the *diastole.* What is called the *impulse* of the heart occurs during the *diastole.* The heart's impulse is the shock communicated by its apex to the walls of the thorax, in the neighborhood of the fifth and sixth ribs. The impulse is not the same as the arterial pulse. The heart emits two sounds, *first* and *second*, followed by an *interval.* The first are the longest. The following table shows the connection of the sounds of the heart with its movements :—

First Sound.—Second stage of ventricular diastole. Ventricular systole, and auricular diastole. Impulse against the chest. Pulse in the arteries.

Second Sound.—First stage of ventricular diastole.

Interval.—Short repose, then auricular systole, and second stage of ventricular diastole, etc.

Each cavity of the heart will hold about two fluid ounces, but it is probable that the ventricles do not entirely empty themselves at each stroke; they will therefore discharge about one and one-half ounces at each pulsation. Reckoning 75 pulsations to the minute, there will pass through the heart in this time 112 ounces or 7 lbs. of blood. The whole quantity of blood in the human body is equal to about one-fifth of its weight, or 28 lbs. in a person weighing 140 lbs. This quantity would therefore pass through the heart once in four minutes, or about fifteen or twenty times an hour. It is very probable that circulation is much more rapid than this estimate. The number of contractions of the heart in a minute is about 70 or 75. The frequency of its action gradually diminishes from the commencement to the end of life. Just after birth it ranges from 140 to 130, in old age 65 to 50. Age, sex, muscular exertion, emotions, and temperament exert a controlling influence over the heart's action. In persons of sanguine temperament the heart beats more frequently than in those of the phlegmatic, and in the female sex more frequently than in the male. Its action is also increased after a meal, and by rising from a recumbent to a sitting or standing posture. The time of day also affects it; the pulse is more frequent in the morning, and becomes gradually slower as the day advances.

The pulse is always a sure index of health or disease. In inflammation and fevers the pulse is much more frequent than during health. When the vital powers decline it becomes frequent and feeble. In nervous affections with more oppression than exhaustion of the forces, the pulse is often remarkably slow.

The membrane lining the interior of the heart is called the *endocardium*, and the enveloping membrane on the exterior the *pericardium*.

DISEASES OF THE HEART AND CIRCULATORY SYSTEM.

PALPITATION.

This is the most common disease of the heart, and may be connected with various structural changes of the organ, yet it frequently exists independently of any organic lesion, and is often sympathetically dependent upon dyspepsia, hypochondria, hysterics, mental agitation, venereal excesses, masturbation, etc. It may also be due to a low and deficient state of the blood, or *anæmia*. The impulse is weak, fluttering, or tumultuous, generally increased by trifling causes. The beats are increased in frequency, sometimes marked by intermission, and occasionally accompanied by a bellows murmur. The complexion is generally pallid and bloodless, the lips and inside of mouth also pale, the pulse quick and jerking, and the patient complains of breathlessness and fainting. He dislikes animal food, but relishes acids. In females the deficiency of menstrual flow is superseded by the whites, or sometimes the flow becomes very profuse.

TREATMENT.—During the paroxysm a compound of yellow jessamine, scull-cap, and ladies'-slipper should be given, in sufficient doses every hour, until relieved. The feet should be bathed in warm water and the patient avoid all exertion or excitement. If due to anæmia, the proper remedies as well as nourishing diet should be prescribed. If coexistent with dyspepsia, hypochondria, etc., the proper treatment for those affections should be instituted.

ANGINA PECTORIS.

This disease presents rather difficult pathological features. By some writers it is called *neuralgia of the heart*. The principal symptoms are, violent pain about the breast bone, extending towards the arms, anxiety, difficulty of breathing, and sense of suffocation. The paroxysm may be brought on by fast walking, over-eating, or violent exercise, but they may also come on when the patient lies quietly in bed. If connected with ossification, or other morbid conditions, it is an affection of great danger.

TREATMENT.—During the paroxysm the most powerful stimulating and narcotic anti-spasmodics are required. The feet should be placed in warm water, a large mustard plaster should be applied over the cardiac region, and one drop of the tincture of aconite may be given every minute or two, until the spasm is relieved. If it is associated with any organic disease of the heart, the proper treatment for such disease should be instituted, and if due to a neuralgic affection of the organ, the proper remedies for neuralgia should be given. Patients suffering from this dangerous disease should lose no time in consulting some well-skilled physician.

PERICARDITIS.

This consists of inflammation of the sac in which the heart is contained. It does not essentially differ from other serous inflammations, as there may be exudation and liquid effusion, the quantity varying from a few ounces to a few pints. The disease is usually ushered in with a slight chill, followed with fever, or it may commence with fainting. Pain, oppression, weight, palpitation, cough, hurried and difficult respiration, frequent and irregular pulse, inability to lie on the left side, headache, delirium, faintness, anxiety, debility, restlessness, and great nervous irritability usually attend the attack. The face and extremities are swollen, and the urine scanty and high-colored. The essential conditions of fever are always present, the pulse sometimes attaining 120 to the minute. If the acute form advances for several weeks it becomes chronic, or may by insidious advances be chronic from the first. The symptoms are nearly the same as in the acute form.

TREATMENT.—The treatment should be commenced by a lobelia emetic, an active purge, and the application of hot packs to the chest. The tincture of veratrum should be given in sufficient quantities to control the inflammation and lessen the action of the heart. Usually, from two to five drops every half hour is sufficient. If associated with rheumatism, colchicum, cannabis sativa, or macrotys racemosa, should be given. In malarial districts, quinine becomes necessary. Blistering or local depletion may be necessary in some cases.

ENDOCARDITIS.

This is an inflammation of the internal lining of the heart. There is at first pain about the heart, whose disordered action may be violent, or else feeble, irregular, and intermitting. There is more or less difficulty of breathing, and the organ gives forth some abnormal sounds, such as the bellows murmur, the rasping and sawing murmur, arising from thickening of, or deposit on, some of the valves. One or more of the above symptoms occurring during the course of acute rheumatism, may be considered a sign of endocarditis. The patient generally lies on his back, and his pain may sometimes be so slight as scarcely to be noticed, but in dangerous cases there is extreme anguish, liable to be followed by orthopnœa, or necessity of being in the erect posture to be able to breathe, followed by restlessness, delirium, and death. The murmurs may occur at any stage of the disease, from the very beginning towards the close.

TREATMENT.—The treatment is essentially the same as for pericarditis in the commencement of the attack, with the exception that it may be necessary to administer stimulants in some cases Leeches may be applied to the cardiac region, and between the shoulders. Digitalis and veratrum should be cautiously administered to control the heart's action. If associated with rheumatism, colchicum should be given. Mustard poultices, blisters or hot packs may be applied to the chest to hasten the absorption of the deposit of lymph.

If *myocarditis*, or inflammation of the entire substance of the heart, complicates either pericarditis or endocarditis, the active treatment advised in the latter diseases will remove it.

CHRONIC VALVULAR DISEASE OF THE HEART.

This frequently results from chronic endocarditis. They may either be contracted or distorted, preventing accurate closure, or ulceration may occur through the valves. Vegetations and a peculiar deposit may take place under the tissue of the valves, and occasionally there is a deposition of cartilaginous or osseous matter, and in rheumatic or gouty subjects, of the urate of soda, or the valves may become atrophied or wasted away. The effects in slight cases may occasion but little difficulty, but in severe it is apt to produce hypertrophy and dilatation, dropsy, local inflammations, and ultimately death. These results are owing to an impediment in the forward movement of the blood, and to the regurgitation of the same, producing an accumulation behind. This is plainly illustrated in an affection of the mitral valve. If its orifice is contracted by deposits, the blood accumulates in the left auricle by the impediment, and distends it; congestion of the pulmonary veins is the consequence; the lungs share in the congestion, and pulmonary apoplexy may be the result. This of course occasions an insufficient supply of blood to the general system, which the heart is willing to relieve, and, therefore, makes greater efforts, but becomes hypertrophied or enlarged in so doing. Again, suppose some insufficiency in the mitral valve, owing to ulceration, for example, the blood will regurgitate into the left auricle at each pulsation, it produces the same effects. If the *semilunar* valves are contracted, a less supply of blood is sent to the general system, but congestion of the heart and consequent enlargement and dilatation of the left ventricle may occur. The general symptoms of valvular disease is difficulty of breathing, increased by muscular efforts, or emotion, palpitations, the pulse intermittent or jerky. Distinctive murmurs accompany these affections; in mitral deficiency we hear a prolonged murmur in a low key, like whispering the word "*who;*" in contraction of the aortic valves we have a comparatively superficial sound like whispering the letter "z;" in regurgitations we hear squashing sounds.

TREATMENT.—The mitigation of the urgent symptoms may be accomplished by ladies'-slipper, hops, or henbane. In violent action of the heart cherry laurel water may be given with the henbane. Hot foot-baths and mustard plasters may also be necessary. In sudden palpitation and difficulty of breathing, the compound spirits of lavender should be given. Collinsonia is the proper remedy if hypertrophy of the valves is suspected. In valvular insufficiency the tonics and a liberal diet should be prescribed. Conium, belladonna, digitalis, irisin, veratrum, stramonium, and cannabis sativa, are also extensively used in various combination, if they are indicated.

ATROPHY OF THE HEART.

This may result from various causes. When it exists, greater resonance accompanies percussion, and the two sounds of the heart will be more feeble, but more distinctly heard. The symptoms are pallor, coldness and dropsy of the extremities, cough, irregular respiration, palpitation, oppression; in females, irregularity or vicarious menstruation. It may occur with the exhausting diseases, as cancer, consumption, diabetes, etc.

TREATMENT.—The patient should avoid all excesses in mental and bodily exercise. The diet should consist of rich animal broth, with a liberal amount of fats and sugar, cod-liver oil, and the tonics should be administered.

HYPERTROPHY AND DILATATION OF THE HEART.

As these are generally coexistent, they should be considered together. The dimensions of the heart may be increased either by augmentation of its muscular walls, or enlargement of its cavities. The former is hypertrophy, the latter dilatation. The most prominent symptom is difficulty of breathing, produced by any exertion; also palpitations, which are sometimes so violent as to shake the whole body. The secondary signs are violent headache, vertigo, buzzing in the ears, flashes of light, pulmonary congestion, pneumonia, apoplexy of the lungs, congestion of the liver, bilious disorders, and general and local dropsy. The patient's suffering is often extreme, and, unable to lie in bed, he is forced to assume constantly a sitting posture, with the body bent forward. Death usually occurs suddenly in syncope or fainting. Valvular disease is the most frequent cause, though they may be caused by rheumatic irritation, excessive exertion of the organs from any cause, as violent exercise, playing on wind instruments, violent passions, intemperance, etc.

TREATMENT.—The exciting cause should be removed, especially valvular disease. The patient's habits of life and occupation should be regulated, and his diet moderated. Mild cathartics should occasionally be given and passive exercise engaged in. Digitalis is the special medicine; cherry laurel water is also used for the same purpose. These should be carefully administered. The tincture of aconite and colchicum should be given where it has resulted from rheumatism. In dilatation the tonics, cod-liver oil, and animal food should be prescribed. Digitalis is also specially required. Wild cherry bark is an excellent tonic, and as nervous symptoms are very apt to be present in females, opium, belladonna, valerian, etc., may be given with advantage. Every effort should be made to enrich the blood.

CYANOSIS, OR BLUE DISEASE.

In this disease the skin bears a leaden or purple tinge over the whole body. There is a reduction of warmth, and labored breathing. It is due to the admixture of blue or venous blood with arterial or red blood, and caused by the right and left sides of the heart remaining open after birth, or by obstruction of the pulmonary artery, thereby withholding the blood from the lungs and preventing arterialization. It is a disease confined to infants, and is almost necessarily fatal.

TREATMENT.—The circulation must be sedated by allowing the child complete rest, or by the careful administration of veratrum ; good food, fresh air, and protection from extremes of heat and cold are necessary. Apply friction to the head and body by some soft cloth. If syncope occurs, the child should be placed in a warm bath, and camphor applied to its nostrils.

The heart is liable to be assailed by other diseases. *Softening* of the heart may take place without inflammation ; it may result in rupture of the heart. Various *indurations* of the heart may occur, as of the fibrous, cartilaginous and osseous character. *Fatty degeneration* is a rare disease. *Tubercle*, *cancer*, and *polypi* are also noticed.

The heart is the most important organ in the body ; hence its diseases to the physician are full of interest. Nothing gives to a person greater anxiety than the suspicion or knowledge that he is affected with heart disease. The dread of sudden death is universal, and so it generally occurs in cardiac diseases. The most important requisite in the treatment is its early application, as most of the diseases can be cured if treatment is bestowed in time, and hence it behooves every one who feels some abnormal action or uneasiness about the heart to engage treatment, or seek competent medical aid as soon as possible. Those who desire to consult me are referred to page 390. My experience in the treatment of heart diseases has been in extent second to none in this country, and the success has been most gratifying.

DISEASES OF THE BLOOD-VESSELS.

Arteritis.

Inflammation of the arteries is rare in the acute form. The symptoms are pain and tenderness along the course of the vessel, attended with a thrill or throbbing. Lymph is effused within the vessel, often producing a complete arrest of the circulation, and resulting in gangrene. It is highly probable that in spontaneous senile gangrene the cause is arteritis. Chronic arteritis is more common, but difficult to discover. Deposits occur in the arteries, exciting ulceration, or ossification may occur in old age.

Treatment.—Give a mild purge, a hot bath, and sufficient veratrum to control the circulation. The inflamed part should be fomented, blistered, or stimulating liniments and counter-irritation may be applied. The alteratives are always indicated.

Aneurism.

This is a pulsating sac, filled with blood, which communicates with an artery. *True* aneurism consists of a sac formed by one or more of the arterial coats. *False* aneurism is owing to a complete division of the arterial coats, either from a wound or external ulceration; the sac formed of cellular tissue. Every artery may be affected with any aneurism, but the aorta, carotids, axillary, brachial, iliacs, femorals, and popliteals are the arteries most commonly affected. The tumor at first is small, gradually increasing, soft and quite compressible, being filled only with fluid blood. It pulsates synchronously with the heart, and is increased by pressure on the side furthest from the heart. A peculiar thrill is imparted to the hand, and which can be heard if the ear is applied. The strength of the part is much impaired as the tumor enlarges, and the circulation in the extremity weaker. During the progress of the tumor the adjacent parts are displaced and absorbed, even bone is rendered carious and absorbed by constant pressure of the aneurism. The pain and numbness increase, and the general health fails, and at length the tumor may burst, opening upon the skin or some internal cavity, and prove fatal.

TREATMENT.—Complete rest, and the frequent application of hot-packs to the tumor should at first be prescribed. A stimulating liniment may be rubbed over the part. One composed of the compound tincture of myrrh and the oil of origanum answers the purpose well. The "Herbal Ointment" is an excellent application. The gentle application of electro-galvanism should be resorted to if the above treatment does not suffice. Pressure by well-secured pads, or by the thumbs and fingers, continued for a long time, is often tried and successful in some cases. If the above treatment fails, some competent surgeon should be consulted, who will in practicable cases ligate the artery. Valsalva had a curious plan of treatment for aneurism. It consisted of repeated blood-letting, with food enough merely to support life. A cure worse than the disease.

PHLEBITIS AND VARICOSE VEINS.

This is an inflammation of the veins. The signs are pain and tenderness in the course of the vessel, which soon becomes cord-like and knotted, by which it may be distinguished from arteritis. There are swelling and redness of the adjacent parts, the redness being in streaks. The limb below the part is swollen, from obstruction of the circulation and effusion of serum. Pus is a frequent production of phlebitis, in which case perfect occlusion of the vein *above* occurs, with the formation of an abscess, or the pus passes into the heart and produces excessive prostration. *Varicose veins* are the sequel generally to phlebitis.

TREATMENT.—The treatment consists in fomentations, leeching, and occasional purging. The alteratives should also be given. The topical application of tinctures of lobelia and arnica are also useful. Rest is enjoined. The abscesses and consequent ulceration should be treated upon general principles. If the veins become varicosed, astringent applications, and careful bandaging, should be resorted to.

The best method of curing varicose veins, however, is by elastic stockings. These give an equable pressure, which can be so regulated as to afford any compression desired, on every part of the leg where the varicose veins exist. If the veins are varicosed throughout the whole length of the limb, the full-length stocking should be worn; if confined only to the leg, the stocking represented on the right-hand side of the cut is alone necessary, and in some cases the knee-caps and anklets are only required, depending upon the situation of the varicose veins. These elastic contrivances are not only radical cures, but patients suffering from varicose veins have no idea what ease and comfort they afford. They give a very agreeable support to the limb, prevent varicose ulcers, besides quickly reducing the enlarged veins to natural size. They are made of the best silk, are very durable, and not so expensive as not to be afforded by the poorest sufferer. All those desiring these admirable contrivances are requested to correspond with the author;—preliminary correspondence as to size, measurement, etc., is in all cases essential to secure that perfect adaptation which is indispensably necessary in order to afford relief and cure. Great harm is done if the elastic appliance is not eligible in every respect, and therefore patients should hesitate before purchasing those inferior, half cotton articles, which are purchasable everywhere; they do not fulfil the conditions required of them, and are capable of doing great injury, owing to the unequal compression they afford. Preliminary correspondence free.

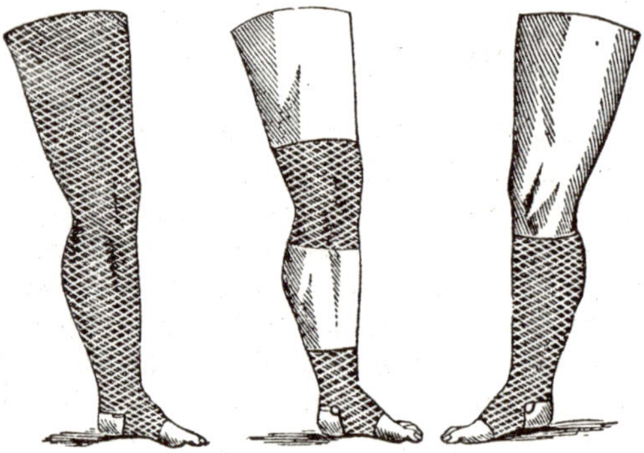

Elastic Stockings, Knee-Caps and Anklets.

Milk Leg (Phlegmasia Dolens).

This is caused by inflammation of the crural veins, hence called *crural phlebitis*. The inflammation is owing to the pressure of the gravid womb. The popular idea that in this disease the woman's milk has fallen into her leg, and which has inflamed, is absurd. The disease begins in from two to seven weeks after delivery, with pain in the lower bowel, groin, or thigh. In several days the pain diminishes, and the limb begins to swell, in the calf first most frequently, and from thence extending upward. The skin becomes entirely white, smooth, and glossy, does not pit when pressed, is painful to the touch, and is hotter than the skin of the other limb. Fever is always present.

TREATMENT.—The patient should lie upon her back, with the swelled limb placed upon pillows, or a bolster, raised so that the foot shall be a little higher than the hip, and she should by no means endeavor to walk until the leg is nearly well. A narrow blister can be applied along the course of the vein, and digitalis may be carefully administered. Take an old flannel petticoat, with the hem cut off, and the gathers let out, and dip it in vinegar and hot water, equal parts, wring it out, and cover the whole limb with it. A blanket or oiled silk may be placed underneath to keep it from wetting the bed. Repeat this and keep it up for six hours, and when it becomes tedious to the patient, it should be removed, and the limb bathed with warm sweet oil, two parts, and laudanum, one part, and then covered with flannel. In two or three hours return to the hot water and vinegar, keep up for five or six hours, then resume the warm sweet oil and laudanum, and in this way alternate until the inflammation is subdued, or until the calf of the limb can be shaken. The bowels should be gently moved, and the diuretics administered, and in cases where the inflammation lasts, and the fever is considerable, veratrum should be given. If recovery does not take place after the active inflammation has subsided, the limb should be entirely enveloped by a spiral bandage, or, what is much better, the full length elastic stocking represented on the foregoing page should be worn. This gives immediate relief, reduces the leg to natural size, and permits the patient to exercise without any injurious results following. Those desiring this indispensable article are requested to correspond with the author.

DISEASES OF THE BLOOD.

SCURVY (SCORBUTUS).

This disease was known to the ancients. The first distinct account of scurvy is contained in the history of the Crusades of Louis IX. against the Saracens of Egypt, during which the French army suffered greatly from it. Lord Anson's voyage, in which more than eighty of every hundred of the original crews perished from the disease, is familiar to every reader of history. This disease illustrates the importance of vegetable food to the human being, as it is a direct result of a diet free from vegetable substances. It used to be very prevalent in the English and American navies, but is now obviated by the ration of lime-juice in the former, and fresh or desiccated vegetables in the latter. It commences with a feeling of languor, or general debility and mental despondency; a sense of fatigue is experienced on the slightest exertion; the face is either pale or sallow, and presents an appearance of puffiness; the gums are swollen, soft, and of a purplish color, and bleed easily; the breath becomes offensive, and an eruption appears on the body. The mucous surfaces frequently bleed, the feet become swollen and hard and painful, and a disposition is evinced to inflammation of a low grade of the viscera, and also to hemorrhagic effusions. The tongue and appetite remain unaffected, and death is produced either by debility or hemorrhage—the intellect remaining sound to the last.

TREATMENT.—Nothing will avail in the absence of fresh vegetable food, and hence the chief treatment consists in giving vegetable food, or the vegetable acid, as citric acid or lemon-juice. Cabbage and potatoes are excellent, and milk is a good article of diet. If fresh vegetables cannot be obtained, dried fruits should be substituted. If the disease has advanced, and there is sponginess of the gums, myricin, rhusin, and hydrastin may be given in combination with capsicum and cream. If active hemorrhage occurs, the oils of turpentine, solidago, and mecca oil may be used to advantage. If chronic blood derangement follows, as is often the case, the alteratives should be given, of which my "Blood Purifier" (see page 471) is the best.

HEMORRHAGES.

BLEEDING FROM THE NOSE (EPISTAXIS).

There is no part of the body more disposed to hemorrhage than the mucous membrane of the nose. The blood effused through this membrane escapes generally through the nostrils, but may enter the mouth through the posterior nares. It is often symptomatic of diseases of the liver, spleen, and other organs, and generally attends the last stages of malignant and low fevers. It may be slight or dangerously profuse. In plethoric or robust patients it constitutes often a means of relief to the vascular system.

TREATMENT.—When it becomes necessary to check the hemorrhage, the patient should be placed in a cool room, the head elevated or held upright, and the feet plunged in warm water containing mustard. The neck should be bared, and cold water aspersed over it and the face. Lemonade and cooling drinks may also be given. When it becomes habitual, or periodic, and especially if it be vicarious of menstruation, it may be anticipated by local depletion on the nape of the neck. In the passive states of the disease, the astringents should be injected into the nose. Tannin, matico, Monsel's solution, etc., are the best.

if it will not stop, the nostrils should be plugged both anteriorly and posteriorly.

HÆMOPTYSIS.

This is a hemorrhage from the respiratory organs. The blood that is expectorated comes from three different sources. It may come from the mucous membrane of the bronchial tubes, from a vessel ulcerated in a tuberculous cavity as in consumption, and from an aneurism of the aorta, or from the large trunks arising from it, in which case it soon proves fatal. Some cases depend on suppression of the menses, and are habitual and not dangerous, but in the majority of cases it is caused by disease of the heart, or consequent to irritation of tubercles. It may be simple, the blood being all spit up, or it may be attended by an infiltration of blood into the minute tubes and air cells, rendering a portion of the lung solid. The symptoms are some degree of pain or oppression at the chest, with cough, which brings up mouthfuls of blood, fluid or clotted. The quantity may vary from a tea-spoonful to several pints, so that the patient may be suffocated by the abundance of the blood.

TREATMENT.—A free current of air should be allowed to pass over the patient, his covering should be light, and a mild purge should be given to him. The feet should be placed in hot water. If dependent upon derangement of the menses, the sitz-bath (hot) should be ordered, and matico or other astringents be given. Or it may be arrested by putting one drachm of the oil of origanum in a pint bottle, and allow the patient to inhale the vapor. If matico, tannin, or other vegetable astringents are not at hand, common salt, acetate of lead, sulphuric acid, and alum may be used in case of emergency. Small doses of digitalis should be given to control the circulation.

HÆMATEMESIS.

This is hemorrhage from the stomach. Whatever irritates the mucous surface of the stomach, or interrupts the return of blood from that organ is liable to cause this disease. Blows and injuries received by the abdomen, violent concussions of the trunk, pressure, intemperance, worms, powerful emetics, suppression of menstrual discharge, application of cold, or of cold and moisture to the lower extremities during perspiration, or the catamenial flow, prolonged constipation, and pregnancy, are all liable to cause it. The blood is usually vomited profusely, is sometimes mixed with food, and generally of dark color. The premonitory symptoms are pain or tension about the stomach, with faintness or a sense of sinking, or of anxiety at this region, flatulent or acrid eructations, lassitude with irregular chills and flushes of heat.

TREATMENT.—Apply ice to the region of the stomach, and give a full dose of the oil of turpentine conjoined with castor oil, to be repeated if rejected. Administer the astringents, in all cases the vegetable, but if not at hand, acetate of lead, creasote, tincture of iron, alum whey, sulphuric acid, etc., can be given. During the discharge total abstinence is to be observed, but afterwards, mild mucilaginous drinks and farinaceous food in small quantity may be given, and the transition to solid and more nutritious food should be carefully conducted.

HÆMATURIA.

The source of the blood voided through the urethra may be either from the kidney, bladder, or urethra. When it proceeds from the kidneys, it is attended with a sense of heat and pain in the loins, and sometimes with coldness of the extremities, and the blood is intimately mixed with the urine. When the disease is in the ureters, there is a sense of pain in their course, and fibrous shreds having the shape of the ureters are voided. When the hemorrhage is from the bladder, it is usually preceded by heaviness and tension in that region, extending to the perineum, groins, and small of back; the urine is passed with difficulty; the blood is little, if at all, combined with the urine. If from the urethra, the blood is red, liquid and pure, and comes away generally drop by drop.

TREATMENT.—This depends upon its seat and cause. If from the kidneys, the oils of origanum, copaiba, cubebs and turpentine should be administered, and hot packs applied externally. If the urine is alkaline, as in typhus fever and scurvy, the acids should be given. If from the bladder or urethra, matico or other vegetable astringents should be injected. The avoidance of stimulants and absolute rest should be insisted on in every case.

DROPSIES.

If in man a large venous trunk is compressed or obliterated, so that the blood no longer circulates through it, while the collateral vessels can relieve but imperfectly, dropsical effusion is sure to take place. The effusion is proportionate to the size and importance of the vein obliterated. If, for instance, in the vena cava, or large vein in the abdomen, an obstacle should prevent the return of the blood, the two lower extremities and the scrotum will become filled with serum. If the trunk of the portal vein is more or less obliterated, the serous collection takes place in the abdomen. If the obstruction occurs at the very centre of circulation, namely the heart, and the return of blood everywhere embarrassed, the dropsy becomes general; hence dropsy is one of the most common symptoms of heart diseases. Dropsy is often caused by cold, applied in such a manner as to check the secretions of the skin; is often connected with eruptive diseases, as scarlatina; it may result from granular degeneration of the kidneys, debility, exhaustion from loss of blood, etc.; or from obstruction to the return of venous blood, owing to tumors, hypertrophy of the liver, glandular enlargements, etc.

BRIGHT'S DISEASE OF THE KIDNEY.

This is a dropsy owing to a disease of the kidneys. Dr. Bright, of England, first pointed out, 1827, the frequent connection which exists between dropsy and what has since been called granular degeneration of the kidneys, or "Bright's Disease." This state of the kidneys is not an inflammation, but a slow degeneration of its structure, commencing by an abnormal deposit of fat in the cells lining the little tubes in the kidneys. It is a degeneration similar to the tubercular deposit, or the fatty liver common in consumption, and may properly receive the name of *fatty kidney*. It is a slow, insidious disease, beginning generally much further back than the patient is aware of. By degrees the tubes of the kidneys become blocked up with excessive fatty deposits; the result of this is, that the tubes become dilated, so as to press on the network of the portal veins which surround them. The veins being thus compressed, the capillaries which open into them are unable to discharge their contents, and so become distended with blood, and either allow serum to exude from their walls, or else burst and admit the escape of red particles and fibrine. This may be illustrated in a familiar way. If the mouth of all the little brooklets that flow into a brook be effectively dammed up, so that the brook received none of their supply, the brooklets by constant accession would naturally overflow their banks and inundate the adjacent land, and the brook go dry. So as the accumulation of the fat goes on, the portal networks of veins and the uriniferous tubes waste away or become atrophied, and hence shrinking of the kidney and deficiency of the kidney ensue. Albumen is always present in the urine in this disease This can be discovered by boiling the urine in a small tube, the albumen becoming like the white of an egg boiled. Urea, a natural constituent of the urine, is deficient.

The symptoms in the first stage are weakness and dyspepsia, and the blood loses its red particles very rapidly, but there is little to call attention to the kidneys. In the second stage the symptoms are a pallid, pasty complexion, a dry hard skin, drowsiness, weakness, indigestion, and frequent nausea, often retching the first thing in the morning, and palpitation of the heart. A most characteristic symptom is that the patient is awakened several times in the night with desire to make water. In the third stage, if the patient is exposed to cold, the kidney becomes congested; anasarca or general dropsy with perhaps ascites, makes its appearance; debility increases, the urinary secretion becomes more inefficient, urea and other excrementitious matter accumulate in the blood; a drowsiness and coma, signs of effusion of blood, are sure precursors of death. It is caused by intemperance, privation of air and light, and neglect of proper exercise; frequent exposure to cold, and the other causes of scrofula and consumption.

TREATMENT.—This is one of those harassing complaints which physicians in family practice seldom have the patience to investigate and manage with sufficient care.

The condition of the stomach, bowels and skin should receive especial attention. Free action of the skin should be maintained, as in this way the kidneys are relieved and the blood purified. Stimulating diuretics should not be used. Mecca oil, tonic teas, etc., may be given. There is no better specific agent than helonin, from three to ten grains a day. Eupurpurin and populin may also be given with good effect. Vapor baths are beneficial, and counter-irritation should be made over the region of the kidneys.

It is my confident belief that this grave disease can be cured in nearly every instance if not too far advanced. I am induced to such a belief by the success that attends my treatment. I should be happy to correspond with any one of my readers who may suspect this affection, and shall cheerfully analyze any urine that may be sent to me for that purpose, as in my laboratory there are all conveniences for that purpose. (See page 390). For those under my treatment the analyses are gratuitously made, but to others a fee of £1 must in all instances be remitted.

ASCITES.

This is a collection of water in the belly, though sometimes the fluid is outside of the peritoneum and next to the muscles. There is a sense of distension and weight, especially on the side on which the patient lies. When the collection is large, the breathing becomes short and difficult, and the swelling is uniform over the whole abdomen. In some instances the fluctuation may be heard when the patient moves about. This sound distinguishes this complaint from pregnancy or peritonitis. There are generally loss of appetite, dry skin, costiveness, scanty urine, oppression of the chest, cough, colic pains, and variable pulse. A frequent cause of this complaint is chronic inflammation of the peritoneum; it is also produced by scarlet fever, hob-nailed liver, and other diseases of that organ—in short, whatever obstructs the portal circulation.

TREATMENT.—The remedies for this disease are mainly diuretics and purgatives. Digitalis is an excellent remedy, but should be cautiously administered. The patient should have as a constant drink an infusion of two parts of hair-cap moss, and one each of juniper berries and dwarf-elder bark; also an infusion of queen of the meadow. The purgatives that produce watery stools, such as elaterium, should be given. The compound infusion of parsley is about the best agent to promote the absorption of the fluid. The skin should be kept well open, and the strictest temperance both in eating and drinking must also be observed. If all medicinal treatment fails, the surgeon should be called, who will perform *paracentesis abdominis*, or tapping the abdomen; but this should be deferred until all other means have failed.

HYDROTHORAX.

This is a dropsy of the pleura, rarely existing as an independent affection, but generally associated with a general dropsical condition of the system. It is particularly liable to be connected with organic heart disease. When the effusion is slight, only a slight uneasiness is felt in the lower part of the chest, but as it increases, the patient suffers uneasiness in assuming the recumbent posture, a cough and difficulty of breathing being the result. The latter often becomes very severe, the face swells, the cheeks assume a purple and the lips a livid hue, the skin is dry, urine scanty, bowels constipated, thirst, and more or less mental excitement ensues.

TREATMENT.—If owing to heart disease, that affection should receive special attention. The fluid may be evacuated by means of small doses of elaterium and podophyllum, followed by a free use of chimaphila, galium aparine, and aralia hispida. Other diuretics may also be used, and the general rules of treatment observed as advised in Ascites.

DROPSY OF THE HEART.

This consists of a collection of fluid within the pericardium. There is a feeling of uneasiness, or pressure in the cardiac region, a slight cough, difficult and irregular respiration, faintness, disinclination to lie down, a feeble pulse, capricious appetite, disturbed sleep and delirium If there is stupor, cold extremities, the perspiration clammy, and the action of the heart very much disordered, it usually proves fatal.

TREATMENT.—Same as for Hydrothorax. Tapping may become necessary in both cases.

DROPSY OF THE OVARIES.

This consists of an accumulation of fluid in one or more cells within the ovary, or in a serous cyst connected with the uterine appendages. The ovary loses its original form and structure, and frequently attains an immense size, containing several gallons of water. The effusion sadly interferes with respiration, and it causes exhaustion and often peritonitis. The serum may exist within the cavity of the abdomen, or be confined within the cystic tumor. As the tumor enlarges, it ascends the pelvis and occupies more and more of the abdominal cavity, and may float loosely in the fluid within it, and form adhesions to the peritoneum, omentum, or neighboring viscera.

TREATMENT.—Galvanism is often very successful. The current should be passed through the tumor, and be as strong as the patient can bear it, and should be passed in all directions for half an hour several times a day. The hydragogue cathartics and diuretics should also be given, and the alteratives administered. The strength of the patient should be well supported.

This disease is curable by medicinal treatment alone in its early stages if properly treated, but may become so far advanced under improper management, that tapping becomes necessary, or, if the patient's strength will allow, the removal of the whole tumor.

The author would be pleased to correspond with any lady suffering from this serious disease.

DROPSY OF THE SCROTUM (HYDROCELE).

This is a collection of water in the membrane which surrounds the testicles. It is often caused by rheumatism, gout, scrofula, etc. In some cases the accumulation is very large. It may be distinguished from scrotal hernia by pressing the tumor towards the anus; if it bounds rapidly forward it is hydrocele.

TREATMENT.—The following is excellent. Take queen of the meadow, one ounce; colt's foot, one-fourth pound; yellow parilla, one-fourth pound. Make one quart of decoction or syrup, and take one table-spoonful three times a day. A suspensory bandage should be worn. These can be had from me at reasonable prices. In some cases the scrotum must be tapped, and the vinous tincture of hemlock bark injected to prevent the return of the effusions.

I have under my treatment at all times many dropsical patients, and if received under my care at a reasonable early stage, no necessity for tapping arises, and the patient is cured by medicinal treatment alone. Any one desirous of consulting me, may refer to page 390 for the necessary question to be answered.

ANATOMY OF THE URINARY ORGANS.

KIDNEYS.

The kidneys are two hard glands for the secretion of urine, placed in each lumbar region, just above the hips; they are outside of the peritoneum, or lining membrane of the abdomen, and surrounded with an abundance of fat. The *right kidney* is rather lower than the left, on account of the superposition of the liver. The *length* is about four in ches, and the breadth two inches. The shape is oval, resembling a bean; the position upright, and the fissure (or *hilum*) is directed to the spinal column. The upper end of the kidney is rather larger than the lower. It is covered by a strong *fibrous capsule*. The color is a reddish brown. Upon making a longitudinal section of the kidney, as represented in cut, two different structures are presented. The internal is of a darker color, and consists of about fifteen of what are called the *cones of Malpighi*,[3] which are arranged in three rows, the apex of each converging towards the hilum. This constitutes the *medullary* portion of the kidneys. The external structure is of lighter color usually, is extremely vascular, and of a granulated arrangement; it constitutes the *cortical* portion. The urine is formed in the tortuous tubes of the cortical substance,[2] between whose walls are a number of small bodies called *corpuscles of Malpighi*. At the apex of each cone is the *papilla renalis*, and in the centre of each papilla is a slight depression, called *foveola*. Each papilla is surrounded by a small membranous cup, called *infundibulum*,[4] into which the urine is first received as it oozes from the orifices of the papillæ. Four or five of these infundibula join to form a common trunk, called *calyx*,[5] and the junction of about three calyces forms a common cavity, called the *pelvis*,[6] which is conoidal in shape, and from which proceeds the ureter,[7] the excretory tube of the kidney, which conveys the urine to the bladder. The ureter is a cylindrical tube of the size of a quill, with thin, extensible walls. It enters the inferior fundus of the bladder very obliquely, and opens by a very small orifice.

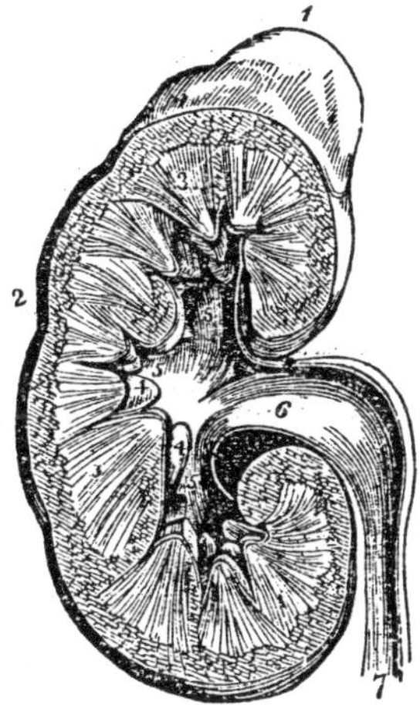

The Kidney.

Just above the kidney, and reposing on its upper extremity, placed one on each side, are two small bodies, varying much in size, called the *supra-renal capsules*.[1] They have no secretion, consequently no duct, but evidently perform important functions in fœtal life, when they are much larger.

BLADDER.

The bladder is a musculo-membranous sac for the reception of urine It is situated in the cavity of the pelvis, behind the pubic bones, and in front of the rectum in the male, but in the female the uterus and vagina are between the rectum and bladder. In shape the bladder is oval, the larger end being downwards; in women it is more spheroidal; in children it is pear-shaped. It is divided into a superior and inferior *fundus*, a *body*, and *neck*.

Its dimensions vary with health and disease. Ordinarily it will hold about a pint. At the neck of the bladder is a circular muscle, called the *sphincter*, which, in a state of contraction, retains the urine in the bladder until the necessity to voiding it arises. The *urethra* is described under anatomy of the sexual organs.

DISEASES OF THE URINARY ORGANS.

NEPHRITIS.

This is inflammation of the kidneys, and which may occur either in its substance, its lining membrane, or in its capsule. The symptoms are deep-seated pain in the small of the back, extending down the groins in one or both sides, increased by pressure; urination either increased or diminished, urine scanty and high-colored, and mixed with blood or gravelly matters. If both kidneys are affected the urine may be suppressed, and comatose symptoms present themselves. Chills, fever, deranged stomach, and constipation nearly always attend it. The testicle is retracted, which distinguishes this disease from lumbago, etc. It runs very rapidly into suppuration, the sign of which is the appearance of pus in the urine.

TREATMENT.—The disease should be controlled by the use of hot packs, vapor baths, lobelia emetics, mild purges, and the internal administration of aconite and veratrum. The mucilaginous drinks should be drunk, and the opiates given if the pain is very severe. In chronic nephritis, where there is debility of the organ, the best remedies are turpentine, copaiba, buchu, uva ursi, pareira brava, and pipsissewa.

DIURESIS.

This is the *diabetes insipidus* of some writers. By this term is understood the excessive secretion of pale, limpid urine, without sugar. The principal symptoms are insatiable thirst and the elimination of a large quantity of urine. These symptoms are usually preceded by a variable appetite, constipation, and derangement of the functions of the skin. The copious flow of urine may only be occasional, following over-mental or physical excitement. It may be distinguished from *diabetes mellitus* by the absence of sugar in the urine.

TREATMENT.—The skin should receive special attention, and excess of drinking should be avoided. The constitutional debility should be overcome with baths, and the general tonics; apocynin, from one-eighth to one-fourth of a grain, four or five times a day, is a specific for this disease.

DIABETES MELLITUS.

This is characterized by increase of urine, containing sugar. The first indications of this disease are languor, dry, and harsh skin, intense thirst, pain in the small of back, constipation, with alternate chill and fever. After a time the general health gives way, and there are muscular weakness, loss of sexual power, pain in the loins, coldness of extremities, a burning sensation in the hands and feet, loss of weight, and a chloroform odor of breath. The gums become spongy, the teeth decay, the mind becomes depressed and irritable, and the appetite voracious. Consumption is often a sequel to this disease. The urine has a sweetish taste, due to the presence of sugar, which can readily be discovered by adding yeast to the urine, which gives rise to various fermentation.

TREATMENT.—A healthy state of the general system should be maintained by fresh air, frequent baths, and a generous diet. No saccharine or starchy articles of food should be eaten. The bowels and liver should be gently stimulated by small doses of leptandrin and leontodin. Great success is obtained by the use of unicorn root. Mecca oil has also been successfully employed in this disease.

Diabetic patients who may desire the author to treat them, may consult him as directed on page 390.

GRAVEL (LITHIASIS).

This disorder consists in the deposition from the urine, within the body, of an insoluble sand-like matter. In health the urine carries off the results of the waste and disintegration of the tissues in a soluble state, but when these matters are in excess the urine frequently deposits them after being voided, on cooling. This often occurs after irregularities of diet, without actually being a morbid condition, but when the accumulation is excessive it causes a serious disease. The gravels are chemically either urates, lithates, phosphates, or oxalates, according to the diathesis of the patient. The passage of gravel or renal calculi from the kidneys to the bladder through the ureters, causes the most excruciating pain. When anything in the bladder, as a mucous shred or a large gravel, acts as a nucleus, the constant accessions to this nucleus form what is known as *stone in the bladder*, which may be of various sizes.

In gravel the patient has a dull aching pain in the back, attended with urgent and frequent desire to urinate, preceded by cutting or scalding pains in the urethra, neck of bladder, or in the course of the ureters In stone we have the same symptoms, but the sudden stoppage of the stream during micturition is always suggestive of its presence in the bladder, and the patient has a constant desire to relieve the pain by pulling at the end of his penis.

TREATMENT.—Diluents should be freely used, and a strict attention paid to diet. Animal food should be sparingly eaten, and alcoholic drinks totally avoided. The chemical nature of the gravel should be ascertained, and when this is done the chemical opposites administered. No treatment will avail, if not in chemical opposition to the diathesis of the patient. If medicinal treatment is ineffectual after a stone has been formed, the surgeon should be consulted, who will remove it by an operation called *lithotrity* or another termed *lithontripsy*.

Unless the stone be too large, my experience is that solvent treatment will prove effectual in nearly every case. The solvent treatment consists, of course, of such herbal agents as are chemically opposed to the nature of the calculus. By such a course of medication my success has been most gratifying.

Ischuria, or Suppression of Urine.

This frequently attends inflammatory diseases, especially acute nephritis. It may either arise from an irritation of the kidney beyond the point of secretion, or from a torpor or paralysis of the kidneys. It is important to distinguish it from *retention of urine*. It is sometimes very dangerous, being attended with vomiting, drowsiness, coma and convulsions. A vicarious secretion from the skin, bowels, etc., is also often established. It is evidently due to a sort of paralysis of the nerve centres.

Treatment.—Leeches may be placed over the loins, and digitalis or squill administered. The demulcent drinks should be freely used. If uric acid is in excess, some carbonate may be given. If dependent upon torpor, the stimulating diuretics, as turpentine, should be used. Frequent hot sitz-baths are also beneficial.

Incontinence of Urine (Enuresis).

This is often associated with some constitutional weakness. The bladder may be exclusively irritated and not be able to hold the urine, or the little circular muscle at the neck of the bladder may be debilitated or paralyzed, owing to acridity of the urine. In some cases it may be owing to debility of the kidneys.

Treatment.—A course of tonics, sea-bathing, cold baths, warm clothing, etc., together with astringents and stimulating diuretics, will usually cure it. Small doses of the extract of belladona will also afford relief. In case of paralysis of the bladder, nux vomica, electricity, counter-irritant application to the spine, and local irritants are necessary.

Cystitis.

This is an inflammation of the bladder. The symptoms are pain above the pubes, tenderness on pressure, the pain extending into the penis, scrotum, and perineum, producing straining and pain in urination ;

sometimes pain over the abdomen, which is swollen, or the inflammation may extend to the peritoneum, causing peritonitis. It may terminate in suppuration, the pus appearing in the urine, or, if the abscess occurs in the coats of the bladder, it may open suddenly. It is caused by direct irritation as by a catheter; also by gonorrhœa, difficult labor, turpentine, cantharides, etc. When the inflammation becomes chronic it is called "*Catarrh of the Bladder.*"

TREATMENT.—Mucilaginous drinks should be freely used, such as decoctions of marsh-mallow, uva ursi, etc. Dover's powder may be given to relieve the pain. About three grains of populin and one-fourth of a grain of gelsemium given three or four times a day, exerts a marked beneficial influence in this disease; linseed oil and essential tincture of hydrangea are also remedies of great value. The chronic form will require special treatment, in accordance to condition and nature of each case.

ANATOMY OF THE NERVOUS SYSTEM.

The principal divisions of the nervous system are the brain, spinal marrow, and nerves. The tissue of this system is included in membranes or sheaths, and consists of two differently colored pulpy materials, one of which is *white* or *medullary*, and the other *gray*, *cortical*, or *cineritious*. The sheath of the nerves is called the *neurilemma*, and the internal material *neurine*. All ganglia and nervous centres consist of a mixture of white fibres and gray globules.

An *anastomosis* is the interchange of fasciculi between two trunks, each fasciculus remaining unaltered, although in contact with another. A combination of anastomoses into a network is called a *plexus*.

SPINAL MARROW.

The spinal marrow is the medullary column included within the bones or vertebræ of the spinal column. It has three coverings: 1st, The *dura mater*, which is a white fibrous membrane, and forms the external; 2d, The *arachnoid*, a serous membrane, forming the middle covering. It is extremely thin and transparent; 3d, The *pia mater*, a cellular membrane, forming the immediate covering. It is very vascular, consisting almost entirely of vessels.

THE BRAIN.

The brain consists of four principal parts: medulla oblongata, pons varolii, cerebrum, and cerebellum. Like the spinal marrow it also has three coverings bearing the same names. The *dura mater* adheres very firmly to the bones of the cranium, and consists of two laminæ, which are divided into folds called *falx cerebri*, *tentorium*, and *falx cerebelli.*

The medulla oblongata is the upper part of the spinal cord; it is conical in shape, and extends from the first bone of the spinal column to the pons varolii. Its divisions are the *corpori pyramidale*, *olivare* and *restiforme*.

The pons varolii is cuboidal in shape, and situated just in front of the medulla.

The cerebrum is the largest mass composing the brain. It is oval in shape, and weighs from three to four pounds. It is divided into two hemispheres, each hemisphere consisting of an anterior, middle, and posterior lobe. The surface presents a number of convolutions, or *gyri*, each separated by deep fissures, or *sulci*. The interior of each hemisphere is medullary in character, and the surface of each convolution is cineritious for the depth of about one-sixth of an inch.

The ventricles of the brain are five in number: they are called the *right* and *left lateral*, the *third*, *fourth*, and *fifth ventricles*.

The more minute anatomy of the cerebrum is exceeding complex, and not of special importance in a popular work of this kind.

The cerebellum constitutes about one-sixth of the brain, and is contained between the occiput and tentorium. It is oblong and flattened in shape, and composed of white and gray substances.

Cranial Nerves.

These are nine in number, and all emerge from the foramina, or opening at the base of the brain. They are designated by their function as well as numerically, viz.: 1st, olfactory; 2d, optic; 3d, motor oculi; 4th, patheticus; 5th, trifacial; 6th, motor externus; 7th, facial and auditory; 8th, pneumogastric, glosso-pharyngeal, and spinal accessory; 9th, hypoglossal.

According to function the cranial nerves may be divided into three classes, viz.: *nerves of special sense*, including the 1st, 2d, and the auditory branch of the 7th; *nerves of motion*, including the 3d, 4th, 6th, facial branch of the 7th and 9th; *compound nerves*, comprising the 8th and 5th.

The principal nerve of the arm is the *brachial;* of the forearm, the *ulnar* and *radial;* of the thigh, the *great sciatic*, which divides, about one-third above the knee, into two large branches, the *peroneal and popliteal;* further on the popliteal is called the *posterior tibial*. In the pelvis there are the *pudic*, *gluteal*, and *lesser ischiatic*.

The *sympathetic nerve* is distributed with all the other nerves of the body, and by means of plexuses supplies all the internal organs.

The nervous system is a complex piece of machinery, and its anatomy requires much study before any competent familiarity with it can be gained. The physician, who has an inadequate knowledge of the anatomy of the nervous system, and philosophy of nervous phenomena, or the physiology pertaining thereto, cannot hope to treat diseases assailing the system with any material success. Competence in this respect is the reward only of a long devotion, and practical experience.

DISEASES OF THE NERVOUS SYSTEM.

INFLAMMATION OF THE BRAIN (CEREBRITIS).

This consists of inflammation of the cerebral substance, and due to long exposure to a vertical sun, the inordinate use of ardent spirits, cold, fright, external injury, the sudden disappearance of an old discharge, and it sometimes occurs as a consequent on small-pox, or erysipelas of the face and scalp, and fevers. The symptoms are violent inflammatory fever, hot and dry skin, flushed countenance, suffused eyes, quick and hard pulse, the arteries of the neck throb, and delirium. The senses are morbidly acute, there being intolerance of light and sound. The person is extremely restless, the muscles of the face are spasmodically contracted, the upper eye-lids hang down, and as the disease progresses, blindness and deafness ensue. The countenance is vacant or idiotic, the eye loses its lustre, the pupils become dilated, and the eyes often squint. In the still more advanced stage, the discharges pass off involuntarily, the countenance becomes pale and sunken, the pulse weak and irregular, the coma more profound, and death soon closes the scene. It is commonly called "Brain Fever."

TREATMENT.—This should be most energetic. Bleeding to fainting has been the practice of many physicians, but I deem it unnecessary, as revulsion can be made by other means. Leeches may, however, be applied to the scalp. The hair should be closely shaved.from the head, and ice, alcohol or ether, with water, applied to the head. The decoction of ladies'-slipper should be given internally. At the outset purgatives should be given. Those that act thoroughly, such as gamboge, colocynth, etc., are the best. The bladder should be emptied every day. In the stage of collapse, stimulants may be given.

APOPLEXY.

This is a condition in which all the functions of animal life are suddenly stopped, except the pulse and the breathing. There is neither thought nor feeling, nor voluntary motion; and the patient suddenly falls down, and lies as if in a deep sleep. The disease assails in three different ways. The first form of attack is a sudden falling down into a state of insensibility and apparently deep sleep, the face being generally flushed, the breathing stertorous, or snoring, the pulse full and not frequent, with occasional convulsions. From this mode of attack death often occurs immediately, but in some cases recovery occurs, with the exception of paralysis of one side, or the loss of speech, or some of the senses. The second mode of attack begins with sudden pain in the head, and the patient becomes pale, faint, sick, and vomits. His pulse is feeble, has a cold skin, and occasionally some convulsions. He may fall down, or be only a little confused, but soon recovers from all the symptoms, except the headache; this will continue, and the patient will sooner or later become heavy, forgetful, unable to connect ideas, and finally sink into insensibility from which he never rises. This mode of invasion, though not so frightful as the first, is of much more serious import.

The third form of attack is where consciousness is retained, but power on one side of the body is suddenly lost. The patient retains his mind, and answers questions rationally, either by signs or words. He may either die soon, or live for years, with imperfect speech, or a leg dragging after him, or an arm hanging uselessly by his side.

Those persons who have large heads, red faces, short and thick necks, and a short, stout, square build, are more predisposed to this disease, than thin, pale and tall persons. Literary men, especially editors, lawyers, doctors, etc., are subject to this disease, owing to mental overwork.

The symptoms preceding an apoplectic attack are headache, vertigo, double vision, faltering speech, inability to remember certain words, sometimes forgetfulness of one's one name, a frequent losing of a train of ideas, and occasionally an unaccountable dread. It is caused by whatever hurries the circulation as strong bodily exercise, emotional excitement, exposure to the sun or severe cold, tight cravats, etc.

TREATMENT.—If the face is turgescent and red, and the temporal arteries throb, and the pulse full and hard, the patient should be placed in a semi-recumbent position, with his head raised, his clothes loosened, particularly his neck-band and shirt collar, and then quickly as possible, cold water or ice should be applied to the head, leeches to the nape of the neck, and mustard plasters to the calves of the leg. Tight ligatures may also be tied around the thighs, sufficiently tight to arrest the venous circulation; they should be removed gradually as consciousness returns. Administer a stimulating purgative, as a few drops of croton oil. Injections may also be given. If the patient is old, and the pulse feeble, the ice applications, ligature, etc., may be omitted, and instead apply warm flannels and warm bricks to the body, and administer camphor. To prevent future attacks, gentle tonics should be given, and the skin kept healthy by daily bathing and friction. The bowels must not be permitted to become costive. The diet should be well regulated. The mind should be kept cheerful and hopeful, and free from all excitement. Intoxicating drinks should be totally avoided, and sexual congress should be of rare occurrence. In fact every thing that might provoke an attack should be avoided.

Congestion of the Brain.

This consists of an accumulation of blood in the cerebral vessels. The countenance is flushed, the eyes suffused, light becomes intolerable, and there is singing in the ears, vertigo, momentary loss of speech, and sometimes delirium. Simple congestion is merely a functional affection, and in a slight or moderate degree involves no immediate danger. It may, however, produce apoplexy and sudden death. It is caused by any mechanical impediment to the return of blood from the head, as tumor of the neck, heart disease, etc. It is a concomitant to nearly every inflammatory cerebral affection.

Treatment.—The treatment consists in diverting the blood from the head by hot mustard foot baths, and an active cathartic. Ice or cold water may also be applied to the head, and the circulation reduced by veratrum. The treatment is the same as advised in apoplexy, in all essential particulars.

Sunstroke.

The injury done to the brain in this case is the same as in apoplexy, with the exception of the clot. It is essentially congestion of the brain. Persons who are exposed by necessity of pursuit to the extreme heat of the sun, should be protected by a wet cloth or cabbage-leaves placed on the head and under a light hat. The symptoms are first dizziness, followed by intense headache. Thirst becomes excessive, the pulse indistinct at the wrist, violent throbbing of the carotid and temporal arteries, and insensibility ensues by a convulsive shivering of the body.

Treatment.—Place the patient immediately in a cool and shady place, and instantly apply, copiously, cold water, or, what is better, pounded ice in a bag, to the head. Make friction over his legs to relieve the congested state of the brain. Application of turpentine by friction on the spine is also of service. Inhalation of ammonia or hartshorn is beneficial, and a small quantity of the carbonate of that substance may be given internally. Continue this treatment until the patient is out of danger, or until death ensues. In plethoric patients, bleeding from the arm is required, and in this instance only is bleeding advisable. After the patient becomes conscious and apparently out of danger, he is to be removed to his home, and a brisk cathartic administered, to effect revulsion. In no case should he be allowed again to expose himself to sun during the first four or five days after the occurrence of the sun stroke. The application of water or ice to the head should be abandoned by gradual increase of temperature, to prevent any reaction

Insanity.

This is an unsound manifestation of intellectual power. The indications which should excite alarm are headache, vertigo, mental confusion, fretful temper, inaptitude for usual occupations, defective articulations, dimness of vision, and flightiness of manner. The patient is also aware that he is not right, he shuns his old friends, has frightful dreams, is tortured with wicked thoughts. If it exists with general paralysis it is frequently incurable. Derangement is manifested in various ways, viz:—

1st. *Mania.*—This is characterized by general delirium, in which the reasoning faculty is disturbed and confused, if not lost, ideas absurd, wandering, or erroneous; conduct violent, excited, and extremely mischievous. The maniac's hair is crisped, he neglects his family and business, suspects his friends, dislikes the light, and certain colors horrify him, his ears are sometimes very red, noise excites and disturbs him, and he has frequent fits of anger and melancholy, without any cause. His delirium extends to all subjects, and the entire intellect, affections and will are in a chaotic wreck.

In *puerperal mania* occurring after delivery, the delirium is frequently extreme, there being a tendency to suicide or child-murder. Maniacs in general have a disposition to murder or suicide.

2d. *Monomania.* This is characterized by mental aberration on one subject. The patient seizes upon a false principle, and draws from it injurious conclusions, which modify and change his whole life and character. In other cases the intellect is sound, but the affections and disposition being perverted, their acts are strange and inconsistent. Attempt is made to justify their hallucinations by plausible reasoning.

3d. *Dementia.* This is a condition in which the weakness of intellect is induced by accident or old age. The ideas are numerous, but vague, confused and wandering; the memory is impaired, and the manners childish, silly and undecided.

4th. *Moral Mania.* Moral insanity is a condition in which there is a perversion of the natural feelings, affections, temper, habits, and moral dispositions. The conduct is eccentric, and an uncontrolable destructive tendency, or a propensity to every species of mischief, are frequently the leading features. A slight insanity is popularly called "a kink in the head;" in Scotland, "a bee in the bonnet."

If insanity is characterized by fear, moroseness and prolonged sadness, it is called *lypemania* or *melancholia.* If religion is the theme of delirium, it is termed *theomania.* If amatory delusions rule, it is called *erotomania.* If the suicidal tendency is strong, it is designated *autophomania*, and if characterized by aversion to man and society, it is called *misanthropia.* If the tendency is to stealing, it constitutes *kleptomania.* *Close confinement*, and *low diet*, such conveniences as prisons afford, are the best cures for this species of mania.

It is a pitiful sight to see the thousand fancies in regard to themselves of the insane. One imagines himself as an inspired individual, and charged with the conversion of the world, while another sincerely believes that the devil has entered into him, and he curses God, himself and the universe. Still another believes that he controls the world, and directs the movements of the planets. One believes that all the wisdom is concentrated in him, and offers to teach the wisest. Another imagines himself some grand king, is proud, withdraws from his fellows, and will allow no one to come in his presence without proper acts of homage. Yet another is Napoleon, or some other great general, and he fights his battles anew, and majestically marshals his imaginary army. *Idiocy* is owing to a congenital deficiency of mind, and in consequence the idiot may often be a deaf-mute, and be governed by insane passions.

The cause of insanity is hereditary predisposition, constant revolution in the mind of some painful thought, injured feelings which cannot be resented, mortified pride, perplexity in business, disappointed affections or ambition, political or religious excitement, loss of friends or property, and in general, whatever worries the mind or creates a deep distress. Another prolific cause is masturbation.

TREATMENT.—The real character of the malady should be ascertained, and, if possible, the pathological condition giving rise to the disorder corrected. Out-door exercise, lively amusements, fresh air and daily bathing, contribute largely to establish a cure. The exciting cause should be removed. The stomach and bowels should receive due attention. The tonics should be given to improve the general health of the patient. Ladies'-slipper, scullcap, cannabis indica, gelsemium, aconite, veratrum, belladonna, quinine, opium and lupulin, stand in good repute for this disorder. The moral treatment should be such as is best adapted to the condition of the patient. It is probably best, when practicable, to place the patient in some well-conducted insane asylum, where he will have proper attendance and treatment. If this is not feasible, the physician should make such arrangements as will best secure the patient, if of vicious disposition, from harming himself or others, but in no case should unnecessary restraint be placed upon the patient.

I have conducted the treatment in many cases of insanity, many of whom I had never seen, and wherever my instructions were faithfully carried out, a cure was generally effected. If any of my readers have relatives or friends who may have become insane, and who may desire to know my opinion of the case, or its chances for cure, and will describe the case to me fully, I will cheerfully state them. (See page 390 for address.)

DELIRIUM TREMENS.

This is also called *mania a potu*, and in common parlance it is the "horrors" or "jim-jams." It is caused by the sudden withdrawal from the habitual or prolonged use of alcoholic stimulation. Its most prominent characteristics are delirious hallucinations, fear, muscular tremors, weakness, watchfulness, and the want of sleep. The symptoms are incessant talking, fidgeting with the hands, trembling of the limbs, a rapid pulse, profuse sweating, and a mingling of the real with the imaginary. The patient's face is pale and sallow, his eye is rolling, quick and expressive, and is busy day and night, and can scarcely be confined to his room. He is unwilling to admit that anything ails him, answers questions rationally, and does whatever he is bidden at the time. Then he begins to wander again, the expression becomes wild, the eyes vacant or staring, and becomes the victim of pitiful and ludicrous illusions of senses, phantasms and hallucinations of every kind; he sees imaginary objects, such as rats, mice, lice, dogs, cats, snakes, and hears and imagines the most extraordinary and absurd delusions. In favorable cases, sleep ends the crisis about the third or fourth day; where death occurs, the delirium is active until sudden suspension of breath ensues.

TREATMENT.—Sleep is the cure for this disease, and opium and its preparations are the sovereign remedies. Give one-third or one-half of a grain of morphia; if this does not produce sleep, give thirty drops of laudanum every two hours till sleep is produced. A draught or two of the patient's accustomed drink may also be given, and large doses of opium may be dispensed with if cold applications are made to the head, and the use of a tepid bath, prolonged for a few hours. Lupulin is also a good remedy.

HEADACHE (CEPHALALGIA).

This, in its widest acceptation, includes all uneasy sensations of the head. It may be confined to one spot, or embrace one side, as in hemicrania; or it may be diffused, and of indefinite extent. It may be felt in the depths of the brain, or only in the scalp and cranium, and continue for an instant, or last for days and weeks. It is usually paroxysmal, and the pain may be simple or very violent. It is a constant attendant to the different forms of inflammation of the brain. It is caused by various conditions; decayed teeth may cause it. When confined to one side, the pain is of a lancinating character; when due to a disordered stomach, it occurs in the forehead and temples; when it occurs from a congestive state of the brain, it is of a dull, heavy, aching character; when due to spinal irritation, there is a protracted pain in the top or back part of the head; and when it is accompanied by nausea and vomiting, it is called "*sick-headache.*"

TREATMENT.—Immediate relief may frequently be obtained by thoroughly evacuating the stomach, and drinking hot tea or coffee, followed by adding ten drops of tincture of belladonna to a tumblerful of water, and taking one tea-spoonful every ten or fifteen minutes. A hot foot-bath and bathing the head in stimulating liniments also afford relief in some cases. If it is due to a full habit, the diet must be regulated. In some bad cases cold applications to the head, leeches to the temples, and hot sinapisms to the spine may be required. Rubbing my "Herbal Ointment" on the forehead, temples, and nape of neck gives instant relief.

HYPOCHONDRIA.

Among the causes of this distressing complaint are disappointment, misfortunes of a heavy character, care, masturbation, excessive mental labor, undue anxiety, costiveness, neglect of cleanliness, indigestion, sedentary occupations, living in close and gloomy apartments, or wet and marshy localities, excessive indulgence in sexual pleasures, or anything which tends to weaken and disturb the nervous system, or over-stimulate the brain. The mental symptoms are countless. The chief one is a constant dread of some unexplainable evil; the patient fears that his wife, if he has one, is unfaithful, or hates him, or that his business is going to ruin, and he will be reduced to beggary, or that his friends despise him, or that he will be charged with the commission of some monstrous crime, or that he has all, or a majority of the worst physical diseases that surgeon or physician was ever summoned to treat. These are the lightest symptoms, and if not immediately attended to, will become aggravated, and go on increasing in violence and extent until the sufferer dies naturally from exhaustion and misery, gets hopelessly insane, or perhaps commits suicide. The organs of sense are more or less deranged, and external sensations are magnified and corrupted even as those of the mind are. Thus, the eye appears to see all sorts of forms which it *does not see*; the smell detects odors which do not exist; the touch demonstrates to the brain objects with which it does not come in contact; the taste is perverted and disordered to an extent which seems, to an uninterested observer, impossible; and the ears convey imaginary sounds of the most perplexing and terrific character. The queer fancies of the hypochondriac are often of such a character as to obliterate pity for the unhappy individual, and provoke both disgust and laughter. Cases have been known where the victim imagined that he was a teapot, or had glass legs which would break upon the lightest exertion, or was made of jelly, and could not move without dissolving into an undistinguishable mass of gelatinous matter, or was as large as an elephant, or as small as a pipe-stem; or had horns growing from the head, or a bottle attached to the end of the nose, or was covered with creeping and venomous insects. Hypochondria is also productive of fainting spells, cold surface of the body, an eye either glassy and unnaturally brilliant, or without any lustre, palpitations, pains in the stomach, pale and livid countenance, and occasional paroxysms of fever.

TREATMENT.—A cure may be effected by the employment of such medicines as will restore tone to the stomach and nervous system, and also by removing, as far as is possible, all the causes which lead to the origin and perpetuation of the malady. Where it is within the scope of the patient's, means he should be kept continually on the move (without fatigue), a constant change of scene being one of the most desirable of self-acting remedies. All allusions to his real or fancied miseries should be avoided, or, if found necessary, of the kindest and most consoling description. It is always the case that the hypochondriac will be the harshest, the most suspicious, and the most ungenerous in every way, towards his best friends. This is an unfailing type of the disease. The friends must bear these annoyances patiently and self-denyingly. To lose one's temper with such a sufferer is to commit a great crime; out-of-door exercise must be as constant as is consistent with the weather and the patient's circumstances. Leave the hypochondriac alone as little as possible. Let him eat and drink but moderately of nourishing but easily-digested food, and above all things keep him from the use of stimulating drinks and tobacco. Music has been found highly beneficial in these cases—anything is good, in fact, which affords lively amusement. A cold or tepid sponge bath should be taken morning and evening, and the rule of "early to bed and early to rise," should never be violated. The bowels must always be kept open—a good passage every twenty-four hours being required—and where the patient is extremely weak, a good substantial tonic, such as "Restorative Assimilant," should be administered three times a day. When the patient has a fainting smell, and thinks he is dying, give him motherwort tea, with spirits of camphor in it, if no other assistance happens to be at hand. This is only general treatment for temporary benefit. To eradicate the disease thoroughly it is necessary to know all about the individual case, and the chief causes of its origin and development. Nature's remedies may then be applied without fear of failure.

NEURALGIA.

This disease affects one tissue only—the nervous, and pain is the only symptom. The pain is of every degree of intensity. It may affect every nerve, but is more commonly confined to the most important. The tearing pain comes on suddenly and in paroxysms. It may be so agonizing as to cause a temporary loss of reason.

When the fifth pair of nerves is affected it is called *tic douleureux;* and *face ache* when confined to the facial nerve and branches. It is called *sciatica* when the pain begins at the hip and follows the course of the sciatic nerve. It may also occur in the female breasts, the womb, in the stomach and bowels, hands and feet, etc.

TREATMENT.—This is palliative and radical. The palliative treatment consists in the administration of aconite, hyoscyamus, ladies'-slipper, belladonna, opium, morphine, lupulin, cicuta, etc. These can either be applied locally, or taken internally. Morphine and aconitin should be injected subcutaneously, and immediate relief follows. In sciatica, blistering along the course of the nerve often cures. Ten grains each of aconitin and extract of belladonna and one drachm of lard, form an excellent ointment for external application. The "Herbal Ointment" (page 472) arrests the pain almost instantly. The radical treatment consists in removing the cause. If due to malarial influence, quinine should be given. If associated with kidney disease, that organ should receive attention. The alteratives are serviceable in many cases.

Bilious Colic.

This is neuralgia of the mesenteric net-work of nerves, or rather hyperæsthesia of the plexus. By hyperæsthesia is meant excessive sensibility or passability. It is characterized by sharp twisting pain extending from the navel to the lower portion of the abdomen. It occurs in paroxysms, and is of a most excruciating character. The patient is restless, hands, feet and cheeks are cold, and the pulse is small and hard. The abdomen is tense and distended; obstinate constipation, and usually nausea and vomiting occur. The fits usually last from a few moments to several hours. The matter vomited up is generally bilious matter.

Treatment.--Administer an active purgative injection immediately, and give internally wild yam, camphor, etc., every fifteen minutes until the pain is relieved. A strong decoction of wild yam root is a specific cure for this affection. Scull-cap and high-cranberry bark are also good. The latter is called *cramp bark* on account of its excellence in spasmodic affections. The vomiting may be checked by laudanum. Hot baths, fomentations, etc., are also useful.

Hiccough.

This consists in spasmodic contraction of the midriff, and a certain degree of constriction, which arrests the air in the wind-pipe, thus producing sudden, short, convulsive inspirations, attended by slight sound, and followed immediately by expiration. It is often a symptom of low forms of fever and inflammatory diseases, or caused by the excessive use of alcohol or tobacco.

Treatment.--When purely nervous, suddenly attracting the mind will cure it. Hence the common advice to the hiccoughing patient, "think of your sweetheart" is so often effectual, because the fond object absorbs the whole mind. When dependent upon a disordered state of the stomach, an emetic will relieve it. In fevers it denotes debility, indicating the need of stimulants.

WHOOPING COUGH (PERTUSSIS).

This is a hyperæsthesia of the pneumo-gastric nerve, and not due to inflammation, as may be supposed. It is a contagious disease. It consists of a convulsive cough, attended by hissing and rattling in the windpipe, and ineffectual efforts to expel the breath. This is repeated until a quantity of thick, tenacious mucus is expectorated, when the breathing again becomes free. The paroxysms apparently threaten suffocation, and the agitation affects the whole body. Blood is sometimes started from the nostrils, but, notwithstanding the violence of the symptoms, it is rarely ever dangerous.

TREATMENT.—An emetic may be given at first. Liniments of olive oil or the "Herbal Ointment" should be applied to the spine. The anti-spasmodics are or course indicated, such as belladonna, a decoction of bitter almond, or of cherry seed, etc. Lobelia is a good remedy, as is also skunk cabbage; daily vapor inhalations are also serviceable; cochineal has a good reputation; it should be used with stillingia.

SPASM OF THE GLOTTIS.

This is also called the *crowing disease* or *false croup*. It is common to children, and rarely occurs in adults. It is a spasmodic disease, and distinguishable from croup by the absence of fever. The child is suddenly taken with an impossibility of taking breath, and struggles convulsively for a time, its head thrown back, face pale, legs and arms stiff, and when it begins to breathe it is of a crowing character.

TREATMENT.—In the paroxysm set the child in an upright position, exposed to a full draught of cool and fresh air, and sprinkle cold water in its face. Loosen all its clothes around the neck, slap it slightly on the back, and apply friction along the spine. If not successful, place it in a warm bath, and then sprinkle cold water in its face. If due to teething, use the proper remedies, and give some gentle physic.

EPILEPSY.

This is characterized by the sudden loss of consciousness and sensibility, accompanied with spasms and convulsions. It comes on suddenly, and epileptics, by the sudden attacks, are at all times in danger. They may be taken while descending a flight of stairs, while traversing the bank of a precipice, while crossing a street crowded with vehicles drawn at full speed, or while in a throng of people whose feet would trample them to death, especially in case of an alarm of fire, a great public meeting or pageant, or other sudden danger. But all those afflicted in this terrible way are actually alive to the dangers of which they are the constant expectants. Epilepsy, in its severer forms, is a terrible disease to witness. It is productive of great distress and misery, and liable to terminate in worse than death, as it is apt, in many cases, to end in fatuity or insanity, and so carrying perpetual anxiety and dismay into all of those families which it has once visited.

The leading symptoms of Epilepsy are, a temporary suspension of consciousness, with clonic spasms, recurring at intervals; but so various are its forms, and so numerous its modifications, that no general description of the disease can be given. I will first describe the most ordinary type of the disease, and then note some of the several variations which occur from the standard type.

A man in the apparent enjoyment of perfect health suddenly utters a loud cry, and falls instantly to the ground, senseless and convulsed. He strains and struggles violently. His breathing is embarrassed and suspended; his face is turgid and livid; he foams at the mouth; a choking sound is heard in his wind-pipe, and he appears to be at the point of death from apnœa, or suspension of breath. By degrees, however, these alarming phenomena diminish, and finally cease, leaving the patient exhausted, heavy, stupid, comatose, or in a death-like condition. His life, however, is no longer threatened, and soon, to all appearances, he is perfectly well. The same train of morbid phenomena recur, again and again, at different, and mostly at irregular intervals, perhaps through a long course of years, notwithstanding the best medical science has been exercised to prevent and cure the distressing malady. This is the most ordinary form of Epilepsy.

The suddenness of the attack is remarkable: in an instant, when it is least expected by himself, or by those around him, in the middle of a sentence or of a gesture, the change takes place, and the unfortunate sufferer is stretched foaming, struggling, and insensible on the earth.

In this country, Epilepsy is commonly called the "*Falling Sickness*," or more vaguely, "*Fits.*" The cry, which is frequently, but not always uttered, is a piercing and terrifying scream. Women have often been thrown into hysterics upon hearing it, and frequently it has caused pregnant females to miscarry. Even the lower animals are often startled, and appalled by a scream so harsh and unnatural, and parrots and other birds have been known to drop from their perch, apparently frightened to death by the appalling sound.

In most of the cases of fits, which have come under my notice and treatment, the first effect of the spasms has been a twisting of the neck, the chin being raised and brought round by a succession of jerks towards the shoulder, while one side of the body is usually more strongly agitated than the other. The features are greatly distorted, the brows knit, the eyes sometimes quiver and roll about, sometimes are fixed and staring, and sometimes are turned up beneath the lids, so that the cornea cannot be seen, but leaving visible the white sclerotica alone; at the same time the mouth is twisted awry, the tongue thrust between the teeth, and, caught by the violent closure of the jaws, is often severely bitten, reddening by blood the foam which issues from the mouth. The hands are firmly clenched and the thumbs bent inwards on the palms, the arms are generally thrown about, striking the chest of the patient with great force. Sometimes he will bruise himself against surrounding objects, or inflict hard knocks on the friends and neighbors who have hastened to his assistance. It frequently happens that the urine and excrements are expelled during the violence of the spasms, and seminal emissions sometimes take place. The spasmodic contraction of the muscles is occasionally so powerful as to dislocate the bones to which they are attached. The teeth have thus been fractured, and the joints of the jaw and of the shoulder put out or dislocated.

This is the most *severe*, yet the most *common* form in which an epileptic attack occurs. Fortunately, there is a large class of cases in which the symptoms are milder. Sometimes there is no convulsion at all, or, at least, is very slight and transient; no turgescence of the face; no foaming of the mouth; no cry; but a sudden suspension of consciousness, a short period of insensibility, a fixed gaze, a totter, perhaps, a look of confusion, but the patient does not fall. This is but momentary. Presently consciousness returns, and the patient resumes the action in which he had been previously engaged, without always being aware that it has been interrupted.

Between these two extremes of epilepsy there are many links or grades. Sometimes the sufferer sinks or slides down quietly without noise; is pale; is not convulsed; but is insensible, much like one in a state of syncope, or fainting.

As it is impossible to give any single description of epilepsy which will include all its varieties, of course it is still more difficult to offer a strict definition of the disease. We can only say it is a malady that causes a sudden loss of sensation and consciousness, with spasmodic contraction of the voluntary muscles, quickly passing into violent convulsive distortions, attended and followed by stupor or sleep, recurring in paroxysms, often more or less regular. Yet all these circumstances may in turn be wanting. There may be no convulsion, no interruption of consciousness, no subsequent coma or stupor, or even a recurrence of the attack.

The duration of the attacks is variable. They seldom continue longer than half an hour; the average duration may be said to be from five to ten minutes. Attacks that spread over three or four hours generally consist of a succession of paroxysms, with indistinct intervals of comatose exhaustion. In the long-continued fits, or in the protracted succession of fits, the patient often dies.

The periods at which the paroxysms return are extremely variable. Most commonly they visit the sufferer at irregular periods of a few months or weeks; sometimes are repeated at intervals of a few days; sometimes every day or every night, and very frequently many times in the twenty-four hours.

The epileptic attack may come on for the first time at *any age.* It may begin in infancy during the first dentition, or teething; more commonly about the age of seven or eight years, during the time of the second dentition; more frequently still, from fourteen to sixteen, shortly before the age of puberty. It is apt to occur for a few years subsequently to this. The first fit may not occur till between thirty and forty; or it may occur at sixty, or even at a later period of life.

TREATMENT.—There is perhaps no disease where a greater diversity of medical treatment has been instituted than in Epilepsy. The whole pharmacopœia has been exhausted, and each remedy extolled for its virtues. One medical man says he cures the disease by trephining; another thinks the oil of turpentine the best remedy; still another recommends the vapor of chloroform. This doctor applies ice, the other cauterizes the back with a hot iron, and yet another speaks highly of a compound of camphor, valerian, assafœtida, naphtha, and oil of cajeput.

Unless rational treatment is employed, the disease cannot be cured. If occurring in infants, it should be ascertained if it is not due to teething or worms, and the proper treatment instituted, if so caused. If connected with derangement of the catamenia, masturbation, or sperma torrhœa, the treatment for these complaints is necessary. The anti spasmodics are indicated in every case, the best of which is blue vervian, although valerian, belladonna, scullcap, etc., are also good. The general condition of the system should receive strict attention.

On page 469 I have given a remedy which will prove in eight cases out of ten a simple and certain cure. I make no secret of its composition. I have sent the prescription to many thousands gratuitously. A fair trial will convince every one that it is one of the most potent remedies ever discovered for the cure of epilepsy, falling sickness, or fits. When this medicine is taken, the spasms gradually grow lighter and lighter, and finally disappear altogether, restoring the patient to the most perfect normal health. Its effect is truly wonderful. The time to accomplish a cure is usually from two to three months.

HYSTERICS.

This is a nervous condition confined to females, though well marked cases of hysteria are occasionally met with in males. The invasion of the disease is sudden and irregular, but in many cases decidedly periodical. The principal characteristics consist in alternate fits of weeping and laughing, with a sensation as if a ball was rolling towards the stomach, chest, and neck, producing a sense of strangulation. Consciousness is lost in violent cases, but it remains clear as a general thing, which distinguishes it from epilepsy. It is dependent upon irregularity of nervous distribution in very impressible persons.

TREATMENT.—During the paroxysms, the feet should be placed in warm water, and a hot mustard plaster applied to the lower part of the abdomen. A decoction of equal parts of ladies'-slipper and scullcap should be given until the spasm subsides. A tea made of ginger and bayberry, the tincture of castor, and assafœtida, are also good. The state of the womb should receive attention, and if dependent upon indigestion and constipation, tonics and laxatives are the proper remedies. I have never met with the annoyance or difficulty in the treatment of this disease that so many practitioners speak of, but regard the disease as easy of cure.

CATALEPSY.

This is an affliction of rare occurrence, and appears to be constitutional, or dependent upon some derangement of the nervous and muscular system which baffles inquiry. The sufferer is suddenly seized by it, and, although powerless to move, or speak, and to all appearance dead, is partially sensible of all that is going on around. In some cases, however, the senses are suspended. The body and limbs are not generally rigid, but will remain in the positions in which the bystanders may place them. Many years ago, when the light of science was not so bright, or shed so extensively as it is now, men and women were buried alive while cataleptic. The catalepsy, or trance, often lasts for weeks, the sufferer, in the meantime, partaking of no nourishment whatever.

"Absence of mind" is a slight form of catalepsy.

TREATMENT.—During the paroxysms the head should be showered with cold water, followed by hot foot-baths and stimulating liniments, with friction to the abdomen and spine. Some aromatic stimulant, as peppermint sling or compound spirits of lavender, should also be administered. For the toning of the nervous system and preventing recurrence of the trance, the "Restorative Assimilant" answers all purposes admirably.

ST. VITUS'S DANCE (CHOREA).

This is characterized by irregular contractions of the voluntary muscles, especially of the face and limbs, there being incomplete subserviency of these muscles to the will. It is a disease which usually occurs before puberty, and is generally connected with torpor of the system and of the digestive organs in particular. The spasms do not continue during sleep, and often, by a strong effort of the will, they can in a measure be controlled. Its duration is long, but usually devoid of danger, unless it merges into organic disease of the nervous centres, or of the heart, or into epilepsy.

TREATMENT.—The general system should be strengthened, and the intestinal canal stimulated. Purgatives once or twice a week, with appropriate regimen, will fulfil these. A mild purgative, like the "Renovating Pill," should be used. The decoction of scullcap and ladies'-slipper is very beneficial. It is cured in a short time by my "Restorative Assimilant."

LOCKED-JAW (TETANUS).

This is a disease of the true spinal system, and is manifested by spasm and rigidity of the voluntary muscles. When the muscles of the neck and face are affected, it is termed *Trismus*, or locked-jaw; when the muscles in front, *Emprosthotonos;* when the muscles of the back, *Opisthotonos;* and when bending to either side, *Pleurosthotonos.*

Tetanus may be either acute or chronic; the former is the most frequent and most formidable; the latter, apt to be partial, milder, and more subject to treatment.

It is called *traumatic* when it follows a wound or injury, and *idiopathic* when of spontaneous origin.

Acute traumatic tetanus is more common in hot climates, and in military practice, and may follow a slight bruise or puncture, especially if some nerve has been injured. The symptoms may appear in a few hours, or in many days; at first, there is a stiffness and soreness about the neck and face, the contraction of the muscles causing a ghastly smile; chewing and swallowing are difficult, the forehead is wrinkled, eyeballs are distorted, nostrils dilated, and the grinning countenance is expressive of horror. Respiration is rapid, the tongue protrudes, and the saliva dribbles. The mind is clear until just before death, which generally takes place in a few days.

TREATMENT.—The indications are to remove all sources of irritation and diminish the spasm. The wound is to be cleansed from all foreign bodies, pus to be discharged by a free incision, if necessary, and warm anodyne poultices and fomentations are to be applied. Excision of the wound, or division of the nerve leading to it, may be done by the surgeon. Nutrition and opium are indispensable; the latter may be used either externally or internally. A lobelia emetic, if it can be administered, should be given, and a brisk purgative should be given. Tobacco either by the mouth, or in enema, is an excellent relaxant. Camphor, assafœtida, etc., may also be used as antispasmodics. Cannabis indica internally, and ice to the spine, have been used advantageously in some cases. If, in opinion of the attending physician, it is necessary, chloroform or ether may be used as an anæsthetic.

PARALYSIS (PALSY).

The most characteristic symptom of cerebral hemorrhage is paralysis.

Very slight effusion produces this effect, and, in general, its intensity is in direct ratio of the extent of the effusion. It also arises from disease of the brain or its membranes, injuries of the brain and spinal cord, diseases of the cord or its membranes, or any injury of the large nervous networks, the action of lead, etc. The nerves of motion as well as those of sensation may be paralyzed, and when it exists on one side of the body it is called *hemiplegia*, and when confined to the lower limbs, *paraplegia*. When the muscles of the mouth or of an extremity are affected, it is called *partial* paralysis, and when both sides, whether in their extent or in some of their parts, are deprived of motion, it is termed *general* paralysis.

At the very moment of the effusion it acquires all at once its highest degree of intensity, then remains stationary or begins to diminish. Sometimes the paralyzed part has not previously experienced any disturbance with respect to either sensation or motion; sometimes, however, the patient has experienced in these parts pricking sensations, numbness, permanent or transient, an unusual feeling of cold, a sense of weight, and a certain degree of debility. The part paralyzed suggests the locality of the effusion or injury, but these are only of interest to the pathologist. When the affected muscles degenerate or atrophy, it is called *wasting palsy*, and when characterized by slow progress, and tremulousness increases to such extent that the agitation prevents sleep, all locomotion, difficulty of chewing and swallowing, etc., it is called *paralysis agitans*.

TREATMENT.—If dependent upon cerebral hemorrhage, the treatment of apoplexy should be instituted, and afterwards the use of derivatives such as purgatives, alteratives, diuretics, etc., and the use of local stimulants. The patient should be restricted in his diet, and all causes of cerebral excitement, whether physical or moral, should be avoided. The bowels should be well acted upon, and the condition of the bladder attended to. When the organic disease is removed, and all symptoms of vascular excitement have subsided, recourse should be had to nux vomica, or strychnine, tonics, and galvanism. In giving strychnine, the lowest dose should be given at first, and cautiously increased. Macrotin, viburnin, xanthoxylin, and rhusin are also good remedies. The local treatment consists in stimulating liniments, blisters to the spine, etc.

Those who may desire my counsel and opinion of their cases, as to nature and curableness, will please write as directed on page 390.

HYDROPHOBIA.

This is caused by the bite of a mad dog or other hydrophobic animals. The human subject is not as liable to hydrophobia as the lower animals, and it is consoling to know that only about one-tenth of those bitten are attacked by hydrophobia.

The interval of the bite and appearance of the disease varies from twelve days to two months. The wound heals like any other bite, but on approach of the disease the scar begins to have sharp pains, and the part feels cold, stiff, or numb. The patient feels a strange anxiety, is depressed in spirit, has an occasional chill, disturbed sleep, and spasmodic twitches. The appetite is lost, and, as the disease progresses, thirst appears, and he attempts to drink; but, the moment the water approaches his mouth, a spasmodic shudder comes over him, he pushes it back with horror, and the awful fact of his condition is known to him, and pitiful expressions escape him. His throat becomes full of glain, viscid mucus, which he continually tries to clear away. He strives to bite his attendants, suffers great depression of spirits, and finally dies from exhaustion, or in a horrible spasm.

TREATMENT.—The wound should be cut out, cups or suction applied to it, or thoroughly cauterized, and the patient should be kept quiet. Copious draughts of whiskey have been advised by some.

The red chickweed or scarlet pimpernel is said to be an absolute remedy. Four ounces of this should be boiled in two quarts of water until reduced to one quart, and a wine-glassful taken twice a day. The wound should also be bathed by the same. The common rose-beetle (*cetonia amata*), found so commonly on rose-bushes, is an effectual remedy. I desire in this connection to draw attention to a most absurd, ridiculous superstition which prevails; that is, if a person be bitten by a dog which is in perfect health, but afterwards goes mad, the person also will be affected, so they insist upon the dog being destroyed, for fear it should go mad at any future period. Instead of this the dog should be carefully taken care of. Patients would then have the satisfaction of knowing that there was nothing wrong with it, and their minds would be at rest.

DISEASES OF THE SKIN.

HUMID TETTER (ECZEMA).

This consists in the appearance of minute shining vesicles, not larger than the head of a small pin, on different portions of the body. They are usually clustered together, and surrounded by a red ring. The fluid in the vesicles becomes opaque in a few days, and finally forms light, thin scales, which fall off. In most cases a fresh crop appears as soon as the first crop is matured, in which case yellow crusts form over the diseased patch, and chronic tetter exists for weeks or months. The red eczema is the worst form of this disease.

TREATMENT.—Low diet, cooling drinks, gentle purgatives and warm baths should be prescribed. The acetic tincture of blood-root should be externally applied. It speedily cures all cases. Celandine, tar, slippery elm poultices, etc., are also useful.

TETTER, SHINGLES (HERPES).

Tetter is a transient non-contagious eruption, consisting of circumscribed red patches, upon each of which are situated clusters of vesicles, about the size of a pea. After a few days the vesicles break, pour out a thin fluid, and form brown or yellow crusts, which fall off about the tenth day, leaving the surface red and irritable. The eruption is attended with heat, tingling, fever, and restlessness, especially at night. *Ringworm* is a curious form of tetter, the inflamed patches being ring-like in form.

TREATMENT.—Light diet, and gentle laxatives. If the patient is old the tonics should be given. The elder-flower ointment is an excellent external application. The acetic tincture of lobelia is also good. Nothing better, however, can be used than the "Herbal Ointment," mentioned on page 472.

ITCH (SCABIES).

This annoying disease is caused by minute white insects, the *acarus scabei* or *sareoptis hominis*, which insinuate themselves beneath the skin. It is said that these insects travel in pairs, male and female, husband and wife evidently, and that the female is very much the smaller. Under the microscope the animal appears as in the cut, which gives a

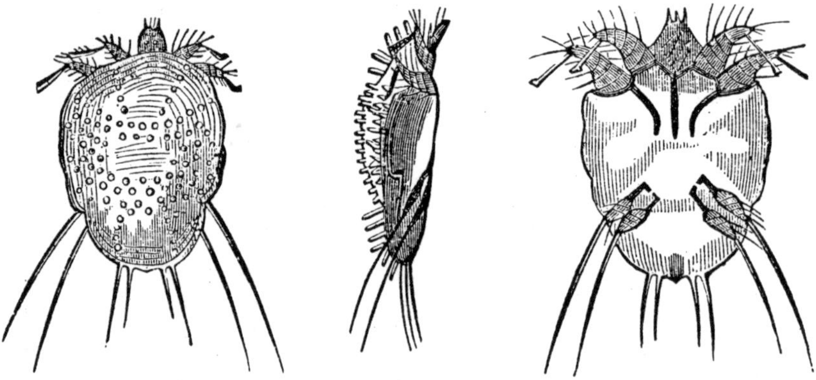

The Itch Insect.

front, back and side view of it. The elegance of the animal is beyond question, and his mode of burrowing under the skin is sagacious. When placed upon the skin he proceeds to make a hole through it, which he does by his head and fore-feet. Into this he insinuates his whole body

Like the mole, he makes a channel many times his own length, at the end excavating a chamber, where he takes his *siesta*, and from whence he saunters forth in quest of provender. As age approaches, tired of the home of his youth, he digs onward, scoops out another, in which he ends his days, beloved and respected by all his neighbors.

Itch is characterized by a vesicular eruption, and makes its appearance between the fingers and in other soft portions of the skin. If the pimples are scratched a watery fluid is poured out which forms small scabs, and if the disease is not cured, extensive sores occur. It is more common among the poor, but James I. of England said that it was only fitted for kings, so excellent is the enjoyment of scratching. It may be a royal luxury, but I am quite sure that persons having the itch would consent for it to be entirely monopolized by kings. A similar disease is caused by the *acarus sacchari*, an insect very common in brown sugar.

TREATMENT.—Whatever kills the little animal will cure the itch. This is best achieved by sulphur. It should be made into an ointment with lard, and thoroughly rubbed into the skin before the fire, morning and evening for a few days. This will put an end to the "squatter sovereignty" of whole colonies. An ointment made from veratrum also does well. Another method is equally if not more efficacious. Rub the entire surface of the body over with soft soap for half an hour—then a warm bath for half an hour, washing it thoroughly off, and exciting the skin to active circulation. Then an ointment, prepared as follows, should be rubbed over the entire surface: Take eight ounces of lard and into it thoroughly rub two ounces of flour of sulphur, and one ounce of carbonate of potash, making an even and uniform mixture, and it is ready for use. This, after it has remained on the skin for three hours, may be well washed off, and the disease is entirely annihilated. In persons of tender skin, or where considerable inflammation has been set up by continued scratching, it may be necessary to anoint with hard soap instead of soft, for it does not contain as much alkali, and leave out the carbonate of potash in the ointment—for reason of its being too stimulating. In these instances, it will take longer to cure the disease, but it is just as certain in its results. This mode of treating this disease is an entirely successful one—and no one need "to scratch" if these simple directions be attended to.

WATERY BLEBS (PEMPHIGUS).

This is characterized by loss of appetite, febrile symptoms, at first, followed by a bright red eruption of a smarting or burning sensation. In the centre of this eruption, minute vesicles appear, which gradually enlarge in blisters in the shape of bubbles and contain a watery fluid. They vary in size from a split pea to that of a hen's egg, and rise very rapidly;

and break in a few days, leaving a raw surface, which soon becomes covered with a crust.

TREATMENT.—The surface of the body should be bathed, and the bowels opened by a gentle purge. The inflamed surface should be covered by a slippery-elm poultice, and be kept moist with tincture of lobelia. When the constitution is feeble, quinine, alnuin, etc., should be given. The diet should receive especial attention, and out-door exercise enjoyed.

RUPIA.

This is a small blister, or vesicle, about the size of a chestnut, which at first contains a darkish fluid, which dries into a crust, falls off, and leaves an indolent ulcer. It is always connected with a vitiated constitution, and is dependent frequently upon imperfect diet, although chronic disease, such as syphilis, phthisis, dyspepsia, and poisonous mineral medicines, not unfrequently produce it.

TREATMENT.—The digestive organs should be corrected, and the blood nourished and enriched by wholesome diet and tonics. The local applications should consist of emollient poultices, and kept constantly moist with the tincture of hydrastin, baptisin, or myrrh. A poultice of equal parts of bayberry, white pond-lily and slippery-elm is very beneficial. The cause, however, is always to be ascertained before the treatment is interposed.

CRUSTED TETTER (IMPETIGO).

The eruption in this disease consists, at first, in slightly elevated pustules or pimples, closely collected together, with an inflamed edge. These break, and the surface becomes red, excoriated, shining, and full of pores, through which a thin, unhealthy fluid is poured out, which gradually hardens into dark, yellowish-green scabs. These scabs sometimes look like honey dried upon the skin, and hence the name of "honey disease." It is very common on the ears and lips of children. It is also called the *milk crust*, when it covers the whole face.

TREATMENT.—Give a purgative, and let the patient take a hot bath. As a local application equal parts of blood-root and white pond-lily, say one ounce, and cider vinegar, six ounces, mix, and let stand twenty-four hours, and apply as a wash with a sponge four or five times a day. The oxide of zinc ointment is also good, but the best and speediest cure is the "Herbal Ointment," described on page 472.

PAPULOUS SCALE (ECTHYMA).

This consists of mattery pimples developed on a highly inflamed skin, appearing chiefly on the extremities and rarely met with in children in the acute form. It is either acute or chronic. The eruption is the acute form is preceded by a slight fever, and in about thirty-six hours red spots appear on the skin, accompanied by heat and tingling On the second day, the centres of these spots are raised by the pus contained, to which the name of *phlyzacious pustule* is given. This stage is accompanied by much pain. Maturation occurs from the fourth to the sixth day, and the disease usually terminates in two weeks. The chronic form is more common, and afflicts young children oftener than adults.

TREATMENT.—For the acute form, low diet, gentle laxatives, and the application of oxide of zinc ointment. The pustulated surface should also be covered with slippery-elm poultices, and kept constantly moist with tincture of lobelia. In the chronic form, in addition to the above, the tonics should be given, and the blood should be enriched by proper medication and nutritious diet.

LEPROSY.

The eruption in this disease makes its appearance as a small red spot, elevated a little above the general skin, usually occurring first on the limbs. The scales occurring on these patches occur in layers, one above the other, and have a bright silvery lustre. This is the *lepra alphoides.* The Hebrew leprosy was a variety of this form. What was known as the *Leuce* was generally not scaly, but consisted of smooth, shining patches, on which the hair turned white and silky, and was totally incurable. When leprosy is of dark livid color, it is called *lepra nigricans,* and when copper-colored, it is due to syphilis, and is termed *lepra syphilitica.* The leprosy of the Arabs is what is known as *Elephantiasis,* and the Greek leprosy includes the varieties met with at the present day. Leprosy is endemic in Egypt, in Java, and certain parts of Norway and Sweden.

TREATMENT.—The means best adapted for its removal, are, a mild, unirritating diet, emollient fomentations, sulphureous baths, fumigations, etc., but often all treatment is ineffectual. A warm solution of the sesquicarbonate of potash is effectual in some cases. An ointment of glycerine and hydrastin, and the acetic tincture of blood-root, are also serviceable, but as a topical remedy, nothing could be superior to my "Herbal Ointment."

DRY TETTER (PSORIASIS).

This differs from leprosy in the eruption being more irregular. The spots sometimes come out in thick clusters, and blend in various ways. The eruption is not circular as in leprosy, but consists of irregular patches of every extent, and the surface is more tender and irritable than in leprosy. There are many varieties of this disease. The

"Baker's Itch," "Grocer's Itch," and "Washerwoman's Scall," are only different varieties of psoriasis.

TREATMENT.—The acetic tincture of blood-root or oxide of zinc ointment, may be applied to the eruption, and the skin should be kept clean, and the pores open. The inflammations may be lessened by emollient and soothing applications. Sea bathing is very good. The general health should be attended to in all cases, and the tonics given in necessary cases.

PITYRIASIS.

This name is from the Greek *pityron*, signifying *bran*. It is characterized by patches of yellowish, or reddish yellow color, covered with fine branny scales, accompanied by smarting, itching, and burning. It may occur at any part of the body, under three or four varieties of form.

TREATMENT.—The treatment advised in psoriasis will answer in this disease.

LUPUS.

This is the "Jacob's Ulcer" of common parlance, and from its rapacity it is named *Lupus*, which is the Latin name for *wolf*. It is also called "noli me tangere," *touch me not*. It occurs in a variety of forms, generally upon the face. It commences by slight thickening and elevation of the skin, usually not larger than a wheat grain. A thin, hard, brownish scab appears on its surface. The disease extends, usually slowly, but sometimes very rapidly, and cases have occurred where the whole nose has been destroyed in a month. It is very rapacious, destroying even the bones in its progress.

TREATMENT.—When it first makes its appearance it should be thoroughly destroyed with caustics, and healed by zinc ointment. At the same time, the alteratives should be given. My "Blood Purifier" (see page 471) is excellent for this purpose. Early institution of treatment will only prevent destruction of tissue.

ELEPHANTIASIS.

This is characterized by the development of tumors upon the skin, varying in size from the head of a pea to that of an apple, or even larger. Eventually these tumors ulcerate, and discharge an unhealthy pus, in some cases affecting the bone, and resulting in mortification and death. It is endemic in Lisbon. At first there is a discoloration of the skin of the face, the lobes of the ear lengthen, and the wings of the nose spread out; then the face becomes tuberculous, the features are puffed out, the lips thicken, the whiskers, eyebrows, and eyelashes fall out. The tubercles ulcerate after some years, there is ozœna, the fingers and toes mortify, and the body exhales a most loathsome odor. This is the leprosy of the ancient Egyptians.

TREATMENT.—The parts should be thoroughly bathed with a strong solution of the sesquicarbonate of potash, and stillingia and other alteratives administered. Where the parts become swollen, painting with the tincture of iron, followed by astringent poultices, has been found very beneficial. When confined to the extremities, amputation may become necessary.

ACNE.

This is a small pimple or tubercle which appears on various parts of the face. The disease leads to no particular evil results, save that it is unpleasant, slightly painful, and disfiguring. It commonly afflicts the young and robust of both sexes, and generally indicates strong passions, and too great an indulgence in animal food, or neglect of ablutions and out-of-door exercise. It is sometimes, in its more severe forms, the consequence of solitary practices. The common form of the disease is an eruption of hard, distinct, inflamed tubercles which remain unchanged for a long time, or else slowly advance to partial suppuration. They are to be seen on the forehead, cheeks, and chin, and sometimes on the nose. It is commonly known as the *brandy face* or *rum blots.*

TREATMENT.—Attention to the general health becomes necessary. It is not well to drive them in by lotions, as they are then liable to break out in some internal organ. Attention to diet, plenty of exercise, a pure imagination, and a clean body, together with open and regular bowels, will soon effect the disappearance of this troublesome enemy of good looks.

WARTS AND CORNS.

Warts consist of collections of hypertrophied cutaneous papillæ, or loops of veins, arteries and nerves. These loops, frequently, without any apparent cause, take on a disposition to grow, and by extending themselves upward, they carry the scarf-skin along with them, which thickens, and the whole forms the wart.

Corns consist in excrescences confined mostly to the toes and soles of the feet, resulting from wearing tight shoes. They occasionally form on the elbows and knees, or on the extremities of the fingers. When occurring between the toes, they are called *soft corns.*

Bunions consist of an enlargement, thickening, and inflammation of the mucous bursa at the side of the ball of the great toe. Occasionally the bursa suppurates, and a fistulous opening left after the pus has evacuated.

TREATMENT.—Corns may be cured by shaving them closely and

applying nitro-muriatic acid or chromic acid ointment. For soft corns acetic acid is better. Warts should be clipped off with the scissors, and chromic acid applied, or any other cauterizing agent will answer. The tincture of thuja is also excellent. Bunions are cured by bathing them frequently in the oil of erigeron.

PRURITIS.

This is dependent upon an altered condition of the nerves of the skin, and consists in a painful sensation of itching. There is no perceptible alteration in the appearance of the skin, and the itching is generally the result of sympathy, through the nerves, with some diseased condition of a distant part. It more frequently affects the fundament, the scrotum, or the vulva of females.

TREATMENT.—The following is usually all the treatment that is required:—Take oleo-resin of lobelia, grs. xx; aconitin, grs. iij; sulphate of sanguinaria, grs. x; glycerine, ℥ ij. Mix. Apply the ointment to the part three or four times a day.. Lead-water and opium are also beneficial.

MACULÆ, OR SPOTS.

This affection, which is characterized by an increased hue of the pigment of the skin, consists of freckles and moles. *Ephelis lenticularis*, or common freckles, appears in small yellowish, brownish, or greenish-yellow, irregular, rounded spots, caused particularly by the influence of the sun's rays upon the parts. It occurs generally in females, owing to their fine skin. *Ephelis hepatica* is observed in females during pregnancy. *Ephelis violacea* is caused by the long use of nitrate of silver. Moles are dark colored patches, usually covered with hair. *Nævi* or *mother's marks* are called aneurisms by anastomosis, or an inter-connection and enlargement of the arterioles of the skin. *Leucopathia*, or *Albinism*, consists of a diminution of the coloring matter of the skin. It is found in all races, but is most striking in the black.

TREATMENT.—Freckles may be removed by keeping out of the sun, and frequently washing the face in a solution of lactic acid. Fresh buttermilk answers the same purpose. The best remedy, however, is to be found in my "Floral Bloom." It quickly removes freckles, moth patches, etc., and makes the skin clear and transparent. Moles and mother's marks belong to surgery, and may in many instances be removed. Albinism is incurable.

SCALLED HEAD (TINEA FAVOSA).

This is caused by an insect by the name of *achorion Schönleinii*. The eruption takes the shape of large flattened pustules, which have an irregular edge, and are surrounded by inflammation. Sometimes they appear first behind the ears, and at other times upon the face, spreading thence to the scalp. The face is usually involved to some extent wherever the eruption may originally show itself. Scalled head is mostly confined among children. In the outset of the disease the pustules on the scalp are generally distinct;—on the face they rise in irregular clusters. They are attended by much itching, and the efforts to relieve this torment hasten their breaking. When broken they discharge a viscid matter and run together, gradually forming sores of a vicious character. These sores are covered by yellowish-greenish scabs which present a revolting appearance.

TREATMENT.—The hair should be shaved close to the scalp, and the head thoroughly washed with soap and water, after which the zinc ointment should be applied in the morning and the tar ointment in the evening. Alteratives should also be given. This course, if persisted in, will remove the disease.

TINEA SYCOSIS.

This is commonly known as "Barber's Itch," and is confined to the face, especially to that portion covered by the beard. It is characterized by inflammation of the hair follicles, causing an eruption of small pustules forming incrustations eventually. It may be consoling to those who suffer with it to know that it is caused by a parasite with the humble name of *microsporon mentagraphytes*.

TREATMENT.—Shave the beard, and paint the part with a strong tincture of iodine for a few days. Follow this with a poultice, composed of equal parts of lobelia, blood-root, myrrh, and slippery-elm. Depilation, or pulling out the beard, may be necessary in some cases to effect the cure.

BALDNESS (ALOPECIA).

This may be partial or general, temporary or permanent, and occur at any period of life. Senile baldness usually takes place gradually, the hair first becoming thin on the crown, or on the temples and forehead. It is owing generally to the general loss of the nutritive functions of the hair, and of the follicular apparatus. Loss of color of the hair (canities) may depend upon advanced age, disease, or deep mental emotion. It usually occurs gradually, after the age of forty. Cases are recorded in which the loss of color was complete in eight days, while in others the hair was almost completely blanched in a single night.

TREATMENT.—If the hair follicles are not destroyed, baldness may be cured. The tincture of cantharides, lac sulphur, shampooing, etc., are each to be recommended. Tonics and strict cleanliness also promotes the growth of the hair. In my "Woodland Balm" (page 473) the bald or gray will find a remedy which has no superior for restoring the hair to a healthy growth and natural color.

ENTOZOA.

These grow in the body without forming attachments to its structures, have an independent life of their own, and possess the power of reproduction and generation. Several species infest the human body, some appearing always in the same organ and some in a particular tissue, and appearing oftenest where that tissue is plentiful. Scarcely any portion of the body is exempt from such growths. Their origin is a subject for two suppositions—that of generative reproduction, and of accidental or spontaneous development of germs that take on modes of life and development characterizing them afterwards. The first supposition is more philosophical, comports more with analogy, and is unquestionably the true theory. The interest attached to these growths, however, is their effect upon the system and cause of disease. Their presence in the system causes morbid phenomena, disordered functional action, and loss of health. The mischief they do in the system depends upon their number, size, rapidity of growth, and species. When numerous or large they imbibe so much nutriment as to rob the system of its necessary sustenance. Their habitation is generally a seat of irritation or inflammation, and more particularly when their location is in a cavity, and when they possess power of motion.

Psychodiara.—*Hydatids.*—These are organized beings, consisting of a globe-like bag of albuminous matter; the texture divided in layers, and containing a limpid, colorless fluid richer in gelatin than albumen. They live by imbibition, have no sensibility or power of motion, and appear more like a vegetable than an animal in their modes of life and reproduction. There are two kinds of hydatids, the *acephalocyst*, or cyst without a head, and the *echinococcus*, which is not different from the other in form but in containing minute animals (vermiculi echinococci) within it. The former is common to the human body, and generated between layers of membrane. The usual abode of hydatids is in the lungs, liver, ovaries, spleen, kidneys, etc. The hydatids occurring in the womb are often mistaken upon expulsion for products of conception, and their presence in that organ often produces similar signs as in pregnancy.

Sterelmintha.—These consist of solid porous texture, perforated by canals or cavities, which serve the purposes of digestion. These animals are hermaphrodite, *i. e.*, having both sexual organs on one individual. The varieties of tapeworm belong to this class. So also the *cysticercus*, which occurs in the muscular structure and in the watery portion of the eye. The liver-fluke—*distoma hepaticum*—also belongs to this class, but which rarely occurs in man, but is supposed to cause the well-known "rot" in sheep.

Cœlelmintha.—This class has a higher organic development than the preceding. It embraces several species of worms having hollow cylindrical bodies, distinct alimentary canals, with a mouth at one extremity and an anus at the other, a nervous system, and the sexual organs on different animals. The common intestinal worms belong to this class; so also the *trichina spiralis*—causing the disease described below which is an animal which exists within the minute, white, ovate cysts imbedded in the muscles. The guinea-worm (*filaria medinensis*), so common to Africa and Asia, but unknown in this country, is a hair-like worm developed beneath the skin, especially in the scrotum and lower extremities. It can be withdrawn when a pustule ensues, by care and patience, wrapping it around a stick until the end appears.

The *strongulus gigas* is an animal that locates itself exclusively in the kidney, and sometimes attains an enormous size. Its body is round, but tapers toward both ends. It sometimes attains a length of three feet, and a thickness of half an inch. It causes impairment of functions, waste of the renal structure, and sometimes inflammation, with pain and bloody urine. It is sometimes expelled through the water passages.

TREATMENT.—The treatment of parasites is indicated by their character or place of abode. If they exist in the alimentary canal, such remedies as are known to expel them should be employed. Anything is a good remedy that is harmless to the system but destructive of life to them. Various agents are poisonous, such as cherry-laurel water, camphor, oil of cubebs, oil of turpentine, copaiba, etc., but these must be employed at proper seasons and in such quantities that they will not harm the general system.

TRICHINIASIS.

This is a disease caused by the *trichina spiralis* which infests various animals, especially swine. If the meat of the hog affected is eaten raw or insufficiently cooked, it is most likely to cause this dangerous disease. Thorough cooking destroys the parasites. The symptoms are extensive gastric disturbance, with nausea and a tendency to vomit; associated with rheumatic pains, stiffness of the muscles, irregular pulse, intermittent fever, which is violently aggravated in paroxysms, thirst, restlessness, nervous excitement, and utter wakefulness. The face generally swells, great prostration ensues, and the patient generally dies in a paralyzed condition.

TREATMENT.—In the early stage an active lobelia emetic should be given, and followed by a full dose of castor oil or spirits of turpentine. An alcoholic vapor bath should be taken, and sufficient veratrum to control the fever. If sleeplessness prevails, opium should be given. The above treatment may be repeated if not at first successful.

THE PROPER CARE OF CHILDREN.

The first requisite of an infant is plenty of pure and fresh air. It should be kept in open air as much as possible, and when in-doors in well-ventilated rooms. When carried in the open air, their heads should not be enveloped in blankets, and when sleeping, their faces should not be covered with the bed-clothes. The infant needs and should have all the oxygen a pure air affords, which is so essential to its proper growth.

The Skin.—The skin of infants should be kept clean, to render them less liable to cutaneous diseases. The unctuous covering of a new-born child should be removed as soon as possible. This can readily be done by smearing it with pure lard, and then washing with white Castile soap and water. Do not use the brown Castile soap, as it contains oxides of iron, which are irritating substances. Infants should be washed every day with warm water, to be followed in course of time with tepid water, then temperate, and finally, at an age of some months, with cold water.

Clothing.—The young child should be amply clothed, care being taken that they are sufficiently loose, to admit free motion in all directions. Flannels should be placed next to the skin in winter, and cotton in summer.

Food.—Proper regimen is of the utmost importance to the health of the young. Until the first teething, the proper and natural food is the mother's milk. If the mother is unable to nurse her child, a wet-nurse should be procured. If the mother's milk is insufficient, cow's milk, sufficiently diluted with water and sweetened with loaf sugar, should be taken in addition. This should be taken from a sucking-bottle, which, when not in use, should be kept in water, to prevent becoming sour. A nursing woman should pay the greatest attention to her health also, and, for obvious reasons, a scrofulous or consumptive mother should never suckle her offspring; she should also place a check upon her passions, as violent passion, grief, envy, hatred, fear, jealousy, etc., tend to derange the character of the milk, and often superinduce disorder of the infant's stomach, and throw it into convulsions. The diet of the mother should receive strict attention. Her drink should be simply water, or weak black tea, and her food plain and wholesome. Pastry and the richer articles of food should not be eaten. She should take daily moderate exercise to induce better assimilation of aliments. When her milk is scanty, a sufficiency can frequently be induced by placing a bread and milk poultice, over which a moderate quantity of mustard is sprinkled, on the breasts.

Weaning.—The child should be weaned after the appearance of its first teeth. Nature then designs it to have different food. Spring and fall are the proper seasons for weaning; no child should be taken from the breast in the midst of summer. The weaning should be a gradual process, and the food to be given should be of the character of milk. Bread and milk, boiled rice and milk, soda-crackers and milk, soft boiled eggs, roasted potatoes and milk, preparations of sago, arrowroot, tapioca, oatmeal gruel, rice pudding, and similar substances are all indicated. My nutritive fluids, given on page 205, can also be given with good service. From these, in course of time, more solid articles of food can be given them. Sugar in moderate quantities is wholesome. Excessive eating should not be suffered. Water is the best drink.

Sleep.—A child should always sleep in a loose gown, to prevent restlessness. Nature should govern its sleep, and which should never be induced by opiates. It should be allowed to sleep to a natural awakening, and should not be aroused for any avoidable purpose. Its covering should be warm but *light*, thus avoiding pressure upon its tender limbs; the infant should lie on its side, alternating at times from right to left, to prevent distortion of the spine. The body should be placed with the head to the north, and this rule applies to all, as the action of electric currents is to the north, thus allowing greater repose to the brain. Strong sunlight or moonshine should be excluded from their sleeping apartments. What I have thus far written is not only preservative of good health, but preventive of many species of illness to which infants are liable. Children are very liable to disease, necessitating great precaution in a variety of matters, the most important of which are the foregoing. When it is known that death destroys about one half of humanity before the age of five years, the physical life of children is of the utmost importance. While young, the moral, intellectual, and religious faculties should be shaped, as the child often indicates the man.

The baby exhibits indisposition by cries, struggles, etc., and if these are carefully noted, ever mother may know what ails the baby.

A baby suffering from stomach-ache sheds tears *copiously*, and utters long and loud cries. As stomach-ache is paroxysmal in character, so will its cries remit, and enjoy repose, to be followed by movements up and down of the legs and the peculiar cry.

To cry in inflammation of the organs of the chest is painful; it therefore does not cry or shed tears, but utters a muttering cry, abruptly completed, and coughs after long breaths.

In diseases of the brain, the child shrieks piercingly, followed by moaning and wailing. In extensive congestion, there is quiet dozing and probably snoring.

Loss of appetite, fretfulness, restlessness, thirst, great heat of skin, are all indications of disease, and require that solicitude and treatment that every fond mother should know how to bestow.

TEETHING.

Many children are lost from teething. The process of dentition often occasions fits. Its symptoms are, swollen and inflamed gums, fever, pain, and heat in the head, sore mouth, etc. Scarification of the gums is often resorted to; but if proper attention be paid to the case in its inception, no such barbarous and injurious method of palliation need be embraced. Bathing the head with diluted spirits, and the feet with warm mustard water; keeping the bowels free and regular by the simplest of herbal laxatives; and placing a plaster (composed of two-thirds flour mustard, one-third flour, and sufficient vinegar to produce the requisite moisture) between the shoulders, will generally obviate all danger and mitigate the pain and suffering. When the speckled sore mouth incidental to teething makes its appearance, treat the child as above, but wash the mouth with a mild solution of borax, and use for diet (if the child be weaned) gum-arabic water, and barley or rice water. If the stomach is acid, and the bowels are griping, administer mild doses of magnesia. Warm baths are always beneficial to children who are teething; but great care should be taken that the little ones do not catch cold after the baths.

The teeth should appear about the sixth month, though it is often later. The two incisors of the lower jaw are generally the first, and then those of the upper jaw follow. Between the twelfth and sixteenth months the grinders come, and next the eye teeth. The others soon follow, so that by the age of two years, the child has its full set of milk teeth, twenty in number. There are instances of children being born with full sets of teeth, as is recorded of Richard III. and Louis XIV.

GENERAL DISEASES.

GOUT.

This is due to the presence of lithic or uric acid in the blood. The attack usually makes its appearance in the night. The patient is first awakened by an intensely burning and wrenching pain in the ball of the great toe, or some other small joint. This pain continues for about twenty-four hours, and is accompanied by fever. It then remits, and the patient may get sleep, though for several successive days he suffers from the attacks. A similar visitation will likely result after a considerable interval. Recovery from the first attack may be complete —the skin peeling off from the red and swollen joint, and leaving it strong and supple as ever; but, after several repetitions of the attacks, the joint becomes stiff, owing to the deposit of lithic acid concretions or *chalk stones.* It is a disease entirely local in its character. It vitiates the blood, affects the general system, and the attack is generally preceded by general symptoms, irritability of temper, unpleasant sensations in the stomach and head, and uncomfortable feelings of body and mind are premonitory symptoms of this disorder. The pain is most excruciating. The stomach, heart, lungs, head, eyes, etc., may also be subject to gouty inflammation. It is caused by luxury and indolence, in the plurality of cases.

TREATMENT.—During the paroxysm the anodynes should be given and applied; subcutaneous injection of morphine is best. The constitutional treatment should be composed of chimaphilin and apocynin in combination; colchicum is also a very good remedy; chloroform liniment may also be externally applied. The patient's habits must be regulated, and his diet simplified, to prevent recurrence of the disease.

Those who may desire consultation with the author, in regard to this disease, are referred to page 390. Consultations, either in person or by letter, from those who may desire treatment, are carefully and gratuitously attended to.

RHEUMATISM.

This very painful affection is most frequently brought on by exposure to wet and cold after violent and fatiguing exercise of the muscles. The acute form is characterized by high fever, with a full bounding pulse, furred tongue, and a profuse sweat which has a sour smell. The urine is scanty and high colored; the joints swell and are slightly red and very tender. The pain is agonizing when the patient attempts to move. If the affection changes from one part to another it is called *metastatic,* and is very dangerous, as it may suddenly seize the lining membrane of the heart, and prove fatal.

The chronic form may follow the acute form, but is more often an independent disease. It differs from the acute form in the absence of fever. The fingers and limbs may frequently be rendered useless by rheumatism, by the great distortion ensuing. It is due to the presence of lactic acid in the blood.

TREATMENT.—The bowels should be evacuated by a purgative, and the tinctures of black cohosh and veratrum given until free perspiration is produced. The tincture of black cohosh, two parts, and tincture of colchicum, one part, in doses of from twenty to forty drops, is also a very valuable remedy. For articular rheumatism the alteratives should be given. My "Blood Purifier" is a sure and efficient cure, and the pain is almost instantly relieved by the application of the "Herbal Ointment" (see page 471).

Electricity may be resorted to in the chronic form. The treatment does not materially differ from that advised in the acute.

Fomentations of hops and cicuta, or stramonium leaves, placed upon the inflamed and swollen joints, will materially relieve the pain.

Rheumatism in the chronic form is often a very difficult disease to cure; but if properly treated, by purely chemical medication, the acid condition of the blood will be negatived, and the patient relieved of his painful malady. Of the thousands of cases that have been under my care, I do not recall one failure.

HIP DISEASE (MORBUS COXARIUS).

This is a disease of the hip-joint, and common to scrofulous children. At first there is slight pain, commonly felt in the knee, lameness, and stumbling in walking, tenderness in the groin, and pain is produced by pressing the head of the bone suddenly against the socket. The limb is longer than the other, which is owing to a depression of the pelvis on the diseased side, the weight of the body being supported on the opposite limb. If the disease is not arrested, destruction of the head of the bone and socket results, and the thigh-bone is drawn up, constituting a spontaneous dislocation. Often an abscess forms and opens externally The toes may be turned inward or outward.

This disease may be positively ascertained in the following way:—Remove the clothing of the patient and place him on any flat surface, as a bench, or table; if he is placed so that the spine everywhere touches the table, the patient's knee on the affected side will be drawn up, the weight of the leg resting on the heel. If now his knee will be pressed down, the spine will be bent inwards, so that it no longer touches the table. This is an unerring diagnosis.

TREATMENT.—At the commencement of the disease a large irritating plaster should be placed over the entire hip, and caused to remain until a thorough counter-irritation is effected, and a discharge ensues. Perfect rest is necessary, and the limb should be confined in a carved splint. Iodine may also be externally applied, and the general health improved by tonics, alteratives, and nutritious food. Counter-extension as advised in cases of fracture is advisable in all cases. A competent surgeon should direct the treatment.

WHITE SWELLING (HYDRARTHRUS).

This disease occurs most frequently about the middle period of life, but is, however, very often seen in children. It will never appear before the age of puberty without a deviation from health, but not always so when it makes its appearance in after-life. It is a disease of the knee-joint characterized by swelling and white color, owing to the tension of the skin. It is of two varieties; both, however, destroy the synovial or articular membrane of the joint. One begins with a trifling stiffness, slight swelling, and in effect reduces the membrane to a pulpy, degenerate mass. The swelling increases gradually, and when the part is touched, it reveals the presence of fluid. Finally the cartilages ulcerate, and the disease assumes such characters that amputation becomes absolutely necessary. The other form begins with pain in the joint, which is severe at one point, and attains its height in a week. It is characterized by inflammation of the synovial membrane, and in a few days the joint becomes swollen from a collection of water.

TREATMENT.—At the commencement bathe the parts with the following liniment :—oil of hemlock, ℥ iv. ; dissolve as much camphor in it as it will take up, and add twelve drops of croton oil, and three drachms of tincture of iodine. Bathe the limb thoroughly, after which apply hot cloths wrung from a strong infusion of arnica flowers and lobelia, and change as often as they grow cool ; with each change apply the liniment. This will arrest the disease if applied at the onset. The patient should be purged, and the compound syrup of chimaphila be administered to him. If the disease is farther advanced, and openings exist, they should be enlarged, and ointments and poultices applied, and the constitution supported by tonics and antiseptics. Splints and entire rest may be necessary in some cases, and when connected with a scrofulous diathesis, my "Blood Purifier" should be taken internally, and the "Herbal Ointment" applied externally. These will quickly eradicate the disease.

HECTIC FEVER.

Hectic fever is remittent, dependent upon local irritation, and rarely. if ever, idiopathic. It is attended by great and increasing debility, a weak, quick pulse, hurried respiration on any exertion, and increased heat of the skin. The febrile exacerbations are preceded by a slight chill, are slight at first, but soon become more evident, especially in the evening. The skin is at first dry, and the increased heat is more evident in the hands and face. The fever terminates in a free, profuse perspiration. The bowels are at first costive, but soon become relaxed, and an exhausting diarrhœa comes on ; the urine is various, generally it is pale, and does not deposit ; while there is generally a pallor of the surface, the cheeks present what is aptly termed the "hectic blush." As the disease advances, the whole frame becomes emaciated, the eyes sink in their orbits, but are brilliant and expressive ; the ankles and legs sometimes swell, and the sleep is feverish and disturbed. Finally the debility becomes so great that the patient expires while making some slight exertion.

Hectic fever accompanies nearly all forms of disease connected with great debility, especially scrofula and consumption. It may also be met with in surgical practice in disease or injury of the joints.

TREATMENT.—This depends much upon the cause or causes which give rise to it. If the digestive mucous membrane is diseased, the treatment consists in strict attention to diet, and in the administration of tonics, diaphoretics, and diuretics. The antiseptics should be given. Strychnine in doses of one-eighth of a grain is decidedly the best agent for this purpose. Cherry-laurel water should also be given. The fever is controlled, like other fevers, with veratrum. If associated with consumption, the "Acacian Balsam" (page 470) will cure it. Stimulants are very serviceable to counteract the debility. Generous diet and cleanliness are not to be neglected.

CURVATURE OF THE SPINE.

Curvature of the spine is due to caries or destruction of the bodies of the vertebræ. There are several varieties of curvature; what is known as lateral curvature consists in the distortion of the spinal column either to the one side or the other. In this case there may be no caries of the spine. It consists in depression of one shoulder, the body being thrown out of its axis, by the curvature. This affection is caused by occupations which keep the body in a laterally distorted position, and tax one side of the body more than the other. It is produced in children who study their lessons at school, with one elbow resting on a high desk, etc. In *Pott's Curvature of the Spine*, the angular curvature is produced by caries of the vertebræ, or ulceration of the substance between the vertebræ, followed by more or less loss of power over the lower extremity. In examining the spine, one or more of the spinous processes is found to project beyond the others. *Hump-backs* are usually caused by curvatures of the spine, but they may also be caused by projection of the sternum, or deviation of the ribs.

TREATMENT.—If associated with scrofula, the treatment for that disease should be instituted. In lateral distortion, calisthenic exercises should be engaged. In Pott's disease extensive counter-irritation should be made over the diseased part, and vigorous tonics given.

The treatment, however, best adapted to obviate all curvatures of the spine, is purely mechanical, and consists of braces, supporters, etc. Nothing else will achieve any satisfactory results. By mechanical appliances the spine is rendered straight, and compelled to maintain that position until a cure is effected. These mechanical appliances should be applied early, and be accurately adjusted and well fitted.

I am constantly applying such appliances in my office, and the results are excellent in nearly all cases. Those who cannot avail themselves of a personal consultation, may send age of patient, nature of curvature height, and measure around the waist, and a suitable appliance will be sent. Preliminary correspondence free.

IMPERFECTIONS OF THE HUMAN FORM.

These embrace those only which are of slighter degree, and of idiopathic origin. They are usually acquired more or less early in life. Not unfrequently they result from bad management of the infant, having its head always too highly bolstered up, and the chest compressed by tight clothing. The school-room, however, is the arena where the human form is robbed the most of its symmetry. It is gratifying to know that greater attention is now paid to this evil, but still to a great extent the seats and desks provided for the pupils are perfect outrages upon their physical natures. The seats are invariably too high and the desks too low, obliging the pupil, for five or six hours, to sit with his head down, his spine curved backwards, and his feet dangling in space. This unnatural position soon causes a loss of erect carriage, and induces stooped shoulders, and incapacious chests. It is but rarely that we see persons having an erect posture in standing or walking, and but few have that prominent chest, so necessary to the perfection and elegance of the human form, and to the full breathing capacity for the lungs. The shoulders should be in the perfect form thrown backwards, and the body erect, the only curve in the spine being the natural inward one in the lumbar portion.

TREATMENT.—Elegance and symmetry of form can only be gained by proper gymnastic and calisthenic exercises. These should be of such a character as to be best adapted to overcome the particular deformity.

Lady's Shoulder Brace Applied.

Gentleman's Shoulder Brace Applied.

In all cases suitable braces should be worn. These gently force back the shoulders, thereby increasing the volume and capacity of the chest, and enable the wearer to maintain the erect posture without fatiguing effort. In all pulmonary diseases, or where there exists an insufficient capacity of the chest, these braces should be worn. In the male they take the place of suspenders, and in the female they can be made to serve the purpose of sustaining the weight of the skirts. Nothing could be more conducive to health than these appliances; they often prevent the onset of consumption in those predisposed hereditarily to that disease. It is a well-known fact that the man or woman having an erect form and expanded chest is much less liable to disease, and at all events possesses greater vigor of health. The reason of this is obvious.

It is particularly advisable that every person having a defective form should wear a shoulder brace. The braces represented in the above cuts are of the author's own invention, and he does not hesitate to claim for them a decided superiority over all other braces for this purpose. They are worn with great comfort, gently obliging the wearer to maintain the erect posture, and enabling him to thoroughly inflate his lungs, which in course of time will lead to permanence of the upright stature with an expanded chest.

All persons desiring these superior braces can obtain them by addressing the author. (See page 389)

Abscess.

An abscess is a collection of pus or matter in the substance of some part of the body. When the matter is poured out from some part, the process is called *suppuration*, when it collects in a tissue, it is an abscess. It commences with all the symptoms of inflammation, fever, pain, redness, and swelling. The centre is firm, with swelling surrounding it. The formation of pus is indicated by rigors, an abatement of fever, and a feeling of weight, tension, and throbbing. The centre softens, which is termed *pointing*, and *fluctuation* is felt. There is a natural tendency to discharge the pus, which is more apt to be towards the skin. It is less apt to open into serous than into mucous tissues. The abscesses that form in scrofulous cases are called *cold*, because the conditions of inflammation are absent. They heal, after the discharge of pus, by a process called *granulation*.

Treatment.—The indication to be fulfilled in the treatment of abscess is to prevent the formation of pus, to evacuate it when formed, and to heal the parts so as to prevent further secretions. To prevent its formation cold applications and leeches should be applied to the part, the patient purged, and restricted to a low diet. When matter is formed warm fomentations and poultices should be applied, to hasten the progress of the pus to the surface. If abscesses distinctly *point* they need not be opened, but allowed to burst themselves, but if they occur in loose cellular tissue, under hard skin, and show a tendency to bur row, they should be evacuated by a free incision. After evacuation the poultices should be continued, or the parts be dressed with stimulating ointments, of which the "Herbal Ointment," page 472, is the best.

FELON (PARONYCHIA).

This is also called *whitlow*, and is an abscess of the fingers, of which there are three kinds, the first situated upon the surface of the skin, the second under the skin, the third within the sheath containing the tendons of the fingers, and sometimes involving the covering of the bone. The latter form is the most terrible, and begins with redness, swelling, and a deep-seated and throbbing pain, which becomes so excruciating as to banish all sleep, and nearly drive the patient to distraction. Relief is only secured by discharge of pus.

TREATMENT.—Carry the hand in a sling and use poultices. A poultice made of equal parts of slippery-elm, poke-root, flaxseed meal, and lobelia seeds, mixed with hot lye, and changed twice a day, is an admirable application. When the pain becomes great, the abscess should be laid open with a knife, cutting down to the bone. Nothing will insure loss of bone but a thorough and deep incision. This is most painful, but will give instant relief. After the evacuation, the treatment is to be followed as in ordinary abscess.

ULCERS.

Ulcers are breaches of continuity of surface, being caused by disease or unrepaired injury. A *simple* or *healthy* ulcer has its surface covered with a thick, creamy, yellow pus, not too profuse, and inodorous. The granulations are small, florid, pointed, sensitive, and vascular. A *scrofulous* ulcer is one occurring in debilitated constitutions, most frequently upon the neck and joints. They originate in the cellular tissue, beneath the skin, exist generally in clusters, and are characterized by imperfect and slow suppuration. An *indolent* ulcer occurs most frequently in the lower extremities of old persons, and is the most common of all ulcers. It is owing most frequently to a sore having been neglected or badly treated. Its surface is smooth, glassy, concave and pale. The discharge is thin and serous, and the surrounding tissue is swollen, hard, and of a dusky-red color. It is painless, and the patient is apt to let it go unnoticed, unless it by accident, exposure, or over exertion, it inflames and becomes painful. An *irritable* ulcer is one having an excess of organizing action, with a deficiency of organizable material. It is superficial, having an equal surface of a dark hue, and often covered with tenacious fibrin. It occurs most frequently near the ankle. It is very sensitive, and attended with great pain. A *phagedenic* ulcer is one of irregular form, with ragged, abrupt edges, and uneven brown surface, looking as if gnawed by an animal. It is attended with burning pain, and great constitutional disturbance. A *varicose* ulcer is dependent upon a varicose condition of the veins, and usually occurs in the leg just above the ankle. They are indolent, and mostly moist on the surface.

TREATMENT.—In the simple ulcer the treatment is simply protective. Water dressings are the best, as they keep the parts clean and remove the liquid pus. The "Herbal Ointment" is equally good. If the granulations become too luxuriant, an astringent wash, or slightly cauterizing them, becomes necessary. In scrofulous ulcers constitutional treatment must be instituted. The soft infiltrated tissues surrounding the ulcers should be destroyed by escharotics, and after the slough is removed, the healthy granulated surface treated as a simple ulcer. In indolent ulcers the sore should at first be cleansed by poultices. Healthy granulation should be aroused by lightly touching the ulcer with nitrate of silver, sulphate of copper, etc., or the same effect may be produced by strips of adhesive plaster being placed over the entire surface of the ulcer. In irritable ulcer the treatment should first be constitutional, and tonics and stimulants administered. The part should be relaxed, rested, and elevated. This should be followed by a light poultice, or warm-water dressing, or if there is great pain, fomentations of the infusion of opium, conium, or belladonna should be applied. In the treatment of phagedenic ulcers, fresh air and good diet are all-important. The secretions must be corrected, and a Dover's powder given at night. The ulcer should be thoroughly destroyed by escharotics, followed by warm poultices. In varicose ulcer cold water, rest, regular bandaging, or laced stocking, constitutes the treatment. *Strapping* with strips of adhesive plaster, by the support afforded, is excellent in all cases of ulcers.

My "Herbal Ointment" (page 472) acts most admirably as a local application in all cases of ulcer. It causes healthy granulation, relieves the pain, and speedily causes union of the edges.

BOILS (FURUNCULUS).

Boils occur most frequently in the young, and in those of plethoric habit, in those parts where the skin is thickest. They are usually gregarious, and depend upon derangement of the stomach and intestines, and frequently succeed eruptive diseases. The swelling is of a conical shape, having a hard, red, and painful base, and a yellow apex. If left to itself it bursts and discharges pus, and a core or slough of cellular tissue; when completely emptied, the heat and pain subside.

TREATMENT.—Poultices and warm fomentations should be applied early, and as soon as pus has formed, the boil should be opened, after which the granulated wound should be dressed with basilicon ointment. If my "Herbal Ointment" is procurable, if may be applied from the first, as it speedily draws the boil to a head, and quickly heals it after discharge.

CARBUNCLE (ANTHRAX).

This is a serious disease; it is a solitary inflammation of the cellular tissue and skin, presenting a flat, spongy swelling of a livid hue, and attended with dull heavy pain. It varies in size, and its progress is slow. Like the boil, it appears more often upon the neck, the shoulders, the back, buttocks, and thighs. The constitutional symptoms are low throughout, and the attendant fever is apt to be typhoid in character; prostration and delirium often terminate the case. It most frequently attacks high livers of an advanced age.

TREATMENT.—During the formation, apply either fomentations and poultices, or cold water dressing. An incision in the form of a cross should be made free and early, which may be followed by caustic applications, in order that the dying parts may thoroughly be removed. After this is done, the wound is to receive ordinary treatment.

CHILBLAIN'S (PERNIO).

This is an affection of the skin, produced by sudden alternations of cold and heat, most commonly affecting the toes, heels, ears, or fingers. It is attended with itching, swelling, pain, and slight redness at first; it may afterwards become of a livid hue, with vesications and ulcerative fissures, which are difficult to heal.

TREATMENT.—Wash the parts thoroughly, and then apply tallow, and if on the hands, draw on a pair of old gloves, especially at night. The "Herbal Ointment" is a sure and rapid cure for chilblains.

BURNS AND SCALDS.

There are three principal divisions of these injuries, which may be produced by hot fluids, vapor, flame, or solids.

1st. Those which produce mere redness and inflammation, terminating in resolution, and perhaps desquamation.

2d. Those causing blisters on the skin, which often dry up and heal; but if the true skin has been injured and inflamed, suppuration, and ulceration will result.

3d. Those causing the death of the part, in which there is not much pain, and which are followed by sloughs.

Extensive burns, even if superficial, are very dangerous, and those upon the trunk are more dangerous than those upon the extremities. The symptoms are paleness and shivering, with a feeble, quick pulse, often prostration, coma, and death. The greatest danger is during the first four or five days, from collapse; subsequently from an affection of the head, chest, or abdomen, or from prostration.

TREATMENT.—Bathing the part in cold water will mitigate the pain, heat, and inflammation. Afterwards it must be protected from the air by raw cotton, or some bland unctuous substance. My "Herbal Ointment" gives instantaneous relief. Glycerine and carbolic acid are used by some, and linseed oil and lime water, or linseed oil, prepared chalk, and vinegar, by others. The indication is only to exclude the air. The blisters should be discharged of their contents, care being taken that the skin is not removed. The nervous excitement is to be calmed by opium, and sinking prevented by stimulants, but care is to be taken that over-stimulation does not result. The separation of sloughs is to be promoted by rest, poultices, and fomentations. In joints passive motion is to be made to prevent stiffness.

GOITRE (BRONCHOCELE)

This is an enlargement of the thyroid gland, an organ that if it performs any functions at all, does so only in fœtal life. It generally commences by moderate increase of the gland, or thickening of the neck, and advances gradually until a portion or the whole gland becomes enormously swollen. It causes dyspnœa, and sometimes obstructs circulation to the brain, when the tumor acquires considerable magnitude. It is more common to females than males, and generally occurs before puberty. The species of idiocy sometimes associated with goitre is called *Cretinism.*

TREATMENT.—Alteratives and discutients. The alteratives, such as stillingia, rock-rose, etc., are to be preferred, and externally iodine may may be applied. Those who may desire my counsel in this disease are referred to page 390.

RUPTURE (HERNIA).

This signifies a protrusion of the abdominal viscera. The predisposing cause is a weakness of the abdominal walls, at the natural openings. This weakness may be increased by injury, disease, or pregnancy, or it may also be due to congenital difficulty. The exciting causes are muscular exertion, jumping, straining, playing on wind instruments, coughing, lifting weights, tight clothes, parturition, straining at stool, etc.

Hernia is divided, according to the site of the protusion, into *inguinal*, *ventro-inguinal*, *umbilical*, *ventral*, *perineal*, *vaginal*, *pudendal*, *thyroideal*, and *ischiatic;* in condition, into *reducible*, *irreducible*, and *strangulated*, and if the contents are entirely intestinal it is called *enterocele*, but if it contains omentum it is termed *epiplocele*.

The symptoms of hernia are a painful swelling forming at some part of the abdomen, which is compressible and soft, and can be made to disappear by pressure in the proper direction, and it often disappears spontaneously. An enterocele is smooth, elastic, and globular, retires suddenly and with a gurgling noise. An epiplocele is more irregular in form, has a doughy feel, and retires slowly without noise.

Reducible hernia is one in which the contents of the sac can be reduced with proper manipulation. *Irreducible* hernia is owing to adhesions, or from membranous bands stretching across the sac, etc., when the contents cannot be replaced; and when the contents of the sac are incarcerated, with inflammation and an interruption to the passage of fæces, it is called *strangulated*. The more common forms are the inguinal and umbilical. Inguinal hernia is called *scrotal* when the intes tine has descended from the groin into the scrotum.

TREATMENT.—The treatment consists in reduction and retention. This can only be achieved in the reducible hernia. Reduction is effected by a manipulation called *taxis*, the patient being placed in a recumbent position, and the muscles of the abdomen relaxed; gentle and steady pressure is made by the hand in the direction of the descent. Retention is effected by continued and suitable pressure by means of the pad of a well-fitting truss. By constant and careful use of a truss, a radical cure may be effected. A lobelia emetic, or the patient may be chloroformed, to relax the muscles, may be resorted to, if replacement cannot be performed without them. In irreducible hernia, the treatment consists in carefully regulating the bowels, avoiding great exertions, and wearing a suitable truss to prevent further protrusion. Strangulated hernia, if it cannot be reduced by taxis, becomes a subject for the surgeon. Radical cures may also be performed by the surgeon.

I have constantly manufactured for my patients a most excellent truss, which effects many cures. It is a light appliance, and occasions no pain or inconvenience to the wearer. It is the most comfortable truss that can be worn, is cleanly and durable, and easily adjusted. It is called the "Champion Truss"—a distinction to which it is clearly entitled. It is the greatest triumph of skill and genius ever attained in this or any other country for the retention and radical cure of hernia or rupture. Its qualities may be briefly stated, as follows, viz. :—

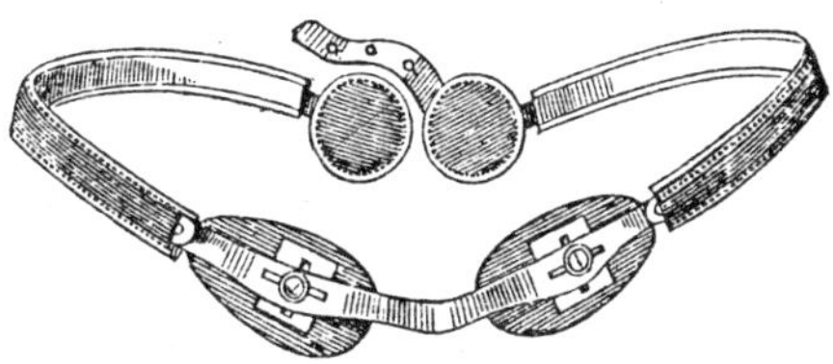

Prof. O. Phelps Brown's Champion Truss.

It is worn with perfect ease and safety.

It keeps its place under all circumstances.

It never gets out of order.

Its pressure is equalized and gentle.

It makes no pressure on the spine.

It is applicable to single or double rupture.

These qualities are all that are required of a truss, either for retention or cure, and any truss lacking in any of them does not fulful its purpose, and is capable of doing great injury. Its perfect adjustment is well represented in the following cuts. The most violent paroxysms

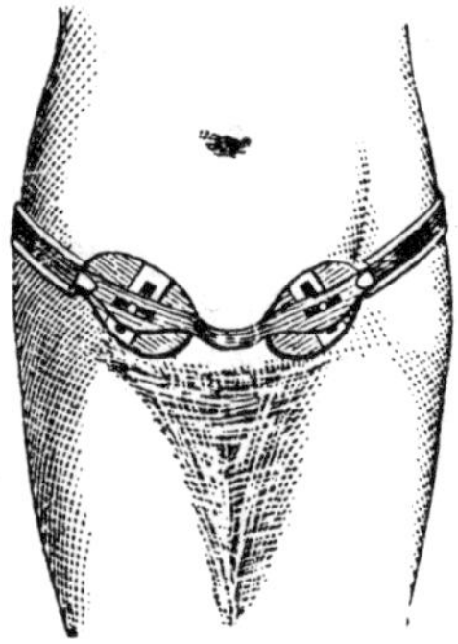

Front View.

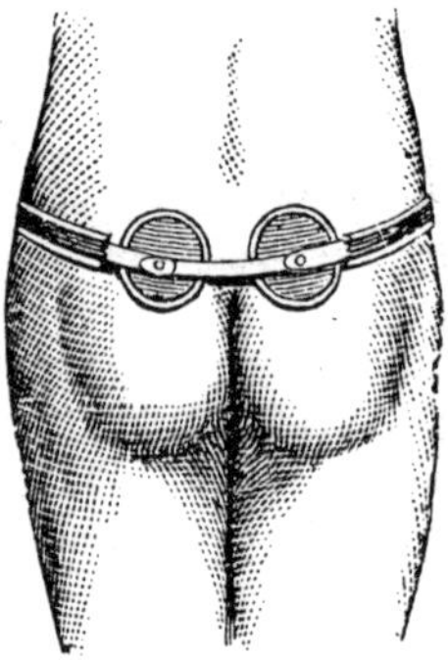

Back View.

of coughing, muscular exertion, falls, etc., will not move it from its properly applied position. This indispensable quality of retention must be possessed by every truss, otherwise it is useless.

Patients desiring the "Champion Truss," will please send the following measurement, viz., around the body where the truss is worn, and state whether right, left, or double. Trusses of the highest mechanical perfection are also furnished for every other variety of rupture. Preliminary correspondence *free* in all cases.

DISEASES OF THE EYE AND EAR.

The eye is one of the most delicate as well as the most complicated organs of the body, and its diseases are but very imperfectly understood by the ordinary practitioner. A great deal of mischief has been done by improper treatment of diseases of the eye, and I may also include the ear, and many persons who now mourn the loss of sight and hearing, partially or wholly so, might yet be in enjoyment of those senses if they but had received the proper treatment. Under this head I shall include those diseases only which are capable of treatment in domestic practice.

CONJUNCTIVITIS.

This is an inflammation of the conjunctiva or mucous membrane of the eyelids. The sensation is as if particles of sand had insinuated themselves beneath the lids, accompanied by heat, pain, and increased lachrymal secretion, also intolerance of light. In severe cases, headache, nausea, constipation, loss of appetite, etc., are present. The causes of this form of inflammation are mostly local, as particles of sand, dust, insects, etc.

TREATMENT.—Remove the cause. If due to foreign particles in the eye, they should be removed. Bathe the eye thoroughly in water, rubbing towards the nose. If iron or steel is suspected, a vial cork, rubbed smooth with flannel, should be touched to all parts of the eye, which will remove the particles. When the eye is relieved, a mild purgative may be given, and cold water applications made to the eye. In severer cases, lotions of nitrate of silver, sulphate of zinc, etc., become necessary.

CATARRHAL OPHTHALMIA.

This is due to exposure to cold. The white of the eye becomes inflamed and very red, and generally there is a thin mucous discharge, which in severe cases becomes thick and purulent. This condition of the eye is accompanied by chilliness, aching of the bones, and some degree of fever.

TREATMENT.—Apply cold soft water to the eyes with little muslin packs, and give a purgative. If this will not relieve the inflammation, cold slippery-elm poultices, or the domestic practice of applying "smear case" to the eyes, may be resorted to. In obstinate or chronic cases a solution of four grains of sulphate of zinc to the ounce of water may be applied two or three times a day with a small brush. The eye should also be bathed with a decoction of golden seal. My "Herbal Ointment" (page 472) is excellent in all ophthalmic diseases.

PURULENT OPHTHALMIA.

The symptoms of this disease peculiar to children are similar to the Catarrhal Ophthalmia of adults. The eyes are kept constantly closed, the lids are red and swollen, and glued together by thick purulent matter becoming dry. The skin is dry and the bowels irregular. It is generally due to exposure to damp and cold, injuries in washing the child, acrid matter, or to a scrofulous constitution.

TREATMENT.—In the treatment of this affection the eyes should be thoroughly washed in a cold, weak solution of hydrastin, four or five times a day. Saturate packs with cold water, containing a little tincture of lobelia, and apply to the eyes and change when they grow warm. The bowels should be kept open with gentle laxatives. Some cases may need a solution of vegetable caustic, sulphate of zinc, or nitrate of silver. If caused by a scrofulous condition, use alteratives, of which the "Compound extract of Rock-rose and Stillingia" is the best (see page 471).

Scrofulous Ophthalmia.

This disease is chiefly confined to children. The child scarcely can bear the light, the lids are spasmodically closed, and the head constantly turned away from the light. The eye is not very red, but a few of the large vessels are considerable injected. It is very liable to recur, and may prove obstinate, and cause ulceration of the cornea.

Treatment.—In this disease it is very important that the general health should be looked after. The local treatment before advised should be resorted to, and the constitutional treatment should be very active and energetic.

Stye (Hordeolum).

This is a small painful pustule on the margin of the eyelid, having its origin in ciliary follicles.

Treatment.—It may usually be cured by applying spirits of hartshorn by means of a small steel needle, puncturing the tumor slightly. If this does not remove the inflammation, slippery-elm poultices should be applied, and tonics and alteratives given.

Amaurosis.

This complaint is due to anæsthesia of the optic nerve. The patient sees objects indistinctly, even when they are lit up by a bright light; they appear surrounded with a fog or mist, and no effort nor the employment of artificial means increase the distinctness. The outlines of objects appear not only indistinct, but also broken, and thus disfigured, the faculty of distinguishing colors is frequently lost, and double vision is not infrequent. This condition, as above described, is more properly *amblyopia*, it is only called *amaurosis* when the vision is entirely lost.

Treatment.—Electro-galvanism is one of the most promising remedies. Powdered bay-berry root, taken as snuff, is occasionally useful. Blisters behind the ear often afford relief. Nux vomica should also be given. The disease is often very obstinate, but I have cured some of the most unpromising cases.

Foreign Bodies in the Eyes.

These should be sought for by inverting the lids, and having the patient turn the eyes in every direction. If it be found to adhere to the mucous membrane of the cornea or conjunctiva, it can usually be removed by a silk handkerchief wrapped around a probe. If lime, mortar, or lye should get into the eye, it should be removed, and the eye washed with a weak solution of vinegar and water. The ensuing inflammation should receive usual treatment. If the foreign bodies enter the interior chamber of the eye, the surgeon should only remove it.

FOREIGN SUBSTANCES IN THE EAR.

Children frequently put peas, beans, kernels of corn, etc., into the ear, which, if allowed to remain, will produce active inflammation. Foreign bodies may also enter the ear by accident. These should all be quickly removed. It should be done by syringing the ear with warm water, or by means of forceps. Excessive accumulation of wax is to be removed by syringing with warm water frequently, and not by ear-scoops.

EAR ACHE (OTALGIA).

This is a neuralgic affection, and is caused by local inflammation, cold and exposure, and carious teeth.

TREATMENT.—If caused by inflammation, a warm poultice of slippery-elm, moistened with laudanum, should be applied, and frequently changed. If caused by carious teeth they should be removed; sweet oil and laudanum dropped in the ear often gives relief, and the common practice of blowing hot tobacco smoke into the ear is also useful.

Many of the eye and ear diseases are surgical in their character, such as strabismus, a few cases of cataract, etc., but a great many of them are amenable to medical treatment. Even cataract, which heretofore was considered eminently surgical, may in many cases be entirely cured by medicinal treatment alone. I have cured a case, in which there was total blindness for ten years, in the short space of two months. The patient ever since is in the full enjoyment of sight. My treatment has also been equally successful in cases of deafness. I regard all cases subject to relief or cure in which the tympanum or drum of the ear is not destroyed. If persons suffering from chronic diseases of the eye or ear will write and state their cases fully to me, I will cheerfully give my opinion by return mail.

MALIGNANT AND VENEREAL DISEASES.

CANCER (CARCINOMA).

This is a malignant tumor. In the first stage it is hard, in the second stage it ulcerates. The seat of cancer is in the female breast, the skin, the tongue, the stomach, the womb, the lips, etc. It rarely occurs in subjects under thirty years of age. It is at first a small hard tumor, movable, but eventually it forms deep and superficial attachments. It grows in general slowly, is irregular in shape, and painful. The pain is mostly sharp, lancinating, and is much increased on pressure. In the course of time the tissue beneath the skin is absorbed, and becomes attached to it, and it presents a bluish, nodulated appearance. Ulceration usually takes place by absorption of the skin, and as sloughing proceeds, the edges become ragged and everted, having a bluish purple color, and discharges a fetid, sanious pus.

There are five varieties of cancer, though microscopically they are essentially the same.

Scirrhus is hard, firm, and transparent, and of a grayish color, occurring most frequently in the female breast, skin, etc.

Encephaloid is soft and brainlike in its appearance, and hemorrhagic in character, frequently met with in the globe of the eye, testes, nares, etc

Colloid resembles glue or honey in the comb, and usually occurs in the internal viscera.

Melanosis, or melanotic cancer, is of a black color, either soft or hard, and occurs mostly upon serous membranes.

Epithelial cancer is usually found upon the lips.

These various forms may exist separately, or one variety may be associated with or take the place of another.

TREATMENT.—As long as this disease was regarded as purely local in character, the only treatment resorted to was extirpation either by cauterizing agents or by the knife ; but since the pathology of the disease is better understood, and its constitutional character ascertained, the treatment employed has been considerably modified. I have long ago held that cancer was a constitutional affection, so instructed my patients, and based my treatment upon that opinion.

It is well to remove the tumor by the knife or cautery, but the liability to recurrence is always great unless constitutional treatment is employed. The cauterizing agents are blood-root and chloride of zinc made into a paste, and then applied to the cancer, the skin having first been removed by a blister. This is reapplied until the whole mass is dead, when in course of time it comes away as a slough. The expressed juices of poke, laurel, blood-root, and yellow-dock answer the same purpose.

The constitutional treatment consists in toning up the general system, abstaining from fatty diet, bathing, and the employment of alterative treatment. Recently, a plant has been brought into notice by the name of *Cundurango* (*Equatoria Garciana*, see page 74) which is destined to revolutionize the treatment of cancer. I have tried it in several cases, and it answered every expectation. I regard it as a virtual specific in cancer, and shall, notwithstanding its very high price, employ it in every case, thereby hoping to make my success in the treatment of this malignant disease more certain. It is a matter of regret that spurious articles are in the market, thus bringing the genuine article, which is yet difficult to obtain, into disrepute.

SYPHILIS.

Syphilis is occasioned by a specific poison which is conveyed by contagion or actual contact. It first shows itself upon the genital organs in the form of a small yellowish pimple, or pimples, the presence of which is at first made manifest by itching and slight soreness. The pimples (called chancres) break, and gradually change into a red, hard-edged shallow ulcer. This ulcer is circular or oval in form, and is surrounded by a ragged border. The skin and tissue in the immediate vicinity become inflamed, and, unless proper remedies be immediately applied, the virus is absorbed into the system, and the consequences are of the most deplorable character. There are many kinds of chancre, viz :—inflammatory, indurated or hard, sloughing or perishing, phagedenic or eating, and gangrenous or likely to mortify. Next in order, if stringent curative measures be not adopted, is the *bubo*, which is a swelling of the glands of the groin, caused by the absorption of the poison. The bubo will usually make its appearance in about a fortnight after the sore is discovered. It advances to suppuration, and also becomes a sore, when it receives the name of "glandular chancre." Sometimes growths resembling certain vegetables appear, in the male, upon the organ and on the membrane lining of the foreskin. In the female, they will be found in and at the entrance of the vagina, and sometimes on the neck of the womb. These are primary symptoms, and, if quickly but radically extirpated or cured, will not result in any very serious constitutional derangement; but if neglected, the virus is absorbed into the blood, and the infection reaches the entire system. When the disease becomes constitutional, the results are most deplorable. The syphilitic ulcer then appears at various parts of the body, more usually upon the arm and forearm, forehead, shin and chest. These ulcers are quite characteristic, so that the experienced surgeon at once knows their specific nature upon sight. The affections of the skin and mucous membrane are called *secondary*, those appearing upon the bones, etc., are *tertiary*. In these advanced stages of the disease the gravity is such as should urge each affected person to employ competent surgical or medical aid, and not longer to postpone such active treatment as is required. Neglect of so important a duty on the part of the patient will result seriously to him, as the progress of the disease is unerringly from bad to worse in every case.

TREATMENT.—In primary syphilis, the chancre should be destroyed effectually by nitrate of silver, nitric acid, or caustic potash, and heal the parts by mild dressing. If this is effectually done, with proper constitutional treatment, no secondary symptoms will supervene.

In secondary and tertiary syphilis the treatment is very important, and must be correct in order to eliminate the disorganizing taint.

The treatment is necessarily alterative and tonic. The following may each be specifically employed, either singly or judiciously combined :— Phytolaccin, corydalin, chimaphilin, tincture of kalmia, menispermin, ceanothus americanus, sarsaparilla, stillingia, and by some iodide of potassium, but never mercury. Mercury in any form is not a specific, and in effects most pernicious. When buboes appear, they should be discussed by a mixture of tincture of iodine, ℥ ij. ; tincture of arnica, ʒ ij. ; tincture of scrophularia, ʒ ij. This should be applied by wetting pads of linen with it and securing them by adhesive strips. If suppuration has taken place, the treatment of abscess is to be employed.

During treatment, the patient should abstain from all fat meats, spirituous liquors, and excesses of every kind.

If any person is conscious that he or she is affected with a syphilitic taint they should never marry, for the offspring will surely be miserable objects of pity, and conjugal bliss very uncertain. The taint must be thoroughly eradicated, so that not a vestige remains, before a marriage, physically pure, can occur.

If rightly treated, syphilis is not a formidable disease to cure, yet how many suffer hopelessly on, after having for years been subjected to mercurial treatment. Purely chemical herbal treatment will only remove the serious disorder from the system, as attested by the thousands of cases under my treatment, in which every trace of the disease has been obliterated from the economy.

GONORRHŒA.

This is vulgarily known as *clap*, so named from the French *clappe*, a bow-string. It received this name on account of the *chordee* occurring in the disease. This is caused by the violence of the inflammation, which abnormally expands the cavernous body of the organ and is painfully drawn downwards, so that the urethra occupies the relative position of the string to a bow-gun.

This is a disease of the mucous membrane which lines the private parts of the male and female, and is communicated as is syphilis, by contagion, or actual contact. It commences with itching and uneasiness about the private parts, and a peculiar feeling of soreness in the urethra, or urinary canal. A scalding sensation is also felt when the patient makes water. In a day or two a whitish matter makes its appearance at the orifice of the urethra, and this will soon increase greatly in quantity, and assume a greenish-yellow color. The parts will be much inflamed, and the urethra will become thickened and very sore. The consistency and quantity of the pus-like discharge vary in different persons. It usually makes its appearance in from three to five days after exposure. It may propagate itself upon other mucous membranes after inoculation.

TREATMENT.—A purgative should be taken at first, and at the same time the parts should be thoroughly packed with cold or hot water. The following are the remedies mostly employed as internal remedies: —Oil of copaiba and cubebs, matico, gelsemin, oil of erigeron, oil of turpentine, etc. These oils should be taken in medium doses, and in emulsion with acacia, etc. The internal injections are vegetable astringents, sugar of lead, sulphate of zinc, etc. The injections should not be strong, and be carefully made, otherwise orchitis may follow. Applying cold water relieves the chordee.

The treatment is not difficult, and, if properly directed, will soon relieve the patient.

GLEET.

This is one of the results of abused or neglected gonorrhœa. It is a continued discharge of a thin and clear character, after the inflammatory and painful early symptoms have disappeared. It is caused by dedebility of the parts, or by unhealthy action of the glands in the urinary passage. It is sometimes, especially in persons of a scrofulous habit, a fixture for years, and constitutes a drain upon the system, the effects of which can only be obviated by the most scrupulous care and attention. The old style of treatment involved the use of cauterizing injections, and the bougie, together with blisters applied to the perinæum. It had the effect of imperfectly remedying, or else of aggravating the complaint, and rendering it next to impossible of cure.

TREATMENT.--Same as for acute gonorrhœa, but it should be more energetic.

Those who may wish to intrust their cases to my treatment, may rest assured that they will be quickly cured, and everything held confidential. The fear of exposure does frequently much mischief, and the dread of losing caste in society, or a feeling of shame, often tempts the sufferer to withhold his case from the family physician for treatment, or he may endure his mental and physical torture in silence as long as he can, and then finally intrust his case to the ignorance of a companion, who may know some recipe, or he may employ the treatment of some incompetent, uneducated physician, found everywhere, especially in large cities, who also maltreats the case, so that finally the disease, which at first was readily curable, has become a very serious affection.

The wrong of such a course is obvious, and I advise the reader, who has or may become unfortunate in this respect, to confide his or her case to some honorable and competent physician, as soon as the disease manifests itself.

DEBILITY OR LOSS OF VITALITY.

This is a condition of the organism characterized by loss of vitality, or deterioration and diminution in the quality and tone of the vital forces. It is one of the chief predisposing causes of disease, and is of itself a condition characterized by all the elements of ill health. The principal causes of debility are improper nourishment, impure air, excessive bodily and mental exercise, want of exercise, long exposure to intense heat or cold, intemperance, depressing states of the mind, and of course a prostrative disease. When not a heritage of the organism, it is generally produced by some flagrant violation of physiological law, depleting the vital forces by the disorganization of organic functions which ensues, or by the loss of vital elements through the eliminating organs, chiefly the kidneys.

That the reader may have a correct understanding of what is meant by vitality, it may be well to give its physiological sense. Though derived from the Latin *vita*, life, it has a somewhat different signification from that which is expressed by the word life. It signifies the constituent principle or essence of life rather than the entity itself. Hence vitality is not properly life, but the element conducive to its perfection and prolongation. It is that principle that gives to the physical organization its vigor, elasticity, and tone, to the mental organs, acuteness, vivacity and sprightliness, and to the whole organism a high standard of health.

If the habits are not in violation of hygiene or physiology, and the expenditure of the vital forces not exceeding the production, the normal condition of the organism would be one of health and vigor, and almost complete immunity from disease. If the expenditure exceeds the production it engenders the condition termed debility. Improper and sinful habits of life, especially in the young, are alarmingly destructive of vitality in consequence of engendering diseases characterized by losses of vital secretions. The intemperate very frequently incur the penalty of over-indulgence in intoxicating beverages by inducing structural diseases of the internal organs, especially Bright's disease of the kidney, wherein the blood becomes devitalized by loss of its albumen through the urine. In the male economy at an age often quite immature there is induced an affection characterized by involuntary expenditure of a secretion, directly by an improper and sinful life. The element thus constantly expended, and which occurs invariably without any exercise of the voluntary powers, is beyond all question the most highly organized and more intrinsically vital than any other secretion of the organism. This affection, peculiarly masculine, is one of the most prolific causes of debility, and is conducive to greater physical misfortune than any other pathological condition induced by violation of physiological laws. The chemical nature of the secretion is highly phosphatic, and as phosphorus is a very important constituent of nerve tissue, its constant involuntary escape from the organism, whether in the urine or otherwise, preys fearfully upon the nerve tissue for phosphatic supply, and eventually, and often quite rapidly, produces atony of the nerve-centres, and a general intonicity of the nervous system, or what is more commonly known as nervous debility. Of the various systems composing the organism the nervous can least afford to lose its vitality, or to become enfeebled. It is the principal or controlling system of the organism, the others being more or less subordinate. If by any depleting causes its just complement of the vital forces becomes reduced, its individual integrity is not alone compromised or destroyed, but muscular action, circulation, digestion, assimilation, and the mental operations also become enfeebled, hence the vital standard of the nervous system is of extreme importance to the general welfare of the whole organism.

Precisely the same pathological condition results from another cause, a sedentary habit of life. It is due to such exciting causes that clergymen and other persons of sedentary habits suffer so frequently from nervous or general debility. When the muscular system is permitted to degenerate from want of proper exercise it gives to the organism a condition of laxity or intonicity which in the male induces the previously mentioned loss of a highly vitalized secretion, and in the female an uncompensated loss of nervo-electric force. Debility is the result in both cases, though the devitalization is more rapid in the male, proportionally to the physical vigor inherent to the different sexes, than in the female. This is explained by the fact that in the male economy a greater loss of the phosphates occurs. In all persons of studious habits, and where bodily exercise is insufficient, the urine is loaded with phosphates, which is indicative of the breaking down of nerve tissue. Consequently in the male there is not only the usual phosphoric loss due to nervous waste, but the super-addition of the involuntary loss of a secretion which, as has been stated, is highly phosphatic in its chemical nature, makes the depletion of the phosphorus essential to a vital condition of the organism, doubly great.

In a debilitated condition of the nervous system, or, as it is usually denominated, nervous debility, from whatever cause the loss of vitality may ensue, there is in general quite a train of symptoms, as may be supposed when this more important part of the economy has become devitalized. This form of debility may usually be recognized by a marked facial expression, a characteristic mannerism, and by a peculiar mental state. The skin of the face is pale and sallow, and usually affected with acne ; there is a dark circle around the orbits, the pupils are dilated and sluggish, the eyes become lustreless, and the face has a haggard, troubled furtive expression. These physiognomic characteristics are due to atony or want of tone in the cerebral nerve-centres, and from the same cause the devitalized patient is listless, shy, retiring and easily confused, society loses its charms, and solitude is preferred, but has, however, no compensating or satisfying influence over the patient. There is a want of steadiness and decision in his locomotion, his inferior extremities are deficient in power, and all the movements are suggestive of a mind ill at ease. The mental operations are confused, speech becomes awkward and often without directness; memory is defective, and the patient is usually absent-minded and given to reverie. Pains in the lumbar region, and a sense of weight and aching in the loins are experienced. The appetite is capricious, and digestion feeble. The mind is deficient in power of attention, the imagination is constantly pervaded with vague erotic dreams, the moral sense is blunted and the perceptions are dull and confused. Pains in the course of the principal nerves and extreme nervous sensibility are experienced. The patient also can fix his mind on any subject with difficulty; his attention wanders, and he is given to day-dreams and erotic visions.

The urine, of course, contains phosphates, the source of which, whether nervous or secretional, is easily determined by analyzation or microscopical examination. Urates are also found in the urine. Those who suspect such vital loss, may with sufficient certainty for all practical purposes ascertain the fact by a simple experiment. The morning urine should be placed in a clean half-pint bottle, and let it stand from forty-eight to seventy-two hours. If there is then found a remarkably peculiar or cloudy sediment or deposit at the bottom, the fact is quite evident that some of the losses alluded to occur, and proper aid should be sought at once.

Such, briefly, are the evidences of a devitalized nervous system. The condition, as is palpable to every one, is fraught with danger to the general welfare, and even to life, if the process of depletion of the vital forces continues too long, or if, by special virulence of the exciting cause, the devitalization is rapid in occurrence. Any loss of vital power should be regarded with solicitude and deep concern by every one who places a proper estimation upon vigor of the organism and its special functions. Careful and judicious treatment must not be neglected, as by such a course only can revitalization be speedily and adequately effected. As soon as loss of vital force becomes apparent, so soon should the services of a competent and experienced physician be engaged. In any stage of devitalization, rehabilitation of the organism with vitality can again be accomplished, the only requirement being employment of competent medical aid, and the exhibition of vitalizing remedies. Revitalization can, however, only be effected by herbal remedies, as their organic nature alone affords the elements required for reendowment of the system with vital force. Minerals are lifeless, and can therefore impart no vital element.

Those desiring to consult the author with reference to debility or loss of vitality from any cause whatever, may refer to page 390, where his mode of treatment is described, and to page 395, where the necessary questions are asked.

SATYRIASIS.

This is an insatiable desire for sexual intercourse, and so called because the satyrs of mythology were greatly addicted to venery. The disease is accompanied by the power of having frequent connection, without exhaustion. It is a species of nervous disease produced by a disordered state of the cerebellum.

TREATMENT.—It can be cured by a low diet, frequent shower baths, physical out-door labor, ice bags to the cerebellum, a hard bed, and hop pillows.

STRICTURE OF THE URETHRA.

This is a diminution or contracted condition of the tube, and may be either *spasmodic* or *permanent*. Spasmodic stricture depends on spasm of the muscles of the perinæum, or upon contraction of the muscular portion of the urethra. Exposure to cold and indulgence in drink favor an attack, which usually occurs after dinner. It generally occurs in persons with permanent obstruction. The urine is suddenly retained; the desire to urinate causes incessant straining, the bladder becomes distended, the countenance anxious, the pulse quick, the skin hot, and at last the urine dribbles, or the bladder may burst, and extravasation occurs into the peritonæum or perinæum. There is another variety of this affection, termed *inflammatory stricture*, caused by abuse of injections, exposure, or intemperance during acute gonorrhœa.

Permanent stricture is a contraction from permanent inflammation, plastic deposit having taken place in the tissue beneath the mucous membrane. The occasion of this inflammation may be gonorrhœa, venery, kicks or blows, riding on horseback, acrid urine, drinking, etc. It is situated most frequently in the membranous portion of the urethra, within a few inches of the glans penis. The extent and degree of contraction vary. Sometimes the stricture is very tight, but limited, as if a thread had been tied around the urethra; more frequently it is of greater extent, containing from a quarter of an inch to several inches. Several strictures may exist at once. Permanent stricture comes on gradually, occurring mostly in middle-aged men. Urination is frequent, tedious, and painful; the stream is thin, twisted, or forked; and a few drops pass after urination, which had collected behind the stricture There is pain in the perinæum, thighs, and loins; erection is often painful; chill and fever constantly occurring as in ague; the testicles, rectum, and bowels sympathize, and the general health is greatly impaired. It is a disease that causes extreme annoyance, pain, and disorder, and should receive early and competent treatment.

TREATMENT.—The indication in spasmodic stricture is to overcome the spasm, and relieve the bladder. This is usually effected by warm hip baths, Dover's powder, laudanum enemata, and cold water upon the genitals. A favorable mental impression is made by pouring water from a can, in a small stream, from some height, into a vessel containing water, in imitation of urination. A few sniffs of ether will usually relax the spasm, but if these means fail, the urine should be drawn of by a catheter.

In permanent stricture *dilatation* by means of flexible bougies is the usual method of cure. Great caution is necessary in the use of these. Some use caustic applications, and in some cases puncturation is resorted to. In some cases opening the urethra may be necessary, as the stricture is so extensive and complete that no other means are available.

These surgical means may at times be necessary, but I have cured very many cases by purely medicinal treatment, and it is very seldom that I employ bougies, but compel absorption of the deposit by alterative treatment. In some cases, however, I frequently combine dilatation with medication. Those desiring consultation are referred to page 390.

PROSTATITIS.

This is inflammation of the prostate gland. It usually accompanies gonorrhœa, but may exist independently. The discharge is similar to that of urethral inflammation, and when the result of chronic inflammation the discharge is called prostatorrhœa. The gland is frequently enlarged. Chronic inflammation is commonly brought on by gleet, stricture, horse exercise, etc., and is most frequently met with in advanced life, and disappears upon the removal of the cause. The gland is also enlarged in old persons—a hypertrophy independent of inflammation. The bladder sympathizes, and becomes irritable ; the urine is fœtid, mucous, and its stains are often retained. It causes most intense suffering.

TREATMENT.—Leeches, rest, counter-irritation, alteratives, laxatives, and enemata constitute the usual treatment. In hypertrophy of the organ, the usual treatment should be instituted. The medicinal treatment, as in stricture, is important, and should only be intrusted to those who fully understand the anatomy of the organ, and the pathology of the disease.

ORCHITIS.

This is the *hernia humoralis* of older writers. *Swelled testicle* is a common accompaniment of mumps. It is often the result of an injury, but oftener of gonorrhœa and its treatment ; exercise, wet and cold often induce it. The organ enlarges greatly fever attends, causing intense pain.

it is usually confined to one of the glands, and mostly the epididymis. The cord is often swollen and painful.

TREATMENT.—Low diet and the recumbent position are essential. The weight of the tumor should be supported by a suspensory bandage. After the acute symptoms have subsided, friction with astringent lotions, and compression by adhesive straps, will be useful. The hardness and swelling are likely to remain unless discussed by the alteratives.

VARICOCELE.

This is a varicose condition of the veins of the spermatic cord. The causes are such as to produce obstruction to the return of blood: constipation, corpulence, tight belts around the abdomen, and warm climate. It is usually an accompaniment of spermatorrhœa. The left side is more frequently affected than the right, because the left spermatic vein is more likely to be compressed by the fæces in the sigmoid or S-shaped flexure of the rectum, and because it is longer and not so direct in its course. The swelling is pear-shaped and feels like a bunch of earth-worms.

TREATMENT.—The cause, if ascertained, should be removed, and the scrotum constantly bathed in cold water, and supported with a suspensory bandage.

The veins are sometimes obliterated by a surgical operation. It can usually be overcome by proper medical treatment, however, and the operation should only be the last resort.

I use for my patients a self-adjusting suspensory bandage, which can be so arranged that any extent of compression can be made, and which in construction is simple and very durable. It is the only perfect suspensory bandage or scrotal supporter made, and the only one from which any great benefit can be expected. It is eminently serviceable in this disease as well as in orchitis, and no one suffering from these diseases should do without them. Sent by mail, postage prepaid, on receipt of 10s.

DISEASES OF THE FEMALE SEXUAL ORGANS.

The genitalia of the female is the controlling centre of her whole economy. If the womb and its appendages are in a healthy state, the female figure preserves its artistic rotundity, her mind its sprightliness. and her humanity its benevolence and sympathy. When diseased, she becomes fretful, peevish, and inconsolable. The province of the physician, therefore, becomes one of great importance, and it is his duty that he should not only thoroughly understand the pathology of uterine diseases, but in his humanity he should combine a fine feeling of compassion, with correct ideas of the treatment required. He should prove worthy of the trust confided to him, in sympathy, considerateness, and skill.

No greater trust can fall upon him; he is not only accountable for the physical welfare of the patient, but bears a further responsibility. If his treatment is not judicious and rational, his patient becomes a victim to a gloomy depression of spirits, and to an irrepressible feeling of languor and misery, that sternly bid away all brightness of life. He will but poorly do his duty if he follows but the beaten track of a routine practice, and, after successive trials, consigns his suffering patient, by pronouncing her incurable, to a condition but little better than the grave. Uterine diseases are not incurable, but when properly treated they yield kindly to medication, as the disposition of all womb affections is to get well, needing but proper medical assistance to stimulate and encourage the forces of recuperation to overcome the assaults of disease. (See page 390)

VULVITIS.

This is characterized by redness and slight tumefaction of skin, covered with mucus, while in neglected cases the parts are found much excoriated. It generally arises from want of cleanliness, or from the acrid character of the vaginal and uterine secretions. It may, however, be produced by excessive sexual intercourse, or a venereal taint. The symptoms consist of great pain and tenderness, a mucous discharge, a smarting in passing urine, and a constant pain about the loins and thighs.

TREATMENT.—This should be treated by hot packs, elm poultices, and a wash of a weak solution of sulphate of zinc, or tincture of myrrh. Quinine, macrotin and leptandrin should be given internally. The parts should be thoroughly cleansed every day.

CLITORITIS.

Inflammation of the clitoris, both acute and chronic, may exist from want of cleanliness, or be produced by masturbation. It is accompanied with burning, itching, and smarting sensations. Enlargement is the usual result of either acute or chronic inflammation, in which case there is extension of the labia, producing irritation, and labial leucorrhœa.

TREATMENT.—When the parts are inflamed, sitz-baths, hot packs, and laxatives will usually relieve it. In case of hypertrophy, it may be painted once or twice a week with a weak tincture of iodine, and the compound syrup of stillingia given internally. When there is extensive enlargement, amputation should be resorted to.

IMPERFORATE HYMEN.

This is not likely to be discovered until the commencement of menstruation. It may then be suspected, if the female has all the symptoms which accompany the menses, without the discharge of the fluid, and if these symptoms should occur at regular periods, accompanied with a sense of weight and fulness of the vagina, especially if an enlargement is perceptible in the lower abdomen, with pain and tenderness.

The symptoms ameliorate in a few days, but return at each menstrual period. If by inspection a hemispherical tumor, of a livid or bluish color, soft and fluctuating, is discovered, the fact is most certain, that it is caused by an imperforate hymen. In most cases the membrane is thin, but it is sometimes from one-fourth to three-eighths of an inch thick.

TREATMENT.—Press the finger against it gently, and attempt to lacerate it by the finger-nail. If it will not yield, perforation should be made by a proper instrument in the hands of a surgeon.

VAGINITIS.

This consists of either acute or chronic inflammation of the vagina. It may be confined entirely to the mucous membrane, or it may extend to the cellular tissue beneath. It is attended with pain, swelling, and redness of the vaginal canal; the mucous membrane is of a vivid red color, and the folds are more developed and prominent than is natural. At the first stage there is an arrest of the secretions, but after a few days serous exudation occurs, which becomes purulent, and of a yellowish or greenish color. The disease may arise from cold, which is the most frequent cause; from injuries to the vagina by violence, excessive indulgence in sexual intercourse, exertion after delivery, high living, etc.

TREATMENT.—A gentle purgative should be taken, and the vagina frequently injected with warm water, the patient kept quiet, and the inflammation controlled by veratrum. Astringent injections are also useful. The chronic form should be treated as vaginal leucorrhœa.

MENSTRUATION.

Though this is not a disease but a healthy function, but as, from various causes, derangement of the function occurs, it is proper that it should be perfectly understood. Menstruation is the term applied to the phenomenon that attends the rupture of what is called the *Graafian follicles* of the ovary, and the discharge of an ova, or egg. It is a bloody discharge from the female genitals—not differing from ordinary blood, excepting that it does not coagulate, and in its peculiar odor. The blood comes from the capillaries of the womb and vagina.

Menophania, or the first appearance of the menses, is usually preceded by a discharge of a fluid whitish matter from the vagina, by nervous excitement, and by vague pains and heaviness in the loins and thighs; numbness of the limbs, and swelling and hardness of the breasts. The first appearance is an evidence of capacity for conception. It generally appears about the age of fourteen, but varies from nine to twenty-four years. In warm climates women begin to menstruate earlier, and cease sooner than in temperate regions; in the cold climates the reverse of this holds as a general rule. The manifestations of approaching puberty are seen in the development of breasts, the expansion of the hips, the rounded contour of the body and limbs,

development of the voice, and the child becomes reserved, and exchanges her plays for the pursuits of womanhood.

More or less indisposition and irritability also precede each successive recurrence of the menstrual flux, such as headache, lassitude, uneasiness, pain in back, loins, etc. The periods succeed each other usually about every twenty-eight days, although it may occur every twenty-two, twenty, eighteen, fifteen, or thirty-two, thirty-five, and forty days. The most important element is the regularity of the return. In temperate climates each menstrual period ordinarily continues from three to six days, and the quantity lost from four to eight ounces. The menses continue to flow from the period of puberty till the age of forty-five or fifty. At the time of its natural cessation, the flow becomes irregular, and this irregularity is accompanied occasionally with symptoms of dropsy, glandular swellings, etc., constituting the *critical period*, *turn*, or *change of life;* yet it does not appear that mortality is increased by it, as vital statistics show that more men die between forty and fifty than women.

It should be the duty of every mother or female in charge of a child, in whom age or actual manifestations suggest the approach of puberty, to acquaint her with the nature of her visitation, and the importance of her conduct in regard to it. She should be taught that it is perfectly natural to all females at a certain period, and that its arrival necessitates caution on her part with regard to exposure to wet or cold. The author has made the acquaintance of the history of many cases of consumption, and other diseases, which were directly induced by folly and ignorance at the first menstrual flow. The child is often kept in extreme ignorance of the liability of womanhood occurring to her at a certain age, and hence when she observes a flow of blood escaping from a part, the delicacy attached to the locality makes her reticent with regard to inquiry or exposure; she naturally becomes alarmed, and most likely attempts to stanch the flow, with bathing or applying cold water to the part, thus doing incalculable mischief.

This purely feminine physiological function should be well studied and understood by all females. At least they should know that the phenomenon is a natural one, liable to disorder, and that the best interests of their general health demand care and prudence on their part to maintain regularity, etc., of the flow. Disregard of such a duty will surely entail much misery.

AMENORRHŒA.

This may occur in three forms. 1st. Where evacuation has never occurred, or *retention of the menses.* 2d. Where there has been no secretion. 3d. Suppression. There are cases where the secretion has been perfect, but the discharge prevented by occlusion of the vagina, or imperforate hymen, etc.; again, secretion may never have occurred, owing to a congenital deficiency of the ovaries; and there are cases where the uterus and ovaries are sound, yet no flow from the vagina. The most common variety, however, is suppression after they had once been regularly established. It may cease by degrees, as in consumptive and scrofulous patients, or occurs as the result of cold, which induces inflammation of the uterus or ovaries. It may also be induced by excessive venery, wet feet, ice water, insufficient clothing, bathing, fear, grief, anxiety, emetics, drastic purgatives, falls, copulation during flow, etc. The symptoms are weight, pain in the head, loins, and uterine regions, hot skin, apoplexy and epilepsy in some cases, vicarious hemorrhages, palpitation of the heart, constipation, chills, loss of appetite, etc.

TREATMENT.—Give a hot foot-bath, if the suppression be recent, and apply hot mustard poultices to the breasts. Internally give tansy, thyme or wintergreen tea, keep the patient warm, and allow but gentle exercise. A compound decoction of seneca, cotton root, and Indian hemp is also very beneficial. In obstinate cases, a hot sitz-bath should be given during the operation of the medicine, so as to centre the blood in the pelvis. If this does not succeed, the system should be invigorated by quinine, blue cohosh, life root, wine, etc., and then the above treatment repeated. The chronic form of the disease should be treated by supporting and invigorating remedies, such as bayberry, black cohosh, sitz baths, galvanism, tonics, etc.

DYSMENORRHŒA.

Painful menstruation occurs generally in single women, and is produced by inflammation or ulceration of the mouth of the womb, neuralgia of the womb during menstruation, masturbation, constipation, and a nervous irritable temperament. The symptoms are restlessness, heat, flushed face, weight and heaviness in the head, pain in the back, and pelvic regions, sometimes so severe as to cause fainting. After a time the pain becomes bearing down, accompanied by a shreddy discharge, or blood-clots. In young and plethoric subjects, but little effect is produced on the general health, but in nervous persons the health fails, and, not unfrequently, consumption ensues. Women subject to dysmenorrhœa are liable to cancer after the turn of life.

TREATMENT.—When the disease is produced by inflammation or ulceration of the mouth of the womb, hot sitz-baths, with hot vaginal injections frequently repeated, in connection with ten or fifteen drops of the tincture of crawley every two or three hours, will usually relieve it. Mild purges should also be taken. When due to neuralgia, black cohosh should be given, and the treatment of neuralgia instituted. Senecin, gossypiin, and gelsemin, are also valuable. When produced by an irritable constitution, ladies'-slipper, scullcap, etc., should be given. Out-door exercises and a nutritious diet should be prescribed.

MENORRHAGIA.

This is characterized by profuse, prolonged, or two frequent menstruation, separately or conjoined. It is accompanied by headache, hot skin, full pulse, weight in the back, hips, loins, pelvis, etc. It is caused by hot rooms, abortions, leucorrhœa, falls, excessive venery, long walks, constipation, etc. The health gives way, the patient becomes bloodless, and exhaustion ensues upon the least exercise.

TREATMENT.—This should be treated by wild cherry, gelsemin, unicorn root, beth root, and injections of a decoction of golden-seal, matico, and cinchona. If the hemorrhage is active, a strong decoction of tannin or cranesbill may be injected, and ten or fifteen grains of cayenne pepper administered. The oil of erigeron is also useful. Tonics should be given in relaxed condition of the system.

VICARIOUS MENSTRUATION.

This is a discharge from some other part than the uterus, usually occurring in the unmarried. In the married, they are usually barren. The blood may escape from any part of the skin or mucous membrane, in the form of bleeding from the nose, lungs, etc.

TREATMENT.—Ten or fifteen drops of the oil of solidago should be given four or five times a day, in connection with sitz-baths, tonics, etc. Life root is especially valuable.

CHLOROSIS.

This is a disease characterized by chronic anæmia, or bloodlessness, affecting females about the age of puberty. In some instances it is undoubtedly dependent upon a nervous affection, but in most instances it is connected with disordered menstruation and sexual causes The red corpuscles of the blood are pale and small, and diminished in numbers. The countenance assumes a wax-like hue, which is so remarkably characteristic, that the disease is called by nurses "*green sickness.*" The appetite is irregular, with craving for particular kinds of food, the urine is thick and full of sediment, and there is usually vertigo, headache, backache, hysterical affections, dysmenorrhœa, and leucorrhœa. The tongue is flaccid and indented at the edges, the pulse is weak and quick, and there is a feeling of general languor, with great indisposition to bodily or mental exercise.

TREATMENT.—When arising from feeble and imperfect digestion, give prickly ash, alder, golden-seal, and nux vomica, cautiously. The animal oils are also very serviceable. The great object in the treatment in this disease is to restore the general health, and not to force menstruation by agents having that power. The patient wants strength and blood, and when that is achieved, menstruation will be natural. Baths, friction, out-door exercise, and a nutritious diet should not be neglected.

CESSATION OF THE MENSES.

We have already stated that this usually occurs between the ages of forty and fifty, but in some cases it occurs much earlier, in others much later. The courses become irregular, often staying away two or three months. Nausea and vomiting, swelling of the abdomen, tenderness of the breasts, etc., are the prominent symptoms. Pregnancy may sometimes be suspected, and there are frequently uterine pains, a dragging sensation in the back and loins, accompanied by violent headache, a loaded tongue, and symptoms of indigestion. A sudden return of the menses mitigates the symptoms, which usually last longer than is natural, and also more profuse.

TREATMENT.—If the symptoms are slight, regulate the bowels and diet, bathe the surface, and occasionally wear a pack, saturated with equal parts of whiskey and water, upon the lower bowel. If more severe, take unicorn root in decoction. Ladies'-slipper, wafer-ash, and black cohosh, are also very good. The tonics should also be given in debilitated subjects. In fact the constitutional symptoms should be met with such remedies as are indicated, as soon as they manifest themselves.

LEUCORRHŒA.

This is commonly known as the *whites.* It consists of a discharge from the vagina, or inner cavity of the womb, of a catarrhal character, varying in color from a light to a yellowish-green, or reddish-brown. It is usually due to inflammation of the mouth and neck of the womb (*cervicitis*), but it is also caused by congestion and inflammation of the interior membrane of the organ (*endo-cervicitis*), in which case it is more serious, and more difficult to cure. There are few females who are not occasionally subject to moderate leucorrhœa. It may be known by the discharge, but also by the attendant pain and a sense of heaviness in the loins, abdomen, and thighs, disordered digestive functions, palpitation of the heart, etc. It causes great impairment of the general health when long continued.

TREATMENT.—Wear flannels next to the skin, and pay attention to the general health. Keep the pores open by the proper medicines. In acute cases inject cold water, and in chronic, warm water. This will modify the inflammation. After this, injections of a strong decoction of golden-seal, white-oak bark, or cinchona, should be frequently used, and witch-hazel taken internally. Dog-wood, bayberry, black and blue cohosh, and gelsemin, are also used for the same purpose. The astringent injections are also serviceable. Rest and quiet are important in the treatment of the disease. Patients should, however, intrust the treatment to an intelligent physician, who should ascertain the cause, when, if the proper treatment is given, the disease will soon be cured.

ULCERATION OF THE WOMB.

This is chiefly confined to the neck of the organ, occurring most frequently in those who have borne children. It is caused by frequent sexual connection, imprudence during menstruation, as standing, walking, lifting, etc., and very often premature efforts after abortion or labor. There is always more or less discharge associated with ulceration, which in quality is mucous, purulent, or starchy, and in color, milky, greenish, yellowish, or brownish,—often tenacious masses of mucus, like starch, come away. It affects the general health similarly to leucorrhœa.

TREATMENT.—Rest should be observed, and sexual indulgence abandoned. The treatment for leucorrhœa should be instituted. Vaginal injections of red-raspberry leaves and golden-seal prove very beneficial in this disease. The constitutional treatment in this disease is more important than any local applications, and should take precedence.

FALLING OF THE WOMB (PROLAPSUS UTERI).

This is denoted by pain in the back and loins, heat in the vagina, painful copulation, painful and irregular menstruation, constipation and diarrhœa in alternation, irritable bladder, etc. The mouth of the womb can be more readily felt than is natural, feeling spongy and hot, and very tender on pressure. It may be ulcerated, and bleed upon the slightest touch. The patient has all the symptoms of dyspepsia, hysteria, neuralgia, palpitation, cough, and difficulty of breathing. It is directly caused by weakness of the broad and lateral ligaments, and remotely by various causes. It is a disease severe in its effects, causing much suffering and impairment of health.

TREATMENT.—The patient should observe perfect quietude. The inflammation and ulceration of the womb treated as previously described. The womb should be gently replaced to its normal position, the bowels kept open by mild laxatives, and the vagina injected with a warm decoction of hemlock and white oak bark. Pessaries do more harm than good, but abdominal supporters to sustain the weight of the bowels should be worn in all cases. (See page 370)

UTERINE DROPSY (HYDROMETRA).

This is an accumulation of fluid in the womb, caused by inflammation and constitutional debility. During the first months the symptoms resemble those of pregnancy; but by introducing the finger, so as to touch the neck of the womb, and pressing the tumor, fluctuation of fluids is felt. The menses are usually suppressed, and general debility will appear, if the disease continues. The patient may die from exhaustion, or the walls of the womb may be ruptured from the pressure of the fluid, causing fatal peritonitis.

TREATMENT.—A tonic and hygienic treatment should be prescribed, and if you can introduce a catheter into the womb and evacuate the fluid, it should be done, but it is better to intrust this to an able physician.

ANTEVERSION AND RETROVERSION.

If the womb falls forward upon the bladder, and towards the pubes, it constitutes *anteversion.* In this case the top or fundus of the womb is turned forward to the bladder, and the mouth towards the rectum. When the womb falls over backwards, between the rectum and the vagina, it is said to be *retroverted.* In this case the fundus is turned towards the rectum, and the neck towards the bladder. If the womb is anteverted and turned upon itself, it is *anteflexed*, and when retroverted and turned upon itself it is called *retroflexion.* These displacements may occur suddenly or gradually, causing great distress. The usual symptoms are costiveness and straining at stool, frequent urination, painful menstruation, pain in the lumbar region, and down the limbs, neuralgia, hysterics, and nervous debility. It is a serious affection, and should receive early attention and proper treatment.

TREATMENT.—The organ is first to be replaced to its normal position, and then the treatment for falling of the womb instituted. Such important diseases should, however, be confided to the care and direction of a competent physician. Great relief is at all times gained by wearing abdominal supporters.

HYDATIDS.

These consist of a formation of small cysts or bladders of water in the uterus, developed from the inner membrane, and vary in size from half a pear to a partridge's egg. They are usually oval, with a thin wall, opaque, and contain a thin fluid. They are most frequently in clusters, and numerous. The symptoms simulate those of early pregnancy, such as nausea, vomiting, enlargement of the womb, fulness of the breasts, suppression of the menses, etc. In a few months, the patient feels a weight and uneasiness about the abdomen, followed by uterine pains, hemorrhage, and expulsion of the hydatids.

TREATMENT.—If the flooding is excessive, control it by injecting vinegar or astringents and administer ten or fifteen drops of the oil of erigeron every fifteen minutes. If the pain is not sufficient to expel the masses, give a warm infusion of blue cohosh or cotton root. Ergot may also be given. After the expulsion the patient should receive tonic treatment.

PREGNANCY AND ITS ACCIDENTS

PREGNANCY.

The first sign of pregnancy is a cessation of the menstrual flow. This will generally be noticed between two and three weeks after conception, and about the same time the woman will discover her breasts to be enlarging, and notice that the rings around the nipple are darker, and cover more space than usual. She will also, to a greater or lesser degree, experience nausea in the morning, and often be afflicted by vomiting, while she will experience dull pains in the "small" of the back, a decided disinclination for exertion, and considerable nervousness. As the womb increases in size and weight (which becomes apparent between the second and third months after conception), it sinks lower into the cavity of the pelvis (or part of the trunk which bounds the abdomen below), and produces much suffering, especially when the pelvis is small or narrow. After the fourth month, the womb, finding insufficient accommodation in the pelvis, mounts higher, and seeks room in the more capacious and yielding belly. Then the distress in the back, and the sickness and vomiting are somewhat modified, or in some comparatively disappear altogether. When the condition of pregnancy is first discovered, the woman, no matter how robust, should avoid all over-exertion or excitement, and should bear in mind constantly St. Paul's motto of "moderation in all things." A state of indolence is productive of disastrous, or, at least, painful consequences. Judicious exercise, and a determination to be cheerful and contented, will do much towards suppressing the usual annoyances of pregnancy, while moping and idling will increase them, and will almost invariably bring about a hard labor. Thus the poor working woman, providing she does not labor *too* hard, or expose herself imprudently to the vicissitudes of the weather, rarely suffers so much in child-bed as the woman who lives only to be petted and admired, and who seldom breathes the air of heaven in its delicious purity. Among the many incidental afflictions of pregnacy, are costiveness and piles. These are produced by the pressure of the enlarging womb upon the lower bowel. This, becoming filled with hardened matter, in turn presses upon the womb, and endeavors to crowd it out of the way. The combined and continual pressure of the womb and bowel upon the water-pipe, causes great difficulty in making water, and their uninterrupted weight upon the ascending veins produces congestion in the lower bowel, and hence the appearance of painful and disagreeable piles. The stomach and bowels should be kept in the best possible order. To prevent or ameliorate piles, use seidlitz powders every day, and inject into the bowels half a pint of pure cold water every morning. With regard to nausea, if it continues after the first three months, eat nothing but plain, yet nourishing food, and use chamomile flower tea as a beverage.

The habit of swathing or bandaging during any period of pregnancy is decidedly injurious, unless the woman be of a very fragile form and debilitated constitution. The child quickens about the end of the fourth month, when its motions will often produce hysterics and fainting fits, and the mother (for such she then is) becomes peevish, irritable, thin, and weak. Great care must be taken to combat this peevishness and irritability by fixing the mind upon pleasant thoughts, and mixing with lively company, if it be available. It will be as well, too, for the woman to lie down a little while, two or three times a day, and not to remain in an erect position too long without taking a little rest. During the last three months, the woman will generally suffer much uneasiness "all over," and will experience trouble in the attempt to get a perfect night's rest. They should not touch opiates under these circumstances. When varicose swellings of the veins of the legs are produced, a good plan is to wear a laced stocking over the affected parts, and this should be adjusted so as not to press too tightly upon the limb. It should be arranged so that the pressure will be equal throughout its length. Sometimes delicate women have convulsive fits in the last stage of pregnancy. These are dangerous, and no time should be lost in calling in an experienced midwife to take charge of the case. However, a two-grain opium pill administered internally, an injection of warm suds, and mustard plasters applied to the feet, and between the shoulders, will not fail of giving speedy relief. Also bathe the feet in warm water. The habitual use of the warm bath will often prevent these convulsions.

Palpitation of the heart, cramps of the legs and thighs, tooth-ache, puffy swellings, suppression of urine (use parsley tea for this), lethargy and headache are always accompaniments of pregnancy. For cramps and swellings, bathe the parts with warm water and red pepper, or mustard. If the swellings are very troublesome, apply fomentations of bitter herbs. In order to prevent sore nipples (which, if neglected, merge into caked and broken breasts), bathe them daily several times with alum-water, or a decoction of white oak bark. This bathing should be commenced about six weeks before confinement. Fox-glove (digitalis) is recommended by many for palpitation of the heart; but I discountenance its use. A little compound spirits of lavender, in water, and moderate doses of Turkey rhubarb will alleviate the attacks.

All pregnant women should wear flannel drawers and keep the feet warm.

All expectant mothers may greatly render a coming labor more easy and painless, if, at about the eighth month, they thoroughly rub my "Herbal Ointment" (see page 472) externally on the abdomen once a day, and continue until labor, and at about the middle of the ninth month they should lubricate the vagina and womb with the ointment. This has the effect of making the mouth more dilatable, the soft parts more yielding, and consequently a safe and comparatively easy labor.

The time of labor to every expectant mother causes constant solicitude, and scarcely any woman approaches the period fearless of the result, but very anxious as to the suffering or safety of life. In the present condition of civilized woman, we well know that the phenomenon of child-birth is attended with pains of an agonizing character, but that the suffering is mostly owing to habits of life, dress, etc., now characterizing woman, is equally certain. It would be an anomaly in nature if a process, so natural to females as child-birth, was originally ordained to be agonizingly painful, and it is quite evident that the pain now characterizing nearly all cases of labor is an infliction imposed by nature in consequence of violation of some of her laws. We are glad to see intelligent women approaching this subject, and have seen no brighter gleam of sunshine than Mrs. Stanton's recent address at San Francisco, which no false delicacy should prevent being reproduced in every paper in the land. She said, "We must educate our daughters that motherhood is grand, and that God never cursed it. And the curse, if it be a curse, may be rolled off, as man has rolled away the curse of labor, as the curse has been rolled from the descendants of Ham." While saying that her mission among woman was to preach a new gospel, she tells the women that, if they suffer, it is not because they are cursed by God, but because they violate his laws. What an incubus it would take from woman could she be educated to know that the pains of maternity are no curse upon her kind. We know that among Indians the squaws do not suffer in child-birth. They will step aside from the ranks, even on the march, and return in a short time bearing with them the new-born child. What an absurdity, then, to suppose that only enlightened Christian women are cursed. But Mrs. Stanton says that one word of fact is worth a volume of philosophy, and gives her experience as follows: "I am the mother of seven children. My girlhood was spent mostly in the open air. I early imbibed the idea that a girl was just as good as a boy, and I carried it out. I would walk five miles before breakfast, or ride ten on horseback. After I was married I wore my clothing sensibly. The weight hung alone on my shoulders. I never compressed my body out of its natural shape. My first four children were born, and I suffered but very little. I then made up my mind that it was totally unnecessary for me to suffer at all; so I dressed lightly, walked every day, lived as much as possible in the open air, ate no condiments or spices, kept quiet, listened to music, looked at pictures, read poetry. The child was born without a particle of pain. I bathed it and dressed it and it weighed ten and one-half pounds. That same day I dined with the family. Everybody said I would die, but I never had a relapse or a moment's inconvenience from it. I know this is not being delicate and refined, but if you would be vigorous and healthy in spite of the diseases of your ancestors and your own disregard of nature's laws, try."

While we heartily endorse all that Mrs. Stanton has said in this matter, we could not advise every mother to "dine with the family" on the day of her labor. It would be an exceedingly dangerous proceeding; but if every woman would be willing to practise the same initiatory training, which is so healthful, because in accordance with physiological laws, there is probably no doubt but that she would also be able to "wash her own baby" and "dine with the family," on even as substantial a dish as pork and beans.

PUERPERAL FEVER.

Child-bed fever is a very fatal disease, and frequently follows parturition. Scrofulous women are peculiarly liable to it. The disease manifests itself in every degree of intensity. The usual symptoms are weight and soreness in the lower part of the abdomen, accompanied by lassitude and debility, capricious appetite, imperfect after-discharge, spongy condition of the gums, constipation, and scanty and high-colored urine. These symptoms continue for two or three days after delivery, when the patient will be seized with chills and rigors. These are soon followed by a hot and pungent skin, pain in the head, nausea, and sometimes vomiting. The pulse becomes hard and quick, respiration rapid, the secretions are arrested, and the pain centres in the lower part of the abdomen and becomes very severe. The bowels are bloated, and very tender, and the lochia or after-discharge is entirely suppressed. In many cases delirium is present, also agitation and a sense of impending death. The worst form is when it presents the appearance of malignant scarlet fever.

TREATMENT.—The bowels should be freely opened with a purgative, after which opium should be administered in tolerably large doses. Warm slippery-elm emulsions should be frequently injected into the vagina, with a view to bring on the lochial discharge. The fever is to be controlled by aconite or veratrum. Tonic stimulants and carminatives should be used, according as the disease shows excitement or depression. In the low form, quinine and camphor are indicated. In the gangrenous form, put charcoal and yeast poultices to the abdomen, and give a decoction of wild indigo in wine and yeast four or five times a day.

Inversion of the Uterus.

This may be partial or complete. When partial, it may be known by the absence of the fundus or top of the womb behind the pubic bones, and the presence of a large solid tumor in the vagina, accompanied by profuse hemorrhage, intense pain in the pelvis, violent straining, vomiting, fainting, cold clammy sweat, and feeble pulse. Complete inversion is recognized by the presence of a reddish livid tumor filling the vagina, and protruding beyond it. It may occur spontaneously in atony of the womb, or from irregular contractions, or it may be caused by violence in extracting the after-birth, shortness of the cord, delivery in the upright position, tumors, etc.

Treatment.—Watch the tumor carefully, and at the moment when there is no contraction, the fundus should be pressed with one finger, and indented like the bottom of a bottle, and make continued pressure until reposition is sure. Then control the hemorrhage, if any is present, with ice to the pelvis, or vinegar injections, and give stimulants if the patient is exhausted.

Miscarriage.

Miscarriage signifies the expulsion of the fœtus from the uterus, before it is sufficiently developed. The causes may be either natural or violent. Among the most prevalent causes, are mercury, constitutional syphilis, either in the father or mother, small pox, sudden and violent excitement of the blood-vessels by surprise, fright, anger, etc. It may also be caused by disease of the embryo, disease of the afterbirth, or direct violence to the abdomen. If it occurs in the early stage, the patient feels languid, uneasy and despondent, and is troubled with alternate chills and flashes of heat; there is nausea, palpitation, pain in the back, and tenderness over the abdomen. The breasts become flabby, and there is more or less hemorrhage. In the more advanced stages, the pains are more severe, and frequently the hemorrhage is so violent that the life of the patient is endangered, unless the proper remedial agents are employed. If miscarriage occurs once, it is liable to recurrence, and hence pregnant women should be very careful.

Treatment.—Those predisposed to miscarriage should carefully avoid purgatives and diuretics, should indulge in no violent exercise, and take a cold sitz-bath every morning on rising, followed by brisk friction with a crash towel. Unicorn root and bayberry should also be taken internally. The pain should be subdued by hyoscyamus, and the hemorrhage checked by the oil of erigeron, or cayenne pepper and matico may be taken. If miscarriage, however, defies this treatment, a physician of ability and reputation should be at once consulted, who will, by his personal attendance, be able to prescribe such remedies as the exigences of the case may require. During convalescence the patient's strength should be maintained to prevent weakness of the womb.

INFLAMMATION AND ABSCESS OF THE BREASTS.

During and after pregnancy the breasts are very liable to become inflamed and sore. The patient shivers, has pain in the head, loss of appetite, is constipated, and her urine is high-colored, and pulse quick. The breasts become red, painful, and swollen, and if the inflammation is allowed to continue, an abscess is formed, which, sooner or later, opens and discharges. Cold during nursing, accumulation of milk, injuries, diseases of the womb, scrofula, etc., are the principal causes.

TREATMENT.—Subdue the inflammation by applying the following:—Take arnica flowers, ℥ j.; lobelia leaves, ℥ ss.; hops, ℥ ij. Make a strong decoction, and apply cloths wrung from it hot as the patient can bear, and repeat every fifteen or twenty minutes. A small dose of aconite may be given internally to control the fever. A mild purgative should also be taken, and if the patient is debilitated, the general tonics should be exhibited. If the abscess, however, will occur, it should be opened, and then poulticed with slippery-elm. For *caked breasts*, apply hot packs, and change them frequently, and between each application bathe the breasts with a liniment composed of equal parts of lime water, sweet-oil, spirits of camphor, and oil of horsemint.

SORE NIPPLES.

This is one of the most common and troublesome difficulties connected with the breasts, after child-birth. It is very frequently caused by want of cleanliness on the part of the mother or child.

TREATMENT.—Wash with castile soap and warm water after each nursing of the child, and then sprinkle the nipple with very fine powdered hemlock bark. Or make and use the following ointment:—Take balsam of fir, ʒ j.; white wax, ʒ ij.; melt together, then add ten grains each of tannin and powdered bayberry. Apply this as often as necessary, previously washing the breasts. Cover the nipple with folds of linen during the intervals of nursing. My Herbal Ointment (page 472), is a speedy cure for this painful affection.

Relaxation of the Abdominal Muscles

One of the most frequent sequels of pregnancy is a permanent relaxation of the abdominal muscles, more or less in degree. The abdomen becomes pendulous, occasioning great inconvenience, suffering, and often inducing malposition of the womb, and other affections.

The only way to remedy this relaxed condition is by artificial support, which is to be kept up until the muscles have again attained their full powers of contraction. Ladies are therefore in the habit of wearing bandages, though these but inadequately supply the necessary support, owing to the difficulty of proper application, so as to secure the equalization of pressure, and the stability of position, necessary. Mechanical appliances should only be used for the purpose of support. These are called *abdominal supporters.* Decidedly the best supporter is the one represented in the cut, an appliance so arranged as to supply the firmest support by means of elastic springs. It gives no uneasiness to the wearer; on the contrary it affords the most comfortable support, enabling the sufferer, who before could scarcely walk, to do so with the utmost facility, occasioning no pain or inconvenience. Supporters are absolutely necessary in all cases, as no medicinal treatment will overcome the relaxation, on account of the constant superimposed pressure of the bowels. These supporters should also be worn in all cases of uterine misplacements, as they afford the greatest relief, and serve as an almost indispensable adjunct to the required medicinal treatment.

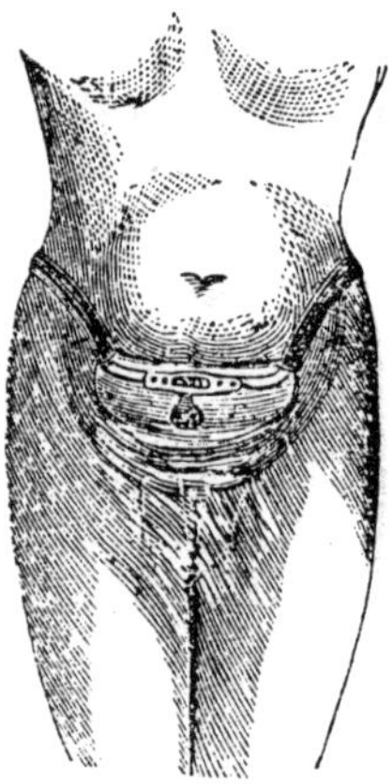

Prof. O. Phelps Brown's Abdominal Supporter.

Another supporter, represented by the adjoining cut, is also a meritorious one, having many excellent qualities. It is especially well adapted to corpulent females. Equality of support under all circumstances is gained by an elastic band in the pad at front. These supporters are the result of thorough study as to the requirements of such appliances, and the author is convinced that they are the best articles for the purpose designed. Their many qualities will at once be apparent both to the professional man or to the patient. Ladies, in need of supporters, may address the author for further particulars. (See page 398)

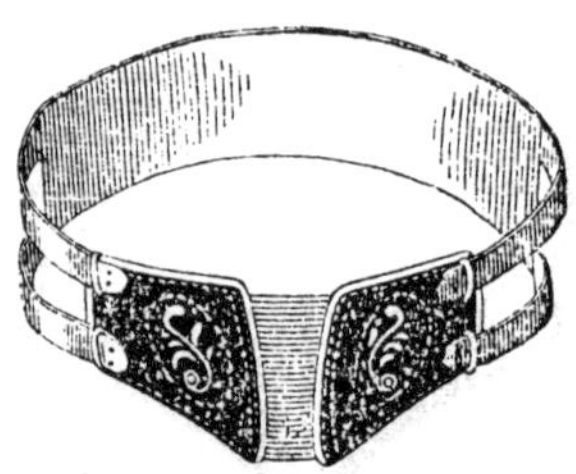

Abdominal Supporter.

The Conduct of a case of Labor.

This should never be attempted except by a physician or competent midwife, but, as it may sometimes take place in railroad cars, in voyages, etc., the duty may fall to the lot of almost any woman or man, and hence it is important that they should know how to proceed. These hints may also be useful to perhaps many in the backwoods, where the population is scarce, and where the nearest doctor lives "a day's journey" away.

How do you Know that the Patient is in Labor?

This the mother frequently knows herself, but she may sometimes be deceived by what are *spurious pains*. If she is in labor, she will have what is called "*come and go*" pains, which at first are moderate and wide apart, but which finally become more intense and succeed each other at shorter intervals. She will describe those as *bearing down* pains, and frequently they are so severe as to cause cries and gestures, the former being of a mourning or complaining character, the other twisting and writhing. She will also have a mucous discharge from the vagina, which is called a "*show.*" She will probably wish to void her urine often, and to relieve her bowels, which should be encouraged. During this stage the mouth of the womb is dilating. Now it will be well for you to pass your finger well up into the vagina, and you will most probably find that the mouth of the womb is dilated, and in extent it depends upon the time at which you may make the examination. When the pains become "thick and fast," you may again make an examination, and you will probably find a fluctuating tumor, which is the *bag of waters*. If this does not burst itself, you may rupture it with your finger, but do not allow yourself to be frightened at the forcible rush of the waters. If you have withdrawn your hand, you may again insert it, and you will most likely find the head about descending into the vagina. If it is the head or breech it will be a natural labor (which I hope it may always be, for I do not believe I could teach you how to proceed in what is called a *preternatural* labor). If the head is there, all right. You may give the soon-to-be-mother your hand, or you may tie a sheet to the bed-post and let her pull at that, or if her husband is present, or if you are he himself, let her press him around the neck whenever an expulsive pain occurs. This will greatly aid her, and you do not know how thankful a woman is in such a case, when she observes apparent assistance on your part. After a few *good* pains, the head of the child will be born, and then the worst is over, for usually one pain more will cause the birth of the whole child.

What will You do Next?

As soon as it is born, you will probably hear the child gasp and cry which is caused by pain ensuing upon sudden expansion of its lungs. If it does not do this, take the child, and shake it gently, give it a few slaps on the buttocks, and empty its mouth of any secretions that may be found there. By doing this, the child may soon cry—when it is all right. If, however, it should not be so easily resuscitated, sprinkle a little water on its face, and if it looks blue in the face, cut the cord, and let it bleed a little; then put your mouth to that of the baby, and while holding its nose shut, blow your own breath into it and fill its lungs, and then press gently on its chest, in imitation of expiration. Do this as long as there is any hope, and your efforts may often be crowned with success. We will suppose, however, that the baby is a struggling, crying, healthy darling. Then, as soon as you do no longer feel the cord pulsate, you can separate it from the mother. To do this take a few strands of thread and tie it round the cord, not so tight as to cut through, about two inches away from the navel. Then take a pair of scissors and cut the cord through about half an inch away from the ligature, not on the side, however, towards the navel; you can put two ligatures on the cord, if you like, and cut between them. Then take the baby away, but be careful how you do it, or else an accident may befall you, and hand it to the proper person to be washed and dressed. The baby is very slippery, so take it up in this way: put its neck between the thumb and forefinger of your left hand, and put the palm of the right under its buttocks; you then have it secure, but do not be too anxious about its safety, or you might choke it

What Next?

You must now pay attention to the exhausted but joyous mother, rejoiced that she has passed such an agony of pain as you can form no conception of, such that you have never felt and never can feel, unless you have been or will be a mother, and yet she will now greet you with a sweet, smiling countenance. Her anxiety, however, is not over until she is relieved of the after-birth. By the time that you have got through with your duty to the baby, you will probably find the after-birth expelled into the vagina, by the *after-pains*. If such is the case, take the cord and pull gently downwards and a little upwards, but by no means pull so hard as to tear the cord, or invert the womb If it will not come, wait, and in a short time try again, and you will most probably find it to come away readily. If you should find her *flooding*, take a rag, saturate it with vinegar, or take a lemon, divest it of its rind, and then pass it into the womb and squeeze it. This causes contraction of the organ, and stops the hemorrhage. You may also apply ice to the spine for this purpose, and if you have ergot in the house, give a pretty large dose of that. After delivery of the after-birth, take a towel, and pass it around the pelvis of the mother, and bind it pretty tightly; cover her up warmly, and allow her to sleep, and so recover strength, as you may suppose that she is very much exhausted by this time.

YOUR WORK IS NOT DONE YET.

The baby has to be washed. This is a tedious job, unless you know how to proceed. All babies are covered with more or less unctuous matter, and this should be removed, or else it is liable to get a skin disease. After you have got your rag (a soft woollen one is the best) and some pretty warm water, smear the child over with pure lard or sweet oil, and then use castile soap and water, and you will soon have it clean. Be careful, however, not to get soap into its eyes, or else you will have to treat it in a few days after for sore eyes. Now you have got it clean, but you must not put on its clothes, until you have dressed the navel, and put on its *belly-band.* To dress the navel, take a well-worn cotton rag, cut it into patches of about four inches in diameter, take three or four of these and cut a hole through the middle of them. Cut also a little bandage, half an inch wide, and wrap it round the navel string, then slip it through the patches, and lay the string pointing towards the left shoulder. Now, put on the woollen belly-band, moderately tight, and secure it with needle and thread, not with pins. You may think this caution unnecessary, but if you had seen as many torn limbs and deep scratches in infants as I have, you would not think so. After this you can put on its whole toilet, and lay it in its proper warm nest--its mother's arms.

But you may think the baby is *hungry*, and that it needs some physic; so you give it some gruel, and follow this up either with castor oil and sugar, molasses, or butter and sugar made into a paste, and force them down the little victim's throat. I say victim, because you could not easily do more harm, and yet this abomination is done every day. If the mother has milk, put it at the breast as soon as you can; if not, let it wait until she has,—it won't starve. It needs no purgative, for the *colostrum* or first of the milk is by nature designed as a laxative, and if it gets that, it will soon have the *black stools*, or discharge of *meconium*, as doctors call it. By no means give it soothing syrups nor spirits, nor put a cap on it, or wash it with spirits. If you take my advice in this matter, the baby will be the better for it, and there will not be a necessity, which is so often the case, of the early exchange of its little dresses for a tiny shroud.

In about twelve hours after delivery the mother may be cleansed, and her bed changed, and light food given to her. She should remain in bed for at least ten days, after which, if she feels strong, she may sit up, but should avoid exertion. If she has insufficient milk, follow advice given on page 328.

Lochia.

For some time after child-bearing, a discharge takes place from the womb which is called lochia. It is at first red; but if all goes well, in a few days the red appearance subsides and gives place to an effusion of a greenish color and a peculiar odor. When the womb is reduced to its original size, the lochia ceases. If it is checked before it should be—and in some women it ought to continue a month—or if the flow proceeds with irregularity, great distress and danger are the consequences. The immoderate flow of the lochia is not so disastrous as the suppression. The latter may be produced by cold, by chilled drink, by mental excitement, or, in fact, by any undue exertion of either mind or body. The results of the suppression of the lochia are great fever, restlessness, heat, pain in the head, back, and loins, delirium, inflammation of the womb, colic pains, costiveness, nervous excitability, muscular contractions, and, in fact, general distress. The first and only thing to be done is to restore the flow. For this purpose, if the patient can bear it, the warm bath must be used; fomentations should be applied to the abdomen; large emollient injections should be given in the rectum, and sudorific medicines (not of a mineral character), assisted by copious diluent drinks, should be administered. The acetate of ammonia will be found very useful. A profuse and general perspiration is the precursor of rapid recovery and safety. While the lochia is apparent the patient must not endeavor to get up, or to undergo any noticeable degree of exertion, or be exposed either to atmospherical changes, or imprudence in diet.

THE TREATMENT IN ACCIDENTS.

The treatment of fractures, dislocations, etc., should always be intrusted to the surgeon, but the emergency of such cases may be so great in certain instances that a few minutes' delay might prove fatal to the patient. Hence I will attempt to instruct the reader how to proceed and what to do *before the doctor comes*. In all cases where surgical help can be procured, it should be done as quickly as possible, but dangerous accidents may occur where surgical aid is impossible to procure, and, therefore, the treatment devolves upon others.

Wounds.

In case of wood-choppers, hunters, etc., away in the backwoods, or in any other case where this precaution is necessary, they should provide themselves always with bandages, Monsel's solution, and a roll of adhesive plaster, and then they are prepared for nearly all cases of accidents that may befall them.

The worst feature about a wound is the bleeding, unless, as in case of gun-shot wound, a vital part is injured. We will suppose, however, that unfortunately one received a wound, either from some sharp instrument, or a gun-shot wound, or some part of his body was lacerated, contused or punctured from some cause, and that the wound was bleeding freely. Before the wound is dressed the character of the bleeding is to be noticed. If the blood is dark-colored and flows regularly in a stream, it is venous blood, and you will be able to control it easily; but if it is bright-scarlet, and spurts out in jets, some artery has been wounded—always a dangerous accident. If the wound is a gun-shot one and received in the trunk, all you can do on the moment is to hermetically seal the wound. Take the adhesive plaster, and cut a piece from it large enough to cover the wound well, and then apply over the wound so as to seal it effectually against escape of blood or entrance of air; or take a rag and shape it in a pledget, and tie it on the wound firmly with a bandage or handkerchief. If internal hemorrhage occurs, you cannot do anything, and the patient will probably die.

If the wound is in the arms or legs, then you can always do something. If the bleeding is venous, you will be able to arrest it by applying cold water. Elevate the limb, and use compression. If this does not arrest it, apply some of the Monsel's Solution, which is a solution of the persulphate of iron, which quickly stanches the blood by coagulation. After the hemorrhage has ceased, apply a bandage. If the blood comes out in jets, you may know that an artery is wounded, and that no time is to be lost. No styptics will arrest hemorrhage from any important artery, but in such cases instantly apply the Spanish windlass, which is made by tying a handkerchief around the limb, and twisting it with a stick, until the hemorrhage ceases. This compression is to be maintained, until the patient can have the attention of a surgeon. Be careful, however, to apply the windlass above the wound towards the heart.

If you have to deal with any ordinary wound, cut, etc., draw the edges together with strips of adhesive plaster, and put on cold water dressings.

FRACTURES.

These accidents often happen where no surgical aid can be conveniently procured. Any one can easily detect a broken bone by the person not being able to raise the limb, by its bending where it ought not, by pain, and by *crepitation*, or crackling sound if the parts are moved. When the bone is merely separated into two parts it is called a *simple* fracture; when an open wound communicates with the fracture it is called *compound;* when the bone is broken into numerous fragments, it is termed *comminuted*, and *complicated* when attended with dislocation, laceration of large vessels, etc.

HEAD.

The bones of the head and face are liable to be broken by blows, falls, etc., and need immediate medical attendance. All you can do before the arrival of the surgeon, is to raise the head, apply cold water, avoid all noise and excitement, and arrest the bleeding by the means heretofore advised.

COLLAR BONE.

This bone is usually broken by violence upon the shoulder, arm, and hand. It is generally broken near the middle of the bone, the part is painful and swollen, and every attempt at motion produces pain; the shoulder is sunken and drawn towards the breast-bone. The patient usually is found supporting the arm with his hand, to relieve the pressure upon the sensitive network of nerves in the armpit.

TREATMENT.—Push the shoulder backwards, and press on the seat of fracture, until you get it in its place. Then make a wedge-shaped pad, and put it in the armpit and secure it there by a bandage, which surrounds the chest. Then bring the elbow to the side, and place the fore-arm in a sling; then take bandages, and secure the whole arm so tightly in that position that it cannot be moved. The surgeon may then be called, or, if the above advice is properly and effectually obeyed, the cure will be a good one.

BROKEN RIBS.

This is known by pain when the patient breathes, or on pressure where the injury has taken place. Crepitation is also felt when the hand is placed over the part during respiration or coughing, and if the pleura is injured, the chest swells, or emphysema appears.

TREATMENT.—If the broken ends project, apply a compress over it; if there is a depression, a compress is to be placed at each extremity. If there is a bruise, apply hot fomentations; then take a bandage six or eight inches wide, and draw it tightly around the chest over the injured part. This gives great relief, as it prevents expansion of the chest in respiration, and holds the broken ends in opposition. Keeping this bandage firmly applied is all that need be done in the way of treatment.

FRACTURE OF THE HUMERUS.

This is the bone between the elbow and shoulder. It may be detected by the ordinary methods.

TREATMENT.—Place the bones in apposition, making sure that it is right, by comparing it with the sound arm. Then take four splints, and put one in front, one behind, and one on each side of the arm. Secure these with a bandage. This dressing will do, until better attention can be given to it by a competent doctor. Place the arm in a sling.

Fracture of the Bones of the Forearm.

There are two bones here, the radius and ulna. They may both be fractured, or only one of them. The fracture is easily detected.

Treatment.—The difficulty here is to observe the space between the bones, which is called the *interosseous* space. The fracture is readily reduced by drawing the arm forwards, and when this is done, press the muscles into the interosseous space. Now, take two splints, well padded on the inside, reaching from the elbow beyond the fingers, put one on the inside and the other on the outside of the forearm, and secure them with a bandage. The arm should be carried in a sling.

Fracture of the Bones in the Hand, Foot, or Ankle.

These solid bones are almost always wounded by such accidents that tend to crush them, as machinery, threshing machines, heavy weights falling on them, etc.

Treatment.—Dress the open wound as any other, then cover the whole hand in several folds of rag, or handkerchief, dipped in cold water.

Fracture at the Hip-Joint.

This is a very serious accident, and liable to occur in aged people. One that receives this injury cannot stand or rise from the ground. If the patient is placed upright the injured limb will be found much shorter than the other, and the foot turned outwards. What is called osseous union rarely if ever occurs in this fracture.

Treatment.—In old persons support the limb by pillows and restrain all motion. This is all you can do. In other cases, make two splints, one reaching from the arm-pit to about six inches longer than the foot, the other from between the legs, extending to the same length. Pad these well, especially at the upper ends. Apply them to the inner and outer side of the leg and secure them with a bandage. Now make a foot-board with two mortised holes in it, through which the splints can pass. Bore holes in the lower ends of the splints every half inch. Put on the foot-board, and attach the foot to it firmly, then pull the foot-board down so as to stretch the leg well, for this secures what is called *extension*, which is necessary in these cases. The splints resting against the arm-pit and perinæum affords what is called *counter-extension*. See in all cases that you have the leg straight.

Fracture of the Thigh-Bone.

Fracture of the shaft of this bone is easily recognized by shortening, crepitation, etc., and you should treat it just the same as advised in the fracture of this bone at the hip-joint. If this fracture should occur away from home, in the fields or elsewhere, get some stiff straw, or bits of very thin board, or if you have a "stove-pipe" hat take that, knock out the crown, take off the rim, and split it up at the sides. Bind these around the limb rather tightly with suspenders, handkerchiefs, or tear your shirt up for bandages. Then you can safely remove the patient to a place where he may receive the proper treatment.

Fracture of the Cap of the Knee or Patella.

This may be broken by muscular contractions or direct violence. Falling on the knee very frequently produces it. There is no crepitation felt in this fracture. The pain is not very severe, but the limb is partially bent, and the patient has no power to extend it.

Treatment.—Keep down the swelling with lotions, etc., and then, by means of strips of adhesive plaster, draw the fragments together and retain them firmly in that position. Prevent motion by putting a long splint on the back of the leg.

Fracture of the Leg.

There are two bones below the knee, the *tibia* and *fibula*, and a fracture, occurring in one or both of them from a fall or direct violence, is a frequent accident, the tibia being most frequently broken. The signs are evident. Crepitation, pain, want of motion, etc., declare it.

Treatment.—When both bones are broken, or when the fibula alone, or when the upper part of the fibula is fractured, the best and most simple apparatus is the fracture-box and pillow. Make a box considerably wider than the leg, with only one end board, and that considerably higher than the sides of the box—the box has no lid. Put a pillow, or little bags of chaff or bran in this; put the broken leg into this; see that it fits well; then secure the foot to the foot-board, so as to prevent lateral inclination.

The great object in the treatment of fractures is to keep the broken ends well together, or in apposition, and keep them there. Nature will do the healing part. In bandaging limbs, be careful that you get them smoothly on the parts, and make allowances for the swelling which occurs. If a bandage is formed too tight, it should be removed, or else mortification of the limb will ensue.

DISLOCATIONS.

The signs of limbs being out of joint are deformity, swelling, and a hollow where none should be, shortening or elongation, pain and immobility of the limb.

Broken Neck, or Back.

This is nearly always accompanied by a fracture. It may be produced by convulsions, falls, hanging, etc. The chances of life are small, on account of injury done to the spinal marrow, or the action of the diaphragm may be suspended by compression of the phrenic nerve.

TREATMENT.—Lay the person (if in the neck) on his back, plant your knees on the patient's shoulders, grasp the head firmly, pull gently, and at the same time put the head into its proper place; but this must be properly and gently done, or else you may do great harm. If in the back, do nothing.

DISLOCATION OF THE JAW.

This is often caused by yawning, by convulsions, or by blows on the chin, when the mouth is wide open. The mouth gapes and cannot be shut, the saliva trickles, there is great pain, and the patient cannot talk.

TREATMENT.—Seat the patient on a low stool, stand in front of him, and then press your thumbs upon the last molar or grinding teeth very firmly. Be careful, however, to have your thumbs well protected with wrappings, or else you may be severely bitten. By doing this you get the articular ends of the jaw-bone from their unnatural position, and reduction is caused by the normal action of the muscles. When you hear the *snap*, you may be sure that the bone is in its proper position. After reduction, the chin should be confined by a bandage for a week or ten days.

DISLOCATION AT THE SHOULDER.

This may be displaced in three directions, viz.: inwards, downwards and backwards. By comparing the injured with the sound shoulder, you may be able to tell that it is a dislocation. Where the head of the bone ought to be, you will find a depression, and you will most likely find a tumor, near the breast, in the arm-pit, or towards the back, according to the manner of dislocation.

TREATMENT.—Lay the person on his back, and sit down beside him on the injured side, and put a round pad in the arm-pit. Then take off your boot, put your foot against the pad, grasp the patient's arm, or tie a towel to it, put it around your neck, and pull in that way. Then while you pull at the arm and push with your foot, tell the patient to turn round, or you may carry the arm across his chest. While this is done, a snap will be heard, and the bone is in its proper place.

DISLOCATIONS AT THE ELBOW.

When both radius and ulna are dislocated, the forearm is bent nearly at a right angle, and is immovable. When the ulna alone is dislocated, there is a tumor projecting posteriorly, the elbow is bent at right angles, and the forearm is turned upwards. The radius is dislocated at the elbow either forwards or backwards. When backwards the head of the bone forms a prominence behind, the arm is bent and the hand prone.

When forwards there is a distinct prominence in front, the arm is slightly bent, and the hand supine.

TREATMENT.—When both bones are dislocated, or in case the ulna is alone out of joint, make forcible extension of the forearm over your knee, placed at the elbow, to make counter-extension. Then bend the forearm while making extension, and reduction will take place. In forward dislocation of the radius make forcible extension, and while doing so, turn the hand from without inwards, called pronation. In backward dislocation make forcible extension, and turn the hand from within outward, or supination. In either case you should press the head of the bone into proper position with your thumb. Then advise rest, cold applications, and a sling.

DISLOCATIONS AT THE WRIST.

The luxation of both bones of the forearm from the bones of the hand is rare. When it occurs forward there is a great projection in front, and the hand is bent backwards; when backwards, the projection is behind, and the hand is flexed. If the radius alone is dislocated the hand will be somewhat twisted. If the ulna is dislocated, it may be easily recognized by a projection on the back of the wrist.

TREATMENT.—The reduction of both bones is effected by making extension and pressure. If either of the bones are dislocated, the reduction is performed in the same manner. Pain, swelling, and stiffness of the joint may follow, which should be obviated by cold applications, rest, lotions, etc., and a light splint may be applied to prevent its recurrence.

DISLOCATION OF THE BONES OF THE HAND.

Displacement of the bones of the carpus or body of the hand rarely occurs. The bones of the fingers are occasionally dislocated, but more frequently the thumb is dislocated backwards.

TREATMENT.—Make extension in a curved line, by means of a narrow bandage or tape, firmly applied by a close-hitch upon the finger.

DISLOCATION OF THE RIBS.

Dislocation of the ribs from the spinal column may sometimes occur by severe falls, or blows upon the back, and from the breast bone, by violent bending of the body backwards. Great pain and difficulty of breathing follow in either case.

TREATMENT.—Tell the patient to take a deep inspiration, and slightly bend the body backwards, and while he does this, make some pressure on the projecting point. After reduction treat the same as for broken ribs.

Dislocation at the Hip.

In this case the leg is shortened and the foot is turned *inwards.* It may be dislocated in five different ways;—upwards and backwards is, however, the most common dislocation. In all cases you may know that displacement has occurred, by comparison with the articulated limb.

Treatment.—The accident is so serious that no attempt should be made at reduction, except by a surgeon, but if it happens when no such aid can be procured, you may proceed as in dislocation of the shoulder. If you cannot make sufficient extension in that way, you may attach pulleys to a towel fastened above the knee, and make counter-extension by means of a folded sheet in the perinæum. After full extension is accomplished, push the head into the socket, or so manipulate the leg that its movements will force reduction. After reduction, the patient should be kept at rest, and walking should not be attempted for several weeks.

Dislocation of the Knee-cap.

This may be dislocated in various directions. It is characterized by the leg being stretched, and a prominence formed by the patella in an abnormal situation.

Treatment.—Raise the patient's leg and rest it upon your shoulder. While in this position, force the bone into its place with the hand.

Dislocation at the Ankle.

This may be forwards, backwards, inwards and outwards, and are the results of severe force. The bones' ends are usually fractured at the same time. It is a very serious accident, and when it occurs to patients whose constitutions are bad amputation may often be necessary.

Treatment.—Reduction is effected by bending at the knee, and while in that position, drawing the foot forwards.

In all cases of dislocations and fracture communicating with joints, the danger is anchylosis or stiffness of the joints. This is to be obviated by what is called *passive motion*, which is to be instituted in all cases, a few weeks after the accident. It is accomplished by taking hold of the limb and moving it in natural directions, as far as consistent, and repeated after suitable intervals. The patient is to be enjoined, also, when practicable, to exercise his limb at the wounded articulation. There are many other fractures and dislocations that I have not spoken of, for the reason that they are all so serious that the treatment should only be attempted by those having the proper anatomical knowledge and surgical skill.

PREVENTION OF EPIDEMIC DISEASES.

The alarming fatality consequent upon an epidemic reign of disease demands the closest scrutiny upon the part of communities, large or small, to guard against its approach or prevalence. Medical skill is unable to cope with the fearful onslaught of epidemics, and in many cases epidemic diseases are of so violent a character that the most vigorous constitutions succumb to the assault, and the profoundest medical skill and most rational medical treatment are unavailing. It is questionable if medical science will ever be able to materially decrease the rate of mortality that usually ensues upon epidemic reign; the subtle ethereal poison causing epidemics being of too violent a character to allow ascendency to be gained by material medicinal agents. Since it is questionable that mastery can be gained by medicinal or therapeutic agents, the proper remedy is suggested, not by investigating the best agents of cure, but in measures of prevention, as the author is quite certain that by proper knowledge and concerted action the spread of an epidemic can be limited, and its onset prevented. Epidemic diseases belong to the class which has been conveniently but inaccurately designated "zymotic." They are generated, according to the most modern physiological doctrine, by a specific poison, introduced into the body from without, which is capable of causing morbid changes in the blood, and of destroying life. The poisons of various epidemic diseases are distinct *inter se;* the contagion of typhus, for instance, being altogether different from that of small-pox, and the contagion of cholera from that of diphtheria, and yet it is plain that they are all somehow related, and capable of gradual transmutation from one type into another. Some ancient types have died out—the black-death, the sweating sickness, and the plague; but new types, undescribed by the old physicians, have arisen. We are able to note remarkable "waves of disease;" at one time the great mortality is from typhus, at another from small-pox, at another from scarlatina. In England they have recently had a succession of epidemic. The outbreak of cholera in 1866 was followed by typhoid fever, and as the latter began to abate in violence, scarlatina appeared in the most malignant form, and attacked the metropolis. This disease had begun a year and a half ago to decline in London, but at the same time it began to spread through other parts of the kingdom, where it has since raged destructively. A little later than the scarlatina, relapsing fever, which has been rare in these countries since 1849, broke out with great severity, also attacking London first, and, when it had spent its force there, extending itself into the provincial towns. Lastly, they have been visited with an epidemic of small-pox more severe than any outbreak of that disease which has been recorded in England during the present generation. And no sooner has the small-pox begun to abate its violence than they are threatened with a return of cholera. This periodicity of disease is yet to be explained; but it is established that, given the same conditions for the reception and propagation of contagion, about the same proportion of lives will be carried away, whether the prevailing epidemic be scarlet fever or typhus, or relapsing fever or small-pox.

The blood-poisoning of the zymotic diseases, which is thus various and changing in type, is traceable, however, to the same class of causes. In some epidemics the germs of contagion are far more volatile than in others, but, in all, we know by experience that, if we can isolate the patient and submit his immediate surroundings to disinfectant agents, we check the spread of the disorder.

Pure air and pure water are irreconcilably hostile to contagious disease. The first duty, therefore, of sanitary administration is the enforcement of effective ventilation, the supply of a fixed quantity of fresh air to every person in every house. This is an innovation which will of course be resisted both by ignorance and self-interest, but no infraction of real liberty will be committed in preventing ignorant or self-interested persons from doing mischief to the community by sowing the seeds of disease broadcast. The next step in the work of prevention is to insist upon a free and well-distributed system of sewers to carry away at once from every habitation the impurities which poison the air, and which, even when they do not directly propagate contagion, insidiously weaken the constitution of those subjected to their influence and prepare them for the reception of the germs of disease. Most country villages and many small towns are almost wholly destitute of systematic drainage, and cesspools, which are the commonest substitutions, are merely traps for infection. The enforcement of drainage and the abolition of cesspools are reforms which experience has shown will never be carried out by the local authorities, and is especially an improvement which ought to be and can be carried by pressure from a strong central executive office. A third precaution is systematic disinfection, not only of everything connected with and surrounding a person suffering from contagious disease, but of all places where dirt unavoidably accumulates, and whence at any time effluvium can be perceived to proceed.

These precautions, however, though valuable in themselves, and also as tending to effect the further object to which we are now able to refer, are quite unavailing unless supplemented by securities for a pure supply of water. Cholera, as we have seen, is held to be propagated almost exclusively through polluted water, and there is scarcely a form of epidemic that is not to some extent disseminated in the same way.

We have stated that it is doubtful if sanitary reform can ever be properly enforced by local authority, and hence advocate that its requirement should be insisted upon by national statutes. The health of any country is as much a principle of political economy as its freedom, and just as worthy, if not more so, of vigilance; and it is to be hoped that the day is not far distant when legislators in every land will see the absolute necessity to enact such laws rendering thorough disinfection and drainage obligatory upon all its citizens. Physicians have long advocated so desirable a reform, and neglected no opportunity to teach the people the virtue of and benefits to be derived from disinfection; but the absence of any epidemic gives a false sense of security, and the advices are unheeded until the deathly blast of the epidemic is upon them, when their folly is exposed and the wisdom of precaution established.

Of the disinfectants, the following are the best:—Chloride of lime, Labarraque's solution, carbolic acid, and bromo-chloralum. Chlorine gas is probably the best, but not so practicable for universal use. Most of them are comparatively cheap, and no household should be without a sufficient quantity.

All cesspools, sinks, etc., should be thoroughly disinfected whenever they become offensive and exhale noxious vapors, and no pools of stagnant water or other filthy places should be permitted to remain undrained for any space of time. If such a desirable reform could become of universal operation, the reign of epidemics would be over and become things of the past.

AUSCULTATION.

This term is applied to the medium of ascertaining the nature and locality of a disease by sound, which can be elicited in two forms, viz., either by the stethoscope, or by percussion; auscul tation is almost invariably adopted for diseases of the chest. It is occasionally used to the abdomen, to diagnose if any enlargement in that locality is due to the existence of wind or water. It is a generally accepted fact that Lænacc made the stethoscope practically available for the investigation of diseases by hearing, and since his days an entire change has taken place in the relative tests for a correct diagnosis in diseases of the chest, and those of the other exceptional few referred to occurring elsewhere, by auscultation. It is much to be regretted that science has not yet, even in this advanced age of scheming, invented a medium by means of which the nature of diseases in the head and abdomen could be determined with a similar proportionate approach to certainty, although the contents of the thorax are beyond the reach of the sense of touch, nevertheless they are now within the limits of the sense of hearing. The lungs occupy the major portion of the chest, and when in a healthy condition, possess a loose spongy feel. The texture of the lungs is made up by a series of cells, some millions in number by computation, like a honey-comb, each connected together by loose cellular tissues. The cells are filled with air, and the consequence of this is, when a moderate tap or blow (percussion) is given upon the ribs, a sound is elicited, varying in intensity and kind to that which would be heard if the lungs were solid bodies. The healthy chest has, by percussion, a uniform resonance, and any variation to this demonstrates the existence of disease; and to ascertain with greater precision its nature and seat, the stethoscope is called into requisition. It may be advantageous to explain what the stethoscope is. It is generally a hollow tube of wood, some a solid, about nine inches in length, and saucer-shaped at each end, and the sounds dependant upon the passing into, and out of, the lungs, pass up the instrument to the ear. The sounds vary according to the nature of the disease. The sounds may be either thos· of air, dry ones, or those of a fluid or rattle, moist ones. The sounds due to the heart's action are very different, and do not depend upon air, but are exclusively attributable to the action of the heart and the circulation of the blood through its different chambers and valves. By percussion, that is, tapping with the fingers over the left side of the chest—the region of the heart—a dull sound is emitted, thus showing the absence of air; and if this dulness exists over a larger space than usual, and attended with other corresponding morbid signs, it shows the probable existence of enlargement of the heart. Enough has now been mentioned for popular purposes about respiratory and cardiac auscultation, both by percussion and the stethoscope, relating to the lungs and heart, the importance of which to a physician, when judiciously applied, cannot be adequately expressed in language, but it may be advantageous to name also concisely that the voice emits various sounds in health and disease, by aid of the stethoscope, which materially assists the physician in determining the character of disease. It would be useless to mention the numerous healthy and diseased sounds of the lungs due to respiration, percussion, and the voice; or of those of the heart, due to percussion or the stethoscope, as they could not be rendered sufficiently explanatory, unless the anatomy and physiology of the various viscera were thoroughly understood, and this is unnecessary for the general purposes indicated in a book which is used only as a public guide to health, and not professionally.

There is a difference of opinion relating to the manner whereby sound is transmitted from the chest to the ear by the stethoscope Some authorities assert that sound is conveyed by the walls of the instrument when a hollow one is used; others declare that sound is propagated by the column of confined air within the stethoscope; hence the reason why some physicians use hollow instruments, whilst others use solid ones; but practically there is, however, little if any real difference.

URINARY DEPOSITS.

Although diseases of the bladder, gravel, &c., and their treatment, have been dilated upon respectively in other parts of the work, practically nevertheless, as diseases of the kidneys and bladder, arising from these deposits, and their fatal tendency, are so common, it is advisable to explain here more fully their character and formation theoretically.

Urinary Deposits.—It is an acknowledged fact, professionally, that fresh urine voided by a healthy person is usually more or less acid, and the acidity is the greatest in urine passed before meals, and it is the least during the digestive process. This is supposed to depend not upon the existence of a free acid, but of some super salts of the alkaline or earthy bases which the urine contains. Both sulphuric and muriatic acids are present in urine, in an extremely diluted condition, of course; but the acids which are generally sought for are uric (lithic) and phosphatic, not only from the great abundance of the former, but because also either acid would be liable to be set free, by uric acid entering more readily into combination with some alkaline or earthy base which the urine contains. The acids do not exist in a free state in healthy urine, but as previously mentioned, in the form of a salt. The usual alkaline bases are soda and ammonia, and the earthy base is lime. The character, formation, and microscopical appearances of urinary deposits vary, as also do the symptoms and treatment. The pinkish sediment in urine is due to lithic acid, and this is the most common kind, and is abundantly demonstrated in the urine of an invalid, when afflicted with acute rheumatism. The whitish sediment is the result of a combination of the phosphates with lime, this kind is usually seen in the urine of persons of advanced age, or in those who have suffered from continuous mental anxiety, or in those whose avocations impose a lasting strain upon the nervous system, thereby incurring a great loss of neurine energy. It is very easy to understand the treatment of lithic deposits, by the administration of alkalies such as saline draughts, the citrate of potash, bicarbonate of potash, or of soda, and the dietetic, in abstinence from acids, and all substances likely to become so. To promote also the removal of acid from the skin, and the free evolution of carbonic acid by the lungs, is an indication of much greater importance; for this object moderate exercise should be used.

In the treatment of whitish deposits a cure will be quickest accomplished by moderate exercise, cessation from labour, especially that of a mental nature, nutritious diet, tonics, sedatives, and the employment of the mind in various forms, either by travelling, music, scenery, &c.

There are other, but very rare, both soluble and insoluble, deposits detected in the urine by chemical tests, and some are observable to the naked eye, whilst a few are only perceptible by the aid of a microscope; these being of such uncommon occurrence, need no further practical comment than a mere mention of their existence.

ANALYSIS OF HEALTHY URINE.

In 1,000 parts.

Water	933·00
Urea (a peculiar compound of Oxygen, Hydrogen, Nitrogen, and Carbon)	30·10
Lactic Acid and Lactate of Ammonia	17·14
Lithic Acid	1·00
Mucus of the Bladder	0·32
Sulphate of Potassa	3·07
Sulphate of Soda	3·16
Phosphate of Soda	2·94
Biphosphate of Ammonia	1·65
Chloride of Sodium	4·45
Hydrochlorate of Ammonia	1·50
Phosphate of Lime and Magnesia....	1·00
Silica	0·03
	1,000·00

Shehberger ascertained the time which several substances take to pass into the kidneys, by experimenting upon a boy who had *inversio vesicæ*, and formed the following table of the results:—

Substance.	Time when first detected in Urine.	Time when it ceased to be perceptible.
Madder	in 15 minutes	in 9 hours.
Indigo	in 15 „	in 4½ „
Rhubarb	in 20 „	in 6⅓ „
Logwood	in 25 „	in 6¾ „

TREATMENT OF CHRONIC DISEASES.

THE AUTHOR'S SPECIALTY.

IMPORTANT TO THE SUFFERING SICK, MALE OR FEMALE.

Chronic Diseases are those that have passed the active or inflammatory stage. Strictly speaking, a disease is not curable until it has passed this stage and become to a certain extent "chronic." The word means "time," and any disease that has had time to pass the active stage, "chronic." The tendency of chronic affections is to recover, and nine out of ten will recover by proper attention to hygienic laws and the right medicine. It would be imprudent, in case of a severe attack of illness, to trust recovery to nature, without availing ourselves of medical advice; without in fact ascertaining the proper remedy, which is surely to be found somewhere in the herbal kingdom. In all cases of chronic disease, a careful diagnosis is absolutely required, as each case is usually accompanied by a variety of sympathetic disorders; hence, it requires the educated and experienced physician to note the variations, detect the complications and identify the locality and extent of the real disorder. Patient and intelligent investigation is absolutely requisite in all cases, as without such a diagnosis the treatment would not be successful.

My specialty is the treatment of chronic disease. I very rarely give advice, unless specially and urgently solicited, with reference to acute affections, and never essay treatment unless the affections be of specific or scrofulous origin, as private diseases, acute phthisis, etc. Aside from these exceptional cases, my professional attention and services are entirely absorbed in the treatment of chronic diseases, and these I can justly claim to treat with unvarying success. This assertion is certainly pardonable when the fact of my success is attested by thousands of former patients in all parts of the world. Early in my professional career it became apparent to me that only as a specialist can any physician hope for either competence or success. Aware of the folly of the attempt to become equally skilful in the treatment of both acute and chronic affections, I made chronic diseases exclusively my study, and devoted for many years all the energies at command in the endeavour to acquaint myself with all the varied and multiform manifestations. No physician, unless he be a prodigy of science, can with equal success treat both acute and chronic affections. If he is animated with the principles of professional integrity, striving to gain absolute competence, he has no time to investigate the characteristics of chronic diseases, should he even have the inclination. The "family physician" deals mostly with acute affections; hence it is necessary to his professional success and reputation to devote his sole attention to the study of acute disorders. It is well known that the highest perfection of mechanism demands the division of labour into special branches, and so it is with the practice of medicine—division into specialties secures greater intelligence, competence, and success of treatment.

It is not necessary that I should particularize each disease for which my advice may be solicited, or for the treatment of which my services may be engaged. I may be consulted with reference to every existing chronic disorder, claiming the requisite ability to give definite and conclusive advice, and provide treatment invariably successful in result, if in my estimation the affection is capable of cure.

Chronic affections are so numerous that the author will allude to the more important only, and such as are fearfully prevalent and destructive.

In the female economy we meet with exceptional diseases not observable in the opposite sex. She, too, by many obscure causes, may sadly destroy her health and capacities of womanhood, and in which condition the same vigilance should be exercised, and the same efficient and reliable medical counsellor should be appealed to. The physical degeneracy is the same, and special treatment no less important than in the analogous condition of the male. Besides this sad affection she suffers untold agony with what are termed *Uterine Diseases.* Vital statisticians assert that there scarcely exists a female in civilized life who does not suffer with uterine disorder at some time of her life, and that as a rule every female is at all times, more or less a sufferer from the womb disease. Why is woman thus fearfully a sufferer? Is it altogether owing to injurious modes of dress, habits of life, and other agencies? Is it not possible that this prevalence of uterine diseases is partially owing to inefficient and irrational treatment? If treatment were competent, this load of suffering would certainly be lighter. These diseases have surely no such pathological character as to render treatment unavailing, and that all that physicians can do is to pronounce them *incurable.*

Proper internal medication in combination with proper hygienic observance, will affect a cure in nearly, if not all, uterine disorders. The long continued suffering, so generally the history of all uterine diseases, is due more to harsh and inappropriate treatment than to any peculiar severity or stubbornness in the morbid elements of the affections themselves. Under proper and skilful treatment, Leucorrhœa, Ulceration, Prolapsus, or Falling of the Womb, the various misplacements of the organ, menstrual disorders, etc., yield kindly, and a cure is speedily effected in all cases.

Diseases affecting the Reproductive System in the male sex are actually the gravest of all, and attended with more sad results than any in the whole catalogue of human afflictions. Their very apparent mildness gives to them a twofold capacity for undermining the constitution and destroying the integrity of the general health, by imperceptible losses through the water or fluids of the body. Patients, before writing, will please save a little of this water in a bottle for twenty-four hours. Write me if there is any sediment, of the colour and quantity, as it will save much loss of time. This disguised or negative feature is always associated with those diseases depending upon disorders of the generative organs, many of which are contracted by dissipated or vicious habits indulged in to a greater or less extent, and patients, though long aware of their indisposition, are not fully conscious of the nature or seriousness of their disease until health is completely broken, the constitution wrecked, and the vitality and vigour of the nervous system utterly destroyed. Long before this one may know that all is not right, but owing to a false delicacy, neglect to employ competent treatment.

Chronic Impotency is one of the most deplorable conditions with which mankind can possibly be afflicted.

Now my success in the treatment of conditions of this class, warrants me in saying that it is just as surely amenable to judicious, well-directed treatment, in accordance with its true pathological character, as any other curable abnormal condition of the sexual organization. The great reason why these diseases have so seldom been successfully treated by the great mass of the profession is, that their pathology has not been properly studied or investigated, and consequently not understood.

The sacral plexus of nerves (with one branch from the lumbar), are the nerves which supply the sexual organization with its vitality.

The sensory nerves convey from the base of the brain, or cerebellum, impressions to these nerve centres, and it is through them that nature asserts its power.

To explain a little more minutely. Whenever a passionate, lascivious thought, or sight, or impression in any form occurs, the sensory nerves convey the impression to the sacral ganglia, and if this nerve centre is active and vigorous, natural results will surely follow; but if it has become atonied, or if it has lost its vitality, of course it cannot act under the impression conveyed to it by the sensory nerves, and this is what constitutes Impotency.

Now, of course, specific medicines, or medicines which have a direct affinity for, or act as a direct stimulus to these nerves, are the only remedies that can be depended upon to restore this lost vitality. Such remedies I claim to make use of in conditions of this class, and my success has proved them to be reliable whenever my directions and instructions have been followed, and my treatment pursued for a reasonable length of time. The specific action of some remedies is too well known to be disputed; quinine, iron, antiseptics, and many others belong to this class.

Now the great majority of diseases we are obliged to treat on general principles, as specifics for all diseases have not yet been discovered; but general treatment would be of no use whatever in conditions of this class; positive, specific treatment is the only available course, and this is what I claim my treatment to be.

It is true, that congenital conditions, or malformations, or organic diseases of the sexual system, may render some cases incurable by any method of treatment, but these cases are extremely rare.

SYPHILIS, that terrible scourge of our large cities, is another disease in which the superiority, nay, even the absolute necessity of specific medication has been clearly established. This formidable disease has assumed alarming proportions in our country, and at this time it cannot be said to be confined to our cities only; for plainly, the rural districts are not exempt from the foul taint. It is its constitutional, secondary and tertiary forms that more particularly demand my attention, and which I am constantly treating with such uniform success. Were this disease confined to its primary stage, it would not be the hydra-headed monster that it now is, but unfortunately its ravages are unlimited; every tissue of the body becomes involved in rapid succession. The throat becomes ulcerated, rendering the breath intolerably offensive; next the glandular system—the glands of the neck; then the cartilaginous tissues, especially of the nose, which soon sinks upon a level with the face, as though it had been battered with a mallet, and finally the bones themselves become spongy, and exostoses supervenes. It would require a large volume to fully describe the ravages of this disease. The number of generations through which it is capable of propagating itself by hereditary descent is unknown—probably unlimited. My specific treatment for the constitutional, secondary and tertiary forms of this disease, may be relied upon with positive certainty to eliminate every particle of this specific contagion from the system, no matter of how long standing.

CHRONIC URINARY DISEASES. This class of diseases has become

alarmingly prevalent in our country, especially among the labouring or active business men of middle age, and those far advanced in years. Diabetes in both its forms, albuminuria, or Bright's disease, ardor urinæ, or irritable bladder; abnormal deposits in the urine; and in the aged, inability to retain the urine, with frequent desire to void it, which when voided flows in a dribbling manner; partial paralysis of the bladder, characterized by inability to evacuate it without considerable effort, accompanied with frequent and sudden cessations of the flow; calculous or gravelly obstructions, etc.

I have made these conditions a special study for years, and I can safely affirm that there are but few cases of this class of diseases that specific medication by nature's remedies will fail to relieve; and I know from experience that there is no class of diseases in which the superiority of specific vegetable medicine is more clearly manifested than in chronic urinary difficulties of every form and type. I have hundreds of testimonials in my possession, conclusively establishing this fact.

CATARRH. This formidable disease is located, primarily, in the pituitary membrane which lines the nasal fossa, and extends to the different cavities communicating with the nose. It is composed of two layers, one fibrous, which is attached to the bones; the other, free and secretory—the seat of smell. This membrane lines all the sinuses of the maxilliary, frontal and ethmoidal bones, and its mucous surface is the primary seat of the catarrhal inflammation, but the fibrous portion is soon involved, and then the discharge becomes pustular and fetid, while all the bones to which this fibrous portion of the membrane is attached become affected, and caries, or slow destruction of the osseous tissues, supervenes; the breath becomes intolerable, and sooner or later all the air passages to and within the lungs become involved; so you can readily see how extensive a disease catarrh is, and how preposterous the idea that a little of somebody's snuff will remove the specific inflammation from all these tortuous winding air-passages, which are so extensive as to make the patient who is badly afflicted with this disease feel as though his whole face was fairly rotten with it. Both local and general treatment of a specific character must positively be resorted to, to remove the septic inflammation, and restore all the tissues to a normal condition.

Specific local treatment, by means of Dr. Lane's Catarrh Cure, and the exhibition of general remedies, which through the circulation and absorbent vessels act as specifics to inflamed mucous membranes, is positively the only reliable treatment for this distressing malady.

My supreme confidence in the healing virtues of herbal medicines was gained only by observing their superiority, and not born of prejudice or antipathy; for in the first few years devoted to the study of medicine, I was taught as others are, to regard the employment of mineral agents as right and advisable. Experience only gave me better knowledge and fuller understanding, and at the present time, should the privilege of employing the medicinal properties of plants be taken away from me, leaving me but the inert and harmful minerals, my professional knowledge would avail me nothing, and I would stand in the presence of disease with fettered hands, helpless as a child, and absolutely without power to mitigate or relieve a single pain or symptom.

I think I can truthfully say that no physician at the present time is treating so many chronic cases as myself. I have for twenty years advertised very largely in all the leading newspapers of the country. I print upwards of three million Shakesperian Almanacs annually for gratuitous distribution. There has been 450,000 "Complete Herbalists" sold within the last twelve years. As I have said before, my specialty has been chronic diseases.

Thousands are led to consult me and my associate physicians for relief, which, owing to our large experience in certain class of complaints, we can guarantee to cure in almost every case. I advertise my family medicines through the chemists, and sell them largely. I I am obliged to have associate physicians to assist me, owing to my business being so large.

All invalids write us unhesitatingly just as they feel in special cases—thus giving us a perfect description of their cases, which enables us to be more successful than we otherwise could be.

Afflicted persons desirous of gaining my advice should give a plain statement of their afflictions; when contracted, the present symptoms, etc.—in fact, everything should be made known to me precisely as would occur by personal interview. The following questions are intended to assist invalids in properly presenting their cases. Answers to all the questions are not necessary.

QUESTIONS FOR REFERENCE.

Designed for those who wish to Consult me with a view to Treatment.

A. What is your age? If known, what is your temperament? Did you arrive at the age of puberty without having had any serious illness or sufficiently so to injure your constitution?

B. Are you afflicted with any chronic form of eruptive diseases? If so, what are its characteristics? Is it scaly or papular (pimples, or pustular) secreting pus? If papular, is it attended with any secretion in the pimples? If so, is the secretion watery? If pustular, do scabs form? Do the scabs drop off and new ones form immediately, or do the pustules heal? What is the colour of these?

C. Is there any hereditary disease in your family, recent or remote?

D. Are you very nervous? If so, can you assign any cause for it? Have you overtaxed yourself with study, or with mental or physical exertion of any kind? Have you any mental trouble? Is your memory or capacity for mental pursuits impaired? Is your sleep disturbed by frightful dreams, or dreams of any kind? If your business through the day has been perplexing, is your sleep disturbed and unrefreshing in consequence of it?

E. Have you any congenital diseases or condition of any kind? that is, any diseased or abnormal condition with which you have been afflicted from birth?

F. Have you always been temperate in your habits? Do you indulge or have you indulged in the use of spirituous liquors of any kind to excess, or of opium in any form, or tobacco?

G. Are you subject to severe attacks of headache, or do you frequently have a dull, heavy, oppressed feeling in the head? If you have either, at what part of the head is the pain most severe, or what part of the head is most liable to attacks of pain? Are you troubled with dizziness of the head, ringing noises in the ears, or specks before the eyes?

H. Have you a disagreeable taste in the mouth, especially in the morning? Are the gums healthy, or are they becoming absorbed, leaving the teeth long and naked? If the latter, do you know whether it is the result of the use of mercury, or of vitiated secretions? Is the tongue coated? Are its tip and edges very red?

I. Do you have any disease of the throat? Are the tonsils very liable to become inflamed and enlarged, causing difficult deglutition? and are you especially liable during cold weather to contract what is called a sore throat?

J. Are you afflicted with a chronic cough? if so, for what length of time have you been troubled with it? At what time of the day do you cough most? Is coughing attended with pain in any part of the chest? if so, what part? Does it cause pain in any part of the chest to inhale a full breath? Have you constant pain in any part of the chest? Is it increased by coughing, and is it always confined to one locality? Do you expectorate much? What is the character of the expectoration? Is it thick and adherent, or is it of a mucous character? Does it sink in water? Do you have turns of perspiring freely at night? Do your feet and ankles swell? and is the swelling edematous?—that is, does it pit on the removal of pressure of the thumb?

K. Do you have any pains or fluttering sensations about the heart? if so, are they constant, or do they come and go at intervals? Do you have palpitation, attended with difficulty of breathing? if so, is it constant or at intervals? If at intervals, of what length of time generally?

L. Is your appetite and digestion good? Are you troubled with collections of wind in the stomach? Does food distress you? if so, what kind of food distresses you most? Does a meat diet give you more pain than a farinaceous one? Do very hot or very cold drinks give you pain in the stomach? Are you constipated? and are you troubled with piles?

M. Have you any pain or weakness in the lower part of your back? Is the voiding of urine attended with pain or smarting? Are you obliged to void it more frequently than is natural? and is it normal in quantity? Does the urine deposit a sediment? if so, what is the character of it?

N. Do you have any rheumatic or neuralgic pains in any part of your body? Are any of the tendons of the extremities contracted? Are you troubled with cramps in the lower extremities when in bed?

O. If a male, have you injured yourself by excesses of any kind, recent or remote. Have you now, or have you had varicocele?

It is not necessary for me to insert here questions which the patient will readily see are inadmissible for a work of this kind, but which are, nevertheless, of great importance; and he can forestall me in this matter by giving me all the information in relation to his condition that will occur to him as being necessary to aid me in forming a correct opinion—the only sure guide to correct and successful treatment.

P. If a female, are you afflicted with uterine derangement in any form—prolapsus, leucorrhœa, ulceration, etc.? Have you passed the climacteric period? If not, is menstruation regular, and normal in quantity and quality? Is it ever attended with severe pain?

Any intelligent female will readily see the absolute necessity that exists for an unreserved history of her case, and a plain statement of the causes which have led her to consult me with a view to obtaining relief.

No false modesty should deter any from making known their exact condition, so that I may be enabled to fully understand the pathology of the case, and to prescribe just what is required to effect the most speedy and decisive results. **It is not necessary by any means that answers to all these questions be given.** The most prominent features of the case are all that I require. It is frequently the case that ladies, in describing their condition, give great prominence to unimportant or merely sympathetic symptoms—slight neuralgic pains in various parts, headache, nervousness, restlessness, and transient or migratory pains—and entirely neglect to say anything about the one great cause of all these unpleasant and sometimes most distressing symptoms—uterine derangement, or an abnormal condition in some form of the sexual organization. No important organ of the body is more intimately connected with the whole sympathetic nervous system, or exercises a greater influence over the other important organs, stomach, liver, lungs and head, and particularly the nerve centres, than the uterus; and when I am told that a lady is suffering from uterine derangement in any form, I know that she is also suffering from many unpleasant, if not distressing sympathetic symptoms. I do not wish to be considered egotistical at all, but after a long and extensive experience, I can positively affirm, that if there is any particular class of diseases in the treatment of which my greatest successes have been achieved, it is in the treatment of diseases incident to females, which have become so prevalent in our country, and which I contend are, as a general thing, treated irrationally, and without any claim to success. While, perhaps, one has been benefitted by the harsh heroic treatment so extensively practised by every medical Tyro at the present time, hundreds have been seriously and permanently injured. My unusual success in the treatment of diseases of this class ought to be sufficient evidence of their curability by a more rational and entirely harmless method of treatment.

In writing for advice, give legibly the post-office, town, and county to which you wish your answer directed, and if medicines are ordered, the name of the station to which they are to be sent.

Remittances should be made in Post Office Money Orders (payable at London General P.O.), wherever there is a Money Order Office. which is now almost universal, there being only a few exceptions. Where these exceptions do exist, REGISTER THE LETTER containing money. Either one of these modes is PERFECTLY SAFE, the Postmaster always giving you a receipt for the money. MEDICINES will not under any circumstances be sent on credit. The Parcel Delivery business has reached *such perfection* within the last few years, that I can almost guarantee a DAILY DELIVERY to every hamlet in the United Kingdom.

ALL LETTERS WILL BE TREATED AS STRICTLY PRIVATE AND CONFIDENTIAL. Invalids on a visit to London may call on me whenever convenient. Office Hours, 10 A.M. to 4 P.M.

Address Prof O. PHELPS BROWN,
61, Chandos Street, Covent Garden, London.

PART III.

THE PHILOSOPHY OF THE SEXES.

Admitting the delicacy of the subject, it is, however, eminently within the province of the medical writer to teach the scientific bearings of the marital prerogative of the sexes, inasmuch as health, as well as civilization, is greatly dependent upon the purity of that relation. While I condemn such literature which is elementarily and purposely suggestive, I have but little sympathy with that prudish modesty which is outraged by everything appertaining to the special characteristics of sex. The author shall, in the consideration of the subject, not attempt to offend healthy conservatism, yet, at the same time, the subject is too important to discuss it with undue reserve or by unintelligent circumlocution. The essays are not written to gratify immoral curiosity, but to edify those who wish to learn and be governed by the correct principles of the philosophy appertaining to the marital union of the sexes. And as this work is specially intended to educate the popular, and not the professional mind, it is proper and quite consonant with every moral consideration, that it should contain such general knowledge as all should know for proper guidance in matters pertaining to the organs of reproduction.

Anatomy of the Male Generative Organs.

If this work was intended exclusively for professional purposes, it would have been quite necessary to give, *in extenso*, the anatomy of the elementary parts entering into the formation of the Male Genitals, and likewise their extraordinary physiological functions, so beautifully adapted for procreative purposes, but as the book is issued simply as a popular Medical Guide, the details of such anatomy cannot here be given, without necessitating the use of such language which would be considered indelicate and unsuited to the public. And supposing that the anatomical parts were demonstrated, the author doubts much whether the reader would understand it sufficiently, unless he were in a dissecting room, and had the parts referred to shown to him in progressive order. Suffice it to say, that there is no distinction between these organs and those of the opposite sex; only in the latter the organs are internal, that is, within the body, whilst in the former (the male) they are external.

Diseases of those parts, from natural, unnatural, infectious, and other causes, are too numerous to dilate upon here, but are dwelt upon elsewhere in the work both fully and explicitly.

Anatomy of the Female Generative Organs.

The same reasons as those given under the head of the preceding chapter are applicable likewise here for the suppression of indelicate explanatory matter, as would be absolutely necessary to demonstrate the organs popularly within the limits of this work, ordained as it is, viz., "A Family Medical Herbal Register."

In excluding such professional language, only useful to the surgeon, the author is sanguine that, apart from the little which would be gained from a knowledge of the anatomy of these parts, if they had been enumerated, it is more than amply compensated for in other parts of the work by a useful record of facts more suited to the public, and appreciated accordingly, referring as it does to all peculiarities and specialities of these organs in both sexes; many of which, it is needless to say, create a vast amount of groundless alarm and apprehension.

Some years ago—but thanks to the Society for the Suppression of Vice—works were published only with the view to intimidate the weak, and with the ulterior mercenary motive of extorting money, under the base garb of a friendly medical monitor, by alluding to some special and confidential matters peculiar to these organs in adults of either sex, in such revolting language, and exaggerating their respective results to a most disgraceful and incorrect extent.

Social Status of the Procreative Organs.

We have now but very briefly, though sufficiently, referred to the genital organs with the same composure and desire to instruct, as when we described the anatomy of the other organs, and I am sure that all of my correct-minded readers have read the same with equal equanimity and desire to learn. It is altogether owing to a false and foolish modesty that everything descriptive of the anatomical differences of the sexes is declared to be indelicate or obscene; but, as previously stated, the anatomy of these parts is quite unnecessary for popular purposes, hence the omission. It is only obscene when used to awaken and excite the imagination to dwell on amatory objects, and not when used for the purposes of legitimate instruction as in these pages. Extreme reticence with regard to matters referring to the genital part of the economy is not always indicative of a pure modesty or continence, nor is it healthy conservatism, but often the promoter of disease and imbecility. This fact leads me to have no sympathy with any prudish illiberality, but forcibly impresses me with the great necessity existing for instruction and enlightenment relative to this part of the economy. I will therefore break loose from the trammels of prudery, and attempt, in a measure, to properly inform my readers, in a discreet manner, if not anatomically, of all the bearings of philosophy relative to the economy of the genitalia, in the succeeding pages. Knowledge of this kind, in obeisance to a proscriptive spirit, is now isolated within a narrow precinct of intelligence, while the demands of the highest welfare of humanity are urgent for universal dissemination. Medical men have long been aware of the necessity of popularising intelligence relative to this subject, but lacked the wisdom to ignore the illiberal countenance that banished it within their own limits of intelligence. If any medical knowledge is worthy of popular acceptance and guidance, it is that pertaining to the genital part of the economy; on no other subject are unprofessional people so ignorant, and no other species of ignorance is conducive to greater misfortunes.

Discussion of this subject in the decorous language of science in a popular work, will not lead to lewdness nor encourage lechery; on the contrary, my convictions are that such information as will be imparted will tend to give a healthy tone to modesty, and encourage continence. This is my purpose, all others I ignore and condemn.

Excessive modesty is often the offspring of ignorance. The physician who is fully acquainted with the anatomy and physiology of the generative organs, finds nothing suggestive in such knowledge; it is to him as common place as the anatomy and physiology of other parts of the economy. And if unprofessional people possessed a proper knowledge of the anatomical features and physiological functions of the reproductive system, any decent and necessary allusion to any part of the same would not be regarded as indelicate or offensive. Such intelligence is not subversive of the moral nature, nor provocative of impure thought; the conventional illiberality deemed proper by certain people, is far more hurtful than judicious instruction. Knowledge with reference to the human economy is capable of great injury if permitted to be buried, and this is as true of the organs in the pelvis as of those in the thoracic region. We should all know, and not be ashamed to admit, when admission is proper and right, that Nature completed her work in case of our own persons; injudicious reservation in this respect does a great deal of harm, as it often obliges the unfortunate to suffer in secret with serious affections, the locality of which makes them ashamed or unwilling to confide in those whose counsels may be of benefit. Few parents have the wisdom to take their children in their confidence, and teach them the evils consequent on solitary indulgence, and but few mothers acquaint their daughters with the phenomenon of womanhood before its appearance. The son is unwilling to seek the counsel of his father, and the daughter does not avail herself of her mother's wisdom and experience. It is the experience of every medical man whose practice extends largely among females, that questions concerning the integrity of the organs in the pelvic cavity are unwillingly answered. What young female is willing to entrust to her medical attendant the knowledge of her disordered menstruation? She refuses to answer his questions, and probably hides her chlorotic face under the bed clothes. The doctor only gains the truth after he is taken to another room, where the mother or nurse acquaints him with the fact. This round-about way of imparting the required information, places the patient in an embarrassing attitude towards her physician, and it would be far better for her own welfare and individual independence did she herself state the fact, and freely and composedly answer the interrogations of her medical attendant. Who can admire the sickly modesty of Dr. Abernethy's patient, who enveloped her wrist in a linen handkerchief before she would permit him to ascertain the condition of her pulse. The Doctor, however, gave the proper rebuke, for he immediately put his hand in his coat-tail, and remarked that "a linen patient requires a woollen physician." Those of the author's sex are also very often uncomfortable in the physician's presence, if questioned with regard to diseases of the generative organs. This is radically wrong, for such timidity and unwillingness induces the patient to defer medical treatment until absolutely driven to it by the extreme gravity the affection assumes. Modesty is an admirable virtue, as far as social intercourse is concerned, but under circumstances requiring medical aid or counsel, the re-establishment of the organs to healthy physiological action should not be embarrassed by a diseased modesty, or timid and foolish reservation. As this work is intended to bear a relation to the reader the same as the physician does to his patient, it is hoped that the knowledge contained in these essays will receive commendation instead of condemnation, that they will be considerably read by all who have need of such intelligence; and that errors of habit may be abandoned, and the proper observance of the laws of health respecting the generative organs be followed instead.

In conclusion, I hope there are not many of my readers who are offended with Nature for making us distinct as to sex, and who endeavour to remedy her mistakes by hushing up the fact altogether.

Preservation of the Health of those Organs.

Complete health of the organs is necessary to the full vigour of the general economy, and it should be the aim and desire of all to maintain the vigor of the genitalia. The male delights in the shapely figure of the person of the female, the full development of her bust, and the vivacity of her spirits, all indicative of a healthy genitalia; and the female takes pride in the male who presents the evidences of a vigorous manhood. This is a natural selection, and no one is indifferent to it.

The greatest requirement is *cleanliness*. Ablutions of these parts should be more frequent than of the body in general. We have seen that in the male the secretion peculiar to these parts is accumulating incessantly. Besides, the locality conduces to an almost constant perspiration. The surface is also studded with numerous sebaceous follicles, whose secretions become quickly very offensive. If these secretions are not removed, they will impede the full development of the organ, as well as abridge their natural functional qualifications. They should therefore be daily cleansed. Cold water is preferable, as it is more stimulating, and possesses greater onic properties than tepid or warm water.

In the female the excessive secretions render cleanliness very important. The vaginal secretions should not be allowed to accumulate at the orifice, as they soon become offensive, and if re-absorbed, impair the general health. There are also many sebaceous follicles, whose secretions should be frequently removed by ablutions. Besides, the urine which passes through the external parts adds constantly to the uncleanly state. It is therefore very important that the parts should be frequently washed, omitting, however, cold water ablutions during the menstrual period.

Nothing is capable of doing greater harm than excesses of any kind, and those organs should not be indulged by any unnatural means. It is promotive of disease, destructive of manhood and healthy womanhood, and, if early engaged in, arrests the full development of the organs of either sex, and so reduces the strength of these organs, that it renders them incapacitated for the purposes which were ordained to them by nature, besides wrecking the nervous system very materially. It is well known that those who have thus been imprudent, having so long been accustomed to excesses of any kind, induce a peculiar and apprehensive weakness of these parts. They have so long been accustomed to the gratification induced by their own electricity, that the magnetism of another body becomes more or less inert in the production of a complete orgasm. The habit is morally and physically pernicious, and its prevalence should be abated by influence of a superior education in these matters.

Undue excitement of the important passion is detrimental in the extreme. Obscene literature and pictures do more harm than merely depraving the moral tastes—they so stimulate the amative passions, that the organs, by the consequent nervous excitement, become debilitated and deprived of their natural vigor. The same effect is produced by association of the sexes, where the mutual conduct is provocative of amative excitement, though modified by forbidden indulgence. Those who have the welfare of the organs in view, are therefore counselled not to permit abnormal excitement of the passions to occur. Females should, likewise, avoid reading obscene literature, from the fact that the constant expenditure of nervous force ensuing upon the engorged condition of her organs is very hurtful. It is a well-known physiological fact, that undue excitement of any passion, such as anger, mirth, etc., is always followed by a certain weakness of the general organism, and the same holds true of the amative passion also.

The occasional desire for congress is purely a natural one, and the most chaste or pure-minded person, sufficiently fortunate to possess healthy organs, cannot rise superior to the desire. It is simply a manifestation of a function of the economy in perfect obedience to a physiological law. It is readily explained. We have seen that semen is the secretory product of a gland (the testes), afterwards deposited in a vesicle; the urine is also secreted by a gland, and deposited likewise in a vesicle (the bladder). When the bladder becomes filled, the afferent nerves distributed to it convey intelligence of the fact to the brain, and a desire for urination arises, which continues as long as the bladder remains charged with urine. This is a natural phenomenon of organic function. In like manner the full seminal vesicles impart the sensation to the nerves distributed to them, which is also conveyed to the brain. What is the result? Naturally, a desire for cohabitation in order to evacuate the charged vesicles. This fact is an unalterable condition of the economy, and it follows that a desire for the evacuation of the vesicles is as much a natural manifestation of functional action as that of relief of the bladder. In the female the hyperæsthetic condition of the nerves distributed to the clitoris, awakens the same desire, which remains as long as the nervous forces are not equalized by the expenditure of a part. It is, therefore, purely a nervous phenomenon in the female. The amative passion is not a cultivated one; it is natural to the human being, and ineradicable by the greatest exercise of continent thought and behaviour, and its gratification is unquestionably hygienic. It is, of course, as subject to rational indulgence as in diet or drink.

We have seen that desires are natural in a healthy condition of either sex, and that a rational indulgence is hygienic, but I earnestly caution every reader to guard against debauching the passion by any unnatural causes or excesses. This indulgence can only be countenanced in marriage. It is therefore the plain duty of every male and female to marry, and as early in life as contingencies will permit. That marriage is hygienic is proved by the fact that married people live longer than the unmarried, a fact that demonstrates the marital privilege as a healthy relation between the sexes. Nature did not design total continence, and such a condition is aversive to the physical and mental well-being of the sexes. Nature, however, provides in this as she does in everything else. The amative passions do not present themselves, or become inconveniently strong in either sex until a full marriageable age is attained.

Marriage.

This is in law the conjugal union of man with woman, and is the only state in which cohabitation is considered proper and irreprehensible. As a legalized custom it is of very ancient origin, and it is doubtful whether even the primitive man was not governed in the intercourse of the sexes by some recognition of the union being confined to one chosen one.

No greater promiscuity can certainly be supposed than occurs in the lower animals, where pairing is the law. The nobler animals, as the lion, elephant, etc., never have but one mate; and even in case of death do not re-mate. As man advanced, civil codes were inaugurated, and certain protection given to the choice of the parties. The earliest civil code regulating marriage of which we have any account was that of Menes, who, Herodotus tells us, was the first of the Pharaohs or native Egyptian kings, and who lived about 3,500 years before Christ. The nature of his code is not known.

The Biblical account extends further back, but it does not appear that any laws existed regulating marriage, but each one was allowed to choose his wife and concubines, and it is supposed that common consent respected the selection. Next Moses gave laws for the government of marriage among the Israelites. The early Greeks followed the code of Cecrops, and the Romans were also governed in their marital relations by stringent laws. In fact the necessity of some law regulating the intercourse between the sexes must have become very apparent to all nations or communities at a very early period. It certainly antedates any legal regulations with regard to the possession of property. It is very probable that every community did by common consent afford to each male one or more females, and the presumption is that such choice or assignment, as the case may have been, was respected by common agreement as inviolable. It is doubtful if ever promiscuity was the law or privilege with any community of men, even in their primitive state. The possession of reason is antagonistic to such a belief; and man was most probably elevated above the beast by the faculty of reason in this respect as in others. Promiscuous sexual intercourse is evidence of debauchery, and a departure from that natural course which is prompted by an innate sense of propriety characterizing mankind. The law is very indefinite with regard to what constitutes a legal marriage. It is an unsettled question, both in England and in this country, whether a marriage solemnized by customary formalities alone is legal, or if one characterized by the mere consent of the parties is illegal. The latter has been held as legal in some instances in both countries. Kent, in his *Commentaries*, lays down the law that contracts made so that either party recognizes it from the moment of contract, and even not followed by cohabitation, amounts to a valid marriage; and also that a contract to be recognized at some future period, and followed by consummation, is equally valid. It is unfortunate that the law is so undecided in this respect. The decisions arrived at, for or against, were not dependent upon any recognized law, but seem to be influenced by the character of the cases, either for favor or discountenance. As long as the law recognizes cohabitation legal only in marriage, it seems to me that if consummated under consent of the parties to bear marital relations with each other, or promise of marriage, the act should be unhesitatingly pronounced as the equivalent of a valid marriage in all instances. If cohabitation is only a marital prerogative the law should not stultify itself by recognizing it as possible to occur in any other relation. If either of the parties are married the law defines it as adultery, and, very properly, defines the punishment It is necessary to the progress of the age that some such principle should be recognized in common law, so as not to subject the decision of the question to the individual opinion of any judge. It would at once obviate the confusion of sentiment now held in regard to it, and besides arrest the decision in test cases from mere caprice of the tribunal. It is certainly as correct a principle as any in common law, and would, in its operations as a statute law, be free from injustice, and capable of doing much good.

POLYGAMY.

This is a state in which a man has at the same time one or more wives, or a woman more than one husband. The latter custom is more properly called polyandry, and prevails in Thibet and a few other places. Polygamy has existed from time immemorial, especially among the nations of the East. In sacred history we find that it prevailed before the flood. Lamech had two wives, and the patriarchs were nearly all polygamists. The custom was tolerated by the laws of Moses, and, in fact, no positive injunction against it is found in the whole of the Old Testament. It is questionable whether more than one was recognized as the *bonâ-fide* wife, the other simply being wives by right of concubinage. But if polygamy was in its strictest sense the legal custom, it soon grew unpopular, for no trace of it is met in the records of the New Testament, where all the passages referring to marriage imply monogamy as alone lawful. The custom has been almost universal in the East, being sanctioned by all the religions existing there. The religion of Mohammed allows four wives, but the permission is rarely exercised except by the rich. The custom is accounted for on the ground of the premature old age of the female in those regions, and also on the ground of excess of the number of females, though the latter, by the authority of recent travellers, is probably not the truth. The marriage code of Fu-hi, who primarily established civilization among the Chinese, gave most probably superiority to but one wife, but raised the concubine to the dignity of a wife to a certain extent.

Among the Greeks, at least of later times, monogamy was the custom, though in the time of Homer polygamy prevailed to some extent. It was not known in the republic of Rome, but during the existence of the empire the prevalence of divorce gave rise to a state almost analogous to it. It prevailed among the barbarous nations of antiquity, excepting the Ger mans, who, according to Tacitus, "were content with a single wife." In some countries more than one wife was allowable if the husband could extend the dowry; a wife without a dowry was considered only a concubine. This was the case in Judea, when it became a dependency of Rome.

In Christian countries polygamy was never tolerated, the tenets of the church forbidding it, though Charlemagne had two wives, and Sigibert and Chilperic also had a plurality. John of Leyden, an Anabaptist leader, was the husband of seventeen wives, and he held that it was his moral right to marry as many as he chose.

In England the punishment of polygamy was originally in the hands of the ecclesiastics. It was considered a capital crime by a statute of Edward I., but it did not come entirely under the control of the temporal power until a statute of James I. made it a felony, punishable with death. George III. made it punishable by imprisonment or transportation for seven years. By the laws of ancient and modern Sweden the penalty is death. The Prussian Code of 1794 subjected the criminal to confinement in a house of correction for not less than two years. In the United States the second marriage is a nullity, and the punishment varies in the different States, though usually imprisonment for a certain period, or fine, or both, is the penalty. The term bigamy is most in use, however, as the plurality seldom extends beyond two. Polygamy has had some defenders even in modern times, most of whom have grounded their defence on the absence of an express prohibition in the Scriptures. Bernard Ochinus, general of the Catholic Order of Capuchins, though afterwards a Protestant, wrote in the sixteenth century a work in which he advocated it. It was also boldly defended by the Rev. M. Madan, in a treatise called *Thelyphthoro*, but limited the privilege to men.

It is the offspring of licentiousness, and its advocates merely wish to give legal color to licentious habits. Every student of history will find that as soon as a nation became morally depraved, polygamy was practised, and that monogamy was the rule in all countries truly civilized. Monogamy is an element of civilization, and, as a true child, fosters and maintains its parent.

Polygamy has of late years been most shamefully revived, and outrageously practised in face of law, by the Mormons. They claim it as a religious duty, and defend the system by claiming that unmarried women can in the future life reach only the position of angels who occupy in the Mormon theocratic system a very subordinate rank, being simply ministering servants to those more worthy, thus proclaiming that it is a virtual necessity of the male to practise the vilest immorality in order to advance the female to the highest place in Heaven.

Mormonism is a religion founded by Joseph Smith, who was born in Sharon, Vt., December 23, 1805, and killed at Carthage, Ill., June 27, 1844. The Smith family removed from Vermont to Palmyra, N. Y., in 1815, and, according to testimony, the reputation of the family was bad, and that Joseph was the worst of the lot. They were untruthful, intemperate, and commonly suspected of vile practices, which were probably true in some cases, and false in others. These statements are not contradicted even by the Mormons. Joseph claims that in 1823 (Sept. 21), he had a vision, in which the angel Moroni appeared to him and made known that in a hill near Manchester, N. Y., he would find a record written on golden plates, giving an account of the ancient inhabitants of America, and the dealings of God with them, and with the record, two transparent stones in silver bows like spectacles, which were anciently called Urim and Thummim, on looking through which the golden plates would become intelligible. These he claimed were placed in his hand September 22, 1827, by the angel of the Lord. The language was called the reformed Egyptian, not then known on earth, and the contents of the plates formed the "Book of Mormon." The book of Mormon has been proven to have been written by Solomon Spaulding. It will thus be seen that Mormonism was the development of a stupendous fraud, and it is exceedingly singular, that a sect of such numbers as Mormonism is now, or has been, could have been formed, when everything connected with it is fraudulent and perniciously immoral. Polygamy was not introduced among the Mormons until 1843, when Smith ordered it as a doctrine of the church by virtue of a revelation. The Mormons also aim to prove its right by claiming that St. Paul's injunction that a bishop "should be the husband of one wife," implies that other men should have as many as they choose, and that if a bishop should be the husband of one wife at least, the passage does not express a prohibition of his having more if he wishes.

It is a most singular fact that a sect like the Mormons could have been established in a country peopled with such law-abiding people as of the United States, and maintain a system of marriage antagonistic to the law and religion of the land. Neither could they have done so, if they had not possessed two great virtues, temperance and industry. It is to be hoped that the legal process now instituted for its abolition will effectually remove the blot from the national escutcheon.

The "Oneida Communists" are essentially polygamic, although they have no marriage system. They do not marry, and ignore all marriage codes. Cohabitation is under no restrictions between the sexes. Marriage is also not observed among the Shakers.

MONOGAMY.

This is the conjugal union of a male with one female only. We have seen that monogamy was co-equal with the dawn of civilization, and that most probably the majority of the males had but one wife, even among polygamic nations. Universal polygamy is practically impossible, the scarcity of females and the poverty of the males forbidding it. The excess of females is not so great in any country as to allow to each male more than one wife, except the male portion is depleted by long and disastrous wars. Monogamy has done more for the elevation of the female than any other custom of civilization. The rich could only afford to practise polygamy, and should the poor imitate the example, it would necessarily subject the wives to a state of serfdom. In the economy of nature it is designed that the male should be the protector of the female, and that by his exertions the provision of food and raiment should be secured. In polygamous nations the female has not attained that social state that she has reached in countries where the male is entitled to but one female as his wife. Woman's highest sphere is not in the Harem or the Zenani, but in that dignified state in which she is the sole connubial companion of but one man. It is debasing to her nature, and subversive of her dignity in the rank of humanity, to make her the equal only with others in the marital union with one male. She becomes only the true, noble, and affectionate being when she is conscious of a superiority to others in the connubial companionship with her accepted one. The female of birds chirps but for her single mate, and she is pugnaciously monogamic as well as virtuous, allowing neither male nor female at or near her home. The spirit of independence she gains by being the mate of but one male gains for her the victory over the intruders.

The physical and mental welfare of the female is also dependent upon monogamic marriage. I have demontrated that temperate indulgence is conducive to the sanitary condition of the sexes, and that absolute abstinence is opposed to the designs of nature. It is also evident that the male is not endowed with greater power, vigor or capacity than the female; therefore, confinement or limitation of the congress to the companionship of one male with one female, as in monogamic marriage, gives the healthy balance to the marital union. The polygamic husband must either suffer from the consequences of excessive indulgence, or his wives from poverty of uxorial gratification; probably both would be the case. Polyandry is equally as proper as polygamy, yet it never in the history of man obtained a permanent foothold. The female is equally capable, if not more so, to capacitate more husbands than one as the male more than one wife, and the physical deterioration would not be greater. The system is more logical than polygamy, because her dependence would be distributed between two or more husbands, in which case she would be better insured against poverty, and her support would be guaranteed by greater probability.

We have now described the history and aspect of the two customs, and will conclude this subject by remarking that a man is morally and physically entitled to but one wife, and that a plurality is a great wrong to the female, and in total opposition to the ordinance of Nature. Wherever polygamy is the custom the female is held in slavish subjection. It only prospers in proportion to the ignorance of the sex. Intelligent and civilized woman will always rebel against such sexual degradation and hymeneal servitude.

Marriage Customs.

It would probably be interesting to many to describe the marriage ceremonies observed by different nations, but to enter into a descriptive detail would occupy too much space. It is sufficient to say that while some wives are wooed and won, others are bought and sold; while in some countries the husband brings the wife to his home, in others, as in Formosa, the daughter brings her husband to her father's house, and is considered one of the family, while the sons, upon marriage, leave the family forever. In civilized countries the ceremonies are either ministerial or magisterial, and are more or less religious in character, while in others less civilized the gaining of a wife depends upon a foot-race, in which the female has the start of one-third the distance of the course, as is the custom in Lapland. In Caffraria the lover must first fight himself into the affections of his lady-love, and if he defeats all his rivals she becomes his wife without further ceremony. Among the Congo tribes a wife is taken upon trial for a year, and if not suited to the standard of taste of the husband he returns her to her parents. In Persia the wife's status depends upon her fruitfulness: if she be barren she can be put aside. In the same country they have also permanent marriages, and marriages for a certain period only—the latter never allowed to exceed ninety years.

In fact the marriage ceremonies differ nearly in all countries. To us some may appear very absurd, and yet our customs may be just as amazing to them. It matters but little how a conjugal union is effected as long as sanctioned by law or custom, and obligates the parties, by common opinion, to observe the duties pertaining to married life.

The Basis of a Happy Marriage.

The state of conjugal union should be the happiest in the whole of the existence of either man or woman, and is such in a congenial marriage. Yet in the history of very many marriages contentment or happiness is palpably absent, and an almost insufferable misery is tho heritage of both parties. It is therefore important that previous to the marital union the parties should take everything in consideration that foreshadows happiness after marriage, as well as everything calculated to despoil conjugal felicity.

The first requisite of congenial marriage is *love.* Without being cemented by this element the conjugal union is sure to be uncongenial. It is the strongest bond, the firmest cord, uniting two hearts inseparably together. Love for the opposite sex has always been a controlling influence with mankind. It is the most elevating of all the emotions, and the purest and tenderest of all sentiments. It exerts a wonderful power, and by its influence the grandest human actions have been achieved. Of what infinite worth it is to either sex to be compensated with a worthy and satisfying love, and how ennobling to the impulses and actions it is to bestow the sentiment upon one worthy to receive and willing to return.

Love is only given to that which we admire and esteem. The man who admires the shapely hand, the comely figure, the pretty foot, the handsome features, the well-formed waist, etc., will naturally love the woman possessing such attractions. The woman will love the man who favorably approaches her standard of conception as to manly excellence and beauty. Others admire moral purity, vivacity of disposition, superior talents, genius, etc., and hence naturally will love the possessors. In fact this proposition is founded upon a law of mind; love cannot be generated by forces that antagonize our ideals of esteem and admiration. The love that engenders matrimonial happiness must be reciprocal. Reciprocity of love will naturally induce matrimonial alliance. It should not be inspired by a passional nature only, nor should it be platonic entirely, but the two intimately blended together will render the love one of adaptation, and secure conjugal placidity. The love that is created in us by the Venus-like form of the female, or Apollo-like character of the male, is not that love that alone insures happiness, the moral and mental nature must also be congenial. Candidates for marriage should carefully consult themselves, and without ulterior motives ascertain if the love they have for the one to be chosen or accepted is adequate to compensate the yearning of this sentiment. If the one selected has all the characteristics that inspire love, that will be the proper one to marry. Love is the main-spring that regulates the harmony of conjugal life, and without it there is a void in the machinery, productive only of jars, convulsive movement, and a grating and inharmonious action. The soul yearns for love and to love, and unless the desire is compensated, human life is a blank, and becomes a purposeless existence. Love ever stimulates the good and suppresses the bad, if kept in a proper channel, and guided by pure affections.

Another requisite of a happy marriage is *health.* No person has a moral right to engage in wedlock who cannot bring to his partner the offering of good health. It may be apparently a cruelty to the consumptive to deny to him the gratification of his affections or passions, but it would be a greater cruelty to encourage him or her in a step the consequences of which would engender anything but happiness. Is it a pleasing thing to contemplate that you throw upon the bosom of your spouse but the body of an invalid, and one that will be the constant object of care and solicitation on the part of either husband or wife? Is it consoling to your justness that you can but offer a limited period of your life to the one of your choice, and that the inevitable consequences of your affection will at an early period leave but one at the hearthstone? Is it encouraging to know that the offspring of your union will in all probability be equally tainted as yourself, and that on those upon whom you conjointly place your hopes and pride are destined to perhaps an early grave? It is intrinsically wrong for those in whom the taint of consumption, scrofula, syphilis, insanity, etc., to marry, unless they feel convinced that by proper medical treatment they have been or can be thoroughly cured. Intermarriage of the cachectic would be far more judicious than the union of the healthy to the diseased. Vigor and debility are constitutional opposites, and cannot exist together in the physical economy, and the marital union of the physically healthy to the physically unhealthy does also produces nothing but discord in the economy of marital existence.

A very important consideration is the knowledge of what marriage really implies. It obliges the encountering of duties and circumstances which press considerations and plans of life upon the most careless minds. The change in the habit and manner of life, the divided responsibility, the inexorable demands of marital duties to be complied with, and various other matters incident to wedded association should be fully pre-considered, and the relation assumed only after thorough deliberation and satisfactory self-examination. It is the duty of the eligible of either sex to marry, but a marital alliance should be consummated intelligently, not thoughtlessly or ignorantly. "Look before you leap," is an adage that has profound significance in its application to candidates for connubial association. If an error is made in selection, scarcely an other error that may be committed by man or woman is so difficult of rectification, and none will result in greater misery, mental anguish, and destruction of all the joys of life. If, on the contrary, the selection or acceptance is wisely and discreetly made on both sides, the conjugal pair will be blest with all the earthly joys capable of attainment.

It is invariably those who thoughtlessly entered into marital companionship that make mistakes. They shrink before the realities incident to married life on their first presentation, simply because they never dreamed, much less thought, that such exigencies are inevitable to the marital sphere. They are ignorant of the duties incumbent upon either husband or wife, hence they leave them unperformed; opportunities for advancement are not improved; neglect becomes the basis of action with only one possible result—marital infelicity. If we trace the cause, we find that in the majority of cases, infelicity is owing to neglect in the performance of marital duty; and this disregard is ascribable to utter ignorance previous to marriage of the duties inherent to the marital sphere; consequently, as soon as they confront the wedded pair they are not met with a fixed determination to discharge them satisfactorily as emergencies will admit, but are shirked and postponed, and finally, when the necessity for action becomes absolute, they are inadequately performed; a fault which is sure to engender dissatisfaction, petulance, or reproach on the part of either husband or wife.

Marriage implies the utter abandonment of the interests and advancement of self to the exclusion of the other marital companion. If circumspect, by noting marital conduct in others, a fair conception of marriage and its consequences will soon be known. Then, the individual must ask himself, or herself: Am I capable and willing to do my duty? Could I rise superior to all the trials, vexations, and perplexities that present themselves to those in marriage? Would I never weary of doing the best under all circumstances? If you can satisfactorily answer these and others, you can enter fitly and nobly into the marital sphere.

Another consideration is *evenness of temper*. In the wooing days every one is a lamb, and only becomes the howling wolf after marriage. Circumstances that ruffle the temper in the presence of the intended are but like the harmless squib, but would become like the explosive torpedo in his or her absence, or in after-marriage. Quarrelling caused by matrimonial differences is the most frequent cause of infelicity, and most of them are caused by an innate irate temper of either the husband or wife. Differences that would be amicably adjusted by the exercise of a little reason and temperance in argument or judgment, are to the irascible the subject for the most vehement and angry logic, and the solution is inevitably discord. It is difficult, I acknowledge, to ascertain previously the mental disposition of persons, when they have occasion to conceal the defect in order to enhance their own interest. It is quite possible that Socrates, when he wooed the *lovely* Xanthippe, deemed her perfection, called her his "darling," his "pet," his "angel," if philosophers ever make use of such endearing expressions. Her conduct evidently deceived him as to her real nature, for the poor old philosopher was egregiously deceived and inexpressibly tortured in his married life by the historically renowned virago and termagant. "Love is blind," but its eyes should not be blindly closed against any such imperfection as naturally tends to destroy wedded bliss. Careful observation in a variety of circumstances will often disclose the real disposition, and the mask is sometimes unwittingly let fall, so that you may gain a cursory glance of the features, which if uncomely, should be enough.

The *tastes* should not be *dissimilar*. Some of them may be unimportant, but others are a fruitful source of disagreement. The social wife will never be contented with the unsocial husband, and the gay husband, though his gayety may not be commendable, will always accuse his wife if she lacks a social disposition to a great extent The religious wife will never excuse a tendency to irreligion in her husband, and though he may be far from being immoral, she is unhappy if he does not participate in her devotions. The one devoted to children will never be happy with one having a natural repugnance for them. In this way we might multiply facts illustrative of the importance of an investigation into the similarity of taste, previous to marriage. Great love, however, overcomes almost every obstacle.

The parties should be nearly of one age, the husband should be the older. The union of the old husband to the young wife, or the reverse, is seldom a happy one. There is seldom that such a marriage occurs in which the incentive is not the wealth of either of the parties. The young graft on the old tree does not thrive well, the vitality required by the one is not afforded by the other. The magnetism of the old is not suited to the young, and there never can be a concord in their union. It is a law of nature that animals of like age should only mate together. The old male bird does not mate with the young female bird, but mating always occurs between those of the same year's brood. It is only in their domestication that they lose this law of instinct, and it is only through a vice of civilization that marriages between the old and young are contracted, in opposition to the original design of sexual union. Such marriages are but seldom the result of a mutual love; one of the party is sure to be actuated by motives other than the one of conjugal happiness, and the union is usually enforced by the opportune chance of enhancement in respect to wealth or station in society. The progeny of such a union is very seldom endowed with either physical or mental vigor, which is easily accounted for. The physiologist knows that the mental emotions of the mother, during the period of pregnancy, is very apt to affect development of the child *in utero*, either favorably or unfavorably. How, then, can a young mother be actually comfortable, how can her emotions be elevated, how can she have that solicitude which is prompted by love, if she bears but little more than respect for her elderly or old husband? She has not that intense solicitude or hope that her child shall be all that is excellent; she has not that incentive of love that prompts her to a revery of desire that her child shall be all that she deems noble and beautiful; her conjugal relation is not calculated to inspire her highest and purest emotions, and the pride of her husband is not great enough for her to yearn for the day when she can present, with all the joys of maternity, an heir to her lord. It is, therefore, a union not calculated to promote domestic contentment, and there must be in the heart of either a husband or wife an aching void, and a longing for other than a senile embrace.

There are other considerations to be viewed before a union is effected. No one should neglect the moral character, the habits of frugality and industry, etc., etc. A marriage should only be consummated when both of the parties are morally certain that they are necessary to each other's existence; that life would be a dreary waste without the oasis of the loved one; that the intended one possesses all you admire and esteem; and that the journey of life in his or her companionship will be one of serenity and happiness;—the union will then, by the endeavors of both, be attended by all the joy, contentment, and happiness that it is in the power of mortals to obtain here below.

I cannot more appropriately close this subject than by quoting an abstract from a well-known author, who presents his case in full color, but it exposes the undercurrent that leads to the marriage-tie only too truthfully. He asks: "Who dared first to say that marriages are made in heaven? We know that there are not only blunders but roguery in the marriage-office. Do not mistakes occur every day, and are not the wrong people coupled? Had heaven anything to do with the bargain by which young Miss Blushrose was sold to old Mr. Hoarfrost? Did heaven order young Miss Fripper to throw over poor Tom Spooner, and marry the wealthy Mr. Bung? You may as well say that horses are sold in heaven, which, as you know, are groomed, are doctored, are chanted on the market, and warranted by dexterous horse-venders as possessing every quality of blood, pace, temper, and age. Against these Mr. Greenhorn has his remedy sometimes; but against a mother who sells a warranted daughter what remedy is there? You have been jockeyed by false representations into bidding for the Cecilia, and the animal is yours for life. She shys, kicks, stumbles, has an infernal temper, is a crib-biter, and she is warranted to you by her mother as the most perfect, good-tempered creature, whom the most timid could manage! You have bought her. She is yours. Heaven bless you! Take her home, and be miserable for the rest of your days. You have no redress. You have done the deed. Marriages were made in heaven, you know; and in yours you were as much sold as Moses Primrose was when he bought the gross of green spectacles."

Marriages are usually contracted to gratify various desires, as love, fortune, or position. The results are most truthfully stated by an eminent divine in the following passages:—

"Who marries for love, takes a wife; who marries for fortune, takes a mistress; who marries for position, takes a lady. You are loved by your wife, regarded by your mistress, tolerated by your lady. You have a wife for yourself, a mistress for your house and friends, a lady for the world and society. Your wife will agree with you, your mistress will rule you, your lady will manage you. Your wife will take care of your household, your mistress of your house, your lady of your appearances. If you are sick, your wife will nurse you, your mistress will visit you, your lady will inquire after your health. You take a walk with your wife, a ride with your mistress, and go to a party with your lady. Your wife will share your grief, your mistress your money, and your lady your debts. If you die, your wife will weep, your mistress lament, and your lady wear mourning. Which will you have?"

To man there is but one choice that he can rationally make, a marriage of love. My female readers, I hope, will also decide rather to wed a husband than the master or the elegant gentleman.

A little foresight, a little prudence, and a little caution, will prevent in most cases the entrance into a marriage which, by the very nature of the alliance, is certain to be an unhappy and improper one.

Married Life.

Two sparrows, votaries of Love,
The Mars and Venus of the grove,
Had been for years such constant mates,
You would have sworn the very Fates
Were impotent to break the bond,
That joined a pair so true and fond:
Together still they sought their food;
Together played in field and wood;
Together built the cosy nest
That served for shelter and for rest;
Together fought the feathered foes
With whom they came to words and blows;
In fine, they lived as lovers ought,
Without a single selfish thought,
Save such as might concern the twain,
Their mutual joy or mutual pain.
At last, one day, they chanced to get
Their feet entangled in a net,
(A vagrant boy had spread the snare
To catch and keep the pretty pair!)
And soon, despite their noisy rage,
They both were prisoned in a cage:
Where—much I grieve the tale to tell—
A sorry scandal now befell;
They scold, recriminate and fight,
Like arrant foes, from morn till night;
Until, at length, the wretched birds
In cruel acts and bitter words
The very furies emulate—
And all their love is turned to hate!

L'ENVOI.

Full many a couple come to strife
And hatred in connubial life,
Whose days of courtship promised fair
As those of this unhappy pair;
But, like the sparrows in my tale,
When trouble comes their tempers fail;
They blame each other for the fate
Which both should strive to mitigate,
With patience helping to endure
The ills that kindness fails to cure!

What an interesting lesson is contained in the above—a lesson that should be well conned and thoroughly learned by every married couple for practical use and guidance.

The physician, in his advices as to the conduct that should be observed by the husband and wife, is more properly confined to physiological aspects, but as the behavior in every respect is so intimately blended, it is not amiss, in a medical work, to state what the conduct should be in general. Unhappiness in wedded life is the result frequently of a couple being joined who should not on any account have been thrown into marital companionship. It is found that they are uncongenial in every respect, and hence the natural and inevitable result is dissension and a mutual regret of marriage. The pharmaceutist knows that if a chemical element is incompatible in a mixture that no amount of shaking, trituration, or commotion that he may produce will make the contrary element act affinitively; on the contrary, the more violent his endeavors the more the incompatibility is manifested. It is precisely so in the union of the man and woman who are by nature and purposes of life incompatible. Discord is evident at the first contact, which in time increases to ebullitions and explosions of temper, and the more they attempt to reconcile their differences the greater they become; the affections are destroyed, and each one becomes conscious that they have made the greatest mistake of their lives. Each blames their misfortune to the other when both are to blame, not so much on account of their combativeness, as that is but a law of their nature, but because neither of them had the wisdom to abstain from entering into the marital relation. It is, of course, commendable that both should be desirous of making the best of their union, and that each should display prudence in their conduct, but in the face of all their endeavors the galling fact of incompatibility is ever present, and no amount of the best efforts will make the union a happy one. If children are born to them they will in all probability be of a vicious nature, lacking in all the noble qualities, and who, born with the innate disposition, and reared and schooled in the midst of family discord, will almost inevitably "go to the bad," thus adding materially to the general misery of the parents, both of whom are ready and honest in their belief and averment that the disposition of the children is the heritage from the other. It is unfortunate that such marriages are consummated, for the diversity in all the actions and purposes of life naturally manifested by both is too great to be reconciled by the most earnest exercise of either prudence or forbearance. Such a union has always been, and will always be, an unhappy one, and the best endeavors will scarcely make it tolerable. It may be poetical to say that such a man and woman are *one*, but they are decidedly *two* on all subjects and conditions of married life.

It is not to be supposed, however, that every infelicitous episode in married life is to be ascribed to incompatibility. The turbulence in many cases is owing to decided misconduct on the part of either husband or wife. Many unions would be very happy if but a generous effort would be made to render it so; but if either one is actuated by a spirit in opposition to mutual confidence, mutual welfare, and mutual enjoyment, it will either create a slavish submission on the part of one, or the assertion of mutual equality. In both cases the result is detri mental to conjugal bliss A tame submission begets disrespect, and the assertion of the right generates the "family jar." In the social and commercial intercourse of man and wife, mutual confidence, mutual endeavor, and mutual benefit should be the objective point. Concealment of purpose is as wrong as deception in action, and neither should be for a moment entertained. The wife should be the possessor of the husband's secrets, and the husband the custodian of the wife's confidences. To be actuated by secrecy either in intent or action is nothing more than duplicity, and an attitude in entire opposition to the spirit of wedded life; but, while the author in every instance advocates an open and candid intercourse between the husband and wife, he can only hurl anathemas upon the one who betrays the confidence. To be worthy of confidence, and to be entrusted with secrets, demands the fidelity that will not betray the one or divulge the other. Deception on the part of either husband or wife will, in spite of all attempts at concealment, often be detected, causing justly indignation and loss of respect. It is an evidence that the one to whom everything should be confided is deemed unworthy of trust, and it puts at an end that harmony and confidence that should exist.

Married couples should most carefully husband their affections for each other. It is a most deplorable fact, that the love between many too soon loses its fervor. This loss is not due to familiarity, nor is it a natural result of daily association; but decidedly the effect of a reprehensible disregard of a mutual endeavor to maintain it. We love only that which is lovely; and the person who makes himself lovely will be loved. It is more frequently the case that the wife loses her husband's affections than the reverse. This is not so much the result of the inferior affectionate nature of man as it is of neglect and imprudence on the part of woman. Women, if they would rule men's hearts, must deserve and unwittingly exact the approval and admiration of their minds. Her variability of temper is most unfortunate. It goes up like a rocket and comes down like an aërolite; a miracle of smiles or weeping Niobe, a driving tempest or a flashing sunbeam. A never-varying, bland, lullaby-sort of temperament is most deplorable; sparkle, buoyancy, and even an irrepressible dash of fun, now and then, are most healthful and appetizing; but mere feminine diplomacy should forbid the not unfrequent dovetailing of winsome caresses and childish poutings on the part of the wife, and so should the whimsical interplay of foolish indulgence and churlish neglect on the part of the husband be abandoned. Principle, not caprice, should be the energizing and controlling motive. The most charming views of wedded life are to be taken from the higher mounts of vision—those of settled design and steady purpose. There must, of course, be mutual concessions and mutual agreements to disagree. There is a way to win by commanding, and a way to command by winning. By the wise interblending of self-centred strength, and a prodigal wifely affection, she may achieve marvels of wifely management. The husband may unconsciously lead; but never essay to drive. At the same time, we are frank enough to confess that there are too many women who need the flaming sword of an archangel to awe and repress them. There is no such thing as conquering them by love; as well prate of love to a blackbird. But if kindness fails, severity will fail all the more surely. Flies still continue to take more kindly to molasses than to vinegar. If they but knew how a cheerful temper, joined with innocence, will make their beauty more attractive, knowledge more delightful, and wit more good-natured, they surely would endeavor to cultivate and cherish it. It is an unquestioned fact that too many wives neglect the most important elements of wifely conduct.

To her is entrusted the care and management of the home—if it is agreeable, it is her work, if it is attractive, it is to her credit alone that it should be ascribed. If the home is not a cheery place, it is because she does not render it so. It is not requisite that elegance and luxury —that only wealth can procure—should characterize it; cleanliness, order, and, above all, her bright, sunny smiles, and cheerful company, adorn it more than the richest household furniture. The atmosphere of the home must not be darkened by the clouds of discontent, perplexity or anger, but lit up by the effulgence of social conviviality, good-nature, and buoyancy of spirit. The husband coming from his daily task must, in return for the bright smiles of the wife and children that welcome him home, throw aside all cares of business, and devote himself to their enjoyment. It will put a new life in him as well as in his wife and children. If exhausted and fatigued, or if his mental energies have been overtaxed, he must not thrust the fact too forcibly upon his family, but on the contrary bring freshness and buoyancy of spirit into the family circle. He must not recuperate his energies at the expense of the vitality of his wife and little ones. The wife should also as early as possible dispense with household duties, and, until the retiring hour, be ever ready to engage in that social communion, which is so healthful, and so conducive to happiness of married life. But how frequently is it the case that the weary husband, who would gladly engage in that relaxation afforded by domestic conference in play, reading, etc., is only beguiled by the din of pots and kettles, the clatter of dishes, the music of a wash-tub, etc., in the kitchen, which often is incessant, until the poor husband, desirous of social comforts, but weary of waiting for them, goes to bed with nothing to lull him to sleep but the confused noises that come from the kitchen, made by his busy and industrious, but indiscreet spouse. We would not deprecate industry on the part of the wife. We well know that many a wife, whose household duties and personal attention to the children absorb most of her time, can find but little opportunity to engage in recreation or social enjoyment, but while we admire thrift, coupled with industrious habits, we cannot but deplore the state which robs from her the best energies, instead of applying some, at least, upon the effort to render the atmosphere of the home, not one of incessant labor only, but also one that is brightened and rendered cheerful by the relaxation afforded by an occasional leisure hour, in which the man, wife, and children are brought in contact, and stimulated and refreshed by social concourse. As well might the husband file his saws, grind his axes, and chop his wood at the same time, as the wife to be continuously drawn from his presence by the labor of the home. It is, we know, not a pleasing contrast, to compare a thrifty and industrious wife with one who is indolent and careless, but we only argue for a limit, as we know that matrimonial happiness, health, and noble qualities of children are dependent in a great measure upon enlivened social intercourse in the family. We would have no wife merit the exclamation of "*How shiftless!*" from an Aunt Priscilla, but they must not be so busy either, that her husband has in her no social companion. Such wives cannot much blame their husbands if they seek social pastime in the club, in the inn, or even in his neighbor's house, where Mrs. Sparkle makes everything so pleasant. It is the duty of the husband, whenever possible, to give his leisure hours to the companionship of his wife and children, but it is also a duty that the wife so arranges everything that they can not only be passed tolerably but agreeably. It should be the effort of both husband and wife to make the home the dearest place on earth to them, and when that is accomplished, connubial happiness is certainly achieved. It is often that the best-meant efforts are fruitless, simply because they are driven in the wrong direction, and the disappointment occurring in consequence of misapplied energy is full hard to bear; but if the married man or woman would study the wants and desires of their consorts a little more, and make earnest effort to supply them, the apple of discord would not be eaten in so many instances.

I cannot two strongly impress the importance of fidelity. Could I have but one word of advice to give to the conjugal pair, I would say:—"*Be true to each other.*" Disloyalty in the marriage bond is the cause of infinite trouble, misery, and ruin. It is the rock upon whose ugly and jagged contour lie the wrecks of numberless matrimonial vessels. Fidelity is the rudder that guides the bark safely through the course, let adversity and ail else assail her, as long as not without her rudder, she will out-ride the storms, and glide triumphantly and peacefully along in smooth water. Disloyalty pitches her at once into the breakers, where she will pitch and toss, heave and thump, and should she even escape, it is only at the expense of important appanages, and most frequently the best directed efforts will not save her from utter ruin.

It is not only the duty of physicians, but of every one who has the welfare of society at heart, to put their voices against the doctrine of "free love," which has of late been promulgated and defended by certain persons who wish to make it a matter of creed or principle of society. It is to the shame of the sex that the majority of its adherents are women, in whom virtue is supposed to have its staunchest defenders and supporters. It is not ostensibly advanced in advocacy of unrestrained sexual commerce, but if thoroughly analyzed, its objective principle amounts to the same. It is a scortatory love at best, and its tendency is to give still greater laxity to the morals of society. It is veiled under the sophistical dogma that every woman, if she desires to become a mother, should be privileged to select her own male to be the father, and that every man should be licensed to choose the woman he desires to be the mother of his progeny. This, they advocate, would insure higher development of the race, and that mankind would soon be superior in intellectual, moral, and physical qualifications. The fact is undeniable that a superior offspring would be the result, if the most eligible individuals would sexually associate, but it could never be accomplished by "free love" practices. It can only be gained by judicious marriage, and in no other way. If the doctrine of unrestrained sexual commerce is best adapted to promote higher development of offspring, it would naturally be exemplified in the issue of those who "*loved not wisely, but too well*," or in those of the lowest grades of society or savage races, where chastity is unknown as a virtue. All the principles of free love characterize such an intercourse· but it has yet to be ascertained whether such progeny are in any respect superior; on the contrary, it is quite probable that they are in many respects inferior. This may be, however, accounted for by the mental emotions of the mother, which are naturally caused by grief, fear, shame, etc. If, even, such unfavorable mental emotions could be removed by sanction from society for such issue, the case would not be modified to a more favorable extent than is now possible by legitimization of offspring by marriage. They also prate of "affinities" and spiritual attraction; but let the candid and virtuous mind investigate the full import of these cohesions, he will find that the spirit of attraction is the cohesive power of gratification of the animal passions. The hideous form of lechery is veiled with but the thinnest gauze; and disguise it as they will, they cannot hide the fact that it is lewdness, and not virtue, which they attempt to honor. The doctrine, if philosophically reviewed, presents no advantages over marriage, but is one pregnant with defects and immoralities, and if carried into effect would unmistakably prove itself to be the death-blow to morality and civilization. The barrier to promiscuity is to be made even more impregnable, and the sacred precinct of sexual congress legitimatized by marriage is not to be over-stepped by the husband or suffered to be invaded by the wife. Lechery has never been, nor can never become a standard principle of moral philosophy, and "free love" is but its synonym.

Is it a consoling picture to those with whom moral rectitude is a cardinal principle to see disloyalty to the marriage-tie openly and shamelessly displayed? Is it ennobling to man's moral nature to cut loose the shackles put upon him by a well-organized society with regard to his conduct in amorous matters? Can it be justified by the most liberal views of right and wrong? Unalterably, no; the man who comes to the abode of his wife, with his lips tainted by contact with others, and yet excited by an unlawful orgasm, commits the greatest offence against his wife, against nature, and against high heaven. The wife who receives the embraces of an unsuspecting husband, while at the same time she is guilty of illicit dealings with others, is worse than the lowest prostitute, and is entitled to no sympathy or condonement. It is only by the most scrupulous adherence to the loyalty that should be observed by man and wife, that marital happiness is to be gained or maintained; infringement is the element of its decay and destruction.

Jealousy is one of the most common visitors at the hearth of a family, and is a great destroyer of its peace. Entertained to a moderate degree it is quite natural, but when it becomes a morbid feeling, it is worthy of severe denunciation. The exhibition of slight jealousy is an unerring manifestation of love, and should be accepted as such by either man or wife. We are jealous of what we love, and unconcerned only about that which we do not appreciate, therefore a certain degree of jealousy entertained by the husband or wife in respect to each other should be elevating to their pride, respectively, and not condemned as a sickly sentimentality. It is only when it becomes a ruling passion that it exerts mischief and discord. When it is so morbid that it becomes a matter of dislike and reproach for the husband to bestow but the ordinary civilities of social intercourse to the opposite sex, or for the wife to receive them, it amounts to but little more than insanity. If the wife is so jealous as to impugn all the motives of the husband, that he dare not even look askance at any other woman, that to speak with other women subject him to one of those infinitely pleasant curtain-lectures, and his personal liberty denied to him with regard to social intercourse, it is then that it becomes disruptive to marital felicity; for the husband, if erring though he be, will surely chafe under the injustice which she will be sure to commit. On the other hand, the jealous husband is just as extravagant in his folly, and instead of guarding his wife's love, takes the best means of repelling it. Confidence, not suspicion, should be the controlling motive, and its mutual entertainment should not be disregarded until the most indubitable proofs are presented to guarantee a disbelief of the partner's honor. Then, if you have bombshells, set them off; but even then, I think, it would comport more with reason and dignity, if the error could be calmly adjudicated, and if that is impossible, a quiet and dignified separation is unquestionably the best course. Reproach, recrimination, and parade of the cause of disruption before the public are by no means a philosophic action, or part of an honorable conduct. It is so with all matrimonial differences, they should not be made public property, for they will surely become disgusting scandal before the scandal-loving people, to be found in every community, are done with them. It will receive such additions, and will be so manipulated and distorted, that, which at its fountain-head was but a peccadillo, will at its terminus be magnified into the greatest crime. What was at first but a slight immorality, is sure to become at the end the grossest violation of decency. If Mr. John Smith in a playful moment is found to kiss Mrs. Sarah Jones, the critics of society will wink and blink, they will hem and haw, look wise, toss their heads superciliously, and before they have ceased their comments, there will be no doubt in their minds but that Mr. Smith and Mrs. Jones were found in *flagrante delicto*. Finally, when the scandal has assumed its worst aspect, some order-loving Christian (!) will with considerable embellishment acquaint Mrs. Smith of her husband's *crime*, and Mr. Jones of his wife's *sins*, and then comes the sequel. The fact would scarcely produce a ruffle, at best but a gentle breeze, but the monster created by scandal produces the commotion of a tornado. Then these vampires who feed upon the peace and reputation of society are satisfied, but they at all times go round like "roaring lions seeking whom they may devour." It is to these scandal-mongers that matrimonial infelicity is often due, from the fact that a husband or a wife may be guided by their opinion rather than to rely implicitly upon each other's honor. If respect is shown to scandal connubial peace is at a discount. The only way to circumvent it, is to isolate adjustment of differences to the family circle, and not allow it to be the property of the unconcerned. The advice of disinterested and honorable people may at times be very serviceable, and not to be disregarded, but to array any or every matrimonial variance before the public for their comments is reprehensibly imprudent and foolish.

It is, however, not to be understood that selfishness should extend to social intercourse with the neighbors, for next to an affectionate family an agreeable neighborhood and good society become objects of desire, because calculated to create happiness. As far as friendship is not abused it should be freely given to the neighbors, and it should be the endeavor of every one to make the relations of a neighborhood of a most friendly and accommodating character. How consoling it is to the bride, who leaves the bosom of her own family and accompanies her husband to a locality where all are strangers, to find in her new home neighbors who manifest a friendly spirit, and are willing to extend cordial greetings to the stranger. She is at once set at ease. The duty that families owe to society is only second in importance to the duty that husband and wife owe to each other, and domestic happiness is not complete unless its social surroundings are congenial and agreeable. An ascetic married life is abusive of the order of nature.

The conjugal pair should in reality be *helpmates.* They should (to use a homely phrase) pull in one direction, and, if the direction is proper and right, pull together. The combination of similar forces has a twofold effect, but forces opposed to each other weakens one and annuls the other, or brings them both to a *quietus.* This simple law of physics is peculiarly applicable to the behavior of the married pair. A harmonious progress requires a combination of purpose and exertion. If the husband is devoted to literature or science, the wife should manifest interest in the same, but if her taste is not for either, she should by no means show displeasure at her husband's devotion to them. It is her duty, in case of improvidence on his part in consequence of his studies, to ask him to improve his negligence, but never in a tone of anger or reproach. The husband should, in like manner, never frown upon any of his wife's delights. If she is devoted to flowers, to music, to painting, etc., it should be he that should stimulate by approval. In case the husband is desirous to accumulate a fortune, and exerts himself to that effect, the wife should not dispirit him, or render his efforts abortive by extravagance. If he is not successful, or fails in business, she should be his comforter and stimulate him to further exertion; and in case the manner of living will in consequence be rendered less luxurious, she should exhibit such a contentment and willingness as to rob the misfortune of half its bitterness. The noble wife is one who does not sink under the crucial test of her husband's misfortunes, but rises to a higher mount of greatness and action by her cheerful resignation to the loss, and encouragement to her husband's drooping spirits. The husband should ever be ready with his approving smiles to cheer his wife's labors, even if to him it appears but a trivial affair. Woman only thrives under the approbation of man, and if that is withheld, especially from the one whom she values most, she soon becomes purposeless and fretful. How many a good wife's heart has been wounded by her husband's indifference with regard to matters which she in her simplicity of heart hoped would delight her companion? It may be but a trifle, but so exceedingly tender is the plant of connubial love, and so susceptible of being lacerated, that "trifles light as air" often impede its growth and embitter its fruit. It is the "*little* foxes that spoil the vines." A single tart remark or unkind tone of voice will penetrate the inner recesses of the heart of the wife who loves, and render her most wretched. *Oneness* should be particularly exhibited in purpose and design, the respective action should be one of accord, and the faculties of each other should be mutually gratified. It is only by such a concert that love is perpetuated and wedlock made an Elysium.

If the husband or wife have vices, the conduct to be pursued is peculiarly delicate. If it is judicious, the vice may be corrected; if otherwise, the habit may become intensified. If the husband is intemperate, the wife should address his highest sentiments, and not attempt to bring about repentance and reform by angry reproach, unkind remarks, or undignified aspersions. No one has a keener sense of his depravity than the drunkard, and he is by no means dead to the finer sensibilities, hence any inhumane treatment, or reproof insulting to inherent dignity, is not calculated to achieve reformation. He is to be approached as a man, his nobility is to be addressed, and his better feelings excited. He is to be shown that he is none the less loved for his noble qualities, that aside from his folly he is still the being who possesses his wife's affections, and that only his vice and not he himself is abhorred. It is only by such a procedure that vices, or a disposition to vice, can be cured. It is the mild and gentle force that works reform, revolutions scarcely ever do.

We have now in many aspects considered the prudent course for the conjugal pair to pursue in search of wedded bliss. We have confined ourselves merely to their social relation, there yet remains for us to discuss a not less important subject, namely, that of connubial commerce. From what we have already written the inference is plain, that we advocate a dignified conduct, benignity of temper, subjection of anger, co-operation of purpose, etc., etc., and though there may be, nay, are, many other rocks upon which the matrimonial bark will impinge, the reflective mind will be guided in his behavior in every possible contingency by what we have more lengthily dwelt upon. The indices to marital happiness are reason, prudence, justice, and equality, and they who shape their course by them must attain the object. It shall now be our purpose to consider a subject that is not less important, and much less understood. In its discussion we will confine ourselves to particulars which married people mostly inquire after, and in which they need the most enlightenment.

The discussion of this delicate relation between the married pair is necessary, inasmuch as the unprofessional have access to scarcely any work of standard value and excellence from which they may gather the knowledge so indispensable, unless they are fortunate enough to have the privilege of reading the works of an extensive medical library. Even if this opportunity is afforded, the truth is not clearly presented to them, as such works are intended usually for the professional reader. I, therefore, am confident that I discharge an important duty, especially as I write particularly for the instruction of the popular mind, in presenting to my many readers the philosophy of that relation legitimatized by marriage. In consideration of the subject, I shall employ plain but decorous language, and attempt to present the facts so that they may be intelligible to all, and yet not wound any of the finer sensibilities of my readers. I have previously stated my aim to be merely to afford instruction to the masses relative to such medical subjects as have never been capably popularized, but have been, and are yet a theme on which incompetent charlatans have so ignorantly dwelt upon, and disseminated so much offensive literature. The medical profession is to blame for this. If they had not neglected to teach the popular mind the physiology of cohabitation, empirics would have found no market for their offensive and pernicious works, excepting, perhaps, among the morally depraved.

The married, which I positively know from the many opportunities afforded me in my professional career, are extremely ignorant of the philosophy and physiology appertaining to the special connubial relation, and absolutely know nothing of the hygienic limit or period. I know also that every married man and woman is extremely anxious to possess proper knowledge. As the access to works of scientific authority is extremely limited, they are led to accept the teachings of ignorant empirics, and thus unwittingly do much that is wrong and hurtful. The diffidence characterizing the marital pair to interrogate the family physician as to the proper course to pursue, also tends to keep them in ignorance. It is only when the abuse of the marital privilege becomes painfully apparent that the physician feels warranted to interpose his cautions, and counsel reform and moderation. This, however, occurs only in exceptional instances, the great majority are uninformed and unadvised, controlled only by self-interpretation of the right or wrong of their conduct, or by such information as is commonly possessed by the heads of families, which is often traditional, and usually faulty in its conclusions.

To supply, then, in a medical work for general circulation, the proper instruction as regards the important marital relation alluded to, needs no further justification, but every person actuated by a catholic spirit will, I am sure, deem the discussion eminently appropriate. The under lying purpose of wedded association is of greater importance than half who assume the relation are aware of. Marriage implies much more than a mere association of the sexes—it is rather an institution devised by society to regulate cohabitation and the propogation of species in the best manner. This is the only legitimate purpose of marriage, as aside from this relation between the sexes, every other one could be secured and maintained without matrimonial ties or obligations. Any system of rules or regulations subserving the purpose of controlling this particular marital relation so as to accord with the best known laws of physiology and hygiene, and best adapted for the requirements of propogation of the species, so that offspring will not be recklessly brought into the world, but calculated to secure to it the highest possible endowment of all the nobler human qualities, is decidedly the best marriage code. As an institution, marriage should be governed more by physiological laws than by statute regulations, and the time may yet come when wilful disregard of physiological laws applicable to the matrimonial association of the sexes will be regarded as reprehensible or criminal as the violation of the statute laws governing the institution. It is then quite important that those in marriage as well as those who contemplate matrimonial alliance, should possess adequate knowledge of the incumbent duties, contemplate the dignity and importance of wedlock, endeavor to promote the grand interests and welfare which the marital pair have at stake, avoid animalization and debasement of the connubial repast, endeavor to fitly endow their offspring, and so conduct themselves throughout the whole course of wedded association, that they may be rewarded with all the manifold blessings that should be gained by the grandest and closest association of human interests, purposes, and hearts.

It should never be forgotten by the married that our passions can be over-indulged precisely the same as our appetites. Hygiene requires that our appetites for food or drink should only be appeased to such an extent as will not create a loathing for that which was eaten or drunk, upon quitting the repast. If indulgence is carried to such an extent it amounts to intemperance and will be followed by the usual consequences of violation of hygienic law. It is precisely so with the marital repast: if the relation is assumed too frequently the temperate limit will be over-reached and hurtful consequences ensue. Excess is not only deleterious because destructive of the natural tone of the excitement, generative of nervous disorder, and other hurtful consequences; it is extremely apt to engender indifference after a certain period on the part of either or both of the conjugal pair. By indifference I mean to express that feeling of insatiety after indulgence, that want of mutual accord, or sense of unsatisfactory awakening of the emotions, which is sure to follow excesses. The desires are present but cannot be satisfactorily appeased, precisely as an appetite for a certain article or kind of food remains unsatiated if not within reach to be partaken of. This condition, directly a sequal to immoderation, is one of the greatest incentives to adultery. I am well satisfied that this unpardonable violation of matrimonial trust and fidelity is, in the majority of instances, due to neglect of observing temperance in the early years of marriage. The results of coitive intemperance should thus be strongly impressed upon the minds of every one married or contemplating marriage, as by moderation they will surely attain a higher altitude of connubial enjoyment besides avoiding the violation of the highest and purest of all human trusts which if committed, is irreparably destructive of the integrity of matrimonial alliance.

The married pair should carefully guard against all excesses. Excess of connubial commerce is a severe tax to the nervous system, and very detrimental to health. The class of diseases met with by the physician, of which the remote cause is immoderation, is scarcely second to none in frequency. Besides, the orgasm is less profound if the banquet is too freely partaken of. The physician is frequently asked the question how often intercourse may be indulged in without injury. To this no answer can be given with numerical preciseness; but both sexes possess an unerring monitor, whose voice they should promptly heed Whenever a sense of exhaustion is felt, after copulation, the violation of a physiological law is made manifest. Intercourse should not be indulged in when it requires fatiguing efforts to accomplish it. It is sure to be followed by exhaustion, and the orgasm is neither elevating or satisfactory, and apt to generate an inharmony quite antagonistic to the designs of nature.

Frequency of indulgence does not only deteriorate the moral tone of reproductive and nervous systems, but it often provides the germinal agencies of serious diseases. The remote cause of insanity and consumption is not infrequently intemperance in marital union. The children who are the products of the earlier periods of married life, at which time coitive intemperance is most frequently indulged, are more mentally imbecile, and more pallid in hue and attenuated in form than those born at a later period. This is in consequence, that, sooner or later, the parents are forced to abstain from excess by the ensuing ruination of health, allowing nature to gather up the shattered powers, and assert anew the control of the organism. In the early years of marriage excesses should therefore be carefully guarded against.

During the period of the catamenial presence, strict continence must be observed by the conjugal pair. I should not give this caution were I not aware that in many instances the marital prerogative is thus grievously abused. Propriety and privilege in this respect are particularly at variance, and duty demands observance of propriety.

During the period of pregnancy the husband's conduct should be characterized by kindness, forbearance, and encouragement. While the germ of an immortal being is in the loins of her he loves, that husband is no more than a brute who would in any way neglect her wishes, or refuse to join with her in the solicitude for its welfare. The expectant mother must also control every appetite or mental passion that might injure the precious trust committed to her. The best and noblest thoughts should occupy her mind, and the purest sentiments prevail in her heart, while the babe is hid beneath it, so that her shortcomings and caprices may not be communicated to the product of her conception. She should be, and her husband should assist her to be, patient under any weariness or sorrow belonging to her condition. She should strengthen her heart against the hour of her labor with the thoughts of joy she shall feel, when her child shall see the light, and the process of maternity fulfilled. It is she who bore and in agony gave birth to the link that unites the parents all the more closely together, and that strengthens the hymeneal compact. To her the husband owes devotion, allegiance, and comforting encouragement. He must make her feel that the joys of maternity are not to be centered entirely in the little helpless babe nestling in her arms, but also her heart is to be rejoiced in witnessing the paternal pride of the product of hymeneal union—the jewel of their conjoint love. The component parts of the family are then complete, the husband, the wife, and the child, nothing is wanting but the coupling of energy and intent, to procure the highest share of human bliss to be obtained on this side of the grave.

The author is prompted, but space will not allow, to give at length his views upon the management of children. On this point husband and wife frequently disagree, and the result of the disagreement is manifested in the child. It is more usually the case that the father is sterner and firmer than the mother, in whose heart the tender elements of humanity prevail. It is, however, not necessary to be stern in the management of children, but an unflinching firmness is at all times essential, and absolutely necessary in both parents to gain a healthy control over their children. Firmness must, however, be exhibited in the same direction, and that direction the right one.

There is a tendency, we think, at the present day to put children too forward, not so much for the sake of showing off their extraordinary merits to an admiring world, as from the better motive of early accustoming them to the conversation of grown people and the usages of society, and of inspiring them with confidence, ease, and self-possession. No doubt these results are very valuable, but the mistake which many people make is in forgetting that children are something like dogs, which require to be very well trained before they can safely be recommended to the familiarity of strangers. And it is to be remembered that the moment children cease to respect any of the grown-up people with whom they associate, not only is the whole benefit of the intercourse lost at once, but real injury is inflicted on the moral tone of the child. For this reason children should be brought as little as possible into the society of men and women who cannot command their respect; while those who can, the influence should be hedged round by all the numerous impalpable barriers which judicious parents know perfectly well how to interpose between children and the most popular and careless of their adult play-fellows. The confidence which well-bred chil dren at once repose in an eligible stranger, without being rude or troublesome, is charming to everybody, who has any natural taste for their society. It is not pleasant, on the other hand, to see children who are shy, timid, and sheepishly speechless in the presence of strangers, but a confidence and unobtrusive ease of manners can be inspired without thrusting them constantly into the society of elders.

Closely allied with the mistaken license allowed to children in matters like the above, is the disposition to laugh at, and thereby to encourage, all traits of singularity, oddness or affectation, which children may exhibit, as marks of genius which ought not to be repressed. Of all the dangerous errors into which parents can fall, this, in our opinion, is the worst. For nothing sc soon hardens into second nature as juvenile eccentricity; and few things are more injurious to success in life than marked oddities of manner and gesture when they reach the point of grotesqueness. The fond parents dote upon the eccentric child as an *original*, but the author in this respect agrees perfectly with Mr. Peter Magnus; he does not see the necessity of originals. And what is more, so many "originals" are only sham ones after all. That is to say, their singularity is merely a bad habit which they can't shake off, and is only very partially innate. When parents see their child doing anything unlike other children, anything queer, surprising, or uncouth, however comic or however clever it may seem, they should never laugh at or applaud it. Children naturally self-willed, and with real natural peculiarities, can soon be broken of such tricks, if treated with absolute indifference. But soon let the idea find its way into their brains that such sallies, naughty though they be, are regarded as marks of genius, and the mischief is done. It is not necessary that parents should engage harsh reproof or exhibit anger to correct such pertness or disposition to oddity, but if approbation is withheld, and probably displeasure shown, the mischief will soon be corrected. Children, like their elders, delight in approbation, and if they can only secure it by doing what is right and proper, the inclination to do that which is wrong or displeasing, is robbed of its greatest incentive.

To come back to the point from which we started—the management, namely, of young children—there is one thing to be laid down: let there be no divided rule in a house. Do not let children see that the father means one thing and the mother another in their bringing up. They see the difference in a moment, and when they do, farewell to all wholesome parental influence. The starting-point of ruined manhood or womanhood, in many cases, is just this diversity of parental control. That mother urges her child towards destruction who offers condolence to it, after reproof or correction by the father, no matter how harsh or cruel it may have been. Such matters must be corrected by conference, at which the children are not present. She is not to show any displeasure at the exercise of authority by the father in the presence of the child; if she does, the child's self-will is gratified by a mother's alliance, and a certain importance is given to the improper conduct of the child, which, in accordance with the human liability to err, is hard to resist. The parents in this respect must be the allies, not the children with the father and mother.

Husbands and mothers may talk too freely before their children, forgetful of their rising intelligence. And, indeed, nothing is more common than to get a wink from the head of the house, implying that you are to be on your guard before Johnny or Tommy, Kitty or Lucy, who are listening open-mouthed to your witty narrative, while they themselves in the next moment will offend against their own precautions in the most barefaced manner by plunging headlong into your domestic controversy, in which, to speak metaphorically, knives are freely used on both sides. Again, parents should be extremely careful in commenting upon the conduct of their neighbors in the society of their children, or that self-same Tom will at the first opportunity acquaint neighbor Jones that, in the opinion of his father, "he is a confounded old fool;" or the same little Kitty will tell Mrs. Robinson that her mother says she is a "lazy, good-for-nothing woman." Trouncing Tommy or Kitty for such imprudence is hardly fair, when the fault lies at the door of the parents. At best, it gives children but a poor example, and instills within them a disrespect of the neighbors, which, probably, they do not deserve, and which may in later years possibly stand in the way of individual advancement. Parents, in rearing their children, have a greater trust than is commonly supposed, and they owe a double duty—one to the child, and the other to society in general. If the child is inclined to vice, the fault lies in many cases with the parents, and the right to thrust upon society either a son or daughter who will constitute but a useless or vicious member thereof, is not properly one of the privileges of humanity. No man has the right to set at large a lot of ferocious animals, who, in the exercise of their ferocity, may do harm to his fellow-men; neither has that parent a moral right to send adrift in the world sons and daughters, who, in the exercise of the vicious culture they have received, prove annoying and harmful to their fellow-beings. There is no deeper stratum of thought in moral economy than this, and none that receives less attention.

It is to mothers that society and mankind are indebted for its morality and uprightness. By her efforts the only real work of reformation can be achieved. The training of children is mainly intrusted to her hands; if her duty is properly performed, the moral tone of society is to be placed to her credit; if carelessly and imprudently attended to, she is the one that is mainly accountable for its vices. It may seem a cruelty to add to the travails of maternity and to her household duties the further responsibility of rearing the moral structure of society; but who is to assume it, if she be not the proper person? The child is, to a certain age, mainly in her presence alone, and this association cannot be shirked or changed; for it is true to a natural law that the mother is to be the closest companion of her children. It is during this period of companionship that the foundation of the moral superstructure is to be laid, and the mother must be the artisan. She may be aided by her husband and others; but the chief duty to form and direct is her own, and the structure she rears, whether good or bad, is her work.

Her duty to her offspring commences at the moment of conception. While the product is yet hidden within the confines of her womb she must have its future welfare at heart, and lend her thoughts only upon that which is good and noble. She should in her mind select the career of the child, and that such a one that is characterized by all the noble qualities, and freedom from vices. Who can gainsay the fact, that when the babe is assuming its physical character, while yet in the mysterious depth of the gravid womb, that the mother is not enabled by the purity of her thoughts and exalted character of her emotions to give it also the endowment of its moral character? Who will deny that the transmission of hereditary qualities give the original bias, which subsequent to birth is hard to overcome? The law of transmitting talent and virtue from mother to child is based on physiological principles, as demonstrable as material matter. I would then say to every expectant mother: Let your thoughts be good, your emotions pure, your imaginations morally exalted; be brave, be strong, be good, and centre all and only the purest feelings upon that helpless atom of humanity reposing in your womb, so that at the hour of your labor you are fortified against its agony by the consciousness that the babe you usher into the world is endowed with qualities, which, by subsequent development and culture, will enable it, when of proper years, to take its place among the good and noble of this earth.

Subsequent to birth the mother must continue her efforts. She must impose barriers against everything that has an unwholesome influence on the moral tone of her child. She must not intrust the training of her precious darlings to nurses or governesses. A mother who reposes the development of character of her children to salaried persons is prostituting the high estate of maternity, and sins against Nature and her God. It is she who must take the hand of the child while yet in its innocence, and lead it in the path of virtue and truth; her hand must remove all the lures and seductive temptations that beset its path, and she alone must assume the cultivation of its moral nature.

Men may build prisons, asylums, reformatories, create midnight missions, etc., but reformation by these means is uncertain, expensive, and at best very ineffectual. It is the hardened criminal they deal with—

one in whom vice has become the second nature. No real reformation is accomplished by any such means, none will ever ensue; and as long as mothers are not alive to the importance of properly training the pliant child, vice will increase and baffle every other mode of reformation. One wiser than myself has said—"Train up a child in a way he should go, and when he is old he will not depart from it." The truth of this is self-evident, and is supported by another, whose figurative language is equally truthful—

"As the twig is bent the tree 's inclined."

It is, therefore, the mother who must nourish the truth in her arms, so that when it leaves them it will walk strongly forth alone, blessing and blest of all men.

Advice to the Childless.

The most impressive words in the whole range of language are Father and Mother. Their full significance is only realized and understood when the prattling babe stretches out its tiny arms and first lispingly pronounces the tender words. The heart must, indeed, be dead to all emotion, which at that moment does not pulsate with pride and exalted love. The first words taught to it, and the first words learned, are those tender names, and the proudest moment of the whole of parentage is when the lesson is learned by, and let fall from, the lips of the smiling babe. The soul is elevated above material things, the tenderest chords of love are vibrated, the joys of the world but this one are forgotten, and the whole heart embraces but the innocent babe that sprung from their loins. The entity of the family is incomplete without children, and the action of its machinery is unharmonious without those little wheels. The integrity is faulty in the absence of offspring; it is like the pillar of which the capital and pedestal exist, but the shaft is wanting to give it dignity. The childless family is not a pleasant one to contemplate; the husband and wife grow old, but there is no young life to inspirit them, or to give cheer to their existence. Childless longevity is at best but a dismal life—there is always an aching void—a palpable evidence of a lacking integer. Barrenness is a condition from which every woman instinctively recoils. The desire for children may or may not be entertained, yet to know that she is incapable of motherhood is to know that she is lacking in the most important element of womanhood. It is a physical condition abhorrent to every female, because she feels that she is beneath the dignity that distinctively characterizes her sex. Motherhood is the ideal state of womanhood, and the yearning for maternity is one born of nature. The woman in whose bosom such a desire makes no response is unworthy of her sex, and she deserves none of the elevated joys and honor which woman is sent here to achieve, and she will reap none. It is the highest honor her sex can reach, as productiveness entitles her to the proud position of one of the prime factors in the propagation of species.

None but physicians know how great the desire for children is in those whose married life has been passed for some time without issue. To them the secret yearnings of their hearts is intrusted, and to their confidence is reposed the animated impulse that is ceaselessly throbbing in the bosom of those whose hearth-stone is desolate, and around which gathers not a child. The outside world may not know of the painful vacancy that is ever confronting them, nor the despair that has possession of their hearts; but the physician, to whose skill they so earnestly appeal to accomplish the realizatian of their hope, is ever, and probably the only *confidante.* He alone knows the elevation of spirits, the fulness of pride, and the intensity of satisfaction that is manifested if he has removed the barrier to productiveness, and that the process of maternity is in progress. But let him say that the barriers to conception are insuperable, it causes a painful despondency, and that exquisite anguish resulting from unappeased yearnings of the soul. It is, however, a providential ordination that few women are hopelessly barren, and but few men unprocreative. Circumstances may for a certain time make them practically unproductive, but such a physical condition can in almost every case be removed by consistent treatment, and by observing such measures and precautions tending to promote fruitfulness. The causes of childlessness with certain married parties are various. It may be due to deformities of the womb, Fallopian tubes, and ovaries of the female; or testes, spermatic cord, and penis of the male. The pathological conditions are many, which occur in both sexes, that prevent conception, while in some cases the anatomy of the parts render conception and child-bearing utterly impossible. It may be caused by stricture of the womb and Fallopian tubes, misplacement of the tubes, adhesions of the uterine walls, etc., etc., or through malformation, as occlusion of the vagina, etc. It may also be due to degeneracy of the testes of the male, epispadias, hypospadias, etc. Conception may also temporarily be prevented by uterine and ovarian diseases, or to a diseased condition of the spermatozoids of the male semen. Unproductiveness is frequently due to a devitalized condition of those animalculoids, in which state they have no fecundating properties. Sterility. dependent upon some vicious conformation of the genital organs of either sex, apparent or concealed, is called *absolute.* Infecundity, due to the conditions already enumerated, are absolute causes of sterility, and can only be removed by medical treatment, which in most cases, if of a rational and appropriate character, can effectually be accomplished. When a female does not conceive with one individual, but has or may with another, the condition is called *relative* sterility. Relative infecundity is frequently met with, and in many cases presents such features that the atociac condition cannot be overcome without calling to aid artificial means. It is often observed that a woman in her second marriage is sterile who in her first marriage was prolific in offspring; again, the widower in his first marriage gave evidence of fecundating power, but in his second alliance no impregnation ensues. Absolute and relative sterility may exist at the same time, thus a female may be married to a man who is physically incapable of impregnating her, yet at the same time the conformation of her genital organs may be such as to render her absolutely sterile. It is therefore necessary in all cases of sterility to fully investigate the causes, both absolute and relative. Sterility in some females is often dependent upon a condition of the womb characterized by membranous menstruation. Conception is prevented in such cases by devitalization of the semen by the vitiated secretion and discharges from the uterine surface. In all cases of absolute sterility, medical treatment offers the only hope of obliteration of the causes. The diseases of the female genitalia which are causative of infecundity must be treated as required by their pathological character; and it is necessary that such treatment should be admirably adapted to the conditions of the case, and most carefully instituted. Such cases should only be intrusted to physicians who by skill and experience have the requisite ability, and who are conversant with the precautions that studiously are to be observed. Improper treatment is exceedingly apt to render sterility an irremediable condition, which under rational treatment would have resulted in the removal of all the barriers to impregnation. If the cause lies in the male, whose formative material is devitalized by a diseased condition of the fabricating organs, seminiferous ducts, or seminal vesicles, medical treatment likewise is the only means of making the patient procreative. The male often renders himself powerless to procreate by imprudence or various excesses, in which case the semen is not fully organized and deficient in procreative elements. All these varied conditions of husband and wife contributing to childlessness are mainly remediable, so that under the care of an intelligent physician parentage to them is not always a forlorn hope. The prospect for issue is favorable in most cases under rational treatment, hence the gloom of the childless need not be perpetual if they but employ the counsel and aid of the competent physician. Neglect of so important a duty is very common, the conjugal pair stolidly agreeing that their childless state is owing to Divine ordinance, little dreaming that their unproductive union is in opposition to the requirements of the Deity, and that the fault of non-conception is due to incapacity and not to dispensation.

Relative sterility is not amenable to medical treatment. The most common cause of infecundity of this character is the want of adaptation or fitness of the genital organs of the conjugal pair to each other. This want of adaptation is a very frequent cause of sterilty, and should receive proper attention by the medical man to whom is intrusted the rectification of an unproductive union. Of itself, inadaptation may not be the cause of the atociac condition, but when associated with an atonic condition of the uterus, procreation rarely, if ever, ensues. It will not be necessary for me to detail the various forms of inadaptation, as the consideration of such causes of sterility more immediately concerns the medical attendant, but it is quite appropriate to make allusion to such causes, as the childless very properly desire information relative to all possible conditions hindering fructification. Self-treatment is not to be thought of; but a proper knowledge of all the physiological or anatomical causes of sterility should be possessed by all in conjugal association, especially by those who have not as yet attained the full measure of matrimonial enjoyment, by reason of an exceptional provision of fate by which their union is left without the graces and endearments of childhood.

One of the most common causes of barrenness is unquestionably what has been already alluded to, atony of the womb or appendages; in fact some pathological condition of the reproductive organs of the female is, in the large majority of cases, the sole cause. Uterine atony, or intonicity of the womb, may be of every degree of intensity—ranging from a slight feebleness to complete exhaustion—the latter condition being known as paralysis of the womb. This atonic state is owing not to any structural or organic disease of the womb itself, but is merely a secondary pathological condition, the actual seat of the disorder being in the sacral plexus, or that nervous net-work situated near the sacrum, from which the genital organs receive their nervous supply. A paralyzed condition of the womb is aptly illustrated by a paralyzed arm or leg; the loss of natural power, motion, or functions resulting from a diseased condition of some cerebral or spinal nerve-centre, and not from any morbid condition of the part affected. In all cases, therefore, where the cause of sterility has been ascertained to be uterine paralysis, the proper treatment is to restore the tonic powers of the sacral plexus. This is best accomplished by the intelligent application of the electric or galvanic current, or by the employment of the appropriate cerebro-spinal tonics and other medicinal agents. The treatment is, however, to be intrusted to careful, able, and experienced physicians.

The physiological function of the womb, favoring the transmission of the male formative material from the *os uteri* to the ovarium, is a certain suction power or intro-staltic motion. This is accomplished by short and wave-like contractions upward of the uterine muscles. In a paralyzed condition of the womb, which is usually of a chronic character, there is a complete absence of this uterine motion, and consequently the respective formative materials necessary for procreation never come in contact.

Membranous menstruation has already been stated as one of the causes of sterility. This painful affection is characterized by either partial or complete denudation of the uterine cavity of its mucous covering at each menstrual period, leaving the uterine walls in an abraded condition, entirely unfitted for the purposes of gestation. Conception may, however, take place in these cases, but at the arrival of the first period for the occurrence of the menstrual exacerbation, the placenta and membranes are dislodged with the mucous membrane.

The childless wife will note that a pathological or abnormal condition of her pelvic organs is relatively the most frequent cause of sterility, all of the affections being characterized by more or less gravity and requiring the most appropriate and energetic treatment in order to restore the organs to health, and at the same time establish functional integrity and maternal capacity. As most of these uterine affections result from a wilful disregard of the laws of health, slavish obedience to the behests of fashion, and bad habits in general, the author hopes that all females, married or unmarried, who properly appreciate the grandeur of womanhood and motherhood will not wilfully violate physiological law, but strenuously endeavor to preserve uterine health and integrity of the maternal capacity.

Congenital phymosis is a condition of the male organ depriving him of procreative power in nearly every instance. The intervention of the prepuce in this case arrests the ejaculatory force of the seminal expenditure, preventing impulsion into the womb. This deformity is easily obliterated by a surgical operation, which is very frequently performed in my office. It causes but little pain, no inconvenience, and heals rapidly. Circumcision among the Jews is a custom having for its object the removal of this frequent obstacle to multiplication, as existing in the male. Infecundity, especially in the earlier years of marriage, is often a consequence of exhaustion, induced by improper excesses. Intemperate indulgence often renders both husband and wife sterile. The semen must, in order to have procreative perfection, necessarily remain in the seminal vesicles for a certain time, where its procreative qualities are fully developed. After its escape from the vesicles, it further receives the intermixture of prostatic fluid, liquefying it to the proper consistence for easy propulsion into the uterine cavity. Marital excess is therefore preventive of full procreative quality of the semen. Excessive indulgence on the part of the wife causes a feebleness of peristaltic motion of the uterine muscles, or, as it may be otherwise termed, the suction power of the womb. Feebleness of the upward propelling forces of the womb and Fallopian tubes is caused by the excesses alluded to, and hence, if even the semen is introduced within the uterine embrace, the absence of retentive power allows its escape through the mouth of the womb. Sterility from such cause can only be overcome by the observance of moderation by the conjugal pair, and in most cases restorative medical treatment becomes also a necessity.

The most susceptible period for the occurrence of conception is immediately after the complete cessation of the menstrual flow. This susceptibility continues for eight or ten days, but is necessarily greatest at an early period after the menstrual discharge. The menstrual flow in its discharge carries away all obstructions that exist in the mouth of the womb, thus facilitating intro-propulsion of the semen, and the womb at that period has also its greatest tonic power. It is, however, not to be supposed that conception will not take place at the period just preceding the menstrual flow; on the contrary, it may occur at any period between the cessation and onset of the catamenial discharge.

It will thus be seen that many causes, both absolute and relative, tend to sterility. In but few cases, however, is sterility a fixed fact, or an irremediable condition. The greatest triumphs achieved by the medical profession were in the study of the causes of sterility, and the best means for their removal. No physician, alive to the importance and exalted character of his calling, should neglect the study of the subject; on the contrary, he should be conversant with all the pathological features sterility presents, and be able to intelligently ascertain the causes. An important trust is confided to his professional care; the intensest longing capable of the human heart depends upon his skill, either to be appeased or unrequited. Professional acumen is in no respect more essential than in this, and the medical counsellor, unworthy of the trust by reason of imperfect knowledge of the subject, does a grievous wrong by attempting treatment, or venturing decisive advice. The childless pair should at all times seek the most intelligent counsel and most competent treatment, and not allow themselves to become victims of despondency before they have made such a definite attempt.

The author has devoted much time and study upon this subject, feeling that no greater field of usefulness is presented to the physician for the exercise of his skill and professional attainments. The success attained in this sphere of professional activity has only been gained at the expense of laborious study and by the advantages conferred by extensive practice. Competence can only be gained by study and experience in every subject of intelligence—proficiency being only the reward of intellectual labor and opportunity for exercise of the secured knowledge.

The author will gladly give advice to those to whom this chapter refers, being justified by previous success and long professional experience to give proper and definite advice and appropriate treatment. Those desiring to avail themselves of such an opportunity are referred to page 390 for guidance as to the proper information to submit for my consideration.

STERILITY AND SPECIAL WEAKNESS OF THE MALE.

By this is generally considered the inability to engage in the virile act. It essentially signifies a loss of the virile powers. Impotency may be either *partial* or *complete*, and, like sterility, *absolute*, and *relative*. The term impotence is frequently used synonomously with sterility; but, as sterility has been considered in another place, we shall discuss the subject in this place only in the sense implying loss of capacity.

The loss of virile power is owing to a variety of causes. The process of loss in idiopathic cases is usually slow, though in some cases invirility ensues quite rapidly. When due to traumatic causes virile power is lost synchronously with the occurrence of the injury. Impotence usually follows injuries received by the spine and base of the brain, but in these cases the loss is not of itself a pathological disorder, but essentially symptomatic of the injury.

The most common cause of impotence is nervous debility, apparent or concealed and unsuspected. It is the usual sequel to that disease, if it is allowed an unchecked career, manifesting itself at first by a slight incapacity, but which gradually progresses until finally the virile power is completely lost. That impotence is the inevitable result to nervous debility is quite natural, the ceaseless waste of such a vital element of the male economy as semen can have no other finality. The general disturbance of the nervous system caused by involuntary spermatic losses is manifested first in the virile organs, as the erectile property of the organ, purely a nervous phenomenon, and consequently any function so directly under the control of nervous power as the erectile quality, is the one first to succumb to nervous disorganization. Impotence in such cases is, therefore, due to feebleness or insufficiency of the nervous stimuli necessary to provoke a copulative aspect of the male organ. This condition of invirility is also caused by immoderate indulgence, the pathological disorder produced being in all respects the same as that following seminal incontinence, though as a general thing masculine power is lost less.rapidly.

Spinal and cerebral diseases are usually associated with a low condition of the virile power. This manifestation is quite in accordance with the physiological laws governing the virile functions, as it will be remembered that the nervous supply that the organs of generation receive is the pudental nerve, which arises from the sacral plexus. This nerve and branches afford the requisite stimuli necessary to promote congestion of the organ, which phenomenon constitutes an erection. The brain gives the necessary sensory stimulus, without which the nerves are not excited to action. Phrenologists place amativeness in the lower lobe of the cerebellum. but it is quite probable that its locality, though most evidently in the base of the brain. is not in that situation. as analogy will not comport with such a view. Observation teaches that the chanticleer is the most amorous of animals, yet anatomists find no lower lobe of the cerebellum in the brain of the fowl. External violence, however, upon the sacral and occipital regions usually cause sexual imbecility, and hence we know that a healthy condition of the base of the brain and sacral plexus is necessary to the existence of virility. Diseases, excessive study, intemperate use of tobacco, violent and prolonged grief, etc., are therefore causes of impotency, from the fact that the cerebral disorganization which follows produces inertia of the nervous stimuli. Apoplexy is also a cause of temporary impotence, in consequence of the paralysis of the sacral plexus ensuing. It is therefore vitally important that in the consideration of any case of impotence every predisposing cause should receive attention, so that restorative efforts are based upon correct principles. No pathological condition requires such nicety of treatment as impotence, and none that will so readily be remedied if the medication is thoroughly adapted to the case. Although impotence is the usual concomitant to long-continued seminal losses, my experience teaches me that a fair proportion of impotent cases are the results of habits and practices which are perfectly legitimate, and to which no shadow of blame or disgrace can be properly attached. It is a well-established fact that too much mental application, also constant confinement within doors in a vitiated atmosphere, or habitual or sudden exposure to heats and colds, or the destroying influences of extreme grief and care, will produce all the evil effects upon the mental and physical organization that are caused by and attributed to solitary habits. Nervous debility, which is quite a common and comprehensive name for all failures of the intellectual or physical organs or faculties to perform their functions properly, is originated and nurtured, in both sexes, by a variety of causes as countless as the leaves of the forest. Consequently, people should not be backward about making their deficiencies of mind or body known to physicians in such a clear and confidential way as to secure to them the full restoration of their normal health and vigor. Any course of life which is inordinately irksome or, involves heavy tasks, is liable to cause the loss of virile power, or especially in middle age, IMPOTENCY, which is the aggravated form of the same difficulty. Thus we find that clergymen, merchants, book-keepers, literary workers, men who are overtaxed by care and labor, lawyers, judges, boys confined too closely at school, young men who seldom take out-of-door exercise, clerks, heads of public departments, and all others who are constantly wearing and tearing both mind and body without seeking the neutralizing aid of *rest*, amusement, and change of scene, are subjected to some of the numerous ills developed in disabilities and incapabilities which impose untold suffering. These ills are the inheritance of everybody physically and mentally overworked, no matter in what capacity they may labor. It is to be lamented that many of these innocent individuals, from the fear of being charged with guilt, suffer long years in silence when the truly judicious course is to engage medical aid as soon as the fact becomes known. The old-class physicians have used the most powerful minerals within their reach, and, with the earnest and honest desire to do good, have accomplished much that has been of *temporary* benefit. But the reaction from the use of these minerals has been, in all instances, of a non-curative character, the patient purchasing for temporary enjoyment many after-years of incapacity and local weakness.

There is nothing so discomforting to man as the loss of virile power. He may not be a sensual being, yet manhood is a pride to him, the possession of which is always a gratifying knowledge. Impotence implies more than mere virile imbecility, it signifies also a loss of vigor and elasticity of the whole organism, and a gloomy state and impairment of the mental faculties. It has elsewhere been observed that the well-being of the whole economy is greatly dependent upon healthy genitalia; and mental composure, vitality and acuteness of intellect, graceful and easy manners, etc., are no less independent of the virile faculties. Impotency is, therefore, always a deplorable condition, and he who permits himself to be long without the legacy of virility, commits a great injury upon his own personal welfare, and places but a poor value upon the choice powers of manhood. Man without virile power is an anomaly; he has lost his status of sex, and is practically a eunuch as long as the unmanly condition is tolerated. There is a higher motive in possession of virile power than the ability to gratify amorous passion. If that alone gave chief value to virility, its loss would be but inconsiderate, but as we have seen that vigorous manhood is consonant to vitality of the mental and physical economics, it gains a value not to be despised, but greatly cherished, even by the most continent and virtuous men. Healthy functions of the genital organs are as requisite to the integrity of the whole organism as healthy functional action of the thoracic and abdominal organs, and any derangement of the pelvic organs is capable of precisely as much, if not more, disorganization of the general health as a disordered digestive or circulatory apparatus. I will close the consideration of this subject by inviting all those who are deficient in masculine tone or capacity to call on me in person or consult me by letter. (See page 385.)

The Philosophy of Generation.

The greatness, importance, and responsibility of the marital relation are but improperly appreciated and understood by the majority of males and females who enter into that relation. There is a momentous duty to be performed, far more important than those generally supposed to be incumbent upon husband and wife. We have in other places considered the more general duties devolving upon husband and wife to be discharged; we will in this place dwell upon a subject which of all others pertaining to the conjugal association of the sexes is the most important, and which as a duty is more universally neglected and improperly performed because the principles and laws governing generation are but imperfectly understood or not at all. The precise question relative to generation which we purpose to discuss is the transmission to children of the best possible mental, physical and moral attainments.

We have in another part of this work stated that the legitimate object of marriage is to legalize the sexual covenant, and to confine it within a healthful and moral atmosphere. This is not only the legitimate, but technically it is the only aspect of which the law takes cognizance. Such a congress is, therefore, legal between a male and female who have been bound together in wedlock. This is all right and proper; but not by mere legalized association can the welfare of the race be best advanced or secured. The distinguishment of animal creation into two sexes was only designed by Nature for one purpose—the multiplication of species; but it never was the purpose of Nature that the sexes should indiscriminately associate, or that the intent and design of multiplication would be fitly subserved in all cases by merely allowing any male to covenant with any female, irrespective of selection. In the lower animals this is avoided by instinct, but in man the restraint is given by the higher impulses of reason. Yet, notwithstanding this high quality in man, the purpose of Nature is often defeated or controverted by wilful disregard of the promptings of an innate intelligence or disobedience to what is known as physiological law.

The first requisite is circumspect marriage. Without the marital union of eligible parties human progress would be slow, or unpromising. A circumspect marriage tends, however, to bring into conjugal union the more highly endowed male with the more highly endowed female; or, in other words, the *best* man would marry only the *best* woman. The man having highly developed physical, mental, and moral, faculties would only be content in marrying a woman with similarly developed faculties, and in such a union we have the basis for highly endowed offspring. In another essay are given the precautions candidates should observe prior to consummating marriage, and if the instructions therein given should be heeded, unfit marriages would be of rarer occurrence.

But in marriage, proper or improper, a duty has to be performed, neglect of which is sinning against the welfare of the whole race. The aim of all married people should be the bringing into the world of healthy children, not physically only, but mentally and morally also. The greatest achievement and proudest monument of parentage is in giving to the world such offspring as will act well their part in the great drama of life. How is it to be done? Can parents so regulate the gestatory process as to give their children at birth the heritage of physical excellence, large mental capacity, and superior moral disposition? Assuredly they can; it requires but willingness and effort in the right direction. The mother who imparts to the being hid away in her loins her personal features, her disposition, etc., can impart much more by proper effort. The father, from whom the male formative material is received, can do much for the welfare of that being evolved from that material. For all that it is, the child is indebted to either one of the parents; from them is received the human qualities it possesses or exhibits. Subsequent care, training, and education may do much, but the original bias is received within the confines of the womb.

Not much need be said as to the transmission of mental superiority to children. If the parents are intelligent and educated, the children will also have large mental capacity. Subsequent mental training will serve to give offspring that mental culture which in the present progressive period of the human race each individual being should possess. Intelligence, not ignorance, now holds sway; and no one can harmoniously glide along with the current of human progress without a cultivated mind. If mothers, therefore, have tastes for the intellectual pursuits, let them not abandon them while another life is developing.

The transmission of moral qualities is more readily accomplished. To what extent they can be transmitted is not readily definable, but it is a well-settled fact in psychology that the moral habit readily descends from parent to child. This fact is exemplified in the history of nearly every family, for in nearly every case the moral tone of the children represents that of the parents, at least as far as disposition is concerned. Vicious association may destroy the moral tone, even if the disposition is unfavorable; but when the disposition is favorable to moral excellence the inclination to vice is strongly curbed, and moral degeneration is not so easily effected, even if the child is surrounded by all the allurements of vice. On the mother, then, a high duty rests—she is chargeable with the moral tone of society, not by neglecting the supervision of the moral faculties of her born children so much as by indifference when a human soul is undergoing intra-uterine development. Motherhood comes to many most unwelcomely; the trials and cares incident to it are not favorably regarded; but there are few women in whom the maternal instinct is so deficient that they would, with sheer malice, endeavor to give birth to a babe so weighted with the destiny of a bad organization, as to make them through life utterly insensible to all the moral relations of life. Yet such a legacy is completely within the power of a mother to give. If she is not elevated by purity of thought and of action, if not ennobled by intensity of maternal feeling, and if not actuated by constant solicitude for the welfare of her unborn babe, the or ganization of the child will be unquestionably vicious. She should remember that the child in uterine life has no blood but that of its mother; all that courses through its veins and arteries also courses through the blood-vessels of the mother. How important it is then for mothers to guard against everything calculated to disturb the harmony and regularity of the vascular current!

The child *in utero* is technically but an appendage or parasite, over which the maternal mind and body exerts a marked influence; consequently, if mothers in the pregnant state pay heed to the moral relations of life, curb for the time any evil disposition they may have, take pleasure only in that which is pure and upright—in short, lead a blameless moral life—they will most surely be blest with offspring in whom the disposition will be kind and the moral tone exalted. Let me then say to expectant mothers: enlighten and elevate the moral sentiments, exercise desirable talents, cultivate beautiful qualities; for if you do, they will certainly bloom in great brilliancy in your children and children's children. So, too, if there exists among the subtleties of your character any dark spot, exert all your moral strength in order to eradicate it. Surround the growing soul with good influences; cultivate all noble impulses, all holy aspirations; breathe into the opening flower, by the magic power of a mother's love, such knowledge and moral legacy as will prepare it for the world in all its antagonisms; and you will see in the final fruit the reward for all your care, self-denial, and self-abnegation. Husbands must learn to recognize this supreme power of their wives over the ante-natal life (both mental and physical), and they must observe such a line of conduct as not to frustrate any endeavor to exercise it rightly, but should give them the best possible conditions to improve it.

How can parents have healthy children? This is a question of such significant importance to married people that it should engage their most earnest thought and liveliest interest, for parents can by judicious care and careful practice endow their offspring with most excellent physical vigor. To effect this it is only necessary that they should themselves be healthy, or to render inert by proper medication the tendency of transmission of any infirmity or disease with which they may themselves be afflicted. The most potential cause of degenerate health in offspring is the ruinous effect of nervous debility. Any male who previous to marriage practised self-abuse, and who married while suffering from the effects of such a pernicious habit, cannot furnish for the purposes of generation such perfection of formative material as will insure full health in the being that evolves therefrom. The seminal liquid is diseased, and carries with it the germs of low vitality and poverty of physical endurance or capacity. For this reason the author discountenances marriage in those who by youthful errors induced the involuntary expenditure of semen, because that affection destroys the instinct of propagation, and renders the sufferer incapable or unfit to afford such formative material as will result in healthy products of conception. I therefore adjure all these suffering from this infirmity not to marry until by proper and skilful treatment a healthy integrity of the organs is fully re-established. If those who are married suffer from the unmanly losses of semen, they should by all means make early endeavors to have their manhood restored in all its fulness. Those who are partially impotent should not neglect to secure the required treatment—such as will restore virile vigor and healthy procreating power. Medical treatment is of the greatest importance, and, assuredly, it is only those who have full manly vigor and integrity that can hope for healthy offspring. It is scarcely an allowable exercise of privilege for any male to marry if suffering from the effects of indiscretions, as it is well known to every physiologist that procreative capacity is lessened thereby, and offspring usually of feeble mind and body and low moral tone. Let all such sufferers then fully appreciate the responsibility of the married state, and only enter its portals with healthy genital organs and proper virile capacity. This advice should be heeded by all who properly estimate marital eligibility. Their first duty is to engage the services of a competent physician, who will by proper treatment restore the proper integrity of the organs, impart the required vigor, and secure the necessary conditions for healthy propagation.

Eligibility for motherhood requires full integrity of womanhood. No healthy babe can be born if its ante-natal life is passed in a diseased uterine cavity. Women suffering from inflammation or ulceration of the mucous membrane lining the uterine cavity cannot possibly give birth to a healthy child. It is then a high duty for all wives to make all possible effort to become sexually healthy, and if they have the prudence to engage the proper herbal treatment they will certainly regain the required feminine vigor and motherhood will be a blessing instead of a curse.

Proper treatment will even avert the transmission of scrofula, epilepsy, consumption, and other diseases capable of hereditation. This must be given while the child is developing within the uterine cavity. The disease in the parent may not be cured, but rational treatment, under the guidance of a skillful physician, can so modify the gestatory process as to effectually prevent the child from being born with a similar diathesis.

This subject is one of the most important within the whole range of medicine, and should engage the interest of all; it concerns not only individual welfare, but the health and the mental and moral well-being of the whole human race.

The author gladly gives advice to those who may need counsel or treatment. Parents who submit their cases for my consideration will be fully advised what course should be pursued. All communications held inviolably secret. (See page 390 for guidance as to consultation.)

DIVORCE.

This implies the separation of the married pair, by legal dissolution of the matrimonial bonds. Divorces are most commonly given by the courts for causes occurring after marriage; but jurists, in treating upon this subject, also include those causes by which a marriage may be rendered null upon antecedent grounds; as where a marriage was accomplished by forcible or fraudulent means, or where, in consequence of near consanguinity, the act of cohabitation between the pair is by law considered incestuous. Where a physical incapacity for marriage prevails in one of the parties, divorces are usually granted by nearly all courts, provided such an incapacity existed previous to marriage.

It is not our purpose, however, to discuss the subject in its legal aspect, however interesting it might be, but to consider it rather in its popular sense. It is not within the province of the medical writer to consider the subject relative to its legal bearings, though he may with propriety give the subject the attention it claims with reference to abuse of the marital privilege. There are practically many divorces between husbands and wives, of which the law takes no cognizance, and for causes for which no court would grant a dispensation. The author is fully aware that the divorce laws are not any too stringent, and probably too facile in many commonwealths; but, while he is by no means in favor of easy divorce laws, he is ready to admit that the strong hand of the law sometimes is not waved to the side of justice, but inflicts intolerable anguish by enforcing a matrimonial existence which in its very nature is adverse to the very spirit and essence of matrimony.

It is practically divorcing the marriage tie when mutual love no longer characterizes the union. The only bond that unites and that makes the union an inseparable one is love, and not the mere formal ceremony of espousal. The law, however, does not and cannot recognize anything but the *vinculum matrimonii* as binding, but the philosopher delves deeper, and while he does not dispute the necessity of legal ceremonies, he nevertheless knows that marriage is in its very essence not such a union as defined by law, but a linking of affections, a union of souls and hearts. Marriage is practically annulled when love is no longer the cord of union; without mutual affection the association becomes intolerable, the higher purposes of the tie are defeated, and the sacred precinct is invaded by elements foreign to the psychical character of the marital atmosphere. Law can, however, not remedy this; the candidates for marriage must, as before advised, exercise such precautions, that they may not deceive themselves, and only form a matrimonial alliance that augurs a congenial wedded life. Divorces cannot be granted for uncongeniality, provided no actual infringement of the marriage bond has been committed, and cannot extend a dispensation because married life is loveless. Abuse of its privileges would follow, and divorce laws should therefore of necessity be stringent, so that marriages be not recklessly contracted, and obliging intended union to be the result of guarded and careful deliberation, as it is easier to prevent mistakes than to rectify them. Negligence of consulting the better knowledge brings its own reward, and, however intolerable the punishment, a separation cannot ensue by virtue of law. Humanity would grant the dissolution of the tie, but the purity and purpose of law must be protected. Stringency must shield it from disgrace, or the possible chance of its becoming the agent whereby injury may be done, or flagrant violations of matrimonial duty may be prompted by its laxity. Every candidate should lose sight of every consideration except that of happiness in married life, and see that no one can exclaim

> "She (or he) whom the law calls yours,
> Is by her (or his) love made mine."

In nearly all courts, adultery is sufficient cause for divorce, and very properly so. It is the most heinous violation of the duty and trust attached to a conjugal union. Everything besides pales in comparison with adultery in the enormity of its malfeasance in the marital sphere. It is such a flagrant abuse of duty and fidelity that the conjugal pair owe to each other, that it has even been recognized by divine law as sufficient cause for divorce, and as long as civilization has a foothold, and morality considered a virtue, so long will adultery be regarded subversive to the integrity of the conjugal union. It is a crime admitting of no extenuation, and incapable of condonement by the morally upright or the virtuous pure. It is the brand that inflames the worst passions in the one who has thus been injured and disgraced by his or her conjugal associate, surely engendering hate and detestation if the proper value is placed upon marital loyalty. The bubble that has just burst is as easily reconstructed as to agair establish confidence, peace and happiness in that family, of which either the husband or wife has sinned. The wound is incurable, and prolongation of the wedded association only aggravates. Therefore, the only remedy is a legal separation from the one who has proved so unworthy of marital trust. It is not enough that the husband and wife should be guiltless of adultery, but their conduct must be such as to arouse no suspicion of neighbors or others. The conduct must be so guarded that loyalty is not doubted, but manifested even under circumstances where the liability to err is great, so that fidelity is established, and suspicion disarmed.

That wife who, by her conduct in society, or in her social intercourse with other men, brings upon her mistrust, and who provokes public scandal by her vagaries and lax conduct, actually debauches her husband's good name, and does him as much injury as she would were she guilty of adultery. She may never have committed the act, and probably never would, but her deportment is such as to lead observers to the opinion that she would prove disloyal if circumstances favored thereby committing a grievous wrong, and staining the honor and good name of her husband to an unwarrantable extent. The man that brings to his bride the legacy of honor and respectability is greatly injured if she by her immoral conduct begets the suspicion as to loyalty of his friends and neighbors, and she is unworthy of his love and protection if she so far forgets her duty as bring a stain upon his character by her own imprudence. She is guilty of adulterous proclivities, which should be considered sufficient cause for divorce, even if adultery cannot be proven. On the other hand, the husband, who by improper behavior in company, is so unguarded as to be suspected for his loyalty and attachment to his wife, is unworthy of her, and cannot justify his conduct by even the most liberal interpretation of the marriage contract. It would, unquestionably, be well if the law would recognize conduct that suggests an adulterous proclivity as sufficient for divorce, even if adultery *per se* could not be proven, as it would most probably have a salutary effect in counteracting the tendency to the degeneracy of modern free-loveism.

The cry of many wives of the present day, who think that their duty to society is paramount to the duty they owe to their husbands is—Would you exclude us from society? Am I to be imprisoned in the home you afford me and not be allowed to receive my friends, or to mingle again with society? No, not at all; the seclusivism of the harem is not calculated to promote the best interests of conjugal life; but it is to be insisted upon that when wives are in society their conduct should be so dignified, so hedged in with propriety, that their reputation remains unsullied, that the most suspicious need not suspect, and that the libertine is given no opportunity to make his offensive proposals, nor his heart gratified by a passive submission to his lascivious conversation, looks, and hints. Cæsar claimed not too much in his requirements of a wife—she should in all respects be above suspicion. The wife's greatest pride should be the observance of such a line of conduct as meets her husband's approval. All her actions should be characterized by purity and fidelity, and no cause should be given for unpleasant comment. Such noble wives are denominated the oppressed, the slaves of men, etc., etc., by the Women's Rights women; but they are not,—they and they only are the idols of men, at least of those whose affections are pure and worth having. The angelic quality of women, so often the theme of poets and lovers, is surely only manifested by the virtuous and in the faithful. The very existence of civilization is dependent upon virtuous women and faithful wives; men may become depraved, but as long as women remain pure, civilization, morality, and religion will be fostered and propagated. If women live the truth and act the truth, humanity will ever be blessed with the benefits of civilization.

To the sterner sex the mantle of virtue is no less becoming; and fidelity is as much of an adornment and requirement to them as of the gentler sex. The libertine is a despicable creature; and the adulterer is so lost to honor and nobility of character, that his presence in the society of the pure and good should be considered an outrage upon decency and propriety. Chastity is a superior virtue, and loyalty in wedlock a noble attribute; and whichever one of the conjugal pair proves reckless to these connubial trusts is unworthy of marital companionship and defiles a sacred institution.

BRIDAL TOURS.

"Some essays have been written on the barbarisms of civilization; many more might be. Many of the habits prevailing in what ought to be our most refined society are at variance with almost elementary ideas of decency. Others are equally marked in their injurious physical tendencies. It is not surprising that clergymen, even when not of the strictest sect, and philosophers of no particular sect at all, have declaimed against fashionable dresses and dances at late hours. But there are other customs against which no church has fulminated its anathemas, the dangers and absurdities of which no fidgety reformer has perceived or noticed. One of these conspicuously is the Bridal Tour.

"Let us illustrate by a typical case. During one of the earliest and coldest 'cold snaps' there comes off a wedding, which, from the official standing of the parties, naturally attracts some attention. We are soon told that the 'happy couple' are off on their wedding trip to—well, not exactly Alaska or Greenland, but a territory nearly as frigid, and that part of the journey is to be made in stages or sleighs. The intense excitement in appropriateness of the proceeding, the wonderful pains taken by these people to make themselves uncomfortable on what is supposed to be the most festive occasion in their lives, would move one to Homeric laughter, did not events disastrous to the health of the conjugal pair usually follow so closely on the heels of bridal tours." If the parties are not as high in the social scale and less wealthy, the mischief done is as great, if not greater, for in their tour they may lack substantial comforts which the wealthy alone can afford. To all married couples a bridal tour seems to be considered as absolutely essential to give the marital union an importance, without which it would, in their opinion, be an unromantic and but partial marriage.

Looking at the custom from an æsthetic and sentimental point of view, nothing can be more repulsive. An American marriage is theoretically a love match, and it is generally so in practice. Now two persons in love want to see as much as possible of each other, and as little as possible of other people. It is to that we find exceptions; there are individuals whose diseased vanity desires to give publicity to every act of their life. It is a misfortune that these vulgarians are not rarer in every class. An instinct of seclusion and modesty should be the general rule, but this absurd custom forces a new-married couple to put on an unnatural restraint on their legitimate affection, or to make themselves ridiculous before the public. Love, both emotional and passionate, is usually most exuberant to those recently joined in wedlock, and philosophy would suggest the exercise to be confined more to seclusion than the sporadic opportunities afforded in a wedding tour.

Now, in the common-sense, practical, man-of-the-world point of view, the fashionable practice is equally objectionable. It is notorious that nothing, except marriage itself, tries the temper more than joint travel. Therefore, at the very outset of their life-partnership, the quality on which the happiness of that union principally depends is put to the rudest strain. The happy couple expose themselves to the insolence of hackmen and hotel-clerks, the discomforts of rail and hotel, irregular hours and uncertain meals. The Irishman, in the song, married a wife to make him "unaisy." A wedding tour on one of our great thoroughfares of travel is admirably contrived to accomplish this result for both parties.

All this, however, it may be suggested, is matter of taste. We cannot expect to shape the caprices of fashion or custom by the dictates of deliberate philosophy. But what follows is not a questionable point of taste or comfort; it is a matter of downright fact, as certain as if it could be mathematically demonstrated.

The consummation of marriage is, with the exception of child-birth, the most critical period, physically, of the woman's life. After the moral and physical excitement which attends it, her system demands rest, repose, quiet, regular and good living, a supporting and restorative way of life. If these can be secured for some weeks, so much the better, but at any rate they are necessary for some days. Her emotional nature attains the highest state of excitement, in consequence of assisting in a repast which is approached only by intense agitation, no matter how much she may feel it to be a legitimate incident to marriage. This makes it doubly exhaustive, and not only her health for the rest of her mortal existence, but the health and strength of her offspring may be, and often are, materially affected by the want of proper care at this time. Instead of which, the bridal tour piles on additional excitement and fatigue, makes regularity of life impossible—in short, the act involves the reverse of all that the rules of health and physiology require. There is an underlying sense of modesty which may urge the bride on to a journey immediately after marriage. The new condition of life exacts changes which she rather would fulfil among strangers than in her own or husband's domicile. It may confuse the modest and retiring woman to assume the conjugal associations in presence of her parents, brothers, and sisters; but as this is one of the modesties not really commendable, however natural it may be, it does not afford sufficient inducement for encountering all the vicissitudes of a wedding tour.

For man too, at this time, repose and calm, though not so necessary, are highly desirable. It constantly happens, in the case of both sexes, that a slight indisposition, which passed unnoticed in the hurry of preparation, is aggravated to a serious and even fatal extent by the excitement, exposure, and neglect consequent on the wedding tour. No man, for instance, would think of postponing his marriage on account of a slight cold. If he stayed quietly at home afterward, and took care of himself, it would pass away like other slight colds; but he goes off on a bridal tour in the depth of winter, and the malady develops into a chronic pulmonary complaint. Nor would a young woman put off her marriage because she felt a little extra lassitude and want of appetite, with an occasional headache, which, however, *may* be premonitory symptoms of typhoid fever. If you take typhoid fever in time, there is nothing specially dangerous about it; care, patience, and slight treatment are only necessary, and it runs its course. But, if neglected at first, it is almost inevitably fatal. Many cases of brides and bridegrooms, in my profesional experience, came under my observation, dying of typhoid fever just after a wedding trip, which had caused the early symptoms to be misunderstood and neglected. And I have known things worse than death to happen—insanity, temporary or permanent, brought on by the extra fatigue and excitement of the wedding journey.

One old New York custom, and probably to some extent prevailing in other places, was infinitely more rational. The new-married couple took up their quarters at the house of the bride's father, and remained there in seclusion for a week. The only fault about this arrangement was the shortness of time, but for a week, at any rate, they had absolute repose and quiet, and enjoyed all the comforts of a home without the trouble of housekeeping. For one week, at least, the inter-communion of the conjugal pair was unhampered, and secured against the criticism and gaze of the public.

The present fashion of bridal tours is an unmeaning and unreasonable imitation of the European, especially the English practice. The original English theory of a wedding trip is, driving in a comfortable carriage, at a rate of speed just sufficient to exhilarate without fatiguing, over good roads, in weather which may be pleasant or unpleasant, but is never dangerously cold or dangerously hot, to some secluded country-place or seaside village, and resting there a month. The new mode of continental tours is in some respects just as absurd as ours, though the advantage of climate lessens the fatigue and physical risk to some extent. The notorious mutability of our climate is in itself reason enough why a bride should not be exposed to the accidents of travel.

It will thus be seen that the medical aspect of a bridal tour is sufficiently important, and the risk incurred sufficiently great, to cause the wedded pair, if they wish to be actuated with impulses of reason and prudence, rather than by the dictates of custom, to pause before they undergo the trials of a wedding journey. It would certainly be more conducive to their health and happiness if they were guided by a better reason in this respect, and leave wedding trips to be indulged in by those who would rather run the risk of injuring their health and general well-being than offend a fashionable practice. It is a fashionable vulgarity, and not prompted by the behests of good-breeding and social dignity.

POISONS AND THEIR ANTIDOTES.

Nothing that appertains to domestic treatment is of greater value than a knowledge of poisons, and the treatment necessary in cases of accidental or premeditated poisoning. So many substances of a poisonous nature are used in manufactures among farmers, mechanics, and also in private houses, it will be useful to have a guide to refer to in case of accident, for in almost every case of poisoning the antidote must be instantly given or else success cannot be expected. In all cases, unless the physician is within immediate call, no time is allowed to engage his services; hence the great importance of every one supplying himself with the requisite knowledge to treat any or all cases of poisoning.

Precaution with regard to poisons is very necessary. In every family, manufactory, etc., where poisons are required and used, the antidotes should also be kept for use whenever occasion calls for them. Again, when poisons are used for any purpose, it is not enough to know that they *are poisonous*, but it should also be known of what they are composed. For instance, corrosive sublimate may be used, and by accident a poisonous dose may be taken of it; but, unless known that it is a preparation of mercury. the treatment must necessarily be of a vague and uncertain character.

As a general rule, in all cases of poisoning, especially if seen immediately after the poison has been swallowed, the indication is to make the person *vomit*. To bring this about give a teaspoonful of mustard in a tumbler of water, or two or three teaspoonfuls of powdered alum in the same way. Vomiting can in all cases be promoted by tickling the throat with a feather.

ARSENIC.

ARTICLES.—Scheele's green, arsenious acid, orpiment, king's yellow, realgar, fly powder, ague drops, arsenical paste and arsenical soap, rat poison.

SYMPTOMS.—Pain and burning in the stomach, dryness of throat, cramps, purging, vomiting, hoarseness and difficulty of speech, eyes red and sparkling, suppression of urine, matter vomited greenish or yellowish.

TREATMENT.—Give large quantities of milk and raw eggs, lime-water, or flour and water. Then castor-oil; or, if tincture of iron is within reach, take from half to a full teaspoonful of it, and mix with it a little bicarbonate of soda or saleratus, and administer it to the person, and follow it with an emetic. This acts as a real antidote—the chemical combination resulting being insoluble in the fluids of the stomach.

ACIDS.

ARTICLES.—Oxalic (salts of sorrel), sulphuric (oil of vitriol), nitric (aquafortis), muriatic (spirit of salt), but not prussic acid.

SYMPTOMS.—These acids are all corrosive, and hence produce horrible burning and sour pain from the mouth downwards. The skin and mucous membrane of the lips, mouth, and throat is eaten away. The patient experiences great thirst, and purges blood, and has excruciating pain in the stomach.

TREATMENT.—Put an ounce of calcined magnesia into a pint of water, and give a wineglassful every two or three minutes. If you cannot get magnesia, use whiting, chalk, soda, or lime-water, or even knock a piece of mortar from the wall, pound it fine, and give it with milk or water. While one person is attending to this, let another cut common soap into small pieces and give a tea-spoonful with water, or a table-spoonful of soft soap. Also give plenty of warm water to drink.

Citric and *acetic* acids are also poisonous in large doses. The treatment is the same as for the above.

ANTIMONY.

ARTICLES.—Tartar emetic, butter of antimony, oxide of antimony.

SYMPTOMS.—Severe vomiting (if this does not occur it should be induced), cramps, faintness, purging, colicky pains, sense of tightness in the chest, recurrence of vomiting repeatedly.

TREATMENT.—Give plenty of strong tea. If no common tea is at hand, use an infusion of oak, elm, sloe, currant, or blackberry bark or leaves, the requirements being a vegetable astringent. If the butter of antimony has been taken, resort to the treatment advised for acids. In all cases the strength should be supported with stimulants.

Bismuth.

Articles.—Nitrate, pearl powder, face powders.

Symptoms.—General inflammation of the whole alimentary canal, suppression of urine, hiccough, vomiting, cramps.

Treatment.—Plenty of milk, flaxseed tea, infusion of slippery elm, marsh mallow.

Copper.

Articles.—Blue copperas, blue verditer, mineral green, verdigris, food cooked in copper vessels, pickles made green by copper.

Symptoms.—Coppery taste in the mouth, tongue dry and parched, very painful colic, bloody stools, convulsions.

Treatment.—Large quantities of milk and white of eggs, afterwards strong tea. *Vinegar should not be given.*

Gold.

Articles.—Chloride of gold, fulminating gold.

Symptoms.—Similar to other irritant poisons. Pink patches about the lips and mouth.

Treatment.—Give sulphate of iron, which decomposes the substances.

Iodine.

Articles.—Iodides of potassium, mercury, iron, or sodium.

Symptoms.—Burning pain in throat, lacerating pain in stomach, heartburn, vomiting, colicky pains, very likely salivation.

Treatment.—Large quantities of starch and water, flour and water, grated potatoes, or anything that you know contains starch. If the iodides are taken in overdose, produce vomiting as soon as possible.

Iron.

Articles.—Sulphate of iron (copperas), green vitriol, chloride of iron.

Symptoms.—Colic pains, constant vomiting and purging, violent pain in throat, coldness of skin, feeble pulse.

Treatment—Give an emetic, afterwards magnesia or carbonate of soda and water. Also mucilaginous drinks

LEAD.

ARTICLES.—Acetate or sugar of lead, white lead, red lead. litharge

SYMPTOMS.—Metallic taste in mouth, pain in stomach and bowels, painful vomiting, often blood, hiccough. If taken for some time, obstinate colic, paralysis, partial or complete; obstinate constipation, diminution of urine.

TREATMENT.—Put two ounces of epsom salts into a pint of water and give a wineglassful every ten minutes until it operates freely. If the solid forms have been taken, give dilute sulphuric acid, but very carefully.

MERCURY.

ARTICLES.—Calomel, corrosive sublimate, red precipitate, vermilion, white precipitate, turbith mineral.

SYMPTOMS.—Harsh metallic astringent taste, burning pain in the stomach, vomiting and purging frequently of bloody matter, tightness and burning in the throat, tendency to doze, stupor.

TREATMENT.—Albumen in some form must be instantly given; either the white of eggs beaten up with water, milk or wheat flour beaten up. Iron filings can also be given. After these give linseed tea.

PHOSPHORUS.

ARTICLES.—Lucifer matches.

SYMPTOMS.—Pain in stomach and bowels, vomiting, diarrhœa, tenderness and tension of the abdomen, great excitement of the whole system.

TREATMENT.—Prompt emetic, copious draughts of warm water containing magnesia, chalk, whiting, or even flour. No oils or fat should be given.

SILVER.

ARTICLES.—Nitrate, or lunar caustic.

SYMPTOMS.—Similar to other irritant poisons, especially arsenic.

TREATMENT.—Give a large teaspoonful of common salt in a glass of water, and repeat this in ten minutes. Then a dose of castor-oil, and linseed tea, or barley water for a drink.

TIN.

ARTICLES.—Chloride, called muriate by dyers, oxide, or putty powder.

SYMPTOMS.—Vomiting, pain in stomach, purging, convulsive twitchings.

TREATMENT.—Milk must be given copiously. The milk may contain magnesia, chalk, or whiting, if handy. Also raw eggs beaten up with water and milk.

ZINC.

ARTICLES.—Sulphate, or white vitriol. Acetate, chloride (Burnett's disinfecting fluid, also used to destroy cancers).

SYMPTOMS.—Violent vomiting, astringent taste, burning pain in stomach, pale countenance, cold extremities, dull eyes.

TREATMENT.—Plenty of milk with white of eggs in it. If it is the sulphate give carbonate of soda. If excessive vomiting occurs, it can be relieved by copious draughts of warm water.

VOLATILE OILS.

ARTICLES.—Creasote, Dippel's animal oil, oil of tar, oil of tobacco, oil of turpentine, fusel oil.

SYMPTOMS.—Burning pain, vomiting, pungent taste, purging. The oils of tobacco and turpentine affect the nervous system, and will be recognized by their peculiar odor in the matter vomited.

TREATMENT.—Creasote is immediately coagulated by albumen, as milk, white of eggs. Dippel's animal oil may be counteracted by dilute sulphuric acid, and castor or linseed oil. For the others give milk, and promote vomiting, and probably some stimulant.

ALKALIES.

AMMONIA.—Spirits of hartshorn, muriate, or sal ammoniac.

POTASSA.—Caustic potash, liquor potassa, carbonate, or pearl ash, salts of tartar, nitrate, or saltpetre, or liver of sulphur.

SYMPTOMS.—Violent, caustic, acrid taste, great heat in throat, destruction of the mucous membrane of mouth and throat, cold sweats, weakness, hiccough, colic pains, bloody stools.

TREATMENT.—Vinegar, lemon juice, citric or tartaric acids. If the free alkalies are taken give castor or linseed oils, which will form soap in combination with them. For saltpetre give a mixture of acacia, marsh-mallow, flax-seed tea, and for liver of sulphur give common salt.

PRUSSIC ACID.

ARTICLES.—Oil of bitter almonds, laurel water, peach-kernels, cyanide of potassium, used by photographers.

SYMPTOMS.—If the quantity be large, death instantly ensues. In smaller quantities, nausea, giddiness, debility, weight and pain in the head.

TREATMENT.—Give spirits of hartshorn very much diluted, and apply a bottle of smelling-salts to the nose, dash cold water on the head, give stimulants, and make the patient stir about.

VEGETABLE POISONS.

Opium.

Articles.—Laudanum, paregoric, black drop, soothing syrups, cordials, syrup of poppies, morphine, Dover's powder, etc.

Symptoms.—Giddiness, stupor, gradually increasing to a deep sleep, pupil of the eyes very small, lips blue, skin cold, heavy, slow breathing.

Treatment. –Make the patient vomit as quickly as possible. If a full-grown person give fifteen grains of sulphate of zinc in a little water, to a young person half the quantity, to an infant a teaspoonful of syrup of ipecac. If these drugs cannot be had, use mustard and warm water, salt and water, and tickle the throat with a feather. After vomiting, give plenty of strong coffee, and place a mustard poultice round the calf of each leg, and if the patient is cold and sinking, give stimulants, and rouse him to walking or running by your assistance. Beat the soles of his feet, dash cold water on the face, and do anything to prevent him from sleeping until the effects are passed off, for if he goes to sleep, it is the sleep of death.

Strychnine.

Articles.—Rat poison, nux vomica, St. Ignatius' bean.

Symptoms.—Lockjaw, twitching of the muscles, convulsions, the body is bent backwards, so as to rest on the feet and head only.

Treatment.—Empty the stomach by an emetic, then give linseed tea or barley water, and to an adult give thirty drops of laudanum, to relieve the spasms. A tea-spoonful of ether can also be given.

Other Poisonous Plants, or Seeds,

Such as false mushrooms, belladonna, henbane, or anything a child may have eaten, or taken in mistake by any person. Vegetable poisons act either as an irritant, acro-narcotic, or narcotic. If it an irritant, the symptoms are an acrid, pungent taste, with more or less bitterness, excessive heat, great dryness of the mouth and throat, with sense of tightness there, violent vomiting, purging, with great pain in the stomach and bowels, breathing often quick and difficult, appearance of intoxication, eye frequently dilated, insensibility resembling death. The symptoms of narcotic poisons are described under opium.

Treatment.—If an irritant and vomiting does occur and continues, render it easier by large draughts of warm water, but if symptoms of insensibility have come on without vomiting, empty the stomach with any emetic that may be at hand,—sulphate of zinc, mustard; and after the operation of the emetic give a sharp purgative. After as much as is possible of the poison is got rid of, very strong coffee, or vinegar diluted with water, may be given with advantage. Camphor mixture with a little ether may be taken frequently, and if the insensibility is considerable, warmth, frictions, and blisters may be employed. For the narcotics proceed as in opium.

Animal Poisons.

Poisonous Fish.—Old wife, crawfish, land crab, gray snapper, hyne, dolphin, conger eel, mussel, barracuda, smooth bottle fish, grooper, rock fish, Spanish mackerel, king fish, bonetta, porgee, tunny, blower, etc.

Symptoms.—In an hour or two, or much sooner after the fish has been eaten, a weight at the stomach comes, with slight vertigo and headache, sense of heat about the head and eyes, considerable thirst, and often an eruption of the skin resembling nettle rash.

Treatment.—Give a brisk emetic. After full vomiting an active purgative should be given. Vinegar and water may be drunk after the above remedies have operated, and the body may be sponged with the same. Water made very sweet with sugar, to which a little ether may be added, may also be drunk freely. If spasms occur, give laudanum.

Poisonous Serpents.—Copperhead, moccasin, viper, black viper, rattlesnake, water viper.

Symptoms.—A sharp pain in the wounded part, which soon extends over the limb or body; great swelling, at first hard and pale, then reddish, livid, and gangrenous in appearance, faintings, vomitings, convulsions, pulse small, breathing difficult, cold sweats, failing sight, and derangement of the intellectual faculties.

Treatment.—Tie a string tightly above the wound, wash it well, apply a cupping glass, or let the person bitten suck the wound well if he can. If lunar caustic or butter of antimony are at hand, rub them well in, to the very bottom of the wound, or take a very small poker, or a steel used for sharpening knives; make the point of this red hot—to a white heat, if you can—and press this for a moment into the wound. This is not such a dreadful operation as it seems to be, for one moment's application is sufficient, and, if the steel is really hot enough, gives scarcely any pain at the time. Small doses of hartshorn may also be given, and if gangrene is threatened, give wine freely. In case of rattlesnake bite, give whiskey freely. Bibron's antidote and the Tanjore Pills may also be used,—the latter carefully, as they contain arsenic.

Poisonous Insects.—Spanish fly, potato fly.

Symptoms.—Nauseous odor of the breath, acrid taste, burning heat in the throat, stomach, and abdomen, bloody vomiting, excruciating pain in the stomach, heat in the bladder strangury or retention of urine, frightful convulsions.

TREATMENT.—Excite vomiting by giving sweet-oil, sugar and water, milk or linseed tea, very freely. Rub camphor dissolved in oil over the belly and thighs.

VENOMOUS INSECTS.—Tarantula, scorpion, hornet, wasp, bee, gnat, gad-fly.

SYMPTOMS.—In general, the sting of these insects occasions only a slight degree of pain and swelling, but occasionally the symptoms are more violent, and sickness and fever are produced by the intensity of the pain.

TREATMENT.—Hartshorn and oil may be rubbed on the affected part, and a piece of rag moistened with the same, or with salt and water, may be kept upon it till the pain is over. A few drops of hartshorn may also be frequently given internally, in a little water. The sting may in general be removed by making strong pressure with the barrel of a watch-key around it.

RABID ANIMALS.—See Hydrophobia, in its proper place among disease.

RECIPES.

In the following pages will be found a variety of recipes, applicable to many diseases and afflictions for which symptomatic treatment is all that is required. They will be found to be very valuable for domestic treatment. They are not all strictly herbal, but essentially eclectic, so as to be easily prepared and the ingredients readily procured. Nothing capable of harm is, however, admitted,—the few mineral substances that are prescribed being only inserted for therapeutic effects, in consequence of their vegetable analogues being hard to procure or difficult to prepare. Availability was studied more than scientific arrangement, though the merit of each is retained. For handy recipes, therefore, the following are sufficiently diversified for a wide range of application.

In complicated cases, or in diseases requiring systematic treatment, recipes are not to be depended upon. Such cases, of course, require treatment in accordance with the demands of the pathological conditions observed in the disease, and which should in all cases be directed by a competent physician. The remedies, for which the recipes are given in this connection, are designed merely for diseases or affections not ordinarily grave in character, or which do not require more than simple medication. Those desiring to make use of them should have them prepared by a druggist, if they do not have the necessary pharmaceutical appliances to insure correct weight, quantity, mixture, division, etc. The purity and worth of the article are also to be ascertained before being administered.

GOLDEN TINCTURE.

No. 1. Balsam of tolu, two ounces; gum guaiacum, two ounces; gum hemlock, two ounces; gum myrrh, two ounces; each coarsely powdered; oil of hemlock, three ounces; oil of wintergreen, two ounces; alcohol, one gallon. Let it stand fourteen days. Shake frequently in the meantime.

Dose.—From one to two teaspoonfuls, according to severity and obstinacy of the case, in half a glass of sweetened water. This mixture has proved highly useful as an internal remedy for rheumatism, colic, pains, chills, soreness, lameness, sour stomach, languor, depressed spirits, palpitations, water brash, flatulency, and a variety of painful affections.

PULMONARY REMEDY.

No. 2. Take of the roots of spikenard, elecampane, comfrey and blood-root: of the leaves and flowers of hoarhound, and of the bark of wild cherry, each one pound. These may all be ground and tinctured, by adding alcohol, water, and sugar sufficient to make three gallons of syrup, or any portion of the above compound may be tinctured in sufficient alcohol to cover them, when the herbs may be boiled until their strength is obtained, and the tincture and watery infusion may be mixed, and a sufficient amount of refined sugar added to make a thick syrup. For coughs and colds, to be taken in teaspoonful doses as required.

LIVER CORDIAL.

No. 3. Thorough-wort, two ounces; ginger, half ounce; cloves, half ounce; extract dandelion, four ounces; water, one and a half pints. Boil to one-third, and add sugar one and one-half pounds, and brandy, one pint.

Dose.—A wineglassful once or twice a day. An excellent cordial cathartic to act upon the liver. The herbs must be gathered at the proper season or they will be worthless.

ANTI-BILIOUS PILL.

No. 4. Aloes, pulverized, five ounces; fine, dry castile soap, half a drachm; gamboge, pulverized, one ounce; colocynth, one ounce; extract of gentian, one ounce; mandrake, one ounce; cayenne pepper, two ounces; oil of peppermint, half a drachm. Mix well together, and form into three-grain pills.

Dose.—Three to five pills.

AN EXPECTORANT.

No. 5. For asthma and cough, to promote expectoration, and remove tightness of the chest, the following is a valuable compound preparation. Fluid extracts of skunk cabbage, one ounce; lobelia, one ounce; blood-root, one ounce; pleurisy-root, one ounce; ginger, one ounce; water, one pint; alcohol, three pints.

Dose.—Two to four teaspoonfuls. (See Fluid Extracts, page 475.)

FOR PRODUCING SLEEP.

No. 6. The following is a useful preparation for producing sleep, in wakeful or excited conditions, viz.: fluid extract of ladies' slipper, one ounce; fluid extract of pleurisy-root, one ounce; fluid extract of skunk cabbage, one ounce; fluid extract scull-cap, one ounce. Mix.

Dose.—Half a drachm to a drachm three times a day.

FOR SICK AND NERVOUS HEADACHE.

No. 7. For sick and nervous headache, dependent on an acid stomach, the following is useful: fluid extract of ladies' slipper, half an ounce; fluid extract of catnip, half an ounce; fluid extract of scull-cap, half an ounce; water, one pint.

Dose.—One to three teaspoonfuls. Mix.

TONIC TINCTURE.

No. 8. Old cider, four gallons; white oak bark, ten ounces; horse-radish root, one pound; seneca snake-root, six ounces; golden seal root, four ounces; cayenne pepper, two ounces; bruise all fine, add the cider, let stand for ten days, frequently shaking up the mixture in the meantime.

Dose.—For an adult, half to two-thirds of a wine-glassful, three times a day

SARSAPARILLA SYRUP.

No. 9. Good sarsaparilla, two pounds; guaiacum, three ounces; rose leaves, two ounces; senna, two ounces; liquorice root, two ounces; oil of sassafras, five drops; oil of aniseed, five drops; oil of wintergreen, three drops; diluted alcohol, ten pints; sugar, eight pounds.

Dose.—A tablespoonful two or three times a day.

RHEUMATIC TINCTURE.

No. 10. Peppermint water, one and one-half ounces; wine of colchicum root, half an ounce; sulphate of morphia, one grain; magnesia, one scruple.

Dose.—One teaspoonful three or four times a day.

FOR BRONCHITIS.

No. 11. Tannin, three grains; extract of belladonna, three-fourths of a grain; extract of conium, two and a half grains; infusion of senna, three ounces; fennel water, one and a half ounces; syrup of marsh-mallow, one and a half ounces. Mix.

Dose.—A tablespoonful to be taken every two hours in chronic bronchitis.

COMPOUND SPIRITS OF LAVENDER.

No. 12. Dried lavender flowers, two drachms; nutmeg, 2 drachms; mace, two drachms; cloves, two ounces; cinnamon, two ounces. Pulverize all these, and add a quart of spirits. Let it then stand for a week, and then strain off the liquid.

Dose.—One or two teaspoonfuls may be taken often in a little water, with loaf sugar. Useful in nervous affections.

NERVE TONIC.

No. 13. Extract of scull-cap, two drachms; extract of chamomile, two drachms; extract of boneset, one drachm; pulverized cayenne, one scruple; quinine, one drachm; oil of valerian, half a drachm. Beat well together, and make ninety pills.

Dose.—For an adult, one pill every two or three hours.

STOMACHIC BITTERS.

No. 14. Gentian root, two ounces; dried orange peel, one ounce; cardamon seed, half an ounce (all bruised); diluted alcohol or common whiskey, one quart. Let it stand for two weeks.

Use.—Dyspepsia, loss of appetite, general weakness, etc.

Dose.—One or two tablespoonfuls in water, three times a day.

FEVER AND AGUE.

No. 15. Take of boneset, two ounces; blue vervain, two ounces; scull-cap, one ounce; Virginia snake-root, half an ounce. Make an infusion, and drink freely while warm. If it produces vomiting, reduce the dose. This will be found highly beneficial. If the bowels are constipated, use one of my "Renovating Pills" every night until all constipation has been removed or remedied.

STRENGTHENING PLASTER.

No. 16. Resin, one pound; beeswax, one ounce; Burgundy pitch, one ounce; mutton tallow, one ounce. Melt them together, and add olive oil, pulverized camphor and sassafras oil, of each one-sixteenth of an ounce, and West India rum, one fluid ounce. Stir well together, pour into cold water, and form into rolls with the hands; spread with a knife on a piece of linen cloth, and apply in weakness of the joints, rheumatism, weak chest, weak back, ulcers. This is an excellent plaster for all such purposes.

ACETIC BLOOD-ROOT SYRUP.

No. 17. Blood-root in powder, one drachm; acetic acid, or vinegar, one pint; water one pint. Add the blood-root to the vinegar and water mixed, and steep for two hours then strain and add two pounds of white sugar, simmer until a syrup is formed.

This is a *specific* remedy for pseudo-membranous croup. It is also used in infantile pneumonia and bronchitis, but the "Acacian Balsam" should be used with it.

Dose.—For croup, from half a teaspoonful to a tablespoonful, but it should not be given in quantities sufficient to provoke vomiting, unless there is imminent danger of suffocation, and then only sufficient to eject the mucus adhering to the upper part of the bronchia and trachea

A GOOD EMETIC.

No. 18. Pulverized lobelia, one ounce; pulverized blood-root, one ounce; pulv. ipecacuanha, six drachms; pulv. cayenne, four scruples; seneca, one scruple. Mix. An excellent emetic in all cases where one is required. My "Renovating Pills" should be used to cleanse the system of all remaining particles of lobelia.

Dose.—Half a teaspoonful in a cup of warm water, and repeat every fifteen minutes until it operates.

NERVE TONIC AND ANTISPASMODIC.

No. 19. High cranberry bark, one ounce; skunk cabbage-root, half an ounce; scull-cap, half an ounce; cardamon seeds, two drachms; pulv. cayenne, two drachms. Put these into a pint of wine. Shake it well every day for three or four days.

Dose.—A tablespoonful four times a day.

DYSENTERY SYRUP.

No. 20. Best Turkey rhubarb, two drachms; leptandrin, two drachms; white sugar, one pound; hot water, one pint. Triturate well together; add essence of peppermint, one drachm; essence of anise, one drachm; tincture of catechu, two drachms.

Dose.—For dysentery, one teaspoonful every half hour.

COUGH PREPARATION.

No. 21. Tincture of lobelia, half an ounce; tincture of blood-root, two ounces; oil of spearmint, half a drachm; molasses, five ounces.

Dose.—Take one-half of a teaspoonful as often as needed. Useful merely as a palliative.

PULMONARY SYRUP.

No. 22. Spikenard root, sixteen ounces; white root, sixteen ounces; blood-root, eight ounces; elecampane, eight ounces; colts-foot, eight ounces; boneset, eight ounces; poplar bark, four ounces; seneca snake-root, two ounces; lobelia, two ounces; slippery elm bark, eight ounces; proof spirits, three gallons. Bruise or pulverize all, and digest in the spirits for fourteen days; then strain, and add white sugar sufficient to form a syrup.

Dose.—A tablespoonful occasionally, in a mucilage of slippery elm.

Use.—This is a fair relief in all coughs and pulmonary affections.

CHRONIC DISEASES OF THE MUCOUS SURFACES.

No. 23. Hard balsam copaiba, three and a half drachms; fresh ground cubebs three and a half drachms; carbonate of ammonia, one drachm. Make one hundred pills.

Dose.—One pill three times a day, between meals.

LINIMENT FOR CHILBLAINS.

No. 24. Sulphuric acid, one drachm; spirits of turpentine, one drachm; olive oil, three drachms. Mix the oil and turpentine first, then gradually add the sulphuric acid.

A valuable liniment for chilblains. To be rubbed on two or three times a day.

LINIMENT FOR NEURALGIA, ETC.

No. 25. Sweet oil, one ounce; water of ammonia, strong, one ounce. Mix. To be rubbed on with a piece of flannel. A temporary relief for crick in the neck, and rheumatic and neuralgic pains.

SLEEPLESSNESS.

No. 26 Camphor, one grain, formed into a pill, followed by a draught of an ounce and a half of the infusion of hops, with five drops of sulphuric ether.

CHRONIC RHEUMATISM.

No. 27. The remedies given below will be found generally useful:

First.—Warm salt bath. When the pain is very severe at night, take tincture of guaiacum, one drachm; tincture of aloes, half a drachm; spirits of turpentine, thirty drops. Mix, and take in a pint of gruel at bedtime.

Second.—Should the pains continue very severe, give the following: Aloes, half a scruple; opium, three grains; syrup of buckthorn sufficient to form a pill mass. Mix, and make three pills; one at bedtime.

Third.—Compound powder of ipecacuanha, eight grains; camphor mixture, one and a half ounces. Mix, and give a draught every night.

Fourth.—Take wine of colchicum seeds, one ounce; give from ten to twenty drops in gruel or water three times a day, with one of the following pills: sulphate of quinia, twenty-four grains; and syrup sufficient to form into twelve pills; *or*.

Fifth.—Iodide of potassium, one drachm; distilled water, two ounces.

Mix, and give a teaspoonful in a wine-glass of water—morning, noon, and night. This seldom ever fails to give relief.

REMEDY FOR BOWEL COMPLAINT.

No. 28. Rhubarb, pulverized, one ounce; saleratus, one teaspoonful: pour on a pint of boiling water. When cold, add a tablespoonful of essence of peppermint.

Dose.—From one to three tablespoonfuls two or three times a day.

WORM MIXTURE.

No. 29. Populin, one drachm; santonine, twenty grains; tincture of pink root, four ounces; neutralizing mixture, one pint. Rub the santonine in the neutralizing mixture, until thoroughly mixed, then add the other ingredients. Excellent for removing worms in children.

Dose.—From thirty to forty drops every half hour, until it acts on the bowels as a purge. If the worms are not removed, repeat every two or three days; but be cautious to get *good* pink root, as much of the plant sold for pink root by the druggists is poisonous. This is inferior, however, to my "Male Fern Vermifuge," see page 471.

PAINFUL MENSTRUATION.

No. 30. Extract of hyoscyamus, gum camphor, and Dover's powder, of each one scruple. Mix, and make into twenty pills.

Dose.—One pill twice a day for painful menstruation.

STOMACH PILL.

No. 31.—Pulverized rhubarb, and guaiacum, of each eight grains; galbanum, two grains; ipecacuanha, two grains. Mix, and make eight pills.

Dose.—Take one or two pills, night and morning. Excellent for a weak stomach, and a bilious condition.

BRONCHIAL TROCHES. (*For Temporary Relief.*)

No. 32. Extract of liquorice, one pound; sugar, one and a half pounds: cubebs, four ounces; gum arabic, four ounces; all pulverized; extract of conium, one ounce. Mix, and take a piece as big as a pea and dissolve it in the mouth, several times a day; rubbing the neck three times a day with the "Herbal Ointment."

DIARRHŒA.

No. 33. Syrup of orange peel, one ounce; acetate of morphia, two grains; tincture of cinnamon, six drachms; tincture of cardamon, two drachms. Mix.

Dose.—A teaspoonful. Valuable in diarrhœa.

NEURALGIA.

No. 34. Tincture of American hellebore, one drachm; tincture of black cohosh, two ounces. Mix.

Dose.—One teaspoonful, from three to six times a day.

PILE OINTMENT.

No. 35. Extract of stramonium, one ounce; extract of tobacco, one ounce; tannin, ten grains. Make an ointment, and bathe or lubricate the parts, if you cannot at once get the "Herbal Ointment."

STOMACHIC PILL.

No. 36. Powdered cayenne pepper, one drachm; rhubarb, two drachms. Make into a mass with syrup, and divide into sixty pills.

Dose.—Two to three every day, an hour before dinner.

AROMATIC BITTERS. (*Stimulant.*)

No. 37. *First.*—ABSINTHIUM (*Wormwood*). Infuse three drachms in twenty ounces of water.

Dose.—From a half to two tablespoonfuls.

Use.—In debilitated state of the digestive organs.

Second.—ACORUS—Calamus (*Sweet flag root*). Infuse one ounce in twenty ounces of water. Joined with other tonics.

Use.—In uneasiness from flatulence.

TONIC TEA. (*Debility.*)

No. 38. Chamomile, scull-cap, and queen of the meadow, each one pound. Reduce them to powder, and mix well together.

Dose.—To one tablespoonful of this powder add one pint of water; make a tea, and drink during the day. This is a good tonic in all cases of debility.

SPICED BITTERS. (*For weak patients.*)

No. 39. Poplar bark, ten pounds; bayberry bark, two pounds; balmony bark, two pounds; golden seal, one pound; cloves, one pound; cayenne pepper, half a pound; loaf sugar, sixteen pounds.

Let these articles all be made fine and well mixed. Put a tablespoonful of this compound, with four ounces of sugar, into a quart of boiling water. Take a wineglassful three times a day before eating, or a teaspoonful of these powders may be taken in a cup of hot water, half an hour before each meal.

TONIC. (*For Chlorosis, or Green Sickness.*)

No. 40. Sulphate of quinia, fifteen grains; diluted sulphuric acid, fifteen drops; compound tincture of cardamon, three drachms; tincture of hops, three drachms; compound infusion of roses, six ounces. Mix.

Dose.—A teaspoonful two or three times a day.

WHOOPING COUGH MIXTURE.

No. 41. Tincture of blood-root, one ounce; tincture of red root, two ounces; tincture of black cohosh, one ounce; tincture of lobelia, half an ounce; tincture of belladonna, twenty drops. Mix, and shake well before using.

Dose.—For a child one year old, fifteen or twenty drops in sweetened water. The fluid extracts (see page 475) can be used instead of the tinctures. Dose, when fluid extracts are used, three to five drops.

TINCTURE FOR FEVER AND AGUE, ETC.

No. 42. Peruvian bark and wild cherry bark, each two ounces; cinnamon, cloves, and nutmeg, each one drachm; wine, two quarts. Let it stand for a few days to extract the strength.

Dose.—A wineglassful every two or three hours.

Use.—A very good remedy for intermittent fever, or fever and ague, after suitable evacuants. It frequently removes the disease when all other means fail.

ANTI-SPASMODICS.

Mistura Camphoræ. (*Aqua Camphora, U. S.*)

No. 43. *First.*—Camphor, two drachms; alcohol, forty drops; carbonate magnesia four drachms; distilled water, two pints.

Dose.—One to two tablespoonfuls.

Use.—In typhoid conditions, with delirium, for after pains. Tinct. Camphoræ Comp. (*Paragoric Elix., Tinct. Opii Camph.*).

Second.—Pulverized opium, one drachm; benzoic acid, one drachm; oil of aniseed, one drachm; sugar, two ounces; camphor, two scruples; diluted alcohol, two pints. Macerate for fourteen days. Half a drachm contains less than one grain of opium.

Dose.—For infants, from five to twenty drops; adults, one to two tablespoonfuls.

Use.—To allay cough or nausea, to check diarrhœa, to relieve pain.

Moschus. Preputial secretion of the musk animal.

Dose and *Form.*—Five to ten grains, in pill, bolus, or emulsion.

Use.—Hiccough, epilepsy, asthma, cough, palpitation.

TONIC AND CATHARTIC.

No. 44. Aloes, gentian, orange peel, juniper berries, and bruised aniseed, each one ounce; gin, one pint. Mix. Macerate for two weeks, and then strain.

Dose.—A tablespoonful once or twice a day. Good for bilious habits.

DISCUTIENT OINTMENT.

(*For scrofulous and glandular tumors.*)

No. 45. Bark of bitter-sweet root, stramonium leaves, cicuta leaves, deadly nightshade, and yellow dock root, each two ounces; lard, one pound. Bruise and simmer the roots and leaves in spirits; then add the lard, and simmer till the ingredients are crisped or thickened into an ointment.

FOR SUPPRESSION OF URINE IN CHILDREN.

No. 46. Oil of solidago, one drachm; alcohol, eight drachms.

Dose.—From five to twenty drops on sugar at a dose, to be repeated at suitable intervals. Proportionably larger doses of this are also very beneficial for flatulence, faintness, etc., in adults.

GARGLES.

No. 47. *First.*—Raspberry leaves, geranium, blackberry root, and leptandria root, each ounce. Mix, and make three pints of strong decoction. Suitable for a gargle.

Second.—Geranium, golden-seal, marsh-mallow, wild indigo root, and rosemary, each half an ounce. Mix, and make one pint of strong infusion. After straining, add two drachms of powdered borax, and one gill of honey. An excellent astringent gargle.

HONEY BALSAM.

No. 48. Balsam of tolu, balsam of fir, each two ounces; opium, two drachms. Dissolve all three in one quart of alcohol.

Dose.—A teaspoonful occasionally. Valuable for the relief of pulmonary diseases.

ANTI-DYSENTERY CORDIAL.

No. 49. Birch bark and peach pits, each two pounds; bayberry bark, half a pound; wild cherry bark, one pound; water, two gallons. Boil down to one and a half gallons, after which add a gallon of good brandy, and loaf sugar sufficient to make it palatable.

Dose.—A wineglassful three or four times a day.

FOR GRAVEL, DROPSY, ETC.

No. 50. Queen of the meadow, milk weed, juniper berries, dwarf elder, spearmint, wild carrot seed, of each two ounces. Put all in a mortar and bruise, and boil the whole in a gallon of water, till half a gallon of the liquid is left, and then strain.

Dose.—Half a pint of the decoction is to be taken several times during the day.

COUGH SYRUP.

No. 51. Acetate of morphia, four grains; tincture of blood-root, two drachms; antimonial wine, three drachms; ipecacuanha, three drachms; syrup of wild cherry, three ounces. Mix.

Dose.—A teaspoonful two or three times a day.

FOR DYSMENORRHŒA.

No. 52. Viburnin, aulophyllin, each one scruple; gelsemin, five grains. Mix, and divide into ten powders. *Dose.*—One every two hours until relieved.

FOR DIARRHŒA.

No. 53. Tincture of catechu, half an ounce; spirits of camphor, tincture of myrrh, and tincture of cayenne, each two drachms. Mix.

Dose.—From half a teaspoonful to a teaspoonful in diarrhœa.

INJECTION.

No. 54. Castor oil, one gill; pulv. cayenne, ten grains; table salt, one teaspoonful molasses, one gill; warm water, one pint. Inject.

FOR THE BLUES, OR LOW SPIRITS.

No. 55. A pleasant cordial for low spirits is the following: aniseed, four drachms; oil of angelica, one drachm; oil of cassia, forty drops; oil of caraway, thirty drops; proof spirits, two gallons. Mix well.

Dose.—Half a tablespoonful in water.

SKIN DISEASES WITH MUCH IRRITATION.

No. 56. Decoctions of bitter-sweet and mallows, of each half a pint; mix, and make a liniment. Use the "Renovating Pills" internally.

CHILBLAIN OINTMENT.

No. 57. Lard, two quarts; turpentine, one pint; camphor, quarter of a pound. Rub into the parts. This will be found a capital remedy.

ACIDITY OF THE STOMACH.

No. 58. Hard wood ashes, one quart; common soot, half a gill; water, six pints. Digest, settle, and filter.

Dose.—Take one tablespoonful three times a day in acidity of the stomach.

HEMORRHOIDS. PILES.

No. 59. Opium, one scruple; pulverized nut-galls, one drachm; ointment althæa. Mix, and anoint the parts.

SORE THROAT.

No. 60. Those subject to sore throat should make a wash of warm water, in which wood ashes have been dissolved, and apply externally every morning. The "Herbal Ointment" should be applied at night, and well rubbed in. If the disease has become permanent or chronic, the "Acacian Balsam" must be used according to directions. (See page 470.)

INJECTION FOR COSTIVENESS.

No. 61. Castor oil, two ounces; tincture of prickly ash bark, half an ounce; compound tincture of Virginia snake root, two drachms; infusion of boneset and senna, equal parts, half a pint. Mix, and inject. It is by no means, however, as good as the "Renovating Pills." See page 473.

TO PRODUCE PERSPIRATION.

No. 62. Blood-root, golden-seal, sumach berries, bayberry bark, of each two drachms; all pulverized. Mix.

Dose.—Make an infusion in a pint of hot water, and give a tablespoonful every half hour.

POULTICE FOR A FESTER.

No. 63. Boil bread in the settlings of strong beer; apply the poultice in the common manner. This has saved many an hour of suffering.

CATAPLASMS, OR POULTICES.

No. 64. May be made by moistening bread crumbs with milk. They may also be made of flaxseed, roasted onions, snake-root, hops, etc.

Poultices are useful in nearly all cases of local inflammation.

TOOTHACHE.

No. 65. Gum opium, gum camphor, spirits of turpentine, each one scruple. Rub in a mortar to a paste. Put it in the hollow tooth.

Use.—This will cure and even prevent the toothache.

A FRAGRANT BREATH.

No. 66. Take sherry wine, one gill; ground cloves and grated nutmeg, each one drachm; cinnamon and bruised caraway seeds, each a quarter of an ounce. Place all these dry substances into the wine or spirits, in a half pint bottle, and let them stand for several days, shaking the bottle every night and morning. Strain off the tincture through linen to get it bright, then add about ten drops of lavender, or five drops of the otto of roses.

A few drops on a lump of sugar dissolved in the mouth, will secure a breath of flowers. It may be also used with advantage on the toothbrush, in lieu of tooth powder, or, mixed with water, it makes an excellent gargle.

FOOT BATH.

No. 67. A bucket of warm water; pulv. cayenne pepper, one tablespoonful; ground mustard, two tablespoonfuls. Mix.

Use.—As a foot bath in suppression of menses.

TO IMPROVE THE VOICE.

No. 68. Beeswax, two drachms; balsam of copaiba, three drachms; powdered liquorice root, four drachms. Melt the copaiba with the wax in a new earthen pipkin. When they are melted, remove them from the fire, and, while in a liquid state, mix in the powdered liquorice.

Make pills of three grains each. Two of these pills to be taken occasionally, or three or four times a day if necessary.

Use.—This is a good remedy for clearing and cleaning the voice, and is much used by professional singers.

HEADACHE. NEURALGIC PAINS.

No. 69. Take of opodeldoc, spirits of wine, sal ammoniac, equal parts, and apply like any other lotion.

STINGS.

No. 70. Bind on the place a thick plaster of common salt or saleratus moistened; it will soon extract the venom.

A STOMACHIC.

No. 71. Fresh ground cubebs.

Dose. From five to twenty grains.

Use.—As a stomachic in disorders of the digestive organs.

FOR FEVERS AND OTHER ACUTE DISEASES.

No. 72. Asclepin, one-half drachm; warm water, four ounces; compound tincture of American hellebore, thirty drops. Dissolve the asclepin in the warm water, and afterwards add the hellebore.

Dose.—From one to three teaspoonfuls once in every two hours as long as the fever is raging. If nausea occurs, omit the medicine until it subsides. Shake the mixture well before using.

OFFENSIVE BREATH.

No. 73. Solution chlorinated of soda, six drops; water, two ounces. Mix.

Use. A sure remedy for an offensive breath emanating from a deranged stomach.

ANTIDOTE FOR RATTLESNAKE POISON.

No. 74. The *Medical Journal* says the following is an infallible cure for the poison of a rattlesnake bite. Iodide of potass, four grains; corrosive sublimate, two grains; bromine, five drachms. Mix together, and keep the mixture in a glass-stoppered vial, well secured.

Dose.—Ten drops of this mixture, diluted with a tablespoonful of brandy, constitutes a dose. The quantity to be repeated, if necessary, according to the exigencies of the case.

FOR CANCER.

No. 75. Take equal parts of fresh poke-weed, yellow dock, and blood-root; evaporate the juice by the means of a sand bath to the consistency of tar. The ointment should be applied, after the cuticle has been removed by a blister, three times a day. The parts should be washed with good French brandy after each application of the ointment. Before this is used, the advice of a physician should first be secured.

FOR HIP DISEASE.

No. 76. Take of iodine, one ounce; phosphate of lime, two ounces, water, one pint. Dissolve the iodine and lime in the water, and add twenty grains of tannin. Inject with a small syringe three or four times a day.

Use.—A valuable injection in hip disease, where the head of the bone is decayed.

FOR BRUISES.

No. 77. Take pulv. slippery elm and pulv. indigo weed, each one pound; gum myrrh, half a pound; pulv. prickly ash, a quarter of a pound. Wet with good brewer's yeast and apply. A very good poultice for bruises.

FOR DIPHTHERIA.

No. 78. Saturated tincture of scrophularia, one drachm, added to half a tumbler of water.

Triturated macrotin, twenty grains, added to a tumblerful of water.

Dose.—One teaspoonful of each every hour.

GARGLE FOR THE ELONGATION OF THE UVULA.

No. 79. Fluid extract of rhus, one drachm; fluid extract of bayberry, two drachms; water, two ounces. Mix, and gargle the throat three or four times a day. Also bathe the throat upon the outside in strong salt and water. (See fluid extracts, page 475.)

FOR BILIOUS COLIC.

No. 80. Fluid extract of wild yam, two ounces; fluid extract of pleurisy root, one ounce. Mix, and take a teaspoonful as often as is required.

TO REMOVE WARTS AND CORNS.

No. 81. Apply the juice of the leaves of the great celandine or tetter-wort, and keep applying until the fungous growth is removed.

FOR THE TEETH.

No. 82. Make charcoal of bread, pulverize it until it is reduced to an impalpable powder, then apply daily, morning and evening, with a soft brush and pure cold water.

Use.—This will keep the teeth white, and cure diseases of the gums.

A GOOD MEDICATED WINE.

No. 83. Take of powdered colchicum seed, two ounces; of sherry wine, twelve fluid ounces. Put them together in a close glass bottle, and let them stand for fourteen days, giving a good shaking every day. Filter through a fine muslin cloth, and drink as required.

INJECTION FOR ASIATIC CHOLERA.

No. 84. Take of water, one fluid ounce; tincture of prickly ash berries, one fluid drachm; tincture of opium, twenty drops. Mix together. Inject in ordinary quantity until the desired effect has been produced.

BLEEDING AT THE NOSE.

No. 85. Powder of rhatany (for internal use), ten grains.

FOR OLD ULCERS.

No. 86. Take of red chickweed, which is common both in America and Europe, the leaves and flowers, and apply in the form of a poultice, frequently changing them.

NATURE'S

HERBAL REMEDIES.

Below will be found a list of Herbal Remedies that have stood the most crucial tests for years, by which their efficacy has been incontestably proven, and their great and deserved popularity established. Their prominence of virtues and popularity have been gained in consequence of being compounded only with the view to having the greatest concentration of curative properties for the diseases they are designed to cure that the profoundest medical skill is able to suggest, and prepared exclusively from herbs selected in localities best calculated for the development of their medicinal properties. Every herbal constituent, before selection, is subjected to a careful analysis, in order to ascertain the precise quantity of medicinal properties, thus enabling me to prepare these remedies of uniform strength, and endowing them with the highest excellence of curative properties. These remedies are in every way superior, and the use of them by invalids is recommended because of their manifest superiority. In these Remedies they will find positive cures for numberless ills, and the supreme confidence with which they are recommended as unfailing specifics is justified by the universal success they have achieved in a countless number of cases where everything else had failed. In brief, they need but an adequate trial to manifest their restorative and health-giving properties.

These medicines can be procured from all respectable chemists throughout the world. They can also be had from the author by remitting price, on receipt of which he will send them by rail.

The Restorative Assimilant.

Price—4*s.* 6*d. per bottle ;* 3 *ditto*, 11*s.*; 6 *ditto*, 20*s.*

This invaluable remedy is a distilled compound, composed of blue-vervain, water pepper, chamomile, etc., and constitutes one of the triumphs of pharmaceutical science. It is an unfailing remedy for Epilepsy or Fits, curing even the most hopeless cases. A cure has been effected in every case in which a proper trial was given to the medicine. It is none the less effectual in Dyspepsia, for which disease it is an actual specific. It speedily cures all bowel complaints, instantly checking diarrhœa, dysentery, and has given great success in cholera.

The Restorative Assimilant is a valuable remedy for almost every disease that afflicts humanity, owing to its powerful tonic properties, and it is a tonic (the only one known) that does not produce constipation. Our physicians call it the great Napoleon tonic. All forms of indigestion are relieved by it at once, and a single bottle is sufficient to give relief in most cases of dyspepsia, no matter of how many years standing.

In all debilitated conditions of the system, the Restorative Assimilant exerts beneficial and invigorating influence; it builds up the system with such astonishing rapidity as to make it one of the most powerful medicines extant. It quickly restores lost appetite—in Diarrhœa and Bowel Complaint it is a sovereign remedy. Its greatest benefit is felt, however, in Nervous Diseases, Epilepsy, Nervous Prostration, Local and General Debility, Loss of Manhood, Female Weakness of every form—in fact wherever a tonic or nervine is required.

There is a large class of persons who, owing to the pressure of steam under which they have travelled in this fast, present age, are troubled with **sleeplessness—another name for nervousness.** This is not considered a real disease, but it is certainly one of the most distressing ailments that afflicts the human family. It seems to be more prevalent among men than women, owing to their more active business lives. Wherever the most blood is attracted, greater activity is the result; thus the brain is the first to realize exhaustion.

One bottle of the Restorative Assimilant, taken according to directions, will positively set the mental house in order. We would not, however, advise this overtaxing experiment too often.

The Acacian Balsam.

Price—*4s. 6d. per bottle; 3 ditto, 11s.; 6 ditto, 20s.*

This is a highly concentrated compound fluid-extract of Aya-pana, Indian Hemp plant, Coca, Nicaya, Lungwort, &c., rendered highly agreeable with the addition of Paraguayan Wild Honey. This unsurpassed remedy affords speedy Relief and Permanent Cure of Consumption, Bronchitis, Asthma, Coughs, Colds, all Diseases of the Lungs, Chest, and Throat. The cures this great remedy performs exceed the most sanguine expectations, and no one should fail to give it a proper trial, if suffering from some disease of the pulmonary organs.

Fully Conscious of its Weighty Meaning, we nevertheless assert, to all consumptives, and to those who fear the approach of the disease, that in the Acacian Balsam they will find a sovereign remedy, which they can take with full and gratifying confidence that the disease will be overcome or averted, and that by its use they will be restored to good health.

Bronchitis.—For all inflammation of the bronchial tubes, the Acacian Balsam is a reliable remedy. Half the usual dose should be taken every few hours. It speedily allays irritation, loosens the chest, suppresses the distressing cough and pain, subdues inflammation and fever, and produces free and easy expectoration, thus throwing off the disease. The Balsam is greatly assisted by the free outward application of the Herbal Ointment to the chest and throat, and by one or two doses of the Renovating Pills, if the bowels are sluggish or costive.

Asthma.—As soon as the spasm comes on, a full dose of the Balsam should be taken, and the Herbal Ointment well rubbed in over the throat and chest. If relief does not immediately follow, one or two doses more of the Balsam should be taken at intervals of half an hour. This treatment is effectual in all cases of this distressing and alarming disease. In Chronic Asthma, the Balsam should be taken in regularly prescribed doses, and the Ointment thoroughly applied to the throat and chest every night, until the disease completely abates. An occasional dose when breathing becomes somewhat distressed, will effectually prevent any recurrence of the affection.

THE BLOOD PURIFIER.

PRICE—4*s.* 6*d. per bottle;* 3 *ditto*, 11*s.;* 6 *ditto*, 20*s.*

This is a compound extract of rock rose, stillingia, &c., and is the best alterative and depurative ever discovered. It is an unfailing cure for scrofula, syphilis, skin diseases, ulcers, sores, glandular swellings, and all other affections owing their existence to depravity of the blood, and derangement of the lymphatic system. It thoroughly eradicates at once and for ever every contaminating element in the system, and as a special and positive antidote to all blood-poisoning material, it is not only unequalled, but far superior to any other known remedy.

The life is the blood, and from the blood we derive our strength. Probably no one at the present day is wholly free from taint or infection of a **scrofulous character.** Liver, stomach, kidneys, bowels, or womb, may just as likely become the headquarters of the deposits of the weakened, fouled, and evil-breeding stream as the lungs, the brain, the joints, for in every part of the human organism will the diseased blood make its presence morbidly known.

Tendencies and predispositions to this prime source of so many evils and dangers should be carefully noted, and where they have culminated in any one or more of the very many shapes that the disease itself assumes, the treatment should be vigorous and decisive.

This medicine is pleasant to take; in fact, it is really aromatic. It produces no unpleasant effect upon the stomach, no matter how long it is taken. It is one of my "Standard Herbal Remedies" which I can guarantee to perform all that is claimed for it, without hesitation.

THE MALE FERN VERMIFUGE.

PRICE—2*s.* 9*d. per bottle;* 3 *ditto*, 7*s.* 6*d.* *When ordered by post the price is* 3*s.* 3*d.*

This is a syrupized compound fluid extract of male fern, pinkroot, kousso, &c., and warranted to expel every species of worms from the intestinal canal almost instantly. It is just as deadly to the dreadful tape-worm as it is to the round, pin, or thread worm, and is the only vermifuge known that is so positively destructive to all worms, and yet so perfectly harmless to the human subject. It causes no disturbance of the system is safe to use, and pleasant to take.

In presenting this Vermifuge to the public, I have the consciousness that it is a prompt, reliable, and efficacious remedy. **It is composed of the best and most efficacious anthelmintic herbs,** and is so compounded and prepared that it is destructive of the parasites without in the least irritating the bowels of the patient.

Symptoms.—The symptoms produced by worms in the intestinal canal are of almost every conceivable variety. The abdomen becomes bloated and prominent, the appetite variable and capricious, the breath offensive, the tongue has a white, coated appearance, and often the upper lip will be much swollen. The eyelids sometimes swell so much that the child can scarcely see, and occasionally swollen patches present themselves in other parts of the body. The child is restless at night and starts frequently when asleep. Paleness around the mouth, extending up the side of the nose, is a common symptom. Itching of the *anus* is indicative of the presence of the small worms. Epilepsy, St. Vitus' Dance, and every form of nervous derangement, often result from irritation. Itching of the nose is a symptom peculiar of worms, and the child is almost incessantly rubbing that member. A choking cough is often present.

The Male Fern Vermifuge is as **pleasant to take as Aromatic Syrup,** and perfectly safe as well as efficient in all cases. It will expel worms from children in five hours.

The Herbal Ointment.

Price—2s. 9d. *per pot; 3 ditto*, 7s. 6d. *When ordered by post the price is* 3s. *per pot.*

This ointment is composed of the extractive virtues of bitter sweet, skunk cabbage, green ozier, lobelia, water pepper, tobacco stems, &c., making it the most elegant and efficacious ointment that the pharmaceutic art is capable of producing. It is capable of a wide range of application, and as an external remedy it can never be equalled in point of virtue. It speedily cures all inflammations, all lung and heart complaints, swellings, croup, ulcers, tumors, abscesses, wens, cuts, wounds, burns, skin diseases, in fact every disorder arising from inflammation, morbid nutrition, &c. It is used in practice by the best physicians in the world, and its praises daily to be heard from those who have tested its great and manifold virtues are almost too remarkable for credence. Its most wondrous efficacy is particularly exhibited in all lung, heart, and spinal diseases, relieving all pain quickly, and curing them in a short space of time.

The penetrative qualities of this wonderful ointment may be readily ascertained in a practical manner; rub it over the stomach upon retiring, and when the fluids of the body are expelled in the morning, the water will be medicated to such an extent as to change its color, and an unmistakable odor of ointment itself will be emitted. It is the only medicine extant that cures disease through the pores with rapidity and certainty.

The Herbal Ointment is a pain-killer in the most extensive sense of that phrase, and will accomplish its work in many cases without the assistance of an internal remedy. It does not banish pain by producing another irritation, nor by benumbing the parts to which it is applied, but removes the cause of the torture by increasing the circulation, and restoring the afflicted parts to their pristine condition of good health. Its ingredients embrace subtle herbal powers, the precise nature of which it would require more room than we can give to explain. Suffice it to say, that where there is soreness, weakness, or a sore or inflammation, there is disorganization of the tissues—the flesh is no longer in a natural state; chemically it has lost something necessary to its natural existence, or is suffering from the invasion of some foreign and corrupt matter.

The Herbal Ointment is so compounded that it immediately supplies what is wanting, and also with the greatest precision, certainty, and celerity, expels, absorbs, destroys, and banishes all corrupt and morbid humors, discharges, gatherings, sores, &c.

The Renovating Pill.

Price—*2s. 9d. per box; 3 ditto, 7s. 6d. When ordered by post the price is 3s. per box; each box contains 60 pills.*

This excellent pill is composed of mandrake, leptandrin, Turkey rhubarb, soapwort, dandelion, &c. It is a purely vegetable concentration for keeping the bowels in natural order, cleansing the system of all impurities, and positively curing costiveness. These pills unload the liver of bilious matter, and by their tonic action upon the alimentary canal they aid digestion, promote assimilation of nutriment, and produce regular and healthy action of the bowels. Their action is thoroughly effective, but so easy and painless that they can be given with great benefit in even the most diseased condition of the intestines.

Much mischief is done in the treatment of constipation. The common opinion is that all the indications are fulfilled if some medicine merely forces the unloading of the bowels. Medicines simply cathartic merely cause movement of the bowels, they correct no morbid condition, consequently their application is followed by even greater costiveness than previous to their use. A remedy to be effectual must be composed of tonic, alterative, corrective, and cathartic properties. These are admirably combined in the Renovating Pill. This Pill will regulate the bowels when all other preparations fail.

These pills, used in connection with the Liver Invigorator, are invaluable to all who suffer from **Bilious and Liver Complaints, Sick Headache,** loss of appetite, drowsiness, giddiness, and especially **Indigestion,** which prevails to an alarming extent in this country at the present day. In ordinary cases the pills alone will effect a cure.

The Woodland Balm.

Price—*2s. 9d. per pot; 3 ditto, 7s. 6d. When ordered by post the price is 3s. per pot.*

This Herbal production is so compounded as to give moisture, warmth, and action to the hair follicles.

The human hair is a vegetable! It may wither and die like a plant! The seeds, however, for its reproduction, never die, and only need the right kind of cultivation to germinate and put forth a new and healthy crop. So like is it to the other vegetable growths that *it has* *been transplanted* from one body to another, and still maintained its vigor, as testified by Profs. Dzoade, Diffenbach, and others. Gray hair is a partial decay—*the sap of the stalk has dried up.*

I can guarantee **The Woodland Balm** to produce *a fine crop of hair* upon any head in a reasonable length of time. It will produce luxuriant beards and moustaches on what are considered beardless faces. For dressing hair, especially *ladies' and children's hair*, its equal has never been known, or approximated to.

It will cure all eruptions upon the head, of every description, and will dispel, like a charm, scald head, scurvy, salt-rheum, barbers' itch, mercurial sores, no matter of how long standing. It removes all unnatural heat, and will eradicate the too strong tendency of blood to the head. One application of the Balm will prove all I have stated above to be strictly true. When all these irritating effects are removed from the head and brain, the hair will generally resume its natural and former color. For many years I have been requested to make the article known to the public, but have strongly refused to do so from the fact that there are so many spurious articles in the market, and thinking the public might deem the WOODLAND BALM no better than the *injurious articles* so extensively advertised throughout the world. I have, however, finally deemed it expedient to give this limited notice in my Herbalist.

LIVER INVIGORATOR.

PRICE—*4s. 6d. per bottle; three bottles in one large*, 11*s*.

This grand specific is a distilled compound, composed of mandrake, gentian, wild yam, dandelion, and other plants valuable for their curative qualities in all bilious disorders. It arrests all inflammatory processes, removes engorgement and all noxious bilious matter, promotes secretion of healthy bile, stimulates and tones the liver, and so invigorates the organ as to speedily restore healthy functional action of both secretion and elimination. It is applicable to all hepatic diseases, and unfailingly efficacious in every case. No class of diseases is more prevalent than hepatic affections, and none, perhaps, attended with more serious effects to the general organism. The Liver Invigorator is a certain curative for these complaints.

Biliousness causes a most unhappy state of mind and body—that is, the liver whose office it is to withdraw the bile from the blood, fails to perform that duty, and the blood having more and more bile in it, becomes more and more impure, thickens more and more, until at length it is almost too thick to flow at all. If this takes place in the chest it is called "congestion of the lungs"; if in the liver, "congestion of the liver"; if in the skull, "congestion of the brain"; if in the whole body, it is "congestive fever," which generally means death. It is, therefore, important that the torpid liver be aroused to healthy action. Two bottles of Liver Invigorator will emulge the liver and restore its activity.

When it will become known that the Herbal Kingdom is capable of affording materials from which a list of remedies like the foregoing, containing every requisite of a remedy—elegance, efficacy, and reliability, can be prepared, there will scarcely be any who will not abandon the use of pernicious mineral drugs, and resort only to the life-giving remedial agents afforded everywhere by plants.

These remedies every one can depend upon—they embody so much virtue that good results must follow. For a more extended description of them, with numerous testimonials, send for my Illustrated Shakespearian Almanack, and Treatise on Foreign and Native Herbal Remedies, send free, post paid, on application.

The remedies will be sent to any address direct from my office, on receipt of price.

Address—FREDK. W. HALE

60, *Chandos Street, Covent Garden, London.*

FREDERICK W. HALE'S

STANDARD FLUID EXTRACTS.

The fluid extract is the most elegant form for administering medicinal agents, being concentrated, and containing just enough alcohol to preserve them from degeneration by age. They can, therefore, be administered in all inflammatory conditions, in which tinctures containing a greater quantity of alcohol are not admissible.

My fluid extracts are superior to any that are manufactured. They are prepared without the aid of heat, in perfect vacuum, and from plants gathered at the proper seasons, in soils best adapted for medicinal perfection, and in climates to which they are indigenous, and in which they attain their richest medicinal development. This is not the case with other manufacturers—they prepare them from plants of indiscriminate selection, which accounts for their frequent worthlessness. These fluid-extracts are guaranteed for high character and reliability, and physicians can depend upon their action with all confidence.

It is my particular desire in preparing them to offer to households good and convenient remedies, by which they can treat all cases of sickness occurring. They will find them, by the aid of this work, very advantageous for domestic medication. To meet the wants of families, the author sells them in standard small quantities, as it is not to be supposed that they desire or have use for such large quantities that physicians or druggists ordinarily purchase.

It will be seen that the list is very complete, and so systematically arranged that no error can occur, as the virtues and doses of each are appended. Those marked with a star * should not be used without the advice of a physician, and even then the administering should be very carefully and watchfully done.

These extracts are sent by rail, on receipt of price, carefully packed in strong boxes. All of them are warranted to possess the highest excellence of virtue, and to exert the full therapeutic effects desired.

Address—Fredk. W. Hale,

61, *Chandos Street, Covent Garden, London.*

FLUID EXTRACTS.

FLUID EXTRACT OF	MEDICINAL PROPERTIES.	DOSE.	Price per oz. s. d.
Aconite* (leaves)	Narcotic and sedative	2 to 5 drops	1 0
Aconite* (root)	" " "	2 or 3 "	1 3
Agrimony	Tonic, alterative, and astringent	30 to 60 "	1 0
American Valerian	Tonic, stimulant, diaphoretic, and antispasmodic	30 to 60 "	1 3
Arnica Flowers	Stimulant and tonic	10 to 30 "	0 9
Avens Root	Tonic and astringent	10 to 30 "	0 9
Balm	Stimulant, diaphoretic, and antispasmodic	30 to 60 "	0 9
Balmony	Tonic, cathartic, and anthelmintic	30 to 60 "	0 9
Barberry	Tonic and laxative	30 to 60 "	0 9
Bayberry	Astringent and stimulant	30 to 60 "	0 9
Belladonna*	Anodyne, relaxant, antispasmodic	2 to 5 "	1 10
Beth Root	Astringent, tonic, antiseptic	30 to 60 "	1 0
Bitter Root	Emetic, diaphoretic, tonic, and laxative	10 to 20 "	1 3
Bittersweet	Narcotic, diuretic, alterative, diaphoretic, discutient	20 to 40 "	1 0
Black Alder	Tonic, alterative, and astringent	30 to 60 "	1 0
Blackberry Root	Astringent	20 to 40 "	0 9
Blood Root	Emetic, diaphoretic, stimulant, tonic	5 to 30 "	1 0
Blue Flag	Cathartic, alterative, sialagogue, diuretic	20 to 40 "	1 0
Boneset	Tonic, aperient, diaphoretic, emetic	30 to 60 "	0 9
Boxwood	Tonic, astringent, antiperiodic, stimulant	20 to 40 "	0 9
Buchu	Diuretic, stimulant, tonic	20 to 40 "	1 10
" Comp.	" " "	10 to 30 "	1 10
Buckhorn	Mucilaginous, tonic, and styptic	30 to 60 "	0 9
Buckthorn	Cathartic	30 to 60 "	1 0
Bugle Weed	Sedative, tonic, astringent, narcotic	30 to 60 "	0 9
Butternut	Cathartic	30 to 60 "	0 9
Button Snakeroot	Diuretic, tonic, stimulant, emmenagogue	30 to 60 "	1 0
Cannabis Indica*	Narcotic, diuretic, diaphoretic	2 to 5 "	4 0
Canella	Aromatic, stimulant, tonic	10 to 20 "	0 9
Centaury	Tonic and antiperiodic	10 to 30 "	0 9
Cinchona (Calisaya)	Tonic, antiperiodic, febrifuge	20 to 40 "	4 0
Chamomile	Tonic, carminative, antispasmodic	30 to 60 "	1 0
Checkerberry	Stimulant, aromatic, astringent	30 to 60 "	0 9
Cherry Bark	Tonic, stimulant, expectorant	20 to 60 "	1 0
" Comp.	" " "	20 to 60 "	1 3
Cleavers	Refrigerant and diuretic	30 to 60 "	0 9
Coca	Tonic and vivifier	30 to 60 "	12 0
Colocynth*	Drastic cathartic	10 to 30 "	2 0
Cohosh, black	Tonic, antispasmodic, diuretic	10 to 30 "	1 3
Cohosh, blue	Emmenagogue, parturient, antispasmodic	10 to 30 "	1 0
Colchicum Root	Sedative, cathartic, diuretic, emetic	3 to 10 "	1 3
" Seeds	" " " "	5 to 15 "	1 6
Coltsfoot	Emollient, demulcent, tonic	30 to 60 "	0 9
Columbo	Bitter tonic	10 to 30 "	1 10
Comfrey	Demulcent and astringent	30 to 60 "	1 0
Conium*	Narcotic	5 to 10 "	1 3
Cotton Root*	Emmenagogue, parturient	30 to 60 "	1 10
Cramp Bark	Antispasmodic	30 to 60 "	0 9
Cranesbill	Astringent	20 to 40 "	1 0
Cubebs	Diuretic, stimulant, tonic	30 to 40 "	1 10

FLUID EXTRACT OF	MEDICINAL PROPERTIES.	DOSE.	Price per oz. s. d.
Culver's Root	Cathartic, cholagogue, tonic	10 to 30 drops	1 3
Cundurango	Alterative, anticarcinomous	10 to 30 "	10 0
Dandelion	Cathartic, tonic, alterative, diuretic	30 to 60 "	1 3
Digitalis*	Sedative, diuretic, diaphoretic	2 to 5 "	1 0
Dragon Root	Expectorant and diaphoretic	10 to 30 "	0 9
Dwarf Elder	Sudorific, diuretic, alterative	30 to 60 "	0 9
Elecampane	Stimulant and tonic	30 to 60 "	0 9
Ergot*	Parturient	10 to 30 "	2 10
Fever few	Emmenagogue, tonic, stimulant	20 to 40 "	0 9
Fireweed	Emetic, cathartic, tonic	30 to 60 "	1 0
Frostwort	Alterative, anti-scrofulous	20 to 40 "	0 9
Garden Celandine	Stimulant, alterative, diuretic, diaphoretic, vulnerary	30 to 60 "	1 0
Gelseminum*	Febrifuge, antispasmodic	5 to 10 "	2 0
Gentian	Bitter tonic	20 to 40 "	1 10
Gillenia	Emetic, cathartic, tonic	30 to 60 "	1 0
Golden Seal	Tonic, calmative	20 to 40 "	1 10
Golden Rod	Stimulant, carminative	30 to 60 "	1 0
Gold Thread	Bitter tonic	20 to 40 "	1 0
Hardhack	Astringent	5 to 15 "	0 8
Hellebore, black*	Antispasmodic, diuretic, emmenagogue	5 to 10 "	1 0
Henbane*	Narcotic	5 to 15 "	2 0
Hop	Tonic, hypnotic, febrifuge, antilithic	30 to 60 "	2 0
Hydrangea	Diuretic, anticalculus	20 to 40 "	1 0
Hyssop	Stimulant, aromatic, tonic	30 to 60 "	0 9
Ignatia Bean*	Cerebro-spinal tonic	3 to 5 "	2 10
Ipecac	Expectorant, emetic	5 to 30 "	5 0
Jalap*	Drastic cathartic	10 to 30 "	2 10
John's Wort	Astringent, sedative, and diuretic	30 to 60 "	1 0
Juniper Berries	Stimulant, carminative, diuretic	30 to 60 "	0 9
Kousso	Anthelmintic, anti-tape-worm	30 to 60 "	2 10
Ladies' Slipper	Tonic, stimulant, diaphoretic, antispasmodic	20 to 40 "	1 3
Life Everlasting	Astringent	30 to 60 "	1 0
Life Root	Diuretic, pectoral, diaphoretic, tonic	10 to 30 "	1 3
Lily Root	Astringent, demulcent, anodyne, anti-scrofulous	10 to 30 "	1 0
Liverwort	Mucilaginous, astringent	1 dram	1 0
Lobelia	Emetic, expectorant, relaxant, antispasmodic, discutient, and anodyne, externally	10 to 30 drops	1 3
Logwood	Tonic, astringent	20 to 40 "	0 9
Lovage (Privet)	Astringent	30 to 60 "	1 0
Lungwort	Demulcent and mucilaginous	30 to 60 "	1 0
Male Fern	Anthelmintic	20 to 40 "	1 10
Mandrake	Cathartic, cholagogue, tonic	10 to 60 "	1 10
Marshmallow	Demulcent and diuretic	20 to 40 "	1 3
Matico	Stimulant, diuretic, astringent, alterative	10 to 30 "	2 0
Motherwort	Emmenagogue, nervine, antispasmodic, laxative	30 to 60 "	1 0
Mugwort	Tonic, narcotic	20 to 40 "	1 0
Nux Vomica*	Cerebro-spinal tonic	3 to 10 "	2 0
Opium, deodorized*	Anodyne	3 to 10 "	2 0
Pareira Brava	Tonic, diuretic, aperient	30 to 60 "	1 10
Pennyroyal	Stimulant, diaphoretic, emmenagogue, and carminative	30 to 60 "	1 0
Pinkroot	Anthelmintic	20 to 40 "	2 0
Pipsissewa	Diuretic, tonic, alterative, astringent	20 to 40 "	1 0
Pleurisy Root	Expectorant, diaphoretic, tonic	20 to 40 "	1 10
Poke Root	Emetic, cathartic, alterative, narcotic	10 to 30 "	1 0
Poplar Bark	Tonic and febrifuge	20 to 40 "	0 9
Prickly Ash	Stimulant, tonic, alterative, sialagogue	10 to 30 "	1 0
Ptelea	Tonic, antiperiodic	10 to 30 "	1 0

FLUID EXTRACT OF	MEDICINAL PROPERTIES.	DOSE.	Price per oz. s. d.
Quassia	Bitter tonic	20 to 40 drops	0 9
Queen of the Meadow	Diuretic, stimulant, tonic	20 to 40 "	0 9
Rhatany	A powerful astringent	20 to 40 "	1 10
Rhubarb	Cathartic	10 to 30 "	2 6
Rosin Weed	Tonic, diaphoretic, alterative	20 to 60 "	1 6
Sage	Tonic, astringent, expectorant, diaphoretic.	30 to 60 "	1 0
Sarsaparilla (American)	Alterative	30 to 60 "	1 3
" (Foreign)	Alterative	30 to 60 "	1 6
Sassafras	Alterative	30 to 60 "	1 0
Savine*	Emmenagogue, diuretic, diaphoretic	10 to 20 "	1 0
Savory	Stimulant, carminative, emmenagogue	20 to 40 "	1 3
Scullcap	Antispasmodic	20 to 40 "	1 0
Seneka	Emetic and cathartic	15 to 30 "	2 0
Senna	Cathartic	30 to 60 "	1 0
Skunk Cabbage	Emetic, stimulant, antispasmodic, discutient, externally	20 to 50 "	1 0
Snake Root	Tonic, diuretic, diaphoretic	10 to 30 "	1 6
Soap Wort	Tonic, diaphoretic, alterative	10 to 60 "	1 0
Solomon's Seal	Tonic, astringent	20 to 40 "	1 0
Spearmint	Carminative	30 to 60 "	1 0
Spikenard	Alterative	30 to 60 "	1 0
Squill	Emetic, expectorant	2 to 15 "	2 0
Stillingia	An unequalled alterative	10 to 30 "	1 6
Stoneroot	Stimulant	10 to 30 "	1 3
Stramonium*	Energetic narcotic	3 to 10 "	1 0
Sumach	Tonic, astringent, antiseptic	30 to 60 "	0 9
Sweet Gale (Myrica)	Astringent and stimulant	30 to 60 "	0 9
Tag Alder	Alterative, emetic, astringent	30 to 60 "	0 9
Tansy	Emmenagogue, diaphoretic	30 to 60 "	0 9
Thoroughwort	Tonic, aperient, diaphoretic, expectorant	30 to 60 "	0 9
Thyme	Emmenagogue, diaphoretic	30 to 60 "	0 9
Turkey Corn	Alterative	10 to 30 "	1 3
Unicorn Root	Tonic, diuretic, sialagogue	30 to 60 "	1 6
Uva Ursi	Astringent and tonic	20 to 40 "	1 6
Valerian	Sedative	20 to 40 "	1 6
Vervain	Tonic, antispasmodic	20 to 40 "	1 3
Veratrum*	Sedative, diaphoretic	2 "	2 0
Wahoo	Tonic, alterative, expectorant	30 to 60 "	1 6
Water Pepper	Stimulant, diuretic, diaphoretic, excellent external remedy	10 to 30 "	0 9
Wild Indigo	Purgative, emetic, stimulant	10 to 30 "	0 9
Wild Yam	Antispasmodic	10 to 30 "	1 0
Witch Hazel	Tonic, astringent, sedative	30 to 60 "	0 9
Wormwood	Tonic, anthelmintic	10 to 30 "	0 9
Wormseed	Anthelmintic	10 to 30 "	1 0
Yarrow	Astringent, diuretic, alterative	10 to 40 "	0 9
Yellow Dock	Alterative, tonic, detergent	30 to 60 "	1 6
Yellow Parilla	Tonic, laxative, alterative	10 to 30 "	1 6

In the administration of these fluid-extracts the minimum dose should first be given, and if the desired effect is not fully responsive, the doses should be gradually increased to the maximum dose. In some cases even larger doses may be required than those given as ordinarily sufficient for inducing their therapeutic effects.

In consequence of trouble in packing, not less than FIVE SHILLINGS' worth of these fluid-extracts will be sent at one time, unless ordered in connection with some of my Standard Remedies. The quantity may either consist of one medicine, or of an indiscriminate selection from the whole list. They are packed in strong bottles, fully labelled, and guaranteed pure. They can only be sent by Rail.

All orders should be addressed to

FREDK. W. HALE
CO, *Chandos Street, Covent Garden, London*

GLOSSARY.

IT is confidently believed that all the technical terms introduced into this work are fully defined in this Glossary. Many of the medical terms are explained where they occur, and even some of those that are here defined are explained at the place where first employed, but are inserted here also, so as to make this Glossary sufficiently complete for ready reference by the most casual reader.

ACRO-NARCOTIC, Medicines that act on the brain, or spinal marrow, or both, but at the same time irritate the parts to which they are applied.

ADJUVANT, A medicine that aids the operation of the principal ingredient of a mixture or compound.

ADYNAMIC, Pertaining to adynamia, or debility of the vital powers.

AERATION, Charging with air; the transformation of venous blood and chyle into arterial blood by respiration; arterialization.

AFFERENT, Conveying inward, nerves that convey impressions towards the nervous centres.

ALBUMEN, The immediate principle of animals and vegetables; it constitutes the chief part of the white of an egg.

ALKALOID, Having the property of or pertaining to an alkali.

ALVINE, Relating to the lower belly, as alvine dejections, etc.

AMAROUS, Bitter.

ANÆSTHETIC, Relating to privation of feeling; a medicine that prevents feeling.

ANÆMIA, A bloodless condition.

ANTAPHRODISIAC, A substance capable of blunting venereal desires.

ANTIPERIODIC, A medicine which possesses the power of arresting morbid periodical movements, as Peruvian bark.

APERIENT, A medicine that gently opens the bowels.

APHONIA, A voiceless condition; loss of voice.

APHRODISIAC, A substance that excites the venereal passions.

ANTISEPTIC, Opposed to putrefaction.

APHTHOUS, Pertaining to aphthæ or thrush.

AREOLAR, Appertaining to an areola, or the space between the fibres, composing organs, or between vessels which interlace each other.

ASTHENIC, Debilitated; pertaining to asthenia, or want of strength.

ATOCIAC, Pertaining to atocia or sterility; sterile.

ATONIC, Wanting tone; weakness of every organ, and particularly of those that are contractile.

ATROPHY, Defective nutrition; a diminution in the bulk of the whole body, or of a part.

BOUGIE, An instrument used for the purpose of dilating the urethra.

CACHECTIC, Belonging or pertaining to cachexia; depraved nutrition or a bad habit of the body.

CADAVEROUS, Pertaining to or resembling the cadaver, or dead body.

CALISTHENIC, Pertaining to calisthenics, or the art of promoting, by appropriate exercises, strength of body and grace of movements.

CAPILLARY, Hair-like; small.

CARIES, Death or decay of a bone.

CARMINATIVE, A remedy that allays pain or promotes the expulsion of flatus, or wind, from the bowels.

CARDIAC, Pertaining to the heart.

CARTILAGE, A solid part of the body of a medium consistence between bone and ligament.

CASEINE, The chief constituent of milk.

CATAMENIAL, Pertaining to catamenia, or menstrual flow.

CATHARSIS, A natural or artificial purgation, or movement of the bowels

CEREBRAL, Pertaining to the brain.

CERVICAL, Pertaining or belonging to the cervix or neck.

CHOLAGOGUE, A medicine that causes a flow of bile.

CHOLESTERINE, An inodorous, insipid substance, forming the crystalline part of a biliary calculus, and contained in neurine and various other tumors; also in the seeds of many plants, olive oil, etc.

CHRONIC, Of long duration.

CHYMIFICATION, Formation of chyme, or the pulp formed by the food and various secretions, after it has been for some time in the stomach.

CLONIC, Irregular convulsive motions; convulsion with alternate relaxation.

COLLIQUATIVE, Profuse; exhausting; a term applied to discharges which produce rapid exhaustion.

COMATOSE, Pertaining to coma, or a profound state of sleep, from which it is difficult to arouse the individual.

CORRIGENT, Corrective; a medicine that mollifies or corrects the action of a pharmaceutical preparation.

DEGLUTITION, The action of swallowing.

DELIRIUM, Straying from the rules of reason; wandering of the mind.

DEOBSTRUENT, A medicine having the power of removing obstructions

DEODORIZED, Deprived of odor or smell.

DESQUAMATION, Exfoliation, or separation of the scarf-skin, in the form of scales.

DETERGENTS, Medicines that cleanse parts, as wounds, ulcers, etc.

DIAGNOSTICATE, Forming a diagnosis or character of a disease by its symptoms.

DIAPHORESIS, A greater degree of perspiration than natural, but less than sweating.

DIATHESIS, Disposition of the body; predisposition to a certain disease.

DISCUTIENT, A medicine having the power to discuss, repel, or resolve tumors.

DIURESIS, A greater discharge of urine than natural.

DRASTIC, Active; a name given to those cathartics that operate powerfully.

DUCT, The canal leading from a gland or vesicle.

DYSPNŒA, Difficulty of breathing.

ECTOZOA, Parasitic animals that infest the exterior of the body, as lice, etc.

EFFERENT, Conveying outwards; nerves that convey nervous stimulus from the brain to other parts.

EFFLUVIA, Emanations, miasms, noxious matter.

EJACULATOR, That which effects the emission of sperm.

EMBRYO, The fecundated germ in the early stages of its development in the womb.

EMULSION, A pharmaceutical preparation, in which oil is suspended in water by means of mucilage.

EMUNCTORY, Any organ whose office it is to excrete or expel matters.

ENDEMIC, Diseases which are owing to some peculiarity in a situation or locality. Thus, ague is endemic in marshy countries.

ENTOZOA, Parasitic animals that infest the interior of the body, as worms.

EPHEMERAL, Of short duration.

EPIGASTRIUM, That portion of the surface of the body lying over the stomach.

EPIDEMIC, A disease that attacks a number of persons at the same time, and referable to some condition of the atmosphere.

EPISPADIAS, A condition of the penis in which the urethra opens at the upper part of the organ.

ERUCTATION, A sonorous emission of flatus, by the mouth, from the stomach.

EXACERBATION, Increase in the symptoms of a disorder; paroxysm.

EXANTHEMATOUS, Relating to the exanthems, or eruptive diseases.

EXCRESCENCE, A tumor which forms at the surface of organs, especially the skin, mucous membranes, and ulcerated surfaces.

EXFOLIATION, The separation of dead portions from the various tissues

EXTRAVASATION, Escape of a fluid from the vessel which contains it, as blood from the veins.

EXUDATION, The oozing of a matter from the pores of a membrane; also the matter that issues in such a manner.

FACIAL, Relating to the face.

FÆCAL, Relating to the fæces or stools.

FALX, A name given to several membranous reflections having the shape of a scythe.

FARINACEOUS, Having the appearance or nature of farina, or the powder obtained by grinding the seeds of certain plants.

FEBRIFUGE, Having the power of abating or driving away fever.

FEBRILE, Relating to or having the character of fever.

FIBRIN, An immediate animal principle entering into the composition of the chyle and the blood; it is the coagulable material of blood.

FLEXOR, Muscles whose office it is to bend certain parts.

FLUCTUATION, The undulation of a fluid which is felt by pressure, properly practised.

FŒTUS, Usually this name is applied to the product of conception after quickening, or more advanced stage of utero-gestation; more vaguely, it is used synonymously with embryo.

FOLLICLE, A small secreting cavity formed by a depression of the skin or mucous membrane.

FUNGOUS, Relating to funga, or certain growths resembling the mushroom, which have no external ulceration, as warts, etc.

GANGLION, A name generally given to a knot-like enlargement in th course of a nerve.

GANGRENE, Privation of life or partial death of an organ; mortification.

GASTRIC, Relating to the stomach.

GELATINE, An immediate animal principle of jelly-like character.

GENITALIA, The genital or sexual organs.

GLAND, Organs which separate from the blood any fluid whatever; a secreting organ; the reddish and spongy, knot-like bodies met with in the course of the lymphatics.

GLUTEN, An immediate principle of vegetables; it is soft, of a grayish white, viscid consistence, and very elastic.

GRANULATION, Granulations are the reddish, conical, flesh-like shoots which form at the surface of wounds and ulcers.

GRAVID, Pregnant.

GRUMOUS, Clotted ; grumous blood is coagulated or clotted blood.

HALLUCINATION, A morbid error in one or more senses ; a delusion.
HELICINE, Resembling in form the tendrils of a vine.
HEMORRHAGE, A flow of blood.
HEPATIC, Relating to the liver.
HYGIENIC, Relating to hygiene, or that part of medicine whose object is the preservation of health.
HYPERTROPHY, The state of a part in which nutrition is performed with greater activity. Unusual bulk of a part.
HYPNOTIC, A medicine having the power to promote or cause sleep.
HYPOSPADIAS, A malformation, in which the urethra opens at the base or beneath the penis.

IDIOPATHIC, A primary disease ; one not dependent on any other.
IDIOSYNCRASY, A peculiarity of constitution, in which one person is affected by an agent which in many others would produce no effect.
INDOLENT, This, in a medical sense, means *painless*.
INDURATION, The hardness which occasionally follows in an inflamed part.
INFUSORIA, The animalcules originating in decomposition of matter.
INGESTA, Substances introduced into the body by the mouth as food.
INSPISSATED, Rendered thick, as an extract.
INTEGUMENT, Anything which serves to cover or envelop.
INTEROSSEOUS, Between the bones.

JACTATION, Extreme anxiety, excessive restlessness—a symptom observed in serious diseases.

KYESTEIN, A peculiar pellicle forming on the urine of a pregnant woman, when allowed to stand for a few days.

LACHRYMAL, Belonging to the tears.
LESION, Derangement, disorder, any morbid change.
LIGAMENT, A fibrous substance, serving to unite bones and to form joints.
LIGATURE, A cord or thread with which an artery or tumor is tied.
LUMBAR, Pertaining to the loins.
LYMPH, A name given to the fluids contained in the lymphatic vessels.
LYMPHATICS, The vessels conveying lymph.

MACERATION, An operation which consists in infusing, usually with heat, a solid substance, so as to extract its virtues.
MAMMARY, Relating to the mammæ, or female breasts.

MASTICATION, The act of chewing.
MATERIA MEDICA, The knowledge of medicines; the substances used as medicines.
MATURATION, The state of an abscess which has reached maturity.
MEDULLA. The base of the brain; marrow.
MENSES, The monthly flow.
MENSTRUAL, Pertaining to the menses.
MENSTRUUM, A solvent; a substance possessing the property of dissolving others.
METASTASIS, Changing from one place to another.
MICTURITION, Urination, discharge of urine.
MUCILAGINOUS, Having the character of mucilage; resembling gum.
MUCUS, The substance found at the surface of mucous membranes.

NARCOTIC, Substances which have the property of stupefying.
NASAL, Relating to the nose.
NAUSEA, Inclination to vomit; sickness of stomach.
NECROSIS, Death of a bone.
NEPHRITIC, Relating to the kidneys.
NERVINE, A medicine which acts on the nervous system.
NEURINE, Relating to the nerves.
NODE, A hard concretion or incrustation gathering around the joints attacked with rheumatism or gout.
NOSOLOGIST, One versed in nosology, or classification of diseases.

OBSTETRICIAN, One skilled, or practising midwifery.
OPHTHALMIA, Relating or belonging to the eye.
ORGASM, The height of venereal excitement in sexual intercourse.
ORTHOPNŒA, Necessity of being in the erect posture to be able to breathe.
OSSEOUS, Relating to or having the character of bones.

PABULUM, Food, aliment.
PAPILLA, An eminence resembling a nipple.
PARACENTESIS, The act of tapping to evacuate a fluid in a cavity, as in dropsy of the abdomen.
PAROXYSM, A periodical exacerbation or fit of a disease.
PARTURIENT, Bringing forth young.
PARTURITION, Delivery, labor, child-birth.
PATHOLOGICAL, Relating to pathology.
PATHOLOGY, A branch of medicine whose object is the knowledge of disease.
PECTIN, A principle which forms the basis of vegetable jelly.

PECTORAL, Relating to the breast; a medicine that relieves or removes affections of the chest.

PELLICLE, A thin skin or membrane, a film.

PERISTALTIC, A motion consisting of alternate contraction and dilatation.

PERITONEUM, The serous membrane lining the abdominal cavity.

PHAGEDENIC, Appearing as if it was gnawed.

PHARMACEUTIC, Relating to pharmacy.

PHARMACOPŒIA, A work containing the formulæ for the preparation, etc., of medicines.

PHARMACY, The art which teaches the knowledge, choice, preservation, preparation, and combination of medicines.

PHLEGMONOUS, Relating to inflammation which is confined to the areolar texture.

PHLYZACIOUS, Relating to tumors formed by the accumulation of a serous fluid under the scarf-skin.

PHYSIOLOGY, The science which teaches the functions of organs or tissues.

PLETHORA, A superabundance of blood.

PNEUMOGASTRIC, Belonging to the lungs and stomach.

PORTAL CIRCULATION, The circulation of blood in the system of vessels in the kidneys and liver.

PTYALISM, Profuse salivation.

PUERPERAL, Relating to child-birth and its consequences.

PULMONARY, Relating or belonging to the lungs.

PURULENT, Having the character of pus.

PUS, The secretion from inflamed textures.

PUSTULE, An elevation of the skin, having an inflamed base.

PYOGENIC, Having a relation to the formation of pus.

REGIMEN, Diet; the rational and methodical use of food.

RENAL, Relating to the kidneys.

RESPIRATION, The function of breathing, by which is accomplished the mixture of venous blood with lymph and chyle.

REVELLENT, Derivative; a remedy causing an abstraction from the morbid condition of some organ or tissue.

REVULSION, The act of turning a disease from a part in which it seems to have taken its seat.

SAC, A bag-like cavity, formed by any serous membrane.

SACCULATED, Enclosed in a sac; having the character of a sac.

SALIVARY, Relating to the saliva; glands whose function it is to secrete saliva.

SANGUINEOUS, Plethoric; relating to the blood.

SCORBUTIC, Relating to, or having the character of scurvy.
SCYBALA, Hard fæcal matter, discharged in round lumps.
SEBACEOUS, Small hollow organs seated in the substance of the skin, and which secrete a matter having a peculiar odor.
SECRETION, An organic function, chiefly confined to the glands; also the matter secreted.
SEPTUM, Partition; a part separating two cavities.
SERUM, The most watery portion of the animal fluids, exhaled by serous membranes.
SINAPISM, A mustard plaster.
SINUS, Any cavity, the interior of which is more expanded than the entrance.
SORDES, The black substance collecting on the teeth in low fevers.
SPASMODIC, Having the character of a spasm.
SPLENETIC, Relating or belonging to the spleen.
SPUTA, Expectorated matter.
SQUAMOUS, Scaly; having the character of scales.
STERCORACEOUS, Fæcal.
STERTOROUS, Of a snoring character.
STRANGURY, Extreme difficulty in evacuating the urine.
STRUMOUS, Scrofulous.
STYPTIC, Astringent; a medicine which stanches the flow of blood.
SUBLUXATION, A sprain; a partial dislocation.
SUDORIFIC, A medicine which provokes sweating.
SUPPURATION, Formation or secretion of pus.
SYNCOPE; Fainting; loss of sensation and motion.
SYNOVIAL, Relating to the membranes lining the joints.

TAXIS, A pressure exerted by the hand on a hernial tumor for the purpose of reducing it.
TISSUE, The various parts which, by union, form the organs.
THORACIC, Relating or belonging to the chest.
TOPICAL, Local; remedies locally applied.
TOXICAL, Poisonous.
TUBERCLE, A tumor in the substance of an organ, as of the lung.

URINE, The secretion of the kidney.
URINARY, Relating to the urine.
UTERUS, The womb.
UTERINE, Relating or belonging to the womb.

VACCINE, Relating to the matter used for vaccination.
VASCULAR, Relating to vessels; arterial, venous or lymphatic.
VENEREAL, Relating to the pleasures of love.

VERTEBRÆ, Bones of the spinal column.

VESICLE, A small bladder or cyst.

VIROSE, Possessed of noxious properties.

VIRUS, Literally, a poison ; an unknown principle, inappreciable by the senses, which is the agent for the transmission of infectious diseases.

VISCERAL, Relating or belonging to the viscera, or entrails.

VULNERARY, Medicines considered capable of favoring the consolidating of wounds ; only a property of plants.

ZYMOTIC, Relating or appertaining to fermentation.

INDEX.